The Great Economists

Linda Yueh is Fellow in Economics at St Edmund Hall, University of Oxford, and Adjunct Professor of Economics at the London Business School. She is also Visiting Senior Fellow at the LSE IDEAS research centre and was Visiting Professor of Economics at Peking University. The former Economics Editor at Bloomberg TV, she also hosted *Talking Business with Linda Yueh* as Chief Business Correspondent for BBC News. She writes for *The Times*, *The New York Times* and the *Financial Times* and has advised the World Economic Forum in Davos and the World Bank. She has written and edited academic books on macroeconomics, globalization and China. This is her first trade book.

The Great Economists

How Their Ideas Can Help Us Today

LINDA YUEH

VIKING
an imprint of
PENGUIN BOOKS

VIKING

UK | USA | Canada | Ireland | Australia
India | New Zealand | South Africa

Viking is part of the Penguin Random House group of companies
whose addresses can be found at global.penguinrandomhouse.com.

First published 2018
001

Set in 12/14.75 pt Bembo Book MT Std
Typeset by Jouve (UK), Milton Keynes
Printed at Thomson Press India Ltd, New Delhi

A CIP catalogue record for this book is available from the British Library

Hardback ISBN: 978–0–241–23497–6
Trade Paperback ISBN: 978–0–241–23498–3

www.greenpenguin.co.uk

MIX
Paper from
responsible sources
FSC® C018179

Penguin Random House is committed to a
sustainable future for our business, our readers
and our planet. This book is made from Forest
Stewardship Council® certified paper.

To my family

Contents

Introduction: Great Economists on Our
    Economic Challenges   1

1. Adam Smith: Should the Government
    Rebalance the Economy?   11

2. David Ricardo: Do Trade Deficits Matter?   32

3. Karl Marx: Can China Become Rich?   51

4. Alfred Marshall: Is Inequality Inevitable?   76

5. Irving Fisher: Are We at Risk of Repeating the 1930s?   95

6. John Maynard Keynes: To Invest or Not to Invest?   123

7. Joseph Schumpeter: What Drives Innovation?   144

8. Friedrich Hayek: What Can We Learn from
    Financial Crises?   172

9. Joan Robinson: Why are Wages so Low?   194

10. Milton Friedman: Are Central Banks Doing Too Much?   213

11. Douglass North: Why are so Few Countries Prosperous?   239

12. Robert Solow: Do We Face a Slow-Growth Future?   265

Epilogue: The Future of Globalization   283

Acknowledgements   299

Glossary   301

Bibliography   303

Notes   313

Index   333

Introduction: Great Economists on Our Economic Challenges

During times of fundamental change, economic expertise is in demand. Who better to help shape our economic future than the Great Economists? Their thinking transformed the modern economy into one characterized by unprecedented prosperity, relatively speaking, in even the poorest countries. Those ideas from the past can help guide us as we confront today's economic challenges.

Now is an ideal time to assess where the world economy is headed. Having come through the global financial crisis of 2008 and the Great Recession that followed it, the US, Britain, the European Union, Japan, China, and others are experiencing significant challenges to growing their economies and generating wealth. America, for long the leading economic engine of the world, faces the prospect of slowing growth as slow wage growth weighs on its future. In Britain, weak productivity growth and the historic referendum of June 2016 that resulted in a vote to leave the European Union will affect the country's economy for years to come. The EU, meanwhile, faces difficult questions about how to reform the euro area's economy to generate growth while sharing a single currency, the euro. Concerns over slow growth have long confronted Japan, which is at the forefront of a number of innovative economic policies to energize its sluggish economy, while China, too, faces structural challenges as it attempts to join the ranks of the world's rich countries. Emerging economies such as those in Asia, Africa, Latin America, and eastern Europe are also in the spotlight. After years of strong growth, they are slowing down, which raises the question whether these nations will have enough economic momentum left to eradicate poverty within their borders. Yet, we also live during a time of rapid technological change, much like the previous Industrial Revolutions that raised our living standards. We'll also consider what drives innovation and how to increase economic growth.

★

Who, then, were these Great Economists whose theories changed the world and whose ideas can help us with our challenges today? It was a difficult choice to make. Applying the criterion that their work must have direct implications for our current economic problems helped a little, but there remain many not on my list who might arguably have been included. Hyman Minsky, for example, who is discussed in the Irving Fisher chapter because the pair's combined thinking helps us better to understand the nature of financial crises. And Paul Samuelson's ideas on the distributional impact of international trade builds on the work of David Ricardo, so his thinking provides considerable insight into how those who have lost out in the globalization process discussed in the Epilogue might better manage their predicament.

This leads on to my second qualifier, which is that my selections also reflect the issues that I have chosen to focus on. Choices had to be made, so I have whittled a huge list down to one that is centred on economic growth – that is, the rate and the quality of development. How economies grow will be affected by the policy choices taken after the worst banking crash in a century and in the context of a globalized world. The 2008 financial crisis and the rise of emerging markets are among the fundamental factors in the past few decades that have transformed and will continue to reshape the world economy. The crisis showed that some of the old ways of growing an economy are unsustainable, while the fast growth of a number of developing countries suggests that it's time to examine how they did that and what it means for big global challenges such as eradicating poverty. Some countries have already confronted some of these issues, and therefore hold potential lessons for other nations. For instance, what can we learn from how the US and UK have been re-examining their growth drivers after the 2008 crisis, or how China has emerged as a major economy so rapidly? Other examples include how Europe is planning to increase investment to boost economic growth, and Japan's attempts to end decades of economic stagnation through massive government intervention. So, the quality and nature of economic growth will be central to this book.

You will note that I have largely chosen economists from an earlier vintage. The Greats, unsurprisingly, tend to focus on big general questions, such as growth, innovation and the nature of markets. Of course, there are eminent economists who are currently working on key problems. Many of the recent Nobel laureates are actively engaged in current policy debates, such as raising economic growth rates and assessing the role of government spending, but their research is rooted in the work of the originators of the general models that form the foundation of economics. This book reveals who those Great Economists were, where their ideas came from and how their insights have shaped economic thinking.

Unsurprisingly, my first subject is Adam Smith. It is almost a truism that all economists first turn to Smith when confronted with an economic question. I was reminded of it recently when I presented a BBC radio programme. I asked an academic why we tend to overlook the dominant services sector and instead focus on manufacturing, which comprises only around one-tenth of the British and American economies. He referred immediately to Adam Smith, who thought that the services sector was unproductive. Smith believed that the sector was comprised of 'buffoons, musicians, opera-singers',[1] whose output could not be traded and therefore did not add to national output in the same way as manufacturing. Smith was, naturally, a product of his times, which witnessed the advent of industrialization that led to an unprecedented increase in incomes and living standards. His 1776 *The Wealth of Nations* is the seminal work on the subject. Smith's legacy is evident in nearly every aspect of economics. We still view the economy through the lens he fashioned.

So, Adam Smith is the first Great Economist in the book. His idea of the 'invisible hand' of market forces – meaning the innate effects of supply and demand, rather than direct intervention by governments or other institutions – is the foundation of economic theory. As I explored in that Radio 4 programme, the British government is trying to rebalance the economy towards making things once again, after the 2008 crisis revealed the downsides of relying too much on financial services. So far they haven't succeeded. A decade later, the services sector has recovered to pre-recession levels, while manufacturing has not. And it's not just Britain. America, China and other major economies are also seeking to rebalance their economies so that they can grow in a more sustainable fashion. What would Adam Smith say about these attempts? How would he reconcile his affinity for manufacturing with an aversion to governments intervening in the workings of the 'invisible hand'?

An economist inspired by Adam Smith later became the father of international trade. In 1817 David Ricardo formalized the theory of comparative advantage that shows how every country benefits from free trade. This is true even if that country is worse than every other country in the world at producing everything. It should still focus on making what it was relatively less bad at, and specializing and trading would benefit it as well as the rest of the world. But, what if the result of trading on the basis of comparative advantage is that countries like America and Britain run persistent trade deficits, meaning that the value of the goods they import outstrips the value of their exports? What would Ricardo advise governments to do?

Karl Marx viewed the Industrial Revolution rather differently from Adam Smith. Although he too experienced the dramatic transformation of Western economies in the nineteenth century, Marx rejected market-driven outcomes and instead favoured collectivization over capitalism. He viewed the market economy as exploitative and unsustainable, and his views led the former Soviet Union and China, among others, to adopt a communist rather than capitalist system.

The collapse of the Soviet Union is generally viewed as an indictment of central planning. By adopting market-oriented reforms, China has emerged as the world's second largest economy. Still, China is undergoing perhaps the most challenging part of its marketization process. How would Marx judge the trail that the Chinese economy is blazing?

On the opposite side of the planning – market spectrum from Karl Marx was his near contemporary Alfred Marshall. Instead of the government running the economy, Marshall formalized how Smith's 'invisible hand' achieves an equilibrium for the economy through market forces. He showed how supply and demand determine the price and quantity of a good. Marshall's belief in a self-correcting market that moves towards an equilibrium means that we only need a *laissez-faire* state. There is no imperative for the government to intervene a great deal in the workings of the market economy, for instance, in the ups and downs of a business cycle. But, how about redistributing income in the face of rising inequality? How would Marshall have viewed inequalities that have burgeoned as the benefits of a growing economy disproportionately accrue to the top 1 per cent?

There's no doubt that inequality is high on the policy agenda, a reminder that we must consider the quality and not just the speed of economic growth. A best-selling book on the topic of inequality is by the French economist Thomas Piketty. Its popularity reflects a widespread concern that inequality is as high now in America as the Gilded Age of the late nineteenth century. A recent economics Nobel laureate, Joseph Stiglitz, has even pointed to inequality as one of the causes of the slow recovery after the Great Recession. So, how would Marshall view the worsening of income inequality which is often perceived as an indictment of capitalism? Are capitalist economies inevitably unequal?

Concerns over economic growth have certainly heated up since the 2008 global financial crisis, which was the worst economic downturn since the Great Depression of the 1930s. America was the epicentre, and Britain was deeply affected. Years later, there are still high levels of debt and less than robust economic growth. Irving Fisher, who lived through it, warned about the danger of the debt-deflation spiral after such crises. It's what Japan has experienced since its early 1990s real estate crash. As debt was repaid, output fell which led to falling prices or deflation and 'lost decades' of growth. What would Fisher advise in order to ensure that countries do not face 'lost decades' of growth? Are we at risk of repeating aspects of the 1930s, which was characterized by a second recession and stagnant income growth?

Arguably the economist who has been most discussed since the recent downturn, when unemployment returned as a worrying problem, is John Maynard Keynes. According to the think tank for the group of developed nations known as the Organisation for Economic Co-operation and Development (OECD), the long-term unemployment rate (a measure of those who have been out of work for more

than one year) had increased by a staggering 77 per cent in the aftermath of the 2008 crisis. Youth unemployment reached double digits
in some European countries such as Spain. It's less of an issue for the
US and UK, but other forms of 'hidden' unemployment, such as
underemployment and part-time work, are concerns. So, the role of
government in promoting employment and reviving growth is front
and centre in public policy.

It is well known that Keynes did not believe in the market's ability
to self-correct, which was the dominant economic thinking at the
time. Instead, he argued for government spending, and incurring a
budget deficit if necessary, to bring the economy back to full employment. His views were shaped by the persistently high unemployment
rates that followed the Great Depression, and Keynes's ideas made
him an influential figure, even posthumously during the post-war
period which saw the birth of large government programmes such as
the welfare state.

In another parallel to today, the dominant economic debate since
the Great Recession of 2009 has been over austerity – cutting government spending and raising taxes to reduce the budget deficit. One
of the results of austerity measures is a huge drop in government/
public/state investment, which hampers economic growth. Looking
ahead, what would Keynes advise today's governments to do about
public investment, an important driver of growth and full employment in the economy?

Another big economic debate is over how to make economies
more productive. Recovery since the financial crisis has been slow by
historical standards. Raising productivity, which has stagnated in
many developed economies, is crucial if the economy is to grow; but
it requires innovation. This may be the most important policy question for advanced economies, and the Great Economist best placed to
address it is Keynes's contemporary and the advocate of 'creative
destruction': Joseph Schumpeter. Schumpeter's theory placed entrepreneurs and innovators at the heart of not just the recovery but
overall economic growth. So, what would he advise governments
do today in order to raise productivity and innovation?

Another influential contributor to economic policy around that time was Friedrich Hayek. Hayek was the standard bearer for free-market economics. He was part of the Austrian School of economics, which rejected, among other theories, the standard explanations of business cycles. Hayek was diametrically opposed to the views of Keynes and believed in the supremacy of market forces. Hayek opposed the use of monetary policy, which is when the cost and quantity of money in the economy is adjusted to influence growth, as well as Keynes's fiscal activism, setting him at odds with much of the economics profession. Although Hayek found an intellectual home at the London School of Economics and Political Science, his theories are still not widely accepted in academia. With capitalism itself now under attack in the aftermath of the Great Recession by the Occupy movement and others, Hayek's ideas have come back into fashion as the search continues for arguments to defend the market system against growing scepticism. Those ideas can help us discern whether there are any lessons to be learned from the financial crisis.

Joan Robinson, another of the twentieth-century's leading lights, is the sole woman among the Greats in this book, which reflects the chronic dearth of women in economics. When I was an economics doctoral student at Oxford University, I found her theories on imperfectly competitive markets highly insightful. For instance, one of the most pressing economic challenges is low wages. The UK has the dubious distinction of being the only one of the G7 group of major economies where average annual wage growth failed to match inflation for much of the decade since the financial crisis. A general lack of growth in 'real wages' is a problem that goes beyond this last recession, and beyond UK shores. Japan and Germany have faced twenty years of stagnant wage growth for those workers earning the median wage, that is to say those whose earnings fall in the middle section of the pay distribution spectrum. Even worse, median wages in the United States have been stagnant for four decades. This is where Joan Robinson's work offers insights. In the two key factor markets, namely capital and labour, Robinson showed how deviations from the assumption of perfect competition, where all markets operate efficiently, can explain low wages and why pay does not reflect the output of workers. We'll ask what remedies Robinson might offer to address the challenge of stagnant wages plaguing major economies.

The next Great Economist certainly did not suffer from a lack of attention. Milton Friedman famously coined the phrase 'Inflation is always and everywhere a monetary phenomenon.' Friedman believed that the amount of money in the economy only affected prices, and therefore inflation, but not national output in the long run, which is the monetarist view of economics captured by his well-known quote. Throughout his long life Friedman remained an advocate of the free market and even initially considered the establishment of America's central bank, the Federal Reserve, to have been a mistake. Although he later accepted that the Fed was necessary to control the money supply, he insisted it should be confined to that role, and not be an activist institution. Unsurprisingly, he disagreed with the Keynesian view that fiscal policies have a lasting impact on the economy.

Part of the Chicago School of economics, in 1963 Friedman co-wrote with Anna Jacobson Schwartz one of the most influential books on monetary policy: *A Monetary History of the United States, 1867–1960*. They revisited the causes of the Great Depression to understand what happened and why it took so long to recover from the 1929 stock market crash. Their conclusion is that monetary policy was the culprit, specifically the Fed prematurely tightening the money supply, which they argued caused the crash and also led to a second economic downturn, known as a 'recession within the Depression', of 1937–38. So, what would Friedman say about the use of 'unconventional' monetary policy in the aftermath of the Great Recession with its parallels to the 1930s? Central banks have now deployed a dazzling array of policies, including quantitative easing (cash injections) and even negative interest rates (where commercial bank deposits at the central bank are being charged) to get more money into the economy. What would Friedman make of the activities of central banks which are largely operating in unknown territory?

The next pair of authors put forward contrasting views about the fundamental drivers of how an economy grows and develops. And both have heavily influenced current policies.

Douglass North deviated from many of his contemporaries in that he believed that institutions mattered for economic development. North's views have gained currency in recent years because standard growth theories haven't been able to explain fully why some countries become rich and others remain poor. Economists have turned to North's work following the Second World War on the role of institutions to understand why so few countries have become wealthy in the post-war period. As a result, institutions such as the rule of law have come to the forefront of development policies. We'll ask how North would reform institutions to promote economic development.

His contemporary Robert Solow holds a different perspective. Solow produced the seminal work on neoclassical economic growth that North deemed to be incomplete. The Solow model aims to explain growth by examining contributions of workers, the investment of firms in the productive capital of an economy and the role of technological progress. Unlike other recessions that saw a V-shaped output drop and quick recovery, the 2008 crisis has seen a sharp fall in national output or GDP (gross domestic product) but a sluggish recovery. Economists have become worried that this is our collective future. There's even a term revived by Harvard economist Lawrence Summers to describe a slow-growth world: 'secular stagnation'. This was a term used by Alvin Hansen in the 1930s after the last systemic banking crisis to describe the resultant slow growth due in part to ageing societies, among other issues.[2] Japan is the forerunner here, as the most aged economy. How would Solow judge the slow post-crisis recovery, and would he agree that we face a slow-growth future? This question is a pervasive one in the coming years for all developed economies.

Finally, the consensus around globalization is under challenge. After decades where opening up to the global economy was the priority for governments around the world, there is growing discontent with the uneven gains from trade. The economy as a whole benefits, but there are still winners and losers within a country. In the recent past, both the US and the UK have seen the public vote against the status quo, including a rejection of current trade arrangements. Would the Great Economists say that globalization is in trouble?

The rapid global economic growth of the post-war period was led in part by the expansion of international trade. So, prosperity is linked to globalization, particularly in the past few decades with the establishment in 1995 of the World Trade Organization (WTO), which has opened global markets. Globalization has linked all of us via the transmission of not just resources but also ideas from around the world. The concept of a bike-sharing programme in London can be picked up quickly around the world and become deployed by an app in Beijing, for instance. But, trade expansion is stalling and the multilateral system is becoming fragmented into an emerging system of regional and bilateral free trade agreements. Moreover, trade deals face voter backlash over the uneven benefits from globalization. What would the Great Economists say about what this means for trade as an engine of economic growth in the future? Most importantly, how should the backlash against globalization be addressed? Nobel laureate Paul Samuelson's work details the uneven effects of trade on workers in an economy. How should the distributional impact, where the entire economy benefits but some (for example manufacturing workers, farmers) lose, be addressed? Their ideas suggest ways to help even out the winners and losers from trade, and can point the way forward for the future of globalization.

This book will seek to uncover some of the answers to the big economic issues affecting all of us by drawing on the insights of the Great Economists. Their collective knowledge has already shaped the policies that governed the world economy during a period in which our living standards have significantly improved: from the Industrial Revolution through the Golden Age of economic growth after the Second World War to the current digital age. Perhaps their insights can help guide our economic future too.

CHAPTER I

Adam Smith: Should the Government Rebalance the Economy?

Widely viewed as the seminal figure in economics, Adam Smith witnessed the beginning of the Industrial Revolution, which fundamentally changed the Western world. During this time and in the decades that followed, Britain became the world's first industrialized economy. This extraordinary period formed the backdrop to one of the most influential books in economics.

Adam Smith's magnum opus, *An Inquiry into the Nature and Causes of the Wealth of Nations*, took a decade to write. It sets out the concept of the 'invisible hand', which refers to the unseen market forces that set prices by equating supply and demand. It has become the mantra for *laissez faire* economics. Even though Smith himself never used that term in that specific way, his writings did envision a limited role for the state:

> The statesman, who should attempt to direct private people in what manner they ought to employ their capitals, would not only load himself with a most unnecessary attention, but assume an authority which could safely be trusted, not only to no single person, but to no council or senate whatever, and which would nowhere be so dangerous as in the hands of a man who had folly and presumption enough to fancy himself fit to exercise it.[1]

Smith was even more dubious when it came to taxation: 'There is no art which one government sooner learns of another than that of draining money from the pockets of the people.'[2]

Adam Smith would view a policymaker who intervened in the operation of market forces with scepticism. Yet, that's what post-industrial nations like Britain and the United States are attempting to do – roll back the deindustrialization process by encouraging manufacturing and reducing the share of national output accounted for by services. This urge to rebalance the economy arose after the 2008 financial crisis which revealed the fragility of a large banking sector that brought the economy to its knees. It led the then-UK Chancellor George Osborne to start wearing hard hats and to promote the 'March of the Makers'. In the US, President Barack Obama invested in advanced or high-tech manufacturing. His successor, Donald Trump, explicitly extolled companies to bring factories back to America.

What would Adam Smith make of these efforts? Should government rebalance the economy towards making things once again? Is it possible to rebalance the economy in countries where the services sector makes up more than three-quarters of national output, as it does in Britain and the US? The answer holds lessons for other economies that may follow those two nations as they embark on the typical economic path of industrialization followed by deindustrialization.

Industrialization, deindustrialization and reindustrialization

Great Britain became the first industrialized nation in the late eighteenth and nineteenth centuries, followed by Germany and the United States. The period, which became known as the Industrial Revolution, saw the economy transformed from an agrarian society into one characterized by factories owned and run by merchants who traded their wares both at home and overseas.

In our own times, Britain and several other advanced economies, including the United States, have experienced yet another fundamental structural change: deindustrialization. Since the 1980s Thatcher-era reforms that liberalized the financial sector – notably the 'Big Bang' of 1986, when markets were opened up to greater competition – Britain has seen industry give way to services. (Relatively speaking, that is. The UK is still the ninth biggest manufacturer in the world, and was in the top five until around 2004.) Similarly, although the US remains the second biggest manufacturer in the world (having been overtaken recently by China), its services economy accounts for the larger part of American national output. In the European Union the services sector makes up 70 per cent of the GDP or national output for the bloc, but the EU also counts among its ranks some of the biggest manufacturing nations in the world, for example Germany, France and Italy. Even the world's biggest manufacturer, China, which is only a middle-income country, has seen its services sector overtake industrial output in the economy.

When countries grow, they tend to industrialize, so they move out of agriculture and into manufacturing, which has higher productivity or output per worker and thus generates higher wages. Industrialization is how countries become middle class and prosper. Deindustrialization then follows. In advanced economies, manufacturing starts to become relatively less important as a share of output once they become richer and services in the business, retail and finance sectors start to dominate the economy while employment shifts from factories to offices or stores.

The 2008 crisis revealed the downside to having an economy with a large financial services sector. Banks had become complex and interconnected, and their business became harder to understand and to regulate. Their responsibility for causing the worst recession in a century prompted calls from the public to regulate the banks more tightly in the US and UK. The crash also led the American and British governments to want more manufacturing, thus they have sought to 'rebalance' the economy towards making things once again.

That's a big task. Manufacturing accounts for around only 11 per cent of Britain's value-added output, while, as noted, the dominant services sector accounts for over three-quarters of the economy. British manufacturing has declined from contributing a quarter of national output in 1980 to 20 per cent in the 1990s to just 12 per cent in the 2000s. It's a similar picture in the US. By contrast, manufacturing still makes up about 20 per cent of the German economy on the same value-added basis. At its peak, financial services alone made up some 8 per cent of UK national output, which is not that much smaller than all of Britain's manufacturing combined. This is the essence of deindustrialization, where industry has given way to a dominant services sector in the same way that agriculture was overtaken by manufacturing during Adam Smith's time.

The question is, can the US, and perhaps the UK, reverse deindustrialization? It's a refrain heard frequently since the crisis. 'Made in America' and 'Made in Britain' are among the phrases uttered by governments and businesses after the worst recession in a century. But, reversing the process of deindustrialization is challenging in a globalized world economy.

Emerging economies like China can produce more cheaply while information and communications technology (ICT) has lowered the costs of logistics, so globalization makes it harder for rich nations to compete with lower-cost producers. In fact, Harvard economist Dani Rodrik even points to 'premature deindustrialization' in some developing countries which are moving from agriculture directly to services due to the forces of globalization, which holds potentially worrying consequences for countries that have yet to gain a firm foothold in the middle-income stratum.

We are in unknown territory. The impetus for deindustrialization is greater in Britain and America than in other nations. After suffering their worst financial crisis in a century, they are anxious for change.

That's not the sole consideration. Adam Smith may be the economist who named the 'invisible hand' that allowed the market to dictate what was produced and how it was priced, but he did not think highly of the services sector. A product of his time, he did not believe that services could produce output that was as valuable as that from a factory or a bakery. In fact, Smith didn't condone much of what makes up the modern economy, for example he wasn't in favour of joint-stock companies, which are the basis of modern-day corporations.

His legacy continues to affect attitudes today. Even the way that national statistics are collected breaks down manufacturing data in great detail while aggregating much of services output. That's probably also because it's hard for statisticians to put a figure on what a consultant contributes while he sits at his computer or what a meeting adds to national output. We've all been in too many of those to know that they are not all productive!

So, should the government be trying to rebalance the economy? Can market forces driven by the 'invisible hand' be reshaped by the state? What would Adam Smith have to say about it all?

The life and times of Adam Smith

Adam Smith was born in 1723 in Kirkcaldy, a seaport near Edinburgh in Scotland. His deceased father was a Customs officer, and his well-to-do family was friendly with members of the Scottish Enlightenment. The Scottish movement paralleled the European Enlightenment, which counted among its ranks writers like Voltaire, and was characterized by a focus on science and rationality. This period has been called the Golden Age of Scotland, and Smith would figure prominently among its leading thinkers as the father of economic science.

Like many early economists, he wasn't taught the subject. Instead, he studied physics and mathematics at Glasgow University from 1737 to 1740. It was at this time that he also developed an interest in Stoic philosophy. Most early economists were also philosophers, among whom the likes of David Hume and John Stuart Mill were influential in shaping economic thinking.

Smith then studied at Balliol College, Oxford University until 1746. As he wasn't a member of the Church of England, he could not matriculate at that time, so was more like a visiting student. Suffice it to say he did not enjoy his time at Oxford: 'The discipline of colleges and universities is in general contrived, not for the benefit of the students, but for the interest, or more properly speaking, for the ease of the masters.'[3]

So, in the tradition of self-learning that has characterized a number of Oxford experiences, Smith spent his time there on the classics and immersed himself in modern languages. Since, in his view: 'In the university of Oxford, the greater part of the public professors have, for these many years, given up altogether even the pretence of teaching.'[4]

Afterwards, Smith returned to Scotland and gave a series of public lectures at Edinburgh University in 1748. It was there that he became friends with David Hume, a leading figure in the Scottish Enlightenment. That was when Smith's views on the 'invisible hand' started to form. He thought government intervention in the economy was a disruption of the 'natural course' of markets, a view which he later developed in *The Wealth of Nations*. His seminal work argued for a limited state that allowed markets to operate freely. As he stressed in one of his lectures: 'Little else is requisite to carry a state to the highest degree of opulence from the lowest barbarism, but peace, easy taxes, and a tolerable administration of justice.'[5]

Smith's successful lectures led to a professorship at his alma mater. From 1751 to 1764 he taught at the University of Glasgow. First, he took up the Chair in Logic, and was subsequently appointed Chair of Moral Philosophy. During this time he gained fame with the publication of his ethics lectures. In 1759 *The Theory of Moral Sentiments* was published, leading him to become a well-known figure in the European Enlightenment. He described his time as an academic as 'by far the most useful, and, therefore, as by far the happiest and most honourable' of his career.[6]

Nevertheless, in 1764 Smith was tempted to leave academia for a lucrative stint as private tutor to the third Duke of Buccleuch, who was the stepson of Charles Townshend, a politician. He accompanied the young duke for a two-year tour abroad, and spent 1764–6 in Paris, Toulouse and Geneva.

It was in France that he came across the Physiocrats, a prominent group of economists, who viewed agriculture, not manufacturing, as the source of wealth. For Smith, this jarred with the British experience of industrialization, and it is somewhat ironic that Smith's arguments in favour of manufacturing over services share some parallels with Physiocrat thinking.

Upon returning to Britain, Smith moved to London and spent 1766–7 researching public finances for Charles Townshend, who was now Chancellor of the Exchequer. He subsequently returned to Kirkcaldy to live with his mother, and focused for the next six years on writing *The Wealth of Nations*. From 1773–6, he returned to London to finish the book. Smith's publication aimed to influence British

MPs to support a peaceful resolution to the American colonies' War of Independence. In the final paragraph of *The Wealth of Nations*, Smith wrote that Britain should 'endeavour to accommodate her future views and designs to the real mediocrity of her circumstances'.[7] It was a sentence retained in all subsequent editions and reflected Smith's enduring belief that the market, and not the state, should dictate economic progress in all respects, including colonialism.

Adam Smith retired in 1776, the year that America declared independence, and he spent the next two years in Kirkcaldy writing another book, on the 'Imitative Arts', which covered painting, music and poetry. But, in 1778, he re-entered public life and became the Commissioner of Customs for Scotland, following in his father's footsteps. He moved to Edinburgh, where he lived again with his mother, Janet Douglas, a cousin who was also the housekeeper, and his heir, a cousin's son, David Douglas, who was to become Lord Reston, a distinguished jurist.

In 1784 he finished the third edition of *The Wealth of Nations*. A few years later, he also completed the sixth edition of *Moral Sentiments*, which included his thoughts on framing a constitution, which was highly topical at the time of the American Revolution as well as burgeoning revolutions on the Continent, notably in France.

Despite his path-breaking work, Adam Smith was highly self-critical of the slow pace of his writing. In 1785 he claimed the 'indolence of old age' and was uncertain that he could finish the 'Imitative Arts' or another book on the theory of jurisprudence. He had envisaged his major works as a trilogy: *Moral Sentiments*, *The Wealth of Nations* and a third book on Law and Jurisprudence, which was never written. Rather surprisingly, Smith expressed disappointment that he had not achieved more, and insisted that his manuscripts should be burned after his death.[8]

Why rebalance the economy?

Before we assess what Adam Smith would have made of the attempt, let's look at why there is a debate over rebalancing the economy. It's an issue that's at the forefront in Britain, a country that has one of the largest services sectors among advanced economies. As noted earlier, even though the US was at the epicentre of the 2008 financial crisis it remains the world's second biggest manufacturer while the UK has slid down the rankings. So Britain's experience in particular holds potential lessons for other countries.

Changing its economic growth drivers is indeed what Britain set out to do after the 2008 financial crisis. It was termed the 'March of the Makers' under the David Cameron government. The UK wants to rebalance its economy towards making things and selling more of its wares overseas. The two are related in the era of globalization, where much of manufacturing output consists of tradable goods. The British government wants to rely less on financial services, given the banking bust of a few years ago, but manufacturing accounts for only around a tenth of the economy, while the services sector accounts for the bulk of national output. Also, Britain, which until recently exported more to Ireland than to the emerging markets dubbed the BRICs (Brazil, Russia, India, China) combined, wants to reorient more towards developing economies and help its companies access the fastest growing markets in the world.

If it is to succeed in this endeavour, it clearly needs to be peddling the right stuff abroad. However, Britain's trade deficit – the difference between the value of imported and exported goods and services – widened precipitously and hit record highs in the years after 2008. That's not a great piece of evidence for the rebalancing efforts. The hope was that with sterling having lost about a quarter of its value at one point after the banking crash, a cheaper currency would boost exports in the same way that it did during the early 1990s when the pound left the exchange rate mechanism (ERM) that had tied it to the German Deutschmark. The last time that Britain had a trade surplus was towards the end of that decade in 1997, on the back of a depreciated pound.

Before then, Britain had run a deficit in its current account, the broadest measure of trade that includes financial flows, every year since 1984. Notably, the deficit in goods trade grew after the late 1990s with further deindustrialization. Recall that manufacturing's contribution to GDP has halved since 1980.

Offsetting part of the overall trade gap is the balance of trade in services, a figure that has been in surplus at least since 1966. Not only is it a long-standing surplus, it is also a large one, typically around 5 per cent of GDP. When the surplus in investment income earned from abroad is included, economic historian Nicholas Crafts points out that the total 'invisible' service trade balance has been in surplus for two centuries, since 1816.[9]

Britain is particularly good at providing services and ranks behind only the US in terms of total service-sector exports globally. These are not just financial services, but a range of business services including legal, accountancy, architecture, design, management consultancy, software and advertising. Also, the trade in services tends to be relatively high valued-added. As competitiveness is derived from quality rather than cost, margins tend to be larger. The fact that UK exports are increasingly represented by high-end manufactures and services might explain why the recent depreciation of sterling has failed to boost trade by as much as was hoped for. Prices still matter, but perhaps not as much as they used to.

One of Britain's problems is that the global trade in services, which it is particularly good at, has not opened up in the same way as manufacturing. Since the Second World War, the global trade in goods has boomed as multilateral organizations such as the World Trade Organization (WTO) and its predecessors have brought down tariffs and removed restrictive practices. The global trade in services, though, has not been liberalized to the same extent and this hurts Britain. By contrast, where the trade in services has opened up, Britain tends to do well. Higher education is a good example of a UK service industry that successfully serves overseas markets.

Thus, rebalancing the economy and reindustrialization are easier said than done. The recovery may have finally taken hold, but which of these businesses are driving it and which sectors have already recovered? The answers reveal that the recovery is not due to the economy's 'rebalancing'.

Manufacturing output as a whole has yet to recover its pre-recession level nearly a decade on. Past recessions have caused major shake-outs in British manufacturing. The industries that survived and prospered in the aftermath have tended to be in more specialized and higher technology niches.

There are pockets of activity which are doing well. The manufacture of alcoholic beverages is above 2008 levels. There are reports that Scottish whisky distillers, who account for a quarter of the UK's food and beverage exports, are even struggling to keep up with strong worldwide demand.

Britain's aerospace industry is also faring well. Rolls-Royce, with manufacturing plants in Derby and Bristol, is one of the world's largest producers of aircraft engines. Farnborough's BAE Systems is among the largest defence contractors in the world and is building new aircraft carriers.

Although the oil and gas industry is running down, operating expenditure in the oil industry has been growing strongly as it becomes more expensive to extract the remaining 'harder to get to' oil. Decommissioning expenditure is also on the rise. Furthermore, British expertise in maintaining extraction equipment, surveying and extracting hydrocarbons from difficult places is in high demand around the world.

Then there's the housing market. Like manufacturing, construction output has struggled even as the economy as a whole has recovered. Housebuilding is in the doldrums. The number of completed new dwellings has hovered around 150,000 per year; this is less than before the crash and far below the 250,000 per year that many experts argue is needed to meet long-term demand.

The services sector as a whole, however, regained and then exceeded its pre-recession level soon after the crash. But it is a large sector, consisting of a myriad of different activities, and its overall success conceals some internal difficulties. Two sectors to have done badly are, unsurprisingly, banking and government administration. In 2015, the latest year for which annual figures are available, financial services output remained depressed relative to its pre-crisis level despite improvements in the pension and insurance categories. In the public administration and defence sector, output had been falling steadily. The government's continuing squeeze on public spending is likely to push this lower.

Output in the telecommunications and information technology industries recovered quickly. The growing appetite for new technologies from households and businesses has continued unabated despite the depth of the recession.

Business and professional services, which includes a broad range of business-to-business services including legal, accountancy, management consultancy, architecture, scientific and technical research and consultancy, administrative and support services, human resources, public relations, and so on, contracted sharply during the recession. Compared to the first quarter of 2008, output was 15 per cent lower by the third quarter of 2009. The downturn was short lived, however, and the sector recovered strongly and now exceeds pre-recession levels.

It's clear, then, that Britain is a services-based economy. Its recovery from the global financial crisis underscores that fact. Although Britain might once have been correctly described as 'the workshop to the world' and 'a nation of shopkeepers', neither statement has been true for a while.

Manufacturing output and retail sales, once the mainstay of the economy, have been usurped by specialists advising the world how and where to invest, organizing their companies, proposing better product designs, writing contracts, preparing accounts and offering technical advice in the worlds of engineering, IT, architecture and finance. The output of these activities takes the form of blueprints, designs, specifications, recommendations, computer code, ideas, reports, databases and the like. Business activity increasingly consists of people sitting in front of computer screens and having meetings to appraise projects.

How hard is it to boost productivity and innovation in services? To what extent do policymakers misunderstand the importance of the services sector? What would it mean for economic growth if services were accurately measured?

It's harder to tailor policies for services than for manufacturing since services are intangible. But, for post-industrial economies, services comprise the bulk of output, so is there much of a choice? Could boosting innovation in services counteract the trend of declining productivity (and therefore stagnant wages) in advanced societies that we will investigate later in the book?

It's challenging to measure what can be produced in an hour by a professional service such as consultancy compared with the manufacture of a widget. For instance, a London consultancy firm doubled the price of the same report after the economy started to recover. As the price is determined by greater demand, the cost of the report rose even though what was supplied remained the same. It's hard to separate out the effects of a price increase or quality improvement. No wonder there are challenges in measuring the biggest part of the economy. Some companies are also doing both manufacturing and services. 'Manu-services' mean that we also underestimate the evolution of companies like Rolls-Royce, who make more money servicing and maintaining their engines than selling the engines themselves and yet continue to be viewed as a manufacturer rather than a supplier of services.

It's not only the output of services that's intangible; the investment is too. Economists are debating whether better measurement of intangible assets would increase GDP. When research and development (R&D) and other intangible investments were included, US GDP was increased by 3 per cent.[10] The OECD estimates that intangible investment, including that in human capital, such as education, and software, is as important as investment in tangible machinery and equipment in the UK.[11] Since 2014, investment in private R&D has been included in UK GDP. By this approach, UK GDP has been increased by around 1.5 per cent.

Intangible investment is what most firms in the services sector do. They invest in people. Most services companies invest in human capital since that's their main asset. Innovation comes from people who provide a service better. Even though the coffee machine is the same, we're aeons away from the tepid brewed coffee that used to be served in cafes as baristas now provide a wide range of espressos and cappuccinos. That intangible investment in their skills to produce a higher quality coffee is hardly measured. If it were, then the puzzle of Britain's slow productivity growth may be easier to solve if services output is actually higher than measured. Sir Martin Sorrell, the chief executive and founder of WPP, one of the world's largest advertising companies, says that his company invests twenty-five times more in human capital such as training programmes than physical capital in the UK. He believes that services such as those his firm offers are undervalued as contributors to growth.

The overall challenge is how to measure accurately the largely invisible output and input from companies in the services sector. That consultancy report that doubled in cost counts as doubled output of a service in official statistics. Does a price increase reflect an improved service or simply a higher bill? There are also meetings that could be done away with, but think about the ones where decisions are made and creative processes start flowing. Are meetings a drain on resources or profitable brainstorming sessions? Such imponderables are why it's difficult to know precisely how much of UK national output is mismeasured. It's certainly worth trying to do better since this invisible part of the economy generates the most employment.

Better measuring of services output would also affect the country's balance of payments. The UK has had a stubbornly high trade deficit despite the depreciation of sterling after the 2008 crisis. There is scope to boost exports of tradable services to help pay for the goods that are imported. Among the world's developing economies there is a growing market for services, including the highly skilled professional variety that Britain specializes in such as education and law. But those same economies also have burgeoning services sectors, so there is competition from those economies to consider if Britain's position as the world's second largest exporter of services is to be safeguarded.

Of course, effectively promoting the services sector abroad and supporting it at home depends on its clear quantification. Perhaps it is the difficulty of doing so that has contributed to policymakers focusing on promoting manufacturing. Whatever the reason, rebalancing the British economy hasn't exactly been successful: services have recovered to pre-crisis levels without too much help or attention from the government, but manufacturing has still to do so nearly a decade after the event.

So, should Britain continue its efforts to rebalance its economy? What would Adam Smith do?

Adam Smith on rebalancing the economy

Adam Smith's economic system is formulated around three pillars: the division of labour, the price mechanism and the medium of exchange (money). Both the price of goods or services and the wages of those who produce them are dictated by the price mechanism (dubbed by Smith as the 'invisible hand'). Money has a role set by the market to pay for goods/services, and its supply should not be distorted by the state, for example via mercantilist policies where the aim of trade is to run a surplus of exports over imports and to increase a country's store of gold and silver.

Let's delve into these concepts to discern how Smith would view the rebalancing debate.

It is clear that Smith was influenced by the rise of factories. He emphasized the efficiency of a division of labour that allowed for specialization within a production process that comprised several elements. Producing a woollen coat, for example, required wool to be gathered, spun, dyed, woven and tailored. Smith used pin-making to illustrate the benefits of specialization. He observed that ten workers each undertaking their specialized tasks could produce 48,000 pins a day whereas a single person undertaking every task might produce only ten, at most two hundred. In Smith's view, specialization led nations to become wealthy.

Smith also said that, because earnings could be exchanged for goods, the price of a good and the allocation of resources must be connected. He believed that every good had a 'natural' price, which was the cost of producing it. He drew a distinction between that price and the market price, the price consumers would be willing to pay for it. Supply and demand thus govern prices and the 'invisible hand' guides the market to an equilibrium.

But Smith was concerned about distortions that could cause the market price to deviate too far from the natural price. In his view, both the state and businesses could distort prices by interfering with market forces, the former by taxation, the latter by keeping prices artificially high. He concluded: 'Upon the whole . . . it is by far the best police [government policy] to leave things to their natural course.'[12]

This approach is known as *laissez-faire*, although Smith himself never used the term in such a specific way. The concept can be traced to English and Dutch thinkers of the seventeenth century who influenced French merchants during the reign of Louis XIV, a monarch who was keen on mercantilist policies and intervening in the economy. Reportedly, when a French minister asked a merchant what the government could do for him, the merchant replied: '*Laissez-nous faire, morbleu, laissez-nous faire!*' or 'Leave us be, dammit, leave us be!'

In terms of Smith's theories, an outcome of the market mechanism is that it allows self-interest to lead producers and customers to produce and purchase efficiently. As he famously observed: 'It is not from the benevolence of the butcher, the brewer, or the baker, that we expect our dinner, but from their regard to their own interest. We address ourselves, not to their humanity but to their self-love, and never talk to them of our own necessities but of their advantages.'[13]

Multiple producers seeking to sell their goods generate competition that moves prices toward an equilibrium. Revenues, in turn, are used to pay wages for workers (who are also consumers), so the economy benefits from every person in a society acting in their self-interest. Smith was not unaware of the ill consequences of self-interest, remarking that those with poor judgement were subject 'to anxiety, to fear, and to sorrow; to diseases, to danger, and to death'.[14] For the most part, though, an individual's ambition for '[p]ower and riches'[15] raised the economic welfare of the society:

> [E]very individual . . . neither intends to promote the public interest, nor knows how much he is promoting it . . . he intends only his own security; and by directing that industry in such a manner as its produce may be of the greatest value, he intends only his own gain, and he is in this, as in many other cases, led by an invisible hand to promote an end which was no part of his intention.[16]

That is the premise of Smith's economic system. His encounter with the French economic movement known as Physiocracy contributed to his views of what it meant for the structure of the economy. Although he disagreed with its emphasis, he built upon its ideas. The Physiocrats valued nature and agriculture, and did not think that manufacturing was productive. In their theories, farming was the sole source of wealth, while everyone else simply consumed what the farmers produced. For Smith, the context was different. Britain was undergoing an industrial revolution whereby manufacturing was increasing both productivity and incomes. Smith even witnessed a nascent consumer revolution as the middle classes began to buy mass-manufactured goods such as clothing.

Thus, Smith pushed these ideas further and crafted an economic system that valued the productive potential of manufacturing and merchants. In book III of *The Wealth of Nations*, 'Of the different Progress of Opulence in different Nations', he argued that, so long as there is no interference, capital will find its way to its most productive use.

After reviewing economic history, Smith argued that one path had led to prosperity: initially agriculture, followed by manufactures and finally foreign trade. Services weren't valued, as Smith could not have conceived of the technological revolution that would allow output from that sector to be traded as a commodity or a manufactured good on such a huge scale as it is today. For him, for example, a Mozart string quartet could be enjoyed only as a performance, not as a download or on a CD. Had Smith lived today, he might have changed his mind to support some services if they could be traded and had lasting value. That would add another reason as to why he would be concerned about the government rebalancing the economy. At its heart, Smith's views are centred on an undistorted market.

For his system to work effectively, there must be competition in the marketplace. But Smith also stipulated that such operations must be within the legislation and rules set by the government. The banking sector serves as a telling example. Smith believed that there should be competition among banks to reduce moral hazard, for example the possibility that banks might behave badly knowing they will be rescued. Government regulation could force banks to be more careful 'by not extending their currency beyond its due proportion to their cash'.[17] In other words, banks should depend on their cash and deposits for their lending operations and not get themselves in trouble by leveraging themselves in complicated ways.

More controversially, and reflecting his concern about banks, Smith supported setting a ceiling for interest rates, so that 'prodigals and projectors' could not take up the credit available and exclude the '[s]ober people' who would use the loans more productively.[18] (His fellow philosopher Jeremy Bentham considered this to be a betrayal of Smith's free-market principles!)

In this respect, Smith would agree with the need to reform financial services after a crisis. He would improve banking supervision and increase competition to ensure that credit flowed freely in the economy. Along these lines, Smith believed that some government intervention was warranted, but he was specific as to which areas. For instance, the state should maintain good transport facilities (roads, canals, navigable rivers), as that would break monopolies and encourage competition. His preference was to see such facilities regulated by local administration, or even deregulated if that lowered the cost of maintenance.[19]

Smith also advocated government spending on education. He worried about the impact of the division of labour on people, particularly of repetitive assembly work: '[The worker] naturally loses, therefore, the habit of such exertion, and generally becomes as stupid and ignorant as it is possible for a human creature to become.'[20] In his view, government had an obligation to counteract this effect with some provision of universal education. Smith also favoured public examinations to maintain educational standards, and focused on science, a feature of the Scottish Enlightenment: 'Science is the great antidote to the poison of enthusiasm and superstition; and where all the superior ranks of people were secured from it, the inferior ranks could not be much exposed to it.'[21]

But Smith also makes clear that there are areas where governments should not intervene, among them placing limits on the mobility of workers and capital, and enacting policies that hinder competition.

In particular, Smith believed that restraints on the freedom of trade and policies that favour some sectors of trade over others would force economic activity into unproductive channels. Government intervention to promote one sector against the market is bound to be less productive than if self-interested individuals were able to decide on merit which businesses to start or where to work or what to trade. Rebalancing the economy would fall foul of Smith's admonitions about governments believing themselves to be capable of choosing the most productive sectors.

The rebalancing argument cannot separate out the domestic sectors of the economy from a country's trade position since specialization within an economy is affected by globalization. When Britain specialized in manufacturing as the earliest industrial power, it imported agricultural goods. Smith certainly saw the interconnections between trade and the structure of the British economy.

In fact, Smith's beliefs about a circumscribed role for the state were influenced by his deep-seated opposition to the mercantilist policies of that time. He strongly objected to mercantilists distorting international trade by seeking to run a surplus.

In book IV of *The Wealth of Nations*, Smith criticizes the 'Mercantile System'. He explains why the policy that tries to improve the trade balance through imposing restrictions was inefficient. He was particularly against the regulation of the British trade in grain. He wasn't alone. It was a general preoccupation of Enlightenment economists to argue against protectionism. Smith viewed protectionist trade policies as diametrically opposed to an efficiently operating market. Smith reserved his severest criticism of mercantilist practices for the way that European merchants exerted their monopoly power in the American colonies, asserting that '[t]o prohibit a great people, however, from making all that they can of every part of their own produce, or from employing their stock and industry in the way that they judge most advantageous to themselves, is a manifest violation of the most sacred rights of mankind'.[22]

Although Smith equated free trade with the exercise of economic freedom, a theme throughout his work, he did make allowances for customs to generate government revenue if necessary:

From the above considerations it appears that Brittain [*sic*] should by all means be made a free port, that there should be no interruptions of any kind made to foreign trade, that if it were possible to defray the expences of government by any other method, all duties, customs, and excise should be abolished, and that free commerce and liberty of exchange should be allowed with all nations and for all things.[23]

Unlike many economists, Smith had the chance to put his theories into action. As the Commissioner of Customs for Scotland, he advocated the removal of all trade barriers, which was qualified only by the need to raise revenue for what he considered to be the proper purposes of governing a country. He supported levying duties on imports and exports at a moderate level, but not so high that smuggling would be profitable. True to his beliefs about government policies not distorting the market, he would set duties to be equal for different producers and importers, so that one group or one country would not have an advantage over another. For instance, he saw the inequity of exempting the product of private brewing and distilling (which was imbibed by the rich) from excise duty, while taxing the preferred tipples of the poor.

Having shown what the wealth of nations consists of, and how growth may be encouraged, or at least not discouraged, by governments, Smith in book V of *The Wealth of Nations* went on to discuss a necessary public expenditure: defence. But he was against the British going to war over its American colonies. He urged legislators to awaken from the 'golden dream' of empire and avoid 'a long, expensive and ruinous war'.[24] Smith had even advocated that colonists be given representation in Parliament. In correspondence with William Strahan MP (who was the publisher of both Smith and Hume) on 26 October 1775, Smith wrote that 'a forced and every day more precarious Monopoly of about 6 or 700,000 Pounds a year of Manufactures, was not worth contending for; [and] that we should preserve the greater part of this Trade even if the ports of America were open to all Nations'.[25]

Unsurprisingly, Smith stressed the economic gains from relinquishing the American colonies. In line with his view that markets operate efficiently, he saw the benefits of trading with America even if it was no longer a colony; indeed, he was willing to trade with anyone. Preferring one country over another was, after all, a product of government policy and distorted Smith's freely competitive markets.

In summary, then, Adam Smith would not have advocated that governments rebalance the economy if doing so meant introducing distortions into the operation of the market. He was particularly vehement when it came to trade, and he viewed such restrictive policies as not just inefficient for the market but also distortionary in terms of trading with other countries.

Neither Britain nor the United States has managed either to rebalance the economy towards manufacturing or to close their trade deficits after the 2008 global financial crisis. Instead, a dominant services sector and a persistent trade deficit continue to characterize these post-industrial economies. Smith wouldn't have been surprised. In his economic model, government cannot fundamentally change the economy; only add distortions to how the market functions.

Smith didn't suggest, however, that a nation's economic strengths could not be *shaped*. He did believe in government regulation and policies designed to improve market efficiency. Britain during his lifetime underwent a significant structural shift that was possible under the conditions set by the state. The advent of the Industrial Revolution itself is an example of how technological progress, which the state can influence, fundamentally altered the nature of an economy and a society. The digital revolution of the twenty-first century might even change the application of Smith's views on the unproductive services sector, since services output doesn't expire on use and we can now, for example, purchase and enjoy ad infinitum copies of our favourite musical performances.

Finally, as for the reshaping of a nation's advantage to be more competitive in a less than free trade system, Smith would certainly advocate for liberalization and opening up. But what if the global system failed to meet his standards? The next chapter explores how our second Great Economist, David Ricardo, would view the currently imperfect international trading regime and whether Britain and America should be worried about their large trade deficits under such a system.

A giant among economists

He may be the father of economics, but, like all economists, Smith was subject to criticism, and not just over advocating that colonists be given representation in Parliament! For instance, his friend and contemporary, David Hume, disputed Smith's claim that the rent of farms would make up a portion of the price of produce. Hume believed that rent would not factor into the price of a good traded in the market because the price is determined solely by quantity supplied and customer demand.

Nevertheless, Adam Smith was an influential if somewhat eccentric figure throughout his life. Among his known eccentricities was his banging his head against the wall while dictating *The Wealth of Nations* (he had to dictate because his handwriting was terrible). And although he had a designated heir, he gave away a great deal of his money, mostly in secret.

His greatest bequest is, of course, to economics. Smith is unquestionably the father of the field whose ideas of a freely competitive market still shape our thinking today. And he believed in human endeavour above all:

> The natural effort of every individual to better his own condition . . .
> is so powerful a principle, that it is alone, and without any assistance,
> not only capable of carrying on the society to wealth and prosperity,
> but of surmounting a hundred impertinent obstructions with which
> the folly of human laws too often incumbers its operations.'[26]

CHAPTER 2

David Ricardo: Do Trade Deficits Matter?

Buying more from the rest of the world than a country sells – does it matter? It's a concern for a number of countries, but most notably for the advanced economies of the US and Britain, which have some of the largest persistent trade deficits. As discussed in the last chapter on Adam Smith, trade is related to being deindustrialized. So, this is a challenge that other economies may well confront as they develop. But, for the UK and US, it is a pressing issue now with potential lessons for other countries. What does a large trade deficit say about the health of the economy?

It's a long-standing issue, but one that has come into the spotlight as Britain's current account deficit, which is the broadest measure that includes trade and investment flows, rose to record highs after the 2008 financial crisis. There is no doubt that there are concerns about the UK's trade deficit. The Bank of England has warned about the consequences if foreigners stop investing in the UK after it leaves the EU, which would make the current account deficit harder to finance.

The United States also has a large trade deficit, but it enjoys the privilege of the US dollar being the world's reserve currency. That means foreigners more readily lend money to America to finance its deficit. But, the dollar's position has been questioned by the rise of currencies such as the Chinese renminbi (RMB).

The heart of the issue is this: does it matter if the US or Britain has a large trade deficit? It's been the case for decades. The geopolitical tensions may be higher, but has the economic sustainability of the deficit changed much?

The question of trade has garnered much analysis over centuries, particularly for the UK. International trade was one of the first topics tackled by economists in the late eighteenth century. The rejection of the protectionist Corn Laws in favour of opening up to the world economy marked the start of an era of globalization which contributed to Britain's prosperity.

It was at that time that the seminal work on international trade was penned by David Ricardo. Ricardo's *On the Principles of Political Economy and Taxation* is considered to be one of the classics in economics.

So, what would Ricardo make of the persistent trade deficits experienced by the UK as well as other deindustrialized nations such as the US? Ricardo's theory of comparative advantage, whereby countries gain from trade even if they are less efficient in all production than their trading partners, has transformed the thinking around international trade and showed why there are significant benefits from globalization. But to understand the context for Ricardo's economic theory, we must first take a look at his life.

The life and times of David Ricardo

Although one of the most influential economists of all time, one whose ideas still permeate the profession today, David Ricardo never went to university. Born in 1772, he was later to be disinherited by his Jewish family when he married a Quaker, Ricardo nevertheless used his father's connections at the London Stock Exchange to strike out on his own. He became one of the wealthiest men in Britain, as well as an economist, and late in life a parliamentarian.

Unlike most economists, Ricardo was a successful investor. He was really a stockbroker, dealing mainly in government bonds like his father. Similar to his near contemporary Nathan Mayer Rothschild, he was what was then known as a 'loan contractor', whereby he contracted to take on large chunks of government-issued debt and then sold them to the market at his own risk. During the Battle of Waterloo he bet against a French victory by investing in British securities. With that one call he became one of the richest men in England. At the time of his death, he was worth around £700,000.[1]

Another sign of his investment skills is that he was also a landlord. By the age of forty-three he had made £600,000 and purchased Gatcombe Park in Gloucestershire, which has been owned by Princess Anne since 1976. Ricardo's decision to buy land might have had to do with wanting to turn himself in a country gentleman. His investments gave him an annual income of some £28,000: £10,000 from his estates, £10,000 from mortgages elsewhere and £8,000 from French stocks. Translated into today's money, his estate was estimated to be worth £350–400 million, with an annual income of roughly £15 million. His wealth and standing contributed to his economic theories, which were based on three classes within a society.

Once Ricardo became wealthy, he focused less on his businesses. He began writing about economics by happenstance. His interest in economics, or what was known then as political economy, was triggered unexpectedly when he happened to pick up Adam Smith's *The Wealth of Nations* while visiting Bath in 1799. It wasn't until a decade later that he would write his first essay on economics. In his late thirties, Ricardo published a series of economic articles in the *Morning Chronicle*. His writings were published a year later as *The High Price of Bullion: A Proof of the Depreciation of Banknotes*. Due to the war with France, England's gold supply was under pressure so the Bank of England had stopped paying its notes in gold. Freed from this constraint, Ricardo argued that there was too much money printed by the central bank, which contributed to the high inflation of the time. This critique in his very first publication brought him to the attention of some of the leading thinkers of the time: Thomas Malthus, Jeremy Bentham and James Mill, father of the prominent philosopher John Stuart Mill.

An increase in tariffs on imported wheat in 1815 under the Corn Laws prompted his next major work, *Essay on the Influence of a Low Price of Corn on the Profits of Stock*. The argument against the protectionist Corn Laws formed the foundation for his future and seminal work that set out the basis for trade models in economics. In 1817, *On *the Principles of Political Economy and Taxation* was published. Not only did Ricardo's arguments lead to the repeal of the Corn Laws, he also became a lawmaker.

By the time that he had published *Principles*, Ricardo was living both in Grosvenor Square in London and Gatcomb Park (the 'e' was added later). He was elected High Sheriff of Gloucestershire in 1818 and entered Parliament that year. He held his seat until his death a few years later.

In 1823, at the relatively young age of fifty-one, he died unexpectedly of an ear infection. He was survived by his wife, Priscilla, and seven of their eight children. Two sons followed him into Parliament. Ricardo's estate was divided among his family, and he also bequeathed some of his fortune to his friends Malthus and Mill.

Ricardo's career as an economist may have been brief but, during it, his theory of comparative advantage cemented his place in history as the father of international trade.

Like Adam Smith, Ricardo lived during a time of vast change. Undoubtedly, his views on trade were shaped by the protectionist debates over agriculture.

To give a sense as to how much the country had changed, less than one-fifth of the English population lived in the northern half of the country in 1751. By the early nineteenth century, that had risen to a quarter of the population owing to industrialization. A third of the population was urban, up from a quarter in 1751. England had become the most urbanized country in western Europe.

The Industrial Revolution caused Britain to become the richest country in Europe, too, but agricultural output grew less rapidly than the expanding population. As a result, there was heavy reliance on imports of food and raw materials. Those two categories made up almost all imports at a time when Britain was the largest trader in the world owing to its colonial empire.

Still, contrary to popular perception, early-nineteenth-century manufacturing remained dwarfed by the retail trade and crafts. The most popular occupations were those of baker, blacksmith, butcher, bricklayer, carpenter, mason, publican, shoemaker, tailor and, of course, shopkeeper. And, despite the country's prosperity, real wage growth, that is wage rises minus inflation, failed to keep pace with production per head from 1760–1850. Consumption per person was even stagnant between 1780 and 1820.[2]

But the fruits of the Industrial Revolution were accruing to some. Landlords were doing well and capital owners too, since they were investing in factories and machines. As a result, inequality increased. In 1810 the top 10 per cent of individuals owned around 85 per cent of the total wealth. This percentage rose to over 90 per cent by 1900. The top 1 per cent of households owned more than 50 per cent of the nation's wealth at the beginning of the nineteenth century, a figure that rose to nearly 70 per cent by the start of the twentieth century.[3] With his fortune of more than £600,000, Ricardo fell short of being counted as one of Britain's 179 millionaires, but was one of the 338 who had at least half a million pounds.

In Ricardo's day, more than one in two of the very wealthy men in Britain were landowners, a statistic all the more surprising because the Industrial Revolution had created fortunes for industrialists. Apart from land, the wealthy were in commerce and finance, for example bankers, brokers, merchants and ship owners. With his origins in the City of London, the financial centre of the world, and his huge country estates, Ricardo had a foot in both camps of the elite of his time. The bottom tier of society was the newly created class of wage earners. By the middle of the nineteenth century, the share of workers earning industrial wages had increased to around 80 per cent, more than doubling in a century.[4] Thus, a simplified three-tiered social structure formed the basis of Ricardo's economic models. For instance, *Principles* sets out a three-class capitalist economy in which the accumulation of capital depends on the profits made by the capitalists running Britain's industries.

Also, Ricardo believed Britain's economic prospects would be determined by the struggle between protectionist landlords and the rest of society. He observed: 'the interest of the landlord is always opposed to the interest of every other class in the community.'[5] Ricardo saw landlords pushing for protectionist laws like the Corn Laws that would help them but harm the economy.

Another important aspect of Ricardo's ideas was that he followed Jeremy Bentham's definition of utility for a society, which advocated the greatest happiness for the greatest number. Thus, he established a utilitarian basis for his argument in favour of free trade. As it was the most productive economic system, trade had the potential to fulfil Bentham's criterion.[6] In Ricardo's model of trade, because the economy as a whole benefits from international trade, the distributional consequences matter less.

His model of trade reflected his belief in the scientific nature of political economy. This was not a widely accepted view. When he entered Parliament, Ricardo was treated with great respect, but not after he proposed a tax on capital to pay off the national debt, something regarded as a 'wild sort of notion' even by his friends.[7] Practically every eighteenth-century economist thought the national debt was a bad idea and that some drastic measures were needed to pay it off. Ricardo's misfortune was that he was perhaps the most cogent.

Attitudes towards him changed after that. He came to be looked upon as a theorist, an epithet not intended as a compliment. Ricardo defended economic theory against those who relied on facts alone. Indeed, according to the economic historian Mark Blaug, 'the divorce between abstract theory and practical work was never more complete than in the heyday of Ricardian economics'.[8] That led to criticism of Ricardo by leading figures such as Walter Bagehot, editor of *The Economist*: 'To the end of his days, indeed, he never comprehended what he was doing. He dealt with abstractions without knowing that they were such; he thoroughly believed that he was dealing with real things.'[9]

The Austrian economist Joseph Schumpeter even coined the term 'Ricardian Vice', which highlighted Ricardo's alleged habit of making 'heroic assumptions'.[10] Schumpeter criticized Ricardo for introducing assumptions into a simplified representation of the economy in order to produce the desired results.[11]

Nevertheless, Ricardo's impact on economics is lasting, and not only in the area of international trade. Ricardo developed the theory of 'economic rent'. As more land is cultivated, farmers plough less productive land. But a bushel of corn sells for the same price, which does not depend on the productivity of the land. So, the farmers do not earn more if they have to work harder to produce a bushel of corn. Thus, only the landowners gain from higher land prices owing to scarcity. They have not exerted any effort to earn the higher rents charged to farmers. This is in line with his view of landowners, of course, that they were rent-seekers. Rent-seeking is one of the most widely used economic concepts today, for example, to explain why political corruption persists in some oil-rich countries, since there is an incentive to seek to hoard the 'rents' from selling oil and not share it with the country as a whole.

Ricardo's model of international trade

David Ricardo's approach to international trade was rooted in his background, while his interest in economics was stimulated by *The Wealth of Nations*, so it is unsurprising that he further developed Adam Smith's approach.

Smith wrote: 'If a foreign country can supply us with a commodity cheaper than we ourselves can make it, better buy it of them . . .'[12] Accordingly, Ricardo focused on what generated efficiency. His focus wasn't on achieving a trade surplus or avoiding a deficit, but on increasing trade which made a nation more productive. Ricardo and Smith both argued against the eighteenth-century mercantilist doctrine that a favourable balance of trade and money, including amassing gold and silver, led to economic growth. They exposed the fallacy that the way to grow was to aim for a trade surplus, instead of working efficiently and producing goods for the economy.

Ricardo's writings on trade were interlinked with his thoughts on the three great contemporary issues of his day: currency stability, national debt and protection of agriculture. International trade theory concerns more than simply looking at how the export or import sector is performing. Instead, he preferred to think of trade as domestic firms and their consumers selling and consuming across national borders. Hence his view that trade analysis ought to be linked to domestic economic policies. The event that shaped Ricardo's views was the parliamentary debate on the protectionist Corn Laws in June 1813, under which tariffs and restrictions were imposed on imported grain in order to keep domestic prices high. (Despite the name, 'corn' then referred to all farmed grains and not just corn.)

In Ricardo's theory, 'general profits must fall, unless there be improvements in agriculture, or corn can be imported at a cheaper price'.[13] Ricardo's model was based on what he had observed. The law of diminishing returns means there is a natural tendency for profit per marginal unit produced to decline, because the unit price will fall as supply increases. So, for Britain, the ability to trade abroad freely, especially in food, was important for economic growth. Ricardo saw a conflict between landowners, who were the proponents of the protectionist Corn Laws, and the rest: '[The landowner's] situation is never so prosperous, as when food is scarce and dear; whereas, all other persons are greatly benefited by procuring food cheap.'[14]

Ricardo and the Corn Laws

By the time of the Corn Laws there had already been a long history of government intervention in Britain. The state was heavily involved in the regulation and taxation of trade throughout the eighteenth and early nineteenth centuries. During the Industrial Revolution, Britain's trade policies were essentially mercantilist. The Corn Laws imposed significant tariffs on agricultural goods, while the Navigation Acts protected shipping by requiring all English trade to use English ships.

Since the reign of William and Mary, the British government had offered financial support to its prime constituency, namely landowners. British cereals were among the most expensive in Europe, yet until 1760 Britain was able to be a major grain exporter owing to government subsidies.[15] In the late eighteenth century there was a brief period of trade liberalization between Britain and France, but this ended with the Napoleonic Wars. This was followed by the reinstatement of the Corn Laws in 1815. Trade was not very free for much of the first half of the nineteenth century.

Adam Smith had excluded food in his defence of free trade. Ricardo, by contrast, was not too concerned about depending on foreign countries for food, noting that even during the Napoleonic Wars, France had continued to export corn to Britain after lobbying by French exporters. Ricardo also rejected the claim that free trade in corn would increase the volatility of food prices. He pointed to Holland, which depended almost wholly on foreign supply, and yet did not experience food price instability.[16]

Ricardo believed that trade brought about specialization, which would raise the efficiency of production. Free trade in corn would, in Ricardo's view, have 'a decided tendency to raise the real wages of labour . . . all capitalists whatever, whether they be farmers, manufacturers, or merchants, will have a great augmentation of profits'.[17] Although some might lose out,[18] the economic gains to the country as a whole were of far greater importance, or, as he put it: 'I shall greatly regret that considerations for any particular class, are allowed to check the progress of the wealth and population of the country.'[19]

Ricardo's campaign against trade restrictions played an important part in the eventual repeal of the Corn Laws in 1846, twenty-three years after his death. In addition, his arguments against the Bank of England issuing too much money led to the Bank Charter Act of 1844, also called the Peel Banking Act, which established a strict anti-inflationary monetary standard for the central bank.

After these two historic policy changes, Britain rapidly became the 'workshop of the world', exporting manufactured goods as befitting the world's first industrial nation. Great Britain became one of the most open major economies in the world, dominating international trade until the rise of the United States.

A tale of two trade deficits

Although Britain remains one of the most globally oriented economies, it has, since its nineteenth-century heyday, also acquired a large trade deficit. The broader concept was discussed in the previous chapter. Here, we look at the issue in depth.

Since the 2008 crisis, Britain's external deficit had hit a record high. The UK's current account deficit at 5.2 per cent of GDP in 2015 was the largest since at least 1948. The current account is a broad measure that includes traded goods and services as well as monies that flow into and out of the country. The deficit thus includes the cross-border movement of monies by large multinational companies, which isn't a source of concern. But the underlying structural trade deficit in goods and services, which excludes money flows, is 2 per cent or so of GDP. That is what warrants discussion. That's why we need to ask whether Britain should be concerned that it consistently buys more from abroad than it sells. Can the UK afford to keep doing this? Is that sizeable trade gap even measured accurately? That second question arises because most of the economy – more than three-quarters of national output – is comprised of services such as education and finance.

The two questions are related. If the biggest part of the British economy isn't accurately measured, then it follows that exports of services are also likely to be imprecisely accounted for. Therefore, it is possible that Britain's trade deficit in goods and services is not as large as it appears in the official statistics, which might make it somewhat less of a worry.

And the UK sells a lot of services overseas. In 2015, the export of services reached a record surplus of over 5 per cent of GDP. That certainly goes against the picture of a worsening overall trade deficit. Trailing only the United States, Britain is the second largest exporter of services in the world. By contrast, trade in goods recorded a record deficit of over 7 per cent of GDP, resulting in a net 2 per cent deficit.

Could the surplus in the services sector eventually push the trade deficit towards balance? That's not entirely unthinkable. Harvard economist Ricardo Hausmann and his co-author Federico Sturzenegger estimate that the large US trade deficit would actually be a surplus if assets that generate revenue but cannot be seen were properly accounted.[20] The same might well be true of the UK.

So, just how poorly is the dominant but not visible part of the UK economy, services, measured? Since the exports of services are called the invisible balance, it certainly increases the likelihood of mismeasurement. There are also 'manu-services', such as the output of firms in the engineering and software sectors that produce both goods and services, and these are easily misclassified by statisticians. If services were measured more accurately, perhaps we could worry a bit less about the trade deficit.

There is also huge scope for growth in the export of services. Unlike in manufacturing, post-war global trade liberalization has not progressed much in services. Nearly all of the global trade in goods is covered by a wide-reaching multilateral agreement overseen by the World Trade Organization (WTO). By contrast, services haven't seen the same degree of opening up of markets. Service-sector liberalization would help ameliorate Britain's and America's trade deficits since they are among the largest services economies. At present, Britain's service exporters face more trade barriers than their counterparts in manufacturing or resources, but if, for example, the Trade in Services Agreement (TiSA) currently being negotiated by some WTO members comes to fruition, then it would open up world markets for trade in services in a similar manner as manufactured goods and services would face far fewer obstacles to trade, which should reduce the UK's deficit.

Services trade is changing even without a new multilateral trade deal. As already noted, emerging markets are increasingly demanding the types of highly skilled professional services that Britain specializes in such as education and law. It may not be enough to overcome the traded goods deficit, but the demand for services is growing.

As in Britain, the majority of the US economy is made up of services like retail, creative industries and banking. Deindustrialization for the past half century has been associated with a loss of well-paid manual jobs and stagnant wages. It's partly related to globalization and the rise of offshoring, the phenomenon whereby nations with cheap labour costs have taken over the production of lower-end manufactured goods.

As in Britain, too, the trade deficit is a long-standing issue for America but there are signs of change. In the past decade, some factories have been returning to US shores. Is American manufacturing undergoing a renaissance? The 'advanced industries' are leading the US recovery, according to the Washington DC think tank, the Brookings Institution.[21] These are industries which invest a great deal in R&D and are more tech-focused. The revival of 'Made in America' was happening before President Donald Trump's 'America First' policy.

Rather unexpectedly, Tennessee is one of the states leading the revival of manufacturing. The largest car factory in North America, owned by Japanese firm Nissan, is located in the home of country music rather than Michigan. Nissan decided to site more of its car production in Tennessee in recent years, exporting to over sixty countries around the world, but the production lines of today are nothing that Henry Ford would recognize. Robotic arms assemble the cars while other robots drive supplies around a factory that is an astounding 5.3 million square feet. So, even as manufacturing expands, fewer workers are needed than before.

It's not only foreign companies that are coming to America. After decades during which production had been leaving the United States, American companies like Stanley Black & Decker, which were manufacturing in countries like China, have been returning. Stanley Black & Decker recently produced their first power tool in the US in over twenty-five years. The catalyst is an almost perfect storm of factors that have boosted American manufacturing. The extraction of oil from the country's shale has lowered energy costs and made the US competitive again. Rising wages in emerging markets such as China is another reason. Stanley Black & Decker calculates that it costs about the same to produce in America as it does in China, once logistics and transport costs are taken into account. Plus, the US has maintained its position as the technology leader, so productivity is high.

As for Tennessee, there is a long history of innovation in the state. Eastern Tennessee is where the atomic bomb was developed. Federal funding now fosters advanced industries, so those with a high proportion of R&D spending, and STEM (science, technology, engineering and mathematics) workers. For instance, the funding for Oak Ridge National Laboratory supports the development of 3D printing (also known as 'additive manufacturing'). This automated process requires only human programming for just one robotic arm to produce the husk of a car, secreting layer upon layer of plastic. The associated manufacturers who supply the parts and distribute the products also benefit. The company working with Oak Ridge to create the plastics that make the car body strong enough to withstand road stress is a reminder that manufacturing is still based in factories, as is clear from the smell of melting plastic and the loud whirling of machines that accompany this high-tech process.

For reshoring and reindustrialization to take hold, therefore, will require people to see industry in a new light. Will Americans really contemplate going back to work on the factory floor? A common concern of companies is the shortage of skilled workers. I conducted an informal survey of students at the University of Tennessee and found that most didn't see their future in manufacturing. Some wanted to finance those plants, while others said that they weren't good enough at mathematics to work in advanced industries. But they all agreed that manufacturing has an image problem: it might have provided suitable employment for their parents' generation, but it was not for them.

Still, the innovation side is flourishing. At Oak Ridge National Lab, a hundred students gather after school each day to compete to build the best robot. One of the signs that I saw said 'Made in America', but in Chinese characters. It's their way of signalling that the 'Made in China' labels in English on their clothes and electronics will soon face some serious competition. Stimulating competition and better economic output is what David Ricardo would have predicted when nations trade and spur each other on.

How advanced manufacturing is changing trade patterns

According to the Brookings Institution, advanced industries such as Nissan's automated factory discussed earlier have grown 30 per cent faster than US GDP since 1980. In an era of slow wage growth, advanced industries also report earnings growth that is five times faster than the average for the US. Since the start of the 2009 Great Recession, these industries have added around a million jobs.

However, the Information Technology and Innovation Foundation attributed the resurgence in manufacturing jobs to a rebound from the depths of recession. That opinion was echoed by the Center for Business and Economic Research at the University of Tennessee. They forecast that manufacturing jobs will decline once again and that industry will return to its long-term trend of winnowing employment in the face of both overseas competition and automation. That's consistent with the long-term trend where American industrial output has increased since 1950 in absolute terms, but has seen its share of GDP fall as services have grown more quickly.

It's a similar pattern in Britain. Like the US, British manufacturing has grown in absolute size over the past few decades. But, as a share of GDP, manufacturing now accounts for about one-tenth of national output. Despite the last recession, Britain is still among the top ten largest manufacturers in the world and the bulk of R&D spending, over 70 per cent, goes into the sector. Compared with its share of GDP, manufacturing makes an outsized contribution to exports, accounting for nearly half of what Britain sells abroad. But the UK still imports more manufactured goods than it exports, so there is a trade deficit. Again like America, the industries that sell overseas tend to be in advanced sectors, so technologically oriented firms with STEM workers constitute the new face of manufacturing too. But there hasn't been a rebound in manufacturing jobs in high-tech sectors like chemicals, pharmaceuticals or the motor industry. Only the aerospace industry has seen job growth nearly a decade after the recession. Also, labour productivity, that is output per worker, is low. Britain ranks above the world average, but lags behind other countries like the US as well as Germany. Could the UK also experience a reshoring of manufacturing? One issue is a scarcity of STEM workers, which is often mentioned as an impediment for UK employers in business surveys.

So, where does this leave advanced economies like Britain and America? Even if manufacturing output is reshored back to the US or the UK, manufacturing is unlikely to become the biggest part of the economy. Employment will also likely face pressure from robotics and automation. Still, the US experience with the reshoring of production holds lessons for Britain and others as to how to become more competitive in high-end manufacturing, which in turn has implications for what drives growth and also a nation's trade position.

In the previous chapter, we learned what Adam Smith would say about governments trying to rebalance their economies. But what about the related issue of setting trade policy? What would David Ricardo advise governments to do in the face of these trends and a large and persistent trade deficit?

Ricardo's theory of comparative advantage

David Ricardo's theory of comparative advantage states that each country should produce and trade what it is relatively least bad at. Even if China can produce everything more cheaply, America should still produce what it is relatively better at, and so should China. Thus, it is in the interests of every country to specialize in terms of what it produces and trade for what it no longer produces as much of. No nation is completely closed off to the world economy (even North Korea trades with China). That is known as 'autarky', where there is no trade. Thus, all countries choose to trade because international trade increases efficiency for an economy as well as consumption for its people.

Ricardo used the examples of English cloth and Portuguese wine to illustrate his theory. If it takes eighty Portuguese labourers to produce wine and ninety to produce cloth, then it should export wine and import cloth since it is more efficient at producing wine than cloth. Portugal should buy cloth from England even if it takes a hundred English workers to produce the cloth. That may seem surprising, but Portugal is more efficient at producing wine, so by specializing in wine, it can produce more and import what it is relatively less good at.

In England's case, it takes more labour to produce both cloth and wine than in Portugal, for example a hundred labourers to produce cloth and 120 to produce wine. So, England should specialize in cloth because it is relatively more efficient at weaving, though it is not an absolute advantage since Portugal can produce both cloth and wine with fewer workers. England would then import wine, which it is less efficient at producing.

By specializing and then trading, both countries can consume more than if they produced everything themselves. It's not an intuitive concept. Nobel laureate Paul Samuelson observed that this fundamental premise of international trade, comparative advantage, was the best example of an economic principle that is undeniably true yet not obvious to intelligent people.[22]

Does Ricardo's comparative advantage help us to understand whether we should be concerned about trade deficits? Firstly, there are criticisms of his theory to note. Ricardo has been accused of neglecting some of the most important issues in international trade, including presenting a static rather than a dynamic model. In Ricardo's model, countries cannot influence their comparative advantage – a country that is richly endowed with natural resources would specialize in agriculture, for example. But sometimes countries shape their comparative advantage in an attempt to influence what they specialize in, for example with government policies that promote certain sectors. This has become known as 'new trade theory'. This extension of Ricardo's model has been developed, notably by Paul Krugman who won the Nobel Prize for his work on a dynamic theory of trade. New trade theory implies for Britain that, even if it's not abundantly endowed with a large population, it can still promote high-tech manufacturing and need not be entirely squeezed out by lower-cost manufacturing nations.

Ricardo was also criticized for making unrealistic assumptions about the immobility of labour and capital. His theory of comparative advantage works because capital is not as freely mobile between countries as it is within a nation. If it were, English capital would move to Portugal and cloth as well as wine would be produced there too. The movement of labour is scarcely mentioned by Ricardo.

This leads to another problem as to whether or not Ricardo was assuming complete or incomplete international specialization. Countries don't usually entirely abandon a sector, so complete specialization is rare. But Ricardo doesn't examine the consequences of incomplete specialization, nor does he work out where prices of traded goods settle and just assumes it's at a mid-point between the prices of the two trading nations.

Perhaps more important than the technical objections is that Ricardo was thought to have ignored the question of the 'distributional' impact of trade as well as the politics of when nations trade. For instance, he assumes full employment and automatic adjustments of sectors of the economy to the introduction of international trade, neither of which is usually the case. Also, he doesn't address what happens to those who become redundant when their industries are abandoned or downsized following specialization. As ever, even though the country is better off, some will benefit more than others.

Ricardo has also been criticized for neglecting the unequal power relations between England and Portugal, the illustrative countries he used in *Principles*. The Cambridge economist Joan Robinson argued the Ricardian tradition would 'imply trade between countries of equal weight and at the same level of development. This rules out imperialism and the use of power to foster economic advantage.'[23] She added:

> in real life Portugal was dependent on British naval support, and it was for this reason that she was obliged to accept conditions of trade which wiped out her production of textiles and inhibited industrial development, so as to make her more dependent than ever.
>
> . . . When [capital] accumulation is brought into the story, it is evident that Portugal is not going to benefit from free trade. Investment in expanding manufactures leads to technical advance, learning by doing, specialization of industries and accelerating accumulation, while investment in wine runs up a blind alley into stagnation.[24]

It's worth pointing out that trade theory accounts for just one chapter in *Principles*. So, had Ricardo focused more on trade and less on the other economic theories in his seminal work, some of these criticisms might have been addressed.

Nevertheless, economists are agreed that Ricardo's theory helps to explain the basis of why and how nations trade. Economists recognize that the country as a whole gains from trade, but there will be losers in the industry in which the nation no longer specializes. They also see that, once politics is considered, less developed economies may struggle with negotiating the terms of trading with richer countries that provide them with aid.

For post-industrial economies like the United Kingdom's, cheaper manufactures from the developing world have made it harder for Britain to compete and hastened the move into services. So, globalization adds to the challenge of rebalancing the economy. Ricardo would see this as inevitable, but also as related issues to be addressed together.

David Ricardo wouldn't focus government policy on the current account deficit alone. The core of Ricardo's theory is that production and exchange were what determined economic prosperity, not the mercantilist policy deployed to foster a trade surplus in his day.[25] This is similar to Adam Smith, who believed that such efforts to promote a favourable balance of trade were 'absurd'.[26]

Like Smith, David Ricardo would instead urge policymakers to look at the health of the domestic economy and not focus solely on the trade position. How efficient a country is at producing goods and services will help determine its comparative advantage, and that leads to its trade balance. Aiming for a trade surplus without examining what needs to be done in the domestic economy to make exports more desirable to the rest of the world would have struck Ricardo as the wrong way to go about it.

Ricardo on whether trade deficits matter

There's no doubt that David Ricardo's theories held sway in his day as they do now. Trade barriers began to decline in the 1830s. In 1843, a weekly magazine titled *The Economist*, which supported the emergence of free trade and markets, was founded by James Wilson. It included work by Wilson's son-in-law Walter Bagehot. After the Corn Laws were repealed in 1846 and Britain became an industrial powerhouse, the rest of the world soon followed. When the United States was founded in the second half of the eighteenth century, tariffs represented nearly 100 per cent of the new government's revenues. By 1910 it was 50 per cent and it's since fallen to less than 2 per cent of the government budget.[27]

But, even as trade barriers persist in services and agriculture, the World Trade Organization's liberalization agenda has stalled in the twenty-first century.

So, in an imperfect global trade regime, America's and Britain's comparative advantage hasn't been able to deliver all of the benefits postulated by Ricardo. He would also be concerned about the lack of a level playing field in international trade. Ricardo would have pushed harder for the opening of global markets, particularly the relatively closed services sector. Services trade liberalization would help both America's and the UK's trade position and the global economy too, since over 70 per cent of world GDP consists of services.

With greater opening of trade and investment in services, Britain's deficit position may improve if its dominant sector can gain greater traction in world markets. In the meantime, Ricardo would not have been excessively concerned about Britain buying more from the rest of the world than it sells. He would have viewed the trade deficit of Britain as symptomatic of the structure of the economy. Specifically, the UK specializes in services, which, unlike manufactured goods, are partly non-tradeable. So, Britain imports goods that contribute to its trade deficit, while what it produces is in part consumed at home. In any case, he would have pushed for the UK to maintain the openness that it has had since the repeal of the Corn Laws. Finally, had Ricardo had the chance to expand his exposition of his trade model, given his recognition of the conflict among classes, he may well also have accepted measures to redistribute the gains from trade away from rent-seekers and more to those harmed. That would help those left behind when an economy begins to specialize in certain sectors and less in others.

The final chapter will tackle this issue and what Ricardo, and the other Great Economists, would say about how to help the losers from trade and what the backlash seen in various advanced economies means for the future of globalization.

CHAPTER 3

Karl Marx: Can China Become Rich?

Karl Marx was one of the most influential, and also one of the most controversial, economists in history. Marx and his collaborator, Friedrich Engels, proclaimed in the opening sentence of the *Communist Manifesto*: 'The history of all hitherto existing society is the history of class struggles.'[1]

Marx was a man of contradictions. He advocated for the working class, but lived in genteel though poor circumstances. That was not uncommon for the time. Most nineteenth century European revolutionaries were middle-class intellectuals and not labourers. For instance, although Jenny Marx was the wife of a revolutionary, she continued to print stationery embossed with 'Baroness von Westphalen'.[2]

Despite Karl Marx's widespread influence, John Stuart Mill, one of the foremost thinkers of that time, had never heard of him,[3] perhaps because Marx published little in English during his lifetime. Marx's seminal book, *Capital*, was published in German. He was well known in German debates, but less so to an English audience.

Posthumously, Marx's theories of communism transformed the economies of some of the largest countries in the world. From Russia to China, communism took hold in some form as these nations sought an alternative to the US-led capitalist model at the start of the twentieth century. The notions of economic equality and communal effort were among the reasons Russia turned to Marx. Their communist revolution in 1917 led to the establishment of the Soviet Union, which vied with the capitalist United States as the economic model *du jour* during the Cold War which lasted from the end of the Second World War until the fall of the Berlin Wall in the late 1980s.

Marx's most notable success is communist China. The world's second largest economy and its most populous nation adopted communism after its 1949 revolution and has remained governed by the Chinese Communist Party ever since. But starting in 1979, when economic stagnation led its leader Deng Xiaoping to adopt reforms, China has moved away from a planned economy towards a more market-based one. These reforms generated remarkable economic growth, which propelled China from being one of the poorest economies in the world to challenger to the United States. But China's transition is ongoing and numerous difficulties remain, including how to sustain economic growth in a system that is still dominated by the communist state in certain sectors.

What would the father of communist ideology make of China's transition to a market economy and its reform challenges? Can a communist country like China grow rich?

The life and times of Karl Marx

Like David Ricardo, Karl Marx came of age during the Industrial Revolution, though in Germany, which it reached later than in Britain. Born in 1818, Marx grew up in Trier, an agrarian town which belatedly experienced industrialization. There was no industry there during his childhood, and not even a railway until 1860. As Marx commented of his hometown: 'there are simply no sources of earning a living on which we can count'.[4] Until the end of the eighteenth century the city was organized in a 'society of orders'. Rights pertained not to individuals but to groups based on birth or religion, and were even set out in legally binding charters. Under this system, Catholic clergy and petty nobles collected payments from peasants. It was far from fair or equitable, which are recurring themes in Marx's communist philosophy.

Marx is usually described as being descended from a long line of Trier rabbis. Marx's Jewish ancestors had to pay special taxes to their lords for the privilege of residing within their territory and were generally restricted in terms of their occupation to commerce and finance. There were often special restrictions on where Jews could dwell and even in their social relations with Christians. In Trier, some Jews paid 'protection money' and an annual 'New Year's Donation'.[5]

This social order came to a violent end after the French Revolution when, in 1797, Trier was annexed to the French Republic, which took the territory from the Holy Roman Empire. It then became a place in which all citizens were equal under the law. In 1812 the Prussian Chancellor Prince Karl August von Hardenberg issued an Edict of Emancipation for Jews, granting them freedom of residence and occupation, and the right to serve in the armed forces. For Heinrich Marx, Karl's father, the French Revolution offered an opportunity. He could become a lawyer, a profession which previously had been closed off to Jews.

But just a few years later, the government backtracked, deciding that Jewish attorneys would not be allowed to work in private practice. Heinrich decided to change his religion. He was not alone. Most of the leading families of the eighteenth-century German Jewish community had converted to Christianity by the 1830s. Most chose Catholicism, but Marx's father opted for Protestantism because he was an adherent of the Enlightenment whose library included works such as Thomas Paine's *Rights of Man*. He was among the Protestant intellectual middle class who wished to reconcile the rationalism of the Enlightenment with religious tenets.

Still, the Marx family were held in esteem. Typical of the German middle class, Heinrich Marx established his law practice with the dowry of his bride, Henriette Pressburg, who came from a well-to-do family. Karl Marx's mother was from the Netherlands and his aunt had married Lion Philips, whose grandsons were the founders of the eponymous Dutch electronics giant. Also, Heinrich Marx received from the Prussian government the title of *Justizrat*, or judicial councillor, which was a highly desired honorific for an attorney. Their family's social position led Karl's sister Louise to reveal later that she was 'extremely embarrassed' to have a communist leader for a brother.[6]

At a time when few were able to enrol in secondary education, Marx studied at the Trier Gymnasium. This preparatory school was at the pinnacle of the German educational system. He studied French instead of Hebrew for his third language after Latin and Greek, reflecting his father's wish that he pursue a legal rather than theological career. It led to French culture and history becoming an integral part of his ideas. He received high grades on his German and Latin exams, but, somewhat ironically, he did poorly in mathematics, an important element of modern economics.

After completing his secondary education, Marx enrolled at the University of Bonn. But, shortly thereafter, in 1836, he left for the University of Berlin and became engaged to Jenny von Westphalen back home in Trier. Her father, Johann Ludwig von Westphalen, was a senior Prussian bureaucrat and aristocrat. Following the suppression of the Revolution of 1848–49 against Prussian rule, her family lived as political refugees in London for a decade while her half-brother Ferdinand was the Prussian Minister of the Interior. But the social differences between the Westphalens and the Marxes were not great. Jenny's father's salary was less than that of Heinrich Marx. Thus, Jenny did not have a substantial dowry and Karl Marx was facing a decade without any income. In that light, his engagement could be considered an act of rebellion against nineteenth-century bourgeois society. There would be more to come.

Marx's PhD thesis was a comparison of the theories of nature found in the writings of Greek philosophers. It was slow going, and by the time Marx had finished it he had exceeded the statutory maximum of four years and had not applied for an extension. He submitted it instead to the University of Jena, the only German university that required neither a residence period nor a formal defence of the dissertation. It also boasted the lowest fees for granting a doctorate, which Marx received in April 1841.

Aged twenty-three, Marx returned to his native region to become a freelance writer after he had encountered the ideas of Georg Wilhelm Friedrich Hegel at university and joined a group known as the Young Hegelians. Formed by students after Hegel's death in 1831, they were a radical group who were disillusioned with the Prussian state and sought to undermine it with revolutionary ideas. Like other Young Hegelians, Marx abandoned any thoughts of an academic career. His father was not upset by his interests, though he believed his son was misguided. But he condemned his son for excessive spending. It led Marx to harbour a sense of grievance that he would not receive financial support during his parents' lifetimes: 'I have had . . . a falling out with my family, and, as long as my mother lives, I have no right to my fortune.'[7] He faced the prospect of no inheritance as well as no assets during a time when he also had little income.

A year later, Karl Marx found his first job. He became the informal editor for six months in 1842–43 of the *Rhineland News*, which introduced him to communist ideas. Marx enjoyed being a newspaper editor. For much of his life, journalism was the base for not only his livelihood but also his political activism. Marx wrote of the economic conditions: 'that Germany is poor in people who are economically independent, that 9/10 of educated young men must beg the state for bread for their future, that our rivers are neglected, that shipping is in wretched condition, that our once blossoming commercial cities are no longer flourishing.'[8]

In 1844 Marx began his lifelong collaboration with Friedrich Engels. Marx was residing then in Paris. He and his new wife had moved there a year earlier as he had few employment options in Germany and they decided to leave for more tolerant France. Engels and Marx had previously corresponded as they shared similar ideas. So, Engels stopped in Paris en route from England to Germany to meet Marx. What was supposed to be a brief encounter ended up lasting ten days.

While working diligently for the family firm in Manchester, Engels became increasingly sympathetic to communism. Manchester was the global symbol and centre of Britain's Industrial Revolution. Engels's mistress was an Irish immigrant named Mary Burns, who had been both a factory worker and a domestic servant. Through her and his work at his family's Ermen & Engels cotton plant, Engels observed that industrialization generated not only enormous wealth but also misery. There was a stark contrast between the suburban homes of the capitalists and the factory workers' slum neighbourhoods. In

1845 he published *The Condition of the Working Class in England* about his experiences, in which he described the exploitation of the industrial workers employed in factories and mills who produced the capitalists' wealth. So, Engels led a double life. He was a typical capitalist with a bourgeois family, but at the same time, he was a revolutionary who associated with and financed politically dangerous people, including Marx.

In January 1845 Karl Marx was expelled from France after the Prussian government protested against some of his commentary. There were standing orders to arrest him should he set foot in Prussian territory. Since he was given just ten days to leave the country, his pregnant wife was left behind to sort out their affairs. The Marx family moved to Belgium, where other German dissidents were residing, and stayed for three years.

By the middle of 1846 Marx had pawned all of their gold and silver due to his worsening financial situation. Engels was in equally difficult circumstances, having moved to Brussels to organize German workers with Marx, and was dependent on a monthly cheque from his father. Marx had to give up his apartment and move into furnished rooms at a hotel which meant employing fewer servants. Throughout his life, Marx's economic 'woes' were a very benign sort of genteel poverty. An additional expense was due to his being an aspiring political leader. Followers expected financial support and being accommodated as guests. Ironically, Marx's anti-bourgeois and communist beliefs made him reluctant to continue to depend on wealthier friends and supporters in Cologne who had previously sent him money. Marx tried to support himself as a freelance author, but press censorship in Germany made it almost impossible for him to get published.

It was at this time that he wrote his best-known work. Asked to do so by the Communist League, Marx penned the *Communist Manifesto* in collaboration with Engels. The pamphlet was published in February 1848 and it concludes: 'Let the ruling classes tremble at a Communistic revolution. The proletarians have nothing to lose but their chains. They have a world to win.'[9]

The final sentence proclaimed: 'Working Men of All Countries,

Unite!'[10] It is sometimes translated as: 'Workers of the World, Unite!' or 'Workers of All Lands, Unite'. This exhortation is engraved on Marx's gravestone.

In the *Manifesto*, Marx and Engels set out a ten-point guide for a future communist government, including the abolition of inheritance rights and the creation of a state bank with a monopoly on credit. Their version of communism stressed the revolutionary process of creating a new regime, which was radically different from competing forms of socialism. In fact, they denounced socialism as simply a merely reactionary critique of capitalism.

Marx expected capitalists to refuse to cooperate with such a communist government. It would result in an economic crisis that would enable the government to undertake more drastic measures. Marx believed that crisis led to revolution, which was what had happened with the overthrow of the monarchy and the proclamation of the First French Republic in 1792. (It was short-lived. In 1804, Napoleon Bonaparte declared himself Emperor of the First Empire of France, which collapsed in 1815.)

In a historical parallel, after the publication of the *Manifesto*, the 1848 Revolution which Marx supported led to the establishment of the Second French Republic. It was a new and radical form of government in Europe, which was welcomed by revolutionaries.

Marx did not have time to celebrate. In March 1848 he was exiled again, this time being given just twenty-four hours to leave Belgium. In fact, the police jailed him and his wife before then. Both were released the next day but had to leave the country immediately with their children, abandoning all their possessions.

Just a few weeks later, however, Marx and the other leading figures of the Communist League were in Paris at the invitation of the French Republic. Germany and Austria were also drawn into the revolutionary movement. It was then possible for exiled German radicals like Marx to return home, so he moved to Cologne and became the editor of the *New Rhineland News*. The post gave him a platform for his *Manifesto* ideas, including a call for a workers' revolution in Germany. It never happened. Instead, Marx stood trial for his insurgent activities and was expelled from Germany the following year.

Along with other activists of the 1848 Revolution, he moved in 1849 to London, which had a liberal policy on political refugees. Marx had fallen out with the Communist League by then. He was only thirty-one and intended to return to Germany and continue his revolutionary activities, but instead he remained in England until his death.

At the time, London had 2.4 million inhabitants, which made it the world's most populous city. The British capital was the centre of capitalism. Whatever happened at the Bank of England and the London Stock Exchange affected the world economy.

Marx spent time in the working-class neighbourhoods of London's East End, which was home to a large number of immigrant Germans. His family lived in Soho, which was then an immigrant, bohemian area of central London. He founded a journal similar to the one that he had edited in Cologne, *The New Rhineland News: Review of Political Economy*, which he sought to circulate in Germany. Meanwhile, the Marx family became increasingly impoverished, Jenny Marx observing: 'Conditions here are completely different from Germany. All six of us live in one room, with a little study attached, and pay more each week than for the largest house in Germany [in one month].'[11]

Although the Marx family struggled to pay for food, the children had a governess and a maid, which was not atypical for those living in genteel poverty. But they suffered tragedies. Three of the four children born in London died before reaching adulthood, while two of the three born in Brussels survived.

Professionally, there were also blows. In 1851 Louis-Napoléon Bonaparte came to power in France through a coup d'état. While serving as President of the French Republic, Napoleon Bonaparte's nephew titled himself Emperor Napoleon III. In reaction, Marx wrote a pamphlet, *The Eighteenth Brumaire of Louis Bonaparte*, which opens with the phrase that history repeats itself 'the first time as tragedy, the second time as farce'.[12] But it had minimal impact due to Marx's exile and the imprisonment of his followers in Cologne.

At least finances soon improved for the Marx family. From 1853 to 1862 Marx was a correspondent for a number of newspapers and was able to move the family to a new home in Kentish Town in north

London. His reporting on the Crimean War of 1853–56 and other foreign events raised his profile, as he wrote observations such as: 'Has [the bourgeoisie] ever affected a progress without dragging individuals and peoples through blood and dirt, through misery and degradation?'[13]

The war confirmed his belief that a revolution would be triggered by economic crisis – and the first global crisis finally occurred in 1857. A crash in railroad stocks in the US led to the Panic of 1857, which dragged down investors not only in America but globally. Banks in England, France and elsewhere in Europe were affected since financial markets had become interlinked. Jenny Marx observed how this crisis ended the long period of gloom for Marx that had lasted since the death of his eight-year-old son in 1855. Engels even told Marx he was concentrating on riding and shooting to prepare for a forthcoming revolution. But economic recovery started a year later in 1858 and the economic crisis did not lead to revolution. It did, however, lead Marx to become politically active once again.

The recession also caused his employer, the *New York Tribune*, to cut back on its European correspondents. As a sign of desperate times, in 1862 Marx even sought a position in business! After being turned down for a job at a London railway in his first foray into the business world, Marx was helped financially once again, and not for the last time, by Engels.

A year later, in November 1863, his mother passed away and Marx obtained his inheritance. Unexpectedly, a political ally, Wilhelm Wolff, also passed away in exile in Manchester and bequeathed to Marx the bulk of his assets. The family was able to move to a larger house, despite the fact that Marx still had no steady income. It was fortunate because Marx experienced a sudden deterioration of his health that year. He suffered from carbuncles, boils on the skin which were worsened by stress. It meant that he became an observer and not an active participant in the political upheavals in the next two years, which included the American Civil War and the Polish uprising against Russia.

Regardless, Marx's influence spread. He became involved with the International Working Men's Association (IWMA), known as the

First International, formed by an array of European workers' societies. It was followed by the 1889 Socialist or Second International, and the Third Communist International of 1919. The IWMA drew from Marx's theories, particularly the two books published in his lifetime: *A Contribution to the Critique of Political Economy* of 1859 and the first volume of *Capital: Critique of Political Economy*, published in 1867. Volumes 2 and 3 of *Capital* were edited by Engels posthumously.

Ironically, Marx's daughter Laura became involved with a radical French student living in exile who was a member of the International Working Men's Association. Marx had some trouble with this since his daughters had been prepared for bourgeois marriages. They eventually married, and Engels ended up supporting their family too.

Marxism

It was after the 1857 global crisis that Marx began writing his treatise on political economy, *A Contribution to the Critique of Political Economy*, which was published two years later. He analysed the ideas of the leading political economists of the day, particularly Adam Smith and his chief disciple, David Ricardo, as well as Thomas Malthus, Jean-Baptiste Say and James and John Stuart Mill, among others.

Somewhat surprisingly, Marx admired Ricardo, calling him 'the greatest economist of the nineteenth century'.[14] Even though Ricardo was a capitalist, Marx shared his belief in a conflictual course of capitalism. Recall from the previous chapter that Ricardo saw an inevitable conflict between the classes due to international trade. At the heart of Marxism was also a complex class society whose inherent inequalities provided the seeds of its self-destruction. Marx predicted that would lead to the end of capitalism; he believed that Ricardo just hadn't taken his analysis to its conclusion.

Marx's 'theory of surplus value' helps explain his involvement with trade unions and how the end of capitalism comes about. He argued that inputs such as machinery, fuel and raw materials made up a growing part of the cost of production relative to the wages paid to workers. Meanwhile, as production became more mechanized, demand for

labour would fall, creating unemployment. The unemployed constituted a 'reserve army', depressing wages for all workers since the
unemployed could be hired to replace any worker who demanded
higher pay. More expensive machinery also meant that factories
needed to run for longer hours to be profitable. By contrast, unions
advocated shorter working hours, which were beneficial for workers
but reduced the capitalists' profit. Marx believed that declining profits
and labour unrest would lead to the end of the capitalist system.

It was the lack of a revolution after the global crisis of 1857 that led
Marx to play down the importance of crises in bringing about the
end of capitalism. Marx had originally predicted the rise of a capitalist system, characterized by unrest and crisis, which would lead to its
destruction. Now he began to stress the importance of inequality,
particularly the misery of the working class. Marx documented the
many instances of exploitation and poverty that existed in stark contrast to the industrial output fuelling the growing wealth of the upper
classes, particularly in Great Britain from the mid-1840s to the mid-
1860s. He cited how, in 1863, a woman was reported to have worked
herself literally to death cleaning dresses for ladies preparing for
a royal ball.[15] (Though he omitted to mention his own financial
dependence on the capitalist Ermen & Engels textile mill and its
workers.)

Marx and Engels thought that revolution would come from the
most advanced economies because that is where the capitalist crisis
was most likely to occur. In their view, workers were unlikely to
attain power peacefully. A violent revolution would follow. Marx
saw a parallel with the Civil War in America, where Southern slave-
holders started a war when anti-slavery advocates came to power.

The end of the nineteenth century was when Marx finally saw his
communist theories in action. The last quarter of the 1800s saw frequent recessions coupled with deflation or falling prices. It has been
dubbed the Long Depression or the Great Depression of the nineteenth century. In the 1870s, economic crises plagued Europe and
North America. Stock market crashes led to deep recessions, which
generated high unemployment, labour unrest and strikes. During the
Long Depression, nineteen socialist and labour parties were founded

in Europe as well as trade federations. So, the downsides of industrialization paved the way for the workers' movement that appeared not only in Europe but also elsewhere in the world.

That was also the period during which Marx's ideas took hold in Russia. Russian was the first language into which *Capital* was translated. One reader was Vladimir Ilich Ulyanov. Although he had never met Marx, Ulyanov helped organize Marxist groups to create the 'St Petersburg League of Struggle for the Emancipation of the Working Class' in 1895. After being jailed and exiled to Siberia for several years, Ulyanov left for western Europe in 1900 to continue his revolutionary efforts and adopted the pseudonym Lenin. In 1903 Lenin met other exiled Russian Marxists in London and established the Bolshevik Party, which differed from socialist parties in that its members advocated revolution to achieve their aims. When the Russian Revolution against Tsar Nicholas II erupted in 1905, Lenin returned home. More than a decade of political unrest followed until 1917, when Lenin seized power. Russia then became the Soviet Union or Union of Soviet Socialist Republics (USSR) in 1922 after Lenin consolidated his position. The Soviet Union was the first Marxist state in what Lenin intended to be a Marxist world.

Lenin's Soviet Union may have been the most prominent adopter of Marxism, but Mao Zedong's China was the most populous. After winning a civil war against the US-supported Kuomintang (the Chinese Nationalist Party led by Chiang Kai-shek), Mao's Soviet-backed Communist Party adopted a communist system in 1949, more than half a century after Marx's death. A falling out with the Soviet Union in the 1950s, though, saw China split from Leninist thought and adopt Maoist doctrines.

Although the Soviet Union had disintegrated by the early 1990s, and Mao's extremist ideas are long gone, China is still run by the Chinese Communist Party. To think about Marx in today's world, we would most usefully look at China, which adapted Marxism into its own form of communism that governs the world's second largest economy.

But China's evolution towards becoming a market-based economy is not what Marx would have envisaged. Unlike Russia, which abandoned communism for democratization alongside the transition to a capitalist system, China retains elements of Marxist thought, including state ownership in key sectors, alongside significant marketization.

China's adoption of market-oriented reforms in 1979 was due to substantial challenges that arose in its centrally planned economy, which had followed communist principles. Economic decline led to the abandonment of a command economy after three decades. It was followed by nearly forty years of remarkable growth that propelled it to rank behind only the US in terms of the size of its economy. To sustain growth for the coming years, China has now embarked on another ambitious set of reforms to join the ranks of rich countries. Average income in China today is still only one-sixth of the US level.

What would Karl Marx make of it all? Is it possible for a communist state to become rich?

China's economic transformation

China has accomplished a remarkable feat in transforming itself from one of the poorest countries in the world into the second largest economy in under four decades. The economy has expanded at an average rate of over 9 per cent per year since market-oriented reforms began in 1979. Chinese statistics aren't the most reliable, but household surveys and others indicate that China has not only doubled its GDP or national output as well as national income every eight years or so, but also lifted hundreds of millions of its citizens out of abject poverty. In the world's most populous nation, with 1.3 billion people or one-fifth of humanity, the World Bank estimates that the country is on its way to ending extreme poverty, in which individuals live on less than $1.90 per day.

China is unusual in that, while it is transitioning from a planned economy that has dismantled many of its state-owned enterprises and banks, it is simultaneously a developing country in which half the population still live in rural areas. China is also an 'open economy' integrated with world markets.

China remains a communist state governed by the Chinese Communist Party. It's therefore unsurprising that the rule of law and other market-supporting institutions, such as private property protection, are weak, as there is no independent judiciary. This gives rise to the so-called 'China paradox', because the country has grown strongly despite not having a well-developed set of institutions. China's economic growth is, therefore, in many respects both impressive and puzzling. It is also, as with other fast-growing economies, not guaranteed in the long term.

An example of China's particular model of growth can be seen in the differences from other developing countries when it started to reform. Unlike them, China was industrialized early on, during the command economy period between 1949 and 1979. China followed Soviet-style industrialization plans in the 1950s and 60s that focused on transforming an agrarian society into an industrialized economy. China's centrally planned system established state-owned enterprises that created industries where none existed before. Since market-oriented reforms were introduced in the late 1970s, China has undergone a reindustrialization process of upgrading obsolete (state-owned) plants and premises into more advanced (largely privately owned) machines and factories. As Adam Smith well knew, industrialization propels faster growth, so China was able to grow faster than most developing nations struggling to industrialize over the past few decades. Industrialization is accompanied by investment in factories, R&D and so on, which gives a further strong boost to growth. Adding capital accumulated from years of investment has accounted for about half of China's economic growth since market-oriented reforms began. In other words, its success can be explained by the standard economic factors such as investment, but with additional features, notably the reindustrialization of what was then a lower-middle-income country, that are specific to its unusual context.

Another example of China's particular growth model is that productivity is also driven by 'factor reallocation', for example labour migrating from less efficient state-owned industries to the more productive private sector. The process of factor reallocation is contained within the industrial sector, so it is not captured by the urbanization and industrialization processes which usually explain how developing countries grow by moving workers from rural and agricultural sectors to urban and manufacturing work.

Moreover, China confounds any straightforward interpretation of the theories that link 'openness' to the global economy with economic growth. These explanations centre on the positive correlation between greater opening and faster development, as expounded by David Ricardo. Economies open to the global economy grow quickly because the experience of exporting and accessing global markets can lead to improvements in competitiveness. Domestic firms can also 'learn' from foreign investors with more advanced technology and managerial know-how. 'Openness' allows a developing country like China to 'catch up' in its growth rate if it can imitate the existing technology embodied in foreign capital and thus grow more quickly, and perhaps even eventually attain the standards of living of advanced economies.[16]

China is open to the global economy, but exercises elements of control that have prevented direct competition from foreign companies in its economy in a number of sectors. It utilizes a policy towards foreign direct investment (FDI) that furthers its own active industrial policies to develop domestic companies and launch them globally as Chinese multinational corporations. As such, the simple openness measures do not fully capture the nature of China's 'open door' policy that introduced market-oriented reforms in the external sector first in 1979, which then accelerated after 1992 and culminated in its joining the World Trade Organization in 2001.

Several metrics are needed to calibrate the influence on growth of opening up the economy to international trade. For instance, at the start of the reform period, when China was a poor country with a low rate of household saving that was only 10 per cent of GDP, foreign investment supplemented domestic investment, accounting for as much as one-third of the total. Since then, household savings have been as high as 50 per cent of GDP, which is arguably too high as the money has been used to fund investments that are not always productive, such as the 'ghost cities' where residential housing is built but not occupied. Foreign direct investment that established Chinese–foreign joint ventures and other foreign-invested enterprises were explicitly geared towards exports and prevented from selling into the domestic market, which protected Chinese industries from foreign competition. They were initially located in Special Economic Zones, which were created as export-processing zones similar to its East Asian neighbours. China thus became integrated with East Asia, as it joined regional and global production chains, and eventually became the world's largest trader. Undoubtedly, foreign investment and export-orientation benefited its economic growth, but China's policies defy easy categorization as they have always been uniquely tailored to the country's circumstances.

By the late 2000s China was contributing to the 'global macroeconomic imbalances', where the countries with significant trade surpluses (China, Asia and the Middle East oil exporters) saw their surpluses grow while the United States experienced larger trade deficits. The global imbalances and other aspects of the 'China effect' (or 'China price' whereby cheap Chinese labour has pushed down global prices for manufactured goods) point to the need to examine China as a large, open economy. In other words, it is similar to the United States in that what China does affects the world economy in a way that most countries do not. So openness has undoubtedly contributed to China's economic growth but in a nuanced manner.

The other part of technological progress needed for economic growth derives from domestic innovation, and not just reliance on foreign technology. Coming up with innovative technologies requires researchers and R&D investment. China has increased its focus on patents and investment in R&D since the mid-1990s in an effort to support economic growth. Although Chinese researchers and scientific personnel are numerous, the evidence regarding how advanced Chinese innovations are remains mixed. Yet this is the crucial area for sustaining China's growth and for it to become a rich nation. Protecting intellectual property is also a concern, exacerbated by China's lack of an effective rule of law, though the situation is improving.

Indeed, one of the most complex areas of Chinese growth is the role of legal institutions. The predominant view is that market-supporting institutions, such as those which protect property rights and provide contracting security, are important for growth. China has been considered paradoxical in having a weak legal system but strong economic growth. However, China as an 'outlier' requires a closer examination as to how markets were enabled, given the poor formal legal system. Specifically, the reliance on relational contracting, so transacting with those whom you trust, can help to reduce dependence on the judicial system which is being gradually improved as more Chinese firms clamour for better protection of their inventions. The institutional theories that deem a good legal system important for growth therefore apply to China, but there are again nuances to take into account.

The role of informal institutions such as social capital also cannot be overlooked. Entrepreneurs in China relied on social networks, known as *guanxi*, to overcome the lack of well-developed legal and financial systems. It is also the case that the cultural proclivity towards interpersonal relationships meant that social capital played a key part in facilitating the development of self-employment and the impressive emergence of the private sector. That China would allow entrepreneurs to emerge within a communist system is, perhaps, not something that Marx would have anticipated.

After reaching 'middle-income status' in the early 2000s, China found that it also needed to rebalance its economy to grow in a more sustainable manner. Its ability to overcome the 'middle-income country trap', whereby countries start to slow after reaching upper middle-income levels and never become rich, depends on it.[17] Poor countries tend to grow through exports and cheap manufacturing. Growth in a middle-income country is driven more by consumption by its own middle class, leading to a diversified economy that is not heavily reliant on exports to consumers in other countries. For China, rebalancing the economy away from old growth drivers will involve boosting domestic demand (consumption, investment in more productive sectors, government spending that provides social services) so that it grows more quickly than exports. China has also shifted towards services so that the 'factory of the world' now has a bigger services sector than manufacturing. China is still upgrading manufacturing, expanding overseas investment and opening up its financial sector further. China is also promoting the internationalization or global use of its currency, the renminbi or RMB. To achieve these aims will also require examining the institutional framework of the economy, including the role of state-owned enterprises and the legal system. The retention of large state-owned firms and the problematic lack of a 'level playing field' for both foreign and domestic private firms vis-à-vis state-controlled companies raise doubts as to the efficiency of China's markets and thus its ability to grow. So, for China to realize its economic potential will require a significant transformation of the structure of its economy.

There's also the issue of financial stability. An economic crisis, depending on the causes, could trigger a long-lasting downturn. Marx would view this as inevitable in a capitalist economy, of course. In China's case, a financial crisis linked to too much debt or some other issue in its banking system would not be surprising. All major economies experience crisis eventually. Estimates of total Chinese debt by the Bank for International Settlements and others place it around 260 per cent of GDP, which is similar to Europe and the United States. But a key difference is the large amount of corporate debt in China, which is more worrying than government debt if there is a risk of large-scale bankruptcies that could bring down the banking system. And part of that debt is owed to the shadow banking system, where lending is done outside of the formal banks. It's a murky sector which includes anyone who lends money without a banking licence, including loan sharks but also others. By definition, shadow banking debt isn't measured accurately, so the overall level of Chinese debt is a source of concern.

The growth of shadow banking is linked to the Chinese government not introducing sufficient competition into the state-owned banking system. A rapidly growing economy, powered increasingly by private entrepreneurs, requires credit. As private firms sought funds that the formal banking system, which predominantly lent to state-owned firms, were reluctant to provide, unlicensed lending grew. Shadow banking took off after the 2008 financial crisis in the

West. As Chinese exports were hit by recession in America and the EU, growth was affected and so the Chinese government encouraged private companies to grow. Some did that by borrowing from shadow banks. Local governments also tried to boost their economies by investing in infrastructure projects, so they too borrowed. They followed the dictates of the central government, which planned for a large fiscal stimulus that relied on localities to find the money and spend it. Because China doesn't have a well-established bond market where local governments can issue debt and borrow to fund their spending, some of them, too, turned to the shadow banking system.

Since the end of the 2009 Great Recession in the West, the Chinese government has been clamping down on shadow banking. China recognizes the dangers of a debt crisis, like the one experienced by Japan in the early 1990s, that could derail its growth for years. A similarity that China shares with Japan is that nearly all of its debt is domestically held. So, a financial crisis there wouldn't necessarily spread far beyond the Chinese border, though there would clearly be a significant impact if the world's second biggest economy were to suffer from a financial crisis severe enough to lead to economic stagnation.

In order to stop borrowers from turning to shadow banking, the government has tried to develop other instruments to allow companies and local governments to borrow, such as building up the bond markets (the market for corporate and government debt). As in other major economies, that would allow companies and local governments to issue bonds or debt and borrow from capital markets rather than shadow banks to fund their growth. Also, if the Chinese banking system was not predominately state-owned, and there was greater competition due to new bank entrants, this would provide another alternative to shadow banking. Reforming the state-owned banks that dominate China's financial system has been ongoing, but progress is slow owing to the powerful vested interests that benefit from running state-owned banks. This is an example where the communal property system hampers the growth of the increasingly marketized economy, and yet reform is difficult in a communist regime.

So, to sustain China's economic growth will require a series of reforms. Some of the challenges that the country faces are related to its communist political system and the retention of state ownership. Can they be overcome? Can a communist state become rich?

Marx and China

China's revolution seemed to fit Marx's paradigm. China's communist revolt in 1949 was led by rural peasants, which differed from the proletarian revolution in 1917 in the USSR. Even though he lived in the world's largest city after 1849, Marx became eventually convinced of the significance of agriculture in a capitalist economy and of the importance of social conflict in the countryside for revolution. In part, he gained these views from the French Physiocrats, David Ricardo and Thomas Malthus, all of whom considered the agricultural sector to be an essential part of the development process, and thus a source of capitalist conflict in Marx's view. In *Capital*, Marx wrote of the labourers, capitalists, and landowners. Yet in the *Communist Manifesto*, written nineteen years before, he focused on two classes in a capitalist society: the bourgeoisie and the proletariat.

Marx's three-class society characterized China better than Russia in this respect. The Soviet Union was formed from a proletariat uprising, while China's communists were people from the countryside who overthrew the landowners in the Chinese civil war. These were the peasant labourers who rose up, under Mao Zedong, against the capitalist and landowning classes. It was the type of revolution that Marx predicted: social conflict between the exploited labourers and the capitalist classes that would lead to the overthrow of the old system and the adoption of a communal or communist system of ownership.

Marx was opposed to private ownership of the means of production and described bankers as 'a class of parasites'.[18] In the *Communist Manifesto* there was a programme which would carve 'despotic inroads on the rights of property, and on the conditions of bourgeois production'.[19] It included:

1. Abolition of property in land and application of all rents of land to public purposes
2. A heavy progressive or graduated income tax
3. Abolition of all right of inheritance
4. Confiscation of the property of all emigrants and rebels
5. Centralization of credit in the hands of the state by means of a national bank with State capital and an exclusive monopoly
6. Centralization of the means of communication and transport in the hands of the State
7. Extension of factories and instruments of production owned by the State; the bringing into cultivation of wastelands and the improvement of the soil generally in accordance with a common plan
8. Equal liability of all to work; establishment of industrial armies, especially for agriculture
9. Combination of agriculture with manufacturing industries; gradual abolition of the distinction between town and country, by a more equitable distribution of the populace over the country
10. Free education for all children in public schools; abolition of child factory labour in its present form; combination of education with industrial production, etc.

During the command economy period that followed the Chinese revolution that spanned three decades from 1949–79, China adopted the Soviet communist model for a time. A Soviet style of central planning was undertaken in the first Five Year Plan in 1953. State-owned enterprises were created from formerly private firms, and centrally administered by about twenty ministries in the State Council, China's top policy body. The Chinese economy was 'Stalinist' in the sense of establishing urban industries, embarking on long-term planning and providing for scientific and technical education. But relations between China and the USSR broke down within a decade. Among their differences was that the Soviet premier Nikita Khrushchev and Mao Zedong differed on the interpretation of Marxism.

Khrushchev even accused China of misusing Soviet aid to fund its 'Great Leap Forward' in 1958, which he described as a 'harebrained' policy to try to industrialize the nation.[20] The disastrous Great Leap Forward, which lasted until 1962, saw tens of millions of Chinese starve as they followed Mao's dictate to smelt their pots in 'backyard furnaces' to create steel for industrial goods and neglected farming the land. They also fell out over relations with the West, for example Mao disagreed with Khrushchev's policy of co-existence with America. By the late 1960s China and the USSR had engaged in border clashes and even reoriented their nuclear missiles towards each other. As Maoist China went its own way after the split with the Soviet Union, Chinese economic policy also diverged from that of the USSR.

Still, China followed some of the principles set out in *The Communist Manifesto* and *Capital*, at least for a time. For instance, Marx believed that a worker's condition could only be improved by abolishing private property, so China created a state-owned sector comprising firms and banks. China ridding itself of private enterprises after 1949 meant state ownership of the means of production, so everyone was a worker as Marx espoused.

Marx also believed that in the initial stages of a communist society, workers would be paid not in money but in notes denoted by labour time. Pay would correspond to hours worked, after a deduction of a 'common fund' for investment and maintenance. These notes could be used to purchase goods, which were in turn priced according to how much labour time had been expended on their production. The system would be egalitarian and there would be no capitalists to exploit workers. China's post-1949 employment system was based on workers receiving work points per day that could be exchanged for goods, a system similar to what Marx had proposed.

Marx had also endorsed women's political participation. Under Chairman Mao, female labour force participation rivalled that of men's. Curiously, though, the same could not be said of wages, even though 'women hold up half the sky' in Maoist China. A woman earned eight work points for a day's labour as compared with ten for a man.[21]

One disadvantage was that no one did much work in a planned economy since work points were awarded every day by the state regardless of what was produced. That was not quite what Marx had predicted. He believed that more labour-time credits would be awarded for more intense work, so workers would be compensated equitably. Marx actually rejected a 'fair' distribution of income. Furthermore, in his system, workers would not receive the full value of their output. The surplus would go to the people collectively for communal services.[22]

But this collectively minded stage was never reached in any of the communist economies. For China and others such as Vietnam, the lack of incentive to work under central planning led to slow economic growth which in turn brought about the need for reforms. It's not what Marx had envisioned. State ownership of industries also led to inefficiencies and persistent shortages since no central planner could effectively set all quantities and prices as well as market supply and demand. China still retains communal ownership of property, at least nominally, since decades-long leases are permitted. The privatization of land in particular and also the reform of the remaining state-owned enterprises are hotly debated because they are sources of inefficiency that hamper economic growth.

One key concept that underpins Marx's analysis that may shed light on some of the reasons for the divergence between theory and reality is the assumption he makes regarding the rate of profit. It was Adam Smith who first asserted the tendency of the rate of profit to fall over time, which was later developed by David Ricardo and John Stuart Mill. A falling rate of profit leads to a 'stationary state' where the economy stops growing because profit has fallen so far that new investments are not profitable. They all saw it as culminating in the stagnation of a capitalist system, although Marx's version foresaw a workers' uprising that would follow thereafter and lead to the establishment of a communist regime.

For China and the USSR, profits fell as predicted. A lack of work incentive led to low productivity. But state-owned enterprises had to meet their production quotas. They tapped state-owned banks for investment funds, which led to increasingly unprofitable investments and a build-up of debt. A lack of profitability pointed to the need for market reforms. Economic stagnation became the trigger for abandoning Marxist principles. Ironically, the outcome predicted for capitalist economies was actually realized in communist ones.

China's transformation into a largely market-based economy, still ruled politically by a communist party, would not have been foreseen by Marx, for whom communism and capitalism could not coexist. Also, China had become very unequal; at one point during its heady growth rates in the early twenty-first century, communist China was more unequal than capitalist America. That was certainly not part of Marx's vision for a communist society. In China's current phase of reforms, as befits a middle-income country, it is seeking to rebalance its growth drivers and rely less on investment and more on consumption; less on exports and more on domestic demand; less on agriculture and lower-end manufacturing and more on high-tech manufacturing and services. This last aspect would have been particularly galling to Marx. His view on service sector workers was unequivocal: 'From the whore to the Pope, there is a mass of such scum.'[23] He shares that in common with Adam Smith. Marx did not see the value of priests or lawyers, since they did not produce anything of value. In his view, these were only exchanges of a service for money. The notion that intangible output can be as valuable as manufactured goods was simply not within the conception of Marx or the other Great Economists who preceded him. In this respect, Marx would not have approved of China's shift towards a service economy and, especially, away from communal production and farming.

Marx would not have recognized China today as an embodiment of his principles. So, it is unlikely that Marx would have condoned China's subsequent move to incorporate market forces into its economy. He might have been intrigued by the continuation of the communist political system governing an economy that shares challenges such as inequality in common with the most capitalistic of economies, the United States. If China overcomes its challenges and becomes rich under capitalism, then perhaps Marx might reconsider the role that his principles played in guiding communist China – because in Marx's theory, after capitalism takes hold, there is always scope for a worker rebellion and revolution in the future.

★

Marx did not live to see a world in which Marxism had taken hold across swathes of the globe, nor the concomitant Cold War which pitted the communist USSR against capitalist America, or China emerging as the world's second economic power. He died in 1883, just over a year after his wife, probably from tuberculosis, the disease that had killed his father and four of his siblings. Karl and Jenny Marx were both buried in Highgate Cemetery in north London.

The 2008 global financial crisis led some to become disillusioned with capitalism, and Marxism is somewhat back into fashion. A book published in the aftermath of the crisis was titled *How Karl Marx Can Save American Capitalism*.[24] That would have resonated with Marx. To varying degrees, the Great Economists were engaged with the policy debates of the day. Adam Smith and David Ricardo both served in government and actively reshaped economic policies, including the repeal of protectionist legislation. Marx, of course, was more revolutionary and would go further, having spent his life organizing workers to rise up against the capitalists. For him, it is evident that economics must move beyond philosophical principles that interpret and only attempt to influence policy. As he said: 'Philosophers have hitherto only interpreted the world; the point is to change it.'[25]

CHAPTER 4

Alfred Marshall: Is Inequality Inevitable?

There's no doubt that inequality is high on the policy agenda. For instance, addressing income inequality is a refrain heard in Britain, whose current prime minister expressed concern for those who are 'just about managing' or, as her speechwriters dubbed them, 'JAMs'. How well people are faring relates to the quality of economic growth, and not just how fast an economy is expanding.

A somewhat surprising best-selling book is on the topic of inequality by the French economist Thomas Piketty. Who would have thought a 685-page book based on detailed economic research would end up on the *New York Times* best-seller list? Its popularity reflects a widespread concern that inequality is as extreme now in America as it was during the Gilded Age of the late nineteenth century. Economics Nobel laureate Joseph Stiglitz is among those who have pointed to inequality as one of the reasons for the slow recovery after the Great Recession of 2009 that followed the global financial crisis. Stiglitz has argued that highly unequal societies recover more slowly since growth mostly benefits the rich, who save more than they spend. And spending, not saving, fuels an economic recovery.[1] Are capitalist economies always unequal? What, if anything, can be done about it? Is it true that, as Winston Churchill observed in 1945 speaking in the House of Commons of the British Parliament: 'The inherent vice of capitalism is the unequal sharing of blessings; the inherent virtue of socialism is the equal sharing of miseries'?

Some time before Churchill's observation, Alfred Marshall

established neoclassical economics. He adapted the classical economics of Adam Smith, David Ricardo and others into a more analytical framework based on *laissez-faire* principles governing the market. Marshall transformed the way that we think about how different factors can change the prices and quantities of goods and services in the economy. This fundamental framework of economics was devised by this Cambridge economist. How would Marshall view the worsening of income inequality under capitalism?

The life and times of Alfred Marshall

Alfred Marshall was born in 1842 in Bermondsey, a lower-class London district, to a clerk at the Bank of England. He was the second of five children and attended a private school. With the help of a scholarship and financial assistance from an uncle, he then attended Cambridge University to study mathematics.

After graduation, he was elected a fellow in 1865 and then appointed in 1868 as Lecturer in the Moral Sciences at St John's College, Cambridge University. There he met his wife, Mary Paley, who had attended his lectures.[2] Her father and great-grandfather were both Cambridge dons (what fellows of Oxbridge – Oxford and Cambridge – colleges are called). She taught economics herself at Newnham, a women's college at Cambridge University. When they married, university regulations forced Marshall to resign his fellowship, and he took up the combined duties of Professor of Political Economy and Principal of Bristol University College, which had been established the previous year and later became the University of Bristol.

His *Economics of Industry* textbook, co-authored with his wife who became the first female lecturer in economics at Bristol and one of the first in Britain, was published in 1879. A couple of years later he resigned from Bristol and they spent a year on the European continent, which was when he began writing his seminal *Principles of Economics*. After their return to the UK, he resumed teaching at Bristol. But it was a brief return.

In 1883 he took up a tutorial fellowship at Balliol College, Oxford

University. Marshall was sceptical about his ability to attract students to study at the university since he did not believe that economics was treated as a serious subject.[3] PPE (philosophy, politics and economics) wasn't established as a formal degree until the 1920s. He was not there long, but, for a few terms at least, Balliol College counted both Marshall and Adam Smith among its fellows! To ease his departure, Marshall leant on John Neville Keynes, the father of John Maynard Keynes, to take his place. Keynes gave it a brief trial but decided that he preferred Cambridge. It is curious to consider whether history would have been different if he had stayed and his son been raised in Oxford.

In 1885, after the rules were changed to allow for marriage, Marshall returned to take up a professorship at Cambridge. This is where most of his career was spent, first as an undergraduate at St John's College from 1861–65, then as a fellow from 1865–77 and after his appointment as Professor of Political Economy in 1885, which he held until his retirement in 1908; he then remained an emeritus fellow until his death in 1924. It was in 1903 that he established what was to become the university's well-regarded economics undergraduate degree and thereby the Faculty of Economics and Politics.

Alfred Marshall was a late-Victorian intellectual. It was a time of political consensus on the major economic issues of the day. There was universal acceptance of free trade, for instance. Recall the abolition of the Corn Laws in 1846 discussed in the Ricardo chapter, which marked the start of an era of free trade. Marshall too defended free trade half a century later, when it was again under threat.

None of the leading economists of that time were supporters of the 'extreme *laissez-faire*' of the Manchester School of the 1830s and 1840s.[4] Those adherents were largely found on the Continent and in North America. Most economists were like Marshall in that they supported a system that included regulation of the workplace and other circumscribed roles for the government.

It wasn't until Marshall reached his forties that consensus on major economic issues began to break down. It was during the Long Depression in the 1880s when economics was being re-examined that Marshall made his seminal contributions. His theories formalized the building blocks of a competitive market economy. Marshall incorporated rigorous analysis that led to more robust conclusions. He pioneered the use of diagrams to illustrate the key concepts of modern economics such as demand and supply, diagrams which are still taught and used today.[5]

By showing how production and consumption were determined for the economy, Marshall's work sharpened debates over what constituted appropriate economic policy. In terms of production, Marshall's diagrams depicted the effects of declining returns to additional units of capital and labour. When the point was reached at which additional cost equalled additional return, he showed that was the equilibrium where the additional or marginal unit should be produced. For instance, a firm will choose to produce a widget up to the point where the cost does not exceed what it can be sold for. How to reach equilibrium is now a basic concept underpinning economics.

As for consumption, his work on marginal utility analysis explains how consumers behave. Each person decides to work or take leisure, knowing the cost is an hour of effort that would have been compensated by wages. There is utility or enjoyment gained from leisure, but that is balanced by the loss of earnings. Adding up every person's utility offers a way of assessing the wellbeing of a society. This is one of the reasons why Marshall once considered naming his subject social economics rather than simply economics.

His textbook *Economics of Industry*, and his diagrams that showed how optimal decisions are made by firms and people, propelled Marshall to rank among the leading English economists of his day. But his seminal work was still to come. Marshall would soon transform the field with his *Principles of Economics*. The first volume was published in July 1890, and it was even compared to Adam Smith's *The Wealth of Nations*. On the centenary of Marshall's birth, *Principles* was described as follows:

> Ideas of this sort might very likely have permeated English political economy in any case. They were in the air. But as a matter of plain historical fact their prevalence is due to Marshall. In its country of origin Alfred Marshall's *Principles* stands with Adam Smith's *Wealth of Nations* and Ricardo's *Principles* as one of the three great watersheds

in the development of economic ideas: with the usual qualifications, we may divide the history of English political economy into three distinct epochs – the Classical, the Ricardian and the Marshallian or reformed-Ricardian . . . it must be accounted as one of the foundation stones of modern American economics.[6]

Similar to Adam Smith with *The Wealth of Nations*, Marshall took a decade to write *Principles*. The planned second volume, though, was abandoned. Instead, Marshall made significant revisions up to and including to the eighth edition, published in 1920. There was a ninth edition, which showed all the amendments made in the previous eight, published posthumously by the Royal Economic Society in 1961 as Volume II. In all, Marshall spent around forty years on his book of diagrams, so around half his life was dedicated to his seminal work.

Not atypically for a late-Victorian, Alfred Marshall's interest in economics was inspired by an interest in welfare and equality of opportunities, which to him were the cornerstones of a prosperous society. It led Marshall to travel to Germany to learn German so that he could read the original writings of Immanuel Kant. He was then also able to read the works of Karl Marx and Ferdinand Lassalle. Marshall would later advise his students:

> We are told sometimes that everyone who strenuously endeavours to promote the social amelioration of the people is a Socialist – at all events, if he believes that much of this work can be better performed by the State than by individual effort. In this sense nearly every economist of the present generation is a Socialist. In this sense I was a Socialist before I knew anything of economics; and, indeed, it was my desire to know what was practicable in social reform by State and other agencies which led me to read Adam Smith and [John Stuart] Mill, Marx and Lassalle, forty years ago. I have since then been steadily growing a more convinced Socialist in this sense of the word . . .[7]

However, he did not accept all of their beliefs, such as communal property or revolution to effect change, as espoused by Karl Marx. Instead, Marshall believed in a prescribed set of roles for the government to improve welfare for the society and provide opportunities. For instance, he supported state provision of universal education so that even the poorest children could gain skills and compete for jobs in the economy. When it came to improving social conditions, Marshall, true to his life's work, believed in the market forces of supply and demand to raise wages for the poor: 'if the numbers of unskilled labourers were to diminish sufficiently, then those who did unskilled work would have to be paid good wages'.[8]

Although Marshall's work was based on utility theory, he didn't adhere to all of those tenets either. Jeremy Bentham's concept underpins utility theory: 'it is the greatest happiness of the greatest number that is the measure of right and wrong'.[9] In *Principles*, Marshall singled out Bentham's influence on the evolution of economics in the nineteenth century.

But Marshall's view was different from Bentham's, or from John Stuart Mill's idea of a utility-maximizing 'economic man'. Marshall was critical of the concept of seeking the greatest happiness for the greatest number. Instead, he argued that the whole might be larger than the sum of its parts. As we'll come to later, this adherence to utility maximization for society as a whole, which pays less attention to the distribution of that utility, may be why inequality has grown so rapidly in some capitalist economies.

For Marshall, interest in inequality and poverty permeated his work. To the Royal Commission on the Aged Poor in 1893 he declared: 'I have devoted myself for the last twenty-five years to the problem of poverty, and very little of my work has been devoted to any inquiry which does not bear upon that.'[10]

So, what would Alfred Marshall make of the growing inequality in the developed world that has seen as much inequality in early twenty-first century America as he witnessed during the Gilded Age?

Growing inequality

Some of the statistics on income inequality that have propelled it up the policy agenda are striking. For instance, the share of income going to the top has grown to the point where the richest 1 per cent of Americans account for a fifth of all the country's income. The richest 10 per cent of Americans account for half of all of the income in that wealthy country.

According to Thomas Piketty, it's slightly better in Europe. Still, in Britain, the top 10 per cent receive over 40 per cent of the income. In Germany and France, it's over one-third. All of these shares in Europe have risen since the 1970s, but not by so much as to rival the Gilded Age. It has in the US, though, which has led some to dub this era as the Second Gilded Age in America.

This phenomenon is not confined to the world's richest countries. Although developing countries have seen poverty fall dramatically, and a billion people have been lifted out of poverty since 1990, income inequality has remained largely unchanged since 1960.[11] Within countries, inequality on average has risen or not improved significantly, not just in the West but also in countries like China. This is while inequality between nations has fallen because of the relatively faster growth of emerging economies, which has narrowed the income gap between developed and developing countries.

Since the 2009 recession, inequality has been an issue particularly in America. During the economic boom of the 1950s in the United States, the top 1 per cent did only a little better than the rest, gaining some 5 per cent of the increased income. But since the Great Recession, the top 1 per cent have accounted for 95 per cent of the income gain, leaving the bottom 99 per cent with just 5 per cent of the gain between them. During recessionary periods, low interest rates make borrowing cheap and drive a recovery which typically boosts stocks. US markets have hit numerous record highs since the 2008 crisis, and such gains predominately go to the half of US households who own stocks. Of the richest 10 per cent of US households, 93 per cent own shares while it's just 11 per cent among the poorest quintile of households.

How much does inequality affect the recovery? The answer is by no means clear cut. Two Nobel Prize winners in economics, Paul Krugman and Joseph Stiglitz, disagree on whether inequality has played an important part in the slow recovery since the 2008 financial crisis.

Stiglitz argues that inequality impedes economic growth. The rich pay less tax than the poor as a share of their income, so growing inequality does not increase tax receipts as much as expected. Also, the poor consume more of their income than the rich. This lower 'marginal propensity to consume' of the rich was originally identified by John Maynard Keynes. In other words, poorer people have less disposable income and spend more of it on necessities like food. Richer people tend to spend proportionately less of their income since they have more money to spend. It implies that raising incomes for the poor would generate proportionately more consumption, which would drive economic growth.

Krugman, on the other hand, says that he hasn't seen evidence that the rich 'under-consume'. In one sense, the rich spend more than the poor. Someone spending 20 per cent of a £10,000 income would add £2,000 to the economy, while someone spending just 3 per cent of £100,000 would add £3,000. Krugman also points out that this comparison is a static one: you can measure how two people with two different levels of income act at any given point in time, but it's harder to predict how a person's spending would change if incomes were raised.

Stiglitz and Krugman may disagree over how much a role inequality plays in the slow recovery, but they agree that high levels of income inequality are a problem for economic as well as social reasons.

Income inequality has been problematic for a long time. Inequality fell after the Gilded Age and the Roaring Twenties, especially during the 1950s and 1960s when per capita GDP, which is a measure of average income, grew well during what's called the Golden Age of economic growth. But beginning in the 1970s, the income gap ceased narrowing, and then started expanding sharply after 1980, until now when America has become more unequal than ever before.

Is the land of opportunity really a society of haves and have-nots? Is the US economy now just enriching the rich? One theme is evident throughout this debate: the rich getting richer has squeezed the middle class. For the first time since at least the early 1970s, there are fewer people in the middle class than in the working and upper classes in the United States.[12] Indeed, within many nations around the world

income inequality has increased, notably the gap between the richest
1 per cent and the rest of society. F. Scott Fitzgerald said that the very
rich are different from you and me. But perhaps the rich are the same
as each other around the world?

Anyone driving through the narrow streets of Shanghai's French
concession will see immediately why the city was once called the
Paris of the East. Ritzy shops like Prada share a block with older
colonial-era houses – a rarity in China, where high-rise apartments
dominate the city skyline. In the 1920s foreigners and Chinese min-
gled in what was considered to be the most cosmopolitan city in Asia.
Now, with the rapid increase in wealth in China, it feels as though it
has entered a Gilded Age.

Nanjing Road is one of its rare pedestrianized areas. It leads west
from the Bund, an esplanade along the Huangpu River, and a
crowded array of shops, hotels and cafes line both sides. Busy at all
times of the day, the newly minted middle class in China is finally
enjoying a lifestyle that the West takes for granted. But there are beg-
gars crouched in the doorways of the designer shops. Communist
China has become as unequal as capitalist America.

It's remarkable that China has more billionaires than the United
States. Their number is also growing at a striking rate. A decade or so
ago, there were just three dollar billionaires in China; there are now
hundreds. That's a huge change in a country whose average income is
the same as Costa Rica's.

The Chinese billionaires on the *Forbes* rich list are becoming ever-
wealthier. The long-standing incumbent at or near the top of the list
is Wang Jianlin, who made his money through the traditional routes
of property and entertainment. Wealth was obliterated during the
Cultural Revolution of the 1960s and 1970s, so the likes of Wang had
to create their fortunes from scratch. He is now China's leading property tycoon and intends to build a global entertainment empire that
will outshine Disney. His business took advantage of the opening of
China's consumer market in the 1990s and the emergence of the new
middle class. A remarkable number of people have been lifted out of

poverty in a generation, and their demand for the offices, entertainment and cinemas Wang Jianlin provides has made him one of the richest men in the world and a celebrity in China. When he steps out of his Rolls-Royce, people stop to photograph him.

A new generation of entrepreneurs have also made their fortunes as a result of the digital revolution. Around a quarter of the newcomers to the *Forbes* rich list have been from China and many are young. They are predominately in the tech sphere, which has produced wealth for not only the younger cohort of businessmen but also those such as Alibaba's Jack Ma after his e-commerce firm's record-busting initial public offering (IPO), when shares issued for the first time to the public on the New York Stock Exchange raised $25 billion.

The entrepreneurs catering to the new middle class were unlike their predecessors, who made their money through real estate, a field requiring good contacts with the Chinese government since most property was state owned. But, like Wang Jianlin and others who took advantage of the privatization of real estate in China in the 1990s, this new generation is following the ongoing shift in the economy towards consumerism as the government seeks to make middle-class consumption the engine of growth rather than investment in property fuelled by corporate debt (see the chapter on Marx).

More than half of China's wealthy are entrepreneurs; the rest comprise investors and a small number of highly paid executives. The common factor is that, in the absence of inherited wealth owing to the Cultural Revolution, they are nearly all self-made men. (Like most of the super-rich around the world, China's billionaires are predominantly male.)

But the next generation is now coming of age; wealth is once again being passed on in China. The inheritors have been dubbed the *fuerdai*, which translates into the 'rich second generation'. The highest-profile cases of wealth inequality are among the children of the super-rich. It's not only the so-called princelings whose parents are Communist Party officials who are attracting attention. It's also those such as Wang Jianlin's son, Wang Sicong, who reveals his lifestyle on his microblog on Weibo, the Chinese version of Twitter. Whereas their parents tend to be frugal, the *fuerdai*, though they may work hard, play hard too. There is criticism in the media of their fast cars and extravagant spending. Their lavish lifestyles don't sit comfortably in a society that still propounds the virtues of socialism. Wang Jianlin told me when I interviewed him for my BBC TV programme that, as societies become middle class, their resentment against the rich grows. He cited Singapore and Hong Kong as societies in which such attitudes have emerged as their societies became better off.

His observation echoes studies that find that inequality and poverty are relative concepts. Indeed, it's not just the absolute difference between the incomes of the rich and the poor that matters for well-being. That's what is typically measured by indicators such as the Gini coefficient: an index that is zero if all individuals have the same income and one if one person has all the income in a country. But, as a society becomes increasingly dominated by a growing middle class, such comparisons are relative. In fact, in developed economies, it is income relative to the median income (the income of the middle person in the range of incomes) that defines poverty. By that gauge, nearly two million pensioners are poor in the UK when measured as those living on less than 60 per cent of the median income (measured as disposable income minus housing costs).

For China, the shifting societal perceptions of inequality follow from its own recent transformation into a middle-class society. It was as recently as 2001 that per capita annual income in China exceeded $1,000, the level that defines the world's poorest countries. It was only in 2010 that Chinese average incomes surpassed $4,000, the level that defines an upper-middle-income society. Even now, China occupies only a mid-table position in the league of countries ranked by average income.

But, of course, the average obscures the distribution of income, and despite its communist system, the past decade or so has seen China become an unequal society. The top 5 per cent of households account for about a quarter of all income. There is a large gap between urban and rural incomes, or urban households earning three times as much as rural ones. The coast also outpaces the interior in terms of wealth. But the pattern of inequality is moderating. Income inequality reached a peak in 2008 and has since declined. Nonetheless, China, like other emerging nations, is a society that has become very unequal in many respects within a short period of time.

Why has inequality risen over the past century?

One of the reasons for high inequality in countries like China is that, as countries industrialize and urbanize, they grow more quickly. Those who move into industry and cities earn more than those who don't, so income inequality tends to increase with economic development. But countries can reduce income inequality through redistributive policies. Without the social welfare system, inequality would be much higher in the US, the UK and much of the rest of Europe. The lack of such a well-established system is one of the factors contributing to China's high levels of inequality.

In developed countries, different forces are at work. First, globalization has pushed down median wages, and those who gain from international trade, namely the skilled workers and owners of capital, have earned more, while the middle- and lower-skilled have lost out in advanced economies. Another factor is something known as 'skill-biased technical change'. As the economy becomes more technologically driven, it's again the most skilled workers who reap the greatest rewards. The two are related, of course.

Thomas Piketty believes that inequality will rise when the returns to capital (r) exceed the growth rate of the economy (g). In this case, holders of capital (property, companies, stocks and so on) will see their incomes rise faster than average incomes in the long run.

Others think differently. In France and Britain, for example, the value of private capital as a share of income has skyrocketed to over 500 per cent since the 1970s, while for the US that ratio is a hefty 400 per cent. As this wealth is passed along, the gap between the rich and the rest grows, so inherited wealth is another explanation for inequality. Paul Krugman has pointed out that around half of the wealthiest ten Americans inherited their wealth.

Earned income is another driver of inequality. For instance, a CEO of America's largest listed (S&P 500) companies earns, on average, over 200 times that of an average worker in the same company. In the 1960s, it was twenty times as much. Why has this happened? Former US Labor Secretary Robert Reich gives decreased unionization weakening the bargaining power over wages of workers as one cause.[13]

It is likely that all these views have some merit, and that there are a number of factors that have contributed to growing inequality. Each of them suggests a different set of policy solutions. For instance, progressive taxes which tax the earnings of the rich at a higher rate than those of the poor would help to address some of the wage gap. If technological change is exacerbating inequality, then the fiscal system could be used to redistribute. That's what the chairman of former US President Obama's Council of Economic Advisers, Jason Furman, says they did. But others, including the founder of Bain Capital, Ed Conard, contend that raising taxes to reduce inequality is not a long-term solution and can harm companies.

And what about global forces at play that are outside government control? Piketty proposes a more radical solution: an internationally coordinated tax on wealth. But Angel Gurría, Secretary-General of the OECD, which is the think tank for advanced economies, disagrees. He says that national, not global, labour market and tax policies are needed to address inequality. Specifically, there should be a cut in taxes to encourage employment, offset by a rise in certain taxes, including green taxes.[14]

There is a divide between those who argue for redistribution through the tax system and those who are against government intervention. Those who favour more government action would also support policies to raise wages, including setting a higher minimum wage and promoting the creation of well-paid, middle-skilled jobs. Others might prefer policies designed to give every person the same opportunities to earn a living and reduce inequality through market forces, rather than taxing and redistributing after the fact. Their concern is that redistributive policies create the wrong incentives by taxing the successful and subsidizing the less well-off, thus discouraging both the rich and the poor to work. As the political joke goes: 'How can you tell the difference between a Republican and a Democrat? When a Republican sees someone drowning, he throws too short a rope and yells "the rest is up to you". A Democrat throws too long a rope and lets go of his end.'

Suffice it to say this is an unsettled debate. So, what would the father of neoclassical economics make of the rise in inequality, which has become such an issue that it has led some to question the validity of a capitalist system that permits it to happen?

Alfred Marshall's views on inequality

Alfred Marshall argued that the role of the state in addressing inequality should include the following considerations:

> Taking it for granted that a more equal distribution of wealth is to be desired, how far would this justify changes in the institutions of property, or limitations of free enterprise even when they would be likely to diminish the aggregate of wealth? In other words, how far should an increase in the income of the poorer classes and a diminution of their work be aimed at, even if it involved some lessening of national material wealth? How far could this be done without injustice, and without slackening the energies of the leaders of progress? How ought the burdens of taxation to be distributed among the different classes of society?[15]

That is the core of the debate. Marshall saw a trade-off between policies to more equally distribute income and the disincentives they create towards work. In his view:

> the chief dangers of socialism lie not in its tendency towards a more equal distribution of income for I can see no harm in that, but in its sterilizing influence on those mental activities which have gradually raised the world from barbarism.[16]

Marshall drew a distinction between production and redistribution, as did John Stuart Mill. Mill had argued in his *Principles of Political Economy* that economic laws governing production were not easy to alter, while redistributive policies were crafted by governments and changeable.[17] But Marshall initially did not support 'fiscal' redistribution through taxes. He viewed income taxes as inefficient because of their effects on work. But after the introduction of a graduated estate duty (higher rates on larger estates) in 1894, the forerunner to an inheritance tax, there was no disincentivizing effect on the willingness to work. That helped change Marshall's mind, since what he had proposed before, encouraging philanthropy, was not enough to reduce inequality.

So, during and after the First World War, Marshall came to believe in the benefits of progressive tax rates. He gradually accepted fiscal redistribution. What he did not support was equalizing income through extensive redistribution. It would at best achieve very limited results. Over the long run, such policies would hurt growth if people were disincentivized to work, and that would mean less money to redistribute. Redistributive programmes today do not go so far as to equalize incomes, in line with Marshall's concerns.

Progressive taxation is one of the standard tools used now to redistribute income. But the extent of redistribution differs across countries. For instance, there is less redistribution in America than in Europe, which has a larger welfare state. Bigger government, though, doesn't sit well with Marshall.

Marshall saw the government's role more as that of regulator than as provider of goods and services. Ensuring that businesses acted lawfully, that products were of good quality and fairly priced were the sorts of tasks that governments should undertake. And there shouldn't be a large number of bureaucrats: 'The function of Government is to govern as little as possible; but not to do as little as possible.'[18]

Marshall also favoured decentralization. He saw the benefits of experimentation and local competition. He strongly opposed local government as a delegated administrator of central government, though. In his view, education and town planning provided the greatest scope for local initiatives. However, larger tasks, such as the supply of water, electricity and gas, were to be undertaken by government only if they could not be undertaken efficiently by the private sector.

Where Marshall believed that government could help to reduce poverty was by improving the skill set of the poor to make them more competitive in the market. As mentioned earlier, he advocated education to make unskilled labour scarcer and thus better rewarded. He also proposed controlling migration to limit competition.

Like other Victorians, Marshall emphasized the impact on a person's character of any policies that sought to reduce poverty and inequality. Concern about being reliant on charity led to an inevitable emphasis on self-help and mutual assistance, which was a Victorian perspective. But Marshall recognized that factors such as insecure employment, unemployment, illness and old age were common among many of the 'deserving' poor.

His student and successor as Professor of Political Economy at Cambridge as well as literary executor, Arthur Cecil Pigou, believed that Marshall would have welcomed the government's efforts in promoting greater income equality after the Second World War. Marshall had become less concerned about the disincentive effects on work, except for a high tax on savings. So, he was more willing to accept socialist-type policies so long as they were not economically harmful. Still, Marshall worried about the negative effect on productivity 'from the deadening influence of bureaucratic methods'.[19] For instance, Marshall opposed nationalization on principle, except for natural monopolies, which are industries such as utilities where it is efficient to have one firm, and only accepted government involvement if it meant the task could be carried out more efficiently. This was in line with his opinion that economic prosperity depended on the forces of competition. So, he would not support socialist experiments in production, but came to accept fiscal policies designed to alleviate poverty. In this respect, a role for the state in the redistribution of income would be acceptable.

So, we might surmise that Marshall would weigh any tax purporting to reduce inequality carefully against the disincentivizing effects. The OECD recommendations of cutting taxes to encourage employment would be in line with Marshall's beliefs. Given his preference for evidence, he would be swayed by the studies of fiscal redistribution policies adopted since the creation of the welfare state after the Second World War. The International Monetary Fund (IMF) has looked at moderatively redistributive taxes and policies and concluded that they do no harm and might help to reduce income inequality.[20]

Marshall would recognize that the decision as to what level of inequality is acceptable would ultimately be a political one where economics merely provides the analytical tools to determine those benefits and costs to be considered. The US is less redistributive than Europe, which has a larger welfare state and some of the most egalitarian societies in the world, notably the Nordic countries. Americans have chosen to focus on promoting equality in opportunity, giving rise to the notion of an American Dream where everyone who works hard can have a house and a good job. China seems to be headed down the American path, with the phrase of the Chinese Dream used to promote similar ideas. But the dramatic rise in inequality in the United States over the past few decades suggests that the American approach is under challenge. Europe has a different problem in that its expensive welfare state, only some of which has to do with redistributive policies, is unaffordable, for example pension payments are increasing due to ageing societies. Thus, re-examining how to address inequality in capitalist economies has become a pressing issue for many countries.

Marshall's legacy

In May 1908, just before his sixty-sixth birthday, Marshall retired as a university professor in order to work on the second volume of his *Principles of Economics*, which he had announced nearly two decades earlier but was yet to complete. (He had wanted to retire earlier, in 1901, but could not afford to do so.) After retirement, though, he abandoned the second volume. In 1910 'Volume I' was removed from the sixth edition of *Principles*. Instead, he wrote three companions between 1919 and 1924.

One reason was, like many renowned economists, Marshall found himself very busy in retirement. In addition to revising *Principles*, he contributed to parliamentary commissions, engaged in correspondence and undertook other activities that took up his time. Mary Paley wrote that her husband said: 'I don't care for living except to work. He said that he was glad to have done all he could to help the world on.'[21] And he did just that. Marshall was active for nearly two decades after retirement. He died at home in 1924, a fortnight before his eighty-second birthday, due to cardiac failure.

The most important economist Marshall taught in his final decade at Cambridge was John Maynard Keynes, who, along with Pigou, became the major link in creating the Cambridge School who followed Marshallian thought. It is well known that Keynes had no formal qualifications in economics, like many Cambridge students at the time. They would formally study mathematics and pick up what they were really interested in along the way. Keynes's economics training consisted of attending Marshall's and Pigou's lectures and supervisions for a term or so, as well as reading Marshall's work. He probably got the best economics education on offer in England. The more specialist London School of Economics and Political Science was only founded in 1895. Thus, there are Marshallian foundations in Keynesian macroeconomics, particularly in terms of the need for economics to provide policy solutions.

This prompted Marshall and some of his contemporaries to alter the name of their subject from political economy to economics. He advocated for the change to avoid associating the subject with political considerations rather than with national objectives. It was not intended to narrow its scope.

As mentioned earlier, he had also considered calling it social economics. Marshall's economic theory was rooted firmly within the social sciences, where human responses to policies must be considered. So, fiscal measures to address inequality, within the context of rising social discontent that made such actions urgent, would have been consistent with his economic beliefs. A capitalist system that produced another Gilded Age, even more unequal than the original during his lifetime, is unlikely to have sat well with Marshall. And he would

certainly have made his views known. His nephew, Claude Guillebaud, recalled the fear associated with an invitation to lunch for
Marshall's students. They could never be certain when Marshall's
intellect would crush them if they expressed an analysis or opinion
that wasn't wholly rigorous.

Although Marshall is viewed as the economist who increased the
rigour of economics, he taught his students to see economics as offering a set of tools and an analytical way of thinking but not to believe
that the textbook reflected the real world. He described his approach
as follows:

> a good mathematical theorem dealing with economic hypotheses
> was very unlikely to be good economics; and I went more and more
> on the rules –

> 1. Use mathematics as a shorthand language, rather than as an
>   engine of inquiry.
> 2. Keep to them till you have done.
> 3. Translate into English.
> 4. Then illustrate by examples that are important in real life.
> 5. Burn the mathematics.
> 6. If you can't succeed in 4, burn 3. This last I did often.[22]

CHAPTER 5

Irving Fisher: Are We at Risk of Repeating the 1930s?

In October 1929, shortly before the Great Crash, the American economist Irving Fisher infamously declared that stocks had reached a 'permanently high plateau'.[1] But just days later, on 24 October, commonly known as Black Thursday, the market dropped. This was just a precursor to a larger fall. The following week, on 29 October, what became known as Black Tuesday, the stock market crashed. Over those few days, the stock market lost a quarter of its value.

Fisher told the shell-shocked audience of the National Association of Credit Men that he believed nothing fundamental had happened, and they should ride out the temporary storm in the markets. He said: 'The trough was close and the ensuing rally will see the markets quickly return to previous highs.'[2] But, as we know, Fisher was wrong. The Great Crash became the Great Depression and the resulting plunge in the markets wiped out his own $10 million fortune. Ever the optimist, or just out of sheer desperation, he continued to predict a recovery in stock markets and the US economy. However, neither would happen until the end of the 1930s.

Fisher's loss was not just financial. His reputation suffered irreparable damage and he found himself marginalized by businessmen and politicians. Few were willing to take seriously somebody who had been so publicly and spectacularly proven wrong, and lost almost everything as a result. Fisher had marked himself out as a loser.

History, though, has been much kinder, and recognized Fisher's huge contribution to economics. The influential Austrian economist Joseph Schumpeter described him as potentially the greatest economist that America has produced.[3] Indeed, a great deal of modern day economics can be traced back to Fisher's work.

He was the first American economist of any standing. In the late nineteenth century, the US had comparatively few economic thinkers. This was largely because the US government intervened little in the economy, so economics had a limited role in policy. Fisher's work marked a turning point where the HQ of academic economics moved from Europe to the US and in doing so firmly aligned economics with mathematics and statistics. In 1930, he was the co-founder and first President of the Econometric Society, which developed the quantitative aspects of economics. Nearly every Nobel laureate in Economic Sciences has been a member.

Fisher viewed economics in the following way:

> The effort of the economist is to *see*, to picture the interplay of economic elements. The more clearly cut these elements appear in his vision, the better; the more elements he can grasp and hold in his mind at once, the better. The economic world is a misty region. The first explorers used unaided vision. Mathematics is the lantern by which what before was dimly visible now looms up in firm, bold outlines. The old phantasmagoria disappear. We see better. We also see further.[4]

It is remarkable just how much of modern economics, taught in university programmes today, was established by Irving Fisher. Yet he is seldom included in books such as this one, or considered by those studying the history of economic thought. This might have been because he never combined his ideas into a unified theory of economics, in comparison to, say, John Maynard Keynes's *General Theory*, which rather stole his limelight. He also had few disciples, working predominantly on his own and rarely supervising graduate students.

The Theory of Interest, published in 1930, is probably the nearest he came to a *General Theory* type of work. In many ways, it drew together previous research, and Fisher came close to anticipating much of the work of macroeconomic theorists of the late 1930s through to the 1950s. But he didn't carry it through. He was not interested in formulating a theory explaining the level of national income and its changes, as Keynes was to do a few years later.[5] By contrast, Fisher never really pushed his work, thinking of it as an academic project rather than of practical value.

His near death from tuberculosis early in his career led him to emphasize intellectual endeavours that he could accomplish in a short time, as he feared he might never complete long-term tasks.[6] Although he failed to meet his target of writing a book a year, he did manage to turn one out for every two years of his working life, along with scores of professional papers as well as hundreds of popular articles.

He was prolific despite being far from a full-time scholar. His academic work was often put to one side while he promoted his many crusades. He was a reasonably well-known public figure, but most non-economists would associate him with his views on public health, his advocacy for the League of Nations and his stance in favour of Prohibition. On top of this, he was also a businessman and director of companies, accumulating a large fortune before being wiped out by the Great Crash.

By almost all accounts, Fisher was a proud man and hated to be proved wrong. The events of the Great Depression were a chastening experience for him, and he sought to understand how and why his wealth had been lost and the economy and stock market failed to break out of the grip of depression. Between 1932 and 1937 he became an unpaid adviser to the US President, first Herbert Hoover and then Franklin D. Roosevelt. He was clearly motivated by a desire to fix the American economy and with it restore his own finances. It spurred his work on 'debt-deflation', the idea that economies can get trapped in a persistent deflationary spiral where prices fall as the economy stalls since people are not consuming and firms are not investing while they repay debt.

His work resonates in the post-2008 crisis period, where the fear of deflation has again returned to the radar of policymakers. Global growth rates have slowed and inflation rates have fallen persistently

below the targets of central banks. Throughout history, episodes of
deflation are very rare. However, Japan's 'lost decades' since the early
1990s have served as a warning of what might happen in the aftermath of a financial crisis.

Since 2008, advanced countries have struggled to recapture pre-
crisis growth trends and inflation rates have slumped around the
world, bringing many countries to the brink of deflation. The large
build-up in public and private sector debt suggests the global economic situation is ripe for the debt-deflation that Fisher described as
the cause of the Great Depression. So, are we at risk of repeating the
experiences of the 1930s? And what might Irving Fisher suggest we
do about it?

The life and times of Irving Fisher

George Whitefield Fisher, Irving Fisher's father, was a pastor in the
New England Puritan Church. He and his wife, Ella, moved to the
First Congregational Church in Saugerties-on-Hudson, New York, in
1865. Fisher was born there two years later.

In 1883 Irving Fisher's father was taken ill with tuberculosis.
Back then this was almost always a death sentence and he was to
succumb in June the following year, shortly after Fisher graduated
high school. As a child, his skill in mathematics helped him to stand
out and he was admitted to Yale University in 1884. This was to be
the beginning of a lifelong affiliation with one of America's foremost
universities.

However, he was now the breadwinner of his family. Apart from
$500 his father had put aside for him, he knew he would have to both
pay his own way at college and support his mother and younger
brother, Herbert. As an undergraduate, he tutored mathematics and
entered competitions, winning prize money in Latin, Greek and
algebra.

His talent was quickly recognized at Yale. After graduating in
1888, he stayed on to do postgraduate study, but his horizons were
much broader than mathematics. It is rumoured he had studied every

natural and social science course available at Yale, and he began to think of a life in law or economics. Fisher revealed: 'How much there is I want to do! I always feel that I haven't time to accomplish what I wish. I want to read much . . . I want to write a great deal. I want to make money.'[7] In 1891 he decided to embark on a PhD in mathematical economics.

His doctoral thesis, titled 'Mathematical Investigations in the Theory of Value and Prices', took only one academic year to complete and was in some ways seminal. In it Fisher created a mechanism to compute the prices and quantities of goods in an economy. It was lauded by Nobel laureate Paul Samuelson as the 'greatest doctoral dissertation in economics ever written' and was a big step forward in the mathematical treatment of economics.[8]

The following year he was appointed to the Yale Mathematics Department. Shortly thereafter he married Margaret Hazard, or Margie as the family called her. Margie's father, Rowland, was a wealthy woollen manufacturer and the 'patriarch' of the small town of Peace Dale, Rhode Island. In the 1860s he had formed his own congregational church and invited George Whitefield Fisher to become its pastor. The Fisher family moved there in August 1868, and this is where Irving Fisher grew up, although he and Margie were not childhood friends.

At Yale, Fisher abstained from student frivolity due to his Puritan upbringing. But in the autumn of 1891, at twenty-four years of age, he was invited to a friend's home for dinner. Margie was there too and, for Fisher, it was love at first sight. Their engagement followed and their wedding took place in June 1893. They spent a fourteen-month honeymoon travelling and working around Europe, a period which also included the birth of the first of their three children.

Fisher returned to Yale in the autumn of 1894 to become an assistant professor in the Mathematics Department. A year later a permanent position arose in the newly established Economics Department and Fisher asked to be considered. After a brief inter-departmental tussle, Economics won out. Fisher was concerned about doing something of practical value, and saw mathematics as too abstract.

At that time, economic thought in US universities was strongly dominated by the German School. Their approach was historically based; theories were acceptable only from those able to demonstrate a thorough grasp of everything that had come before. Fisher, though, was at the vanguard of mathematical economics, which marked him out as a radical and was to ultimately set him apart from his own faculty.

It is perhaps ironic that having fought so hard to get him, the Economics Department was to then have a very marginal relationship with Fisher. He was not impressed with his fellow academics. He thought that they preferred to hide in the classroom rather than apply their subject matter to improving the human condition. Despite his long affiliation to Yale, he was rarely there, taught few classes and did not in general get on well with his colleagues.

In 1898 he was appointed professor and given lifetime tenure on $3,000 per year (about $85,000 in today's money). Things were looking up. His wife's family were wealthy, and money left in trust to Margie enabled them to lead a very comfortable life. Their house, at 460 Prospect Street in New Haven, had been a wedding gift from the Hazard family. It was large, fully kitted out and attended to by a number of servants. Fisher could also afford to hire his own secretaries to help him in his academic and campaign work.

But as Fisher was embarking on a successful and happy professional and family life, disaster struck. At the age of thirty he fell seriously ill with TB. He believed that his father had somehow passed on the disease to him and that it had remained dormant until then. It took him three years to beat the illness and recover his strength, but it was to be a life-changing event.

Fisher had revered his father and, although not overtly religious himself, he had inherited his strong moral and Puritan standards. Particularly after the trauma of years of illness, he became obsessed with diet and health. He did not smoke, or drink alcohol, coffee or tea; he never ate chocolate, and only rarely meat. He would arise at 7 a.m. each day and jog around the neighbourhood before a light breakfast. He exercised again around noon in his home gym or yard.

Often in the late afternoon he walked or jogged in a park. By 10.30 p.m., he was in bed after some calisthenics. He maintained his fitness regime when he travelled and insisted on his precise diet. On occasion he would even enter hotel kitchens to give specific instructions to the chefs.[9]

He was to become well known throughout America as a health guru. In 1915 he co-authored a book, *How to Live*, setting out basic rules of public hygiene. In total 400,000 copies were sold in the US and it was translated into ten languages. None of his economics writing was as successful. Fisher gave his royalties of $75,000 to the Life Extension Institute, an organization he co-founded two years earlier to promote healthy living and encourage frequent medical check-ups.

Some of his associations were controversial. He was president of the American Eugenics Society and the Eugenics Research Association. His belief in eugenics was based on the maintenance and improvement of the human race. However, he either did not seem to acknowledge or turned a blind eye to the links it had to racial supremacists.

One of his main crusades in life concerned Prohibition. The Eighteenth Amendment to the US Constitution, in effect from 1920, prohibited alcoholic beverages and was in place for thirteen years until it was repealed by the Twenty-First Amendment. He viewed alcohol as a poison that undermined productivity. Drinking alcohol was akin to self-harm. It was in the interest of the economy and society as a whole to abstain. His 1926 book *Prohibition at its Worst* argued that, even though Prohibition did not work perfectly – he was unhappy with the crime and bootlegging it generated – society was still better off than if alcohol were legalized. The problems were not with Prohibition per se, but because it had been introduced too quickly and before the public has been sufficiently educated in its merits. He tended to support presidential candidates in favour of the 18th Amendment outlawing alcohol and never reconciled himself to its repeal in 1933.[10]

His campaigns and activism in public affairs stemmed from his belief that economists should serve the public. And perhaps from a distrust of the political system:

> Our society will always remain an unstable and explosive compound as long as political power is vested in the masses and economic power in the classes. In the end one of these powers will rule. Either the plutocracy will buy up the democracy or the democracy will vote away the plutocracy. In the meantime the corrupt politician will thrive as a concealed broker between the two.[11]

Fisher was also aware of the foibles of economists:

> Academic economists, from their very openmindedness, are apt to be carried off, unawares, by the bias of the community in which they live.
>
> Economists whose social world is Wall Street are very apt to take the Wall Street point of view, while economists at state universities situated in farming districts are apt to be partisans of the agricultural interests.[12]

The Fisher family lived a comfortable life in New Haven. As a professor at Yale, Irving Fisher earned a salary which would have given him a better than middle-class income. In addition, his earnings were supplemented by his many other activities. But he also had expenses, particularly a growing number of staff and secretaries, to whom he would delegate a great deal. But the fact that he lived in a large house with many servants, and that his children were privately educated, was more of a reflection of the wealth he married into. It would not have escaped his notice that his wife's money was to a great extent maintaining his family's standard of living.

Fisher always thought that invention would be the key to making a personal fortune. He had tried many times, but his visible index card system was the breakthrough. It was a simple idea. He cut a notch at the bottom of an index card. These could be attached to a metal strip and mounted vertically, horizontally or even on a circular drum. It was a much more efficient way of finding records than flipping through boxes of cards. The concept had come to him in 1910, but he couldn't find anybody to manufacture the device. Eventually, in 1915, he decided to manufacture it himself, although he had no interest in the day-to-day running of the company, a task he delegated to managers and staff.

By 1919 the Index Visible Company was still struggling to turn a profit, despite a Fisher family investment of over $35,000. But his idea, which he had wisely patented, was practical as well as simple, and as the US economy grew quickly, and record-keeping became vital, it was adopted in companies across the country. As the Roaring Twenties gathered momentum, so did the Index Visible Company's profits. In the early 1920s he opened an office in New York, and even persuaded the state's telephone company to adopt the system.

In 1925, he sold his business to the company that was to later merge into Remington Rand. The company and patents were valued at $660,000, plus he received stock in the new company. At the age of fifty-eight, he had at last made a small fortune from his own endeavours. However, turning a small fortune into a large fortune required something extraordinary, and this came courtesy of a rampant bull market in stocks.

Fisher had invested heavily in the stock market, tending to favour start-up companies with innovative products. All proceeds and dividends were reinvested in the rapidly rising market. But he went further. He borrowed money to purchase stocks, a practice known as buying on margin that essentially allows an investor to leverage their portfolio. For example, suppose you buy $10,000 of stock, putting down only $1,000 of your own capital and borrowing the balance. If the market rises by 20 per cent, you are now getting a return of $2,000 (less interest on the $9,000 dollar loan) on your $1,000 investment. By leveraging yourself in this way, it is perfectly possible to generate a large paper fortune very quickly from a strongly rising market, and Fisher was estimated to have accumulated a staggering $10 million in this manner.

The downside to margin buying is revealed when the market falls, and assets become worth less than the amount of debt incurred in purchasing them. Borrowing to invest and being leveraged bring extraordinary gains in the good times, but result in potentially devastating losses should things go awry.

Fisher's behaviour in the late 1920s in many ways foreshadowed what would happen to the financial sector as a whole nearly a century later. Institutions that are highly leveraged and look sound can suddenly find themselves in a distressed position when the assets they hold become worthless. And in 1929, as the market crashed, Fisher was brought to financial ruin.

He had been a strong advocate of the rising bull market throughout the 1920s. At the end of 1928, he wrote a piece for the *New York Herald* predicting the continuance of the bull market through 1929. When, at the start of 1929, a growing minority voiced concern about a coming crash, Fisher remained steadfastly confident about the market. There is no doubt he was giving his honest opinion, but unfortunately it was catastrophically misguided. Ironically, he would later blame speculation by others about the value of stocks as the root cause of the Great Crash.

Another irony was that Fisher had pioneered the development of economic data. The Index Number Institute (INI) that he established in 1923 published weekly and monthly indicators of economic activity and prices. As such, Fisher should have been well placed to observe the vulnerabilities and imbalances afflicting the economy in agriculture, housing and manufacturing.

As history tells us, 29 October 1929 or Black Tuesday was not the worst of it. The market would continue to drop for a further three weeks. As the banks started to fail, crash would turn into depression. In 1929 there were 659 bank failures; this number would rise eightfold during the next three years.

The crash had a devastating impact on the Fisher family finances. His creditors came calling, but all he had to pay them with were stocks that were of little worth. On top of this the US tax authority, the Internal Revenue Service (IRS), was to pursue him over income he had not reported in the boom years.

Once again it was the Hazard family fortune that would provide the lifeline. Fisher's sister-in-law, Caroline, who was eleven years senior to Margie, had inherited the bulk of the family fortune. The crash had hit her extremely hard, but because her wealth was substantial she remained a rich woman. She lent Fisher stock to use as collateral for more loans to pay off his original creditors. Without this help in buttressing his financial position, it is likely the Fishers would have gone bankrupt in 1930. Over the course of the next decade, he would continuously turn to his sister-in-law to avoid bankruptcy, although Caroline's main concern was probably the welfare of her younger sister. As the requests for assistance came one after another, she grew tired of dealing with Fisher and even though he was family, she turned over her financial relations with him to her representatives.

In 1935, at the age of sixty-eight, Fisher reached Yale's compulsory retirement age. Now unable to pay the mortgage on 460 Prospect Street, he sold the house to the university, who allowed him and Margie to remain as life tenants. Eventually, even the rent became too much, and he was obliged to leave the house for the apartment in which he lived his final days.

Would it not have been better for Fisher to declare bankruptcy in 1930? In doing so, he would have lost both his house and his stock portfolio, neither of which was he eager to do. He never stopped believing the economy would turn upwards sooner rather than later, and with it the value of his stocks. He still saw an economic and financial recovery as the most likely solution to his financial troubles. His optimism was impressive. Unfortunately, every time he asserted that a turning point had been reached, things generally turned out to get even worse.

By 1941 Fisher had assets estimated at $244,000 but owed $1.1 million, including almost $1 million to his sister-in-law. This put his net worth in the red to the tune of $870,000. When Caroline Hazard died in March 1945, she forgave the debt in her will.

Irving Fisher's imprint on economics

In 1903, after returning to Yale upon his recovery from TB, Irving Fisher made some of his most valuable contributions to economics. He published two books of note: *The Nature of Capital and Income* in 1906 and *The Rate of Interest* in 1907. These books, which linked investment and the interest rate, formed the basis for his best-known work in economic theory, *The Theory of Interest*, published in 1930.

However, perhaps his most influential contribution concerned his Equation of Exchange, which sought to predict what might happen to prices when the money supply changed. It had been known for centuries that there existed a relationship between the amount of money in the economy and prices, commonly known as the Quantity Theory of Money. The long inflationary periods of the sixteenth and seventeenth centuries in Europe had coincided with the discoveries of Brazilian gold and Peruvian silver. Although the relationship had become part of conventional wisdom, until Fisher it had never been formalized or put to practical use.

The essence of the Equation of Exchange, written algebraically as $MV = PQ$, is that the total amount of money changing hands in the economy is equal to the total value of goods and services sold. On the left-hand side of the equation is the total money supply (M) multiplied by the velocity of circulation (V), a measure of how frequently money circulates in the economy. On the right-hand side is total spending on all the goods and services in the economy, given by the total quantity sold (Q) multiplied by the selling price (P). Although Fisher was not the first to formalize the relationship – $MV = PQ$ had already been written down by the Canadian-American astronomer and mathematician Simon Newcomb in his 1885 *Principles of Political Economy*[13] – it was he who both furnished the theory with a purpose and came up with the statistical methodology to validate it.

Fisher believed that, in the long run, the velocity of circulation is determined by institutional factors such as habits, business practices and systems of payment and credit. He also assumed that the output of the economy was determined by labour and capital; factors which are not related to prices or the money supply. So, if V and Q are fixed, and MV = PQ, there must be a direct association between changes in the money supply (M) and the price level (P). This was the essence of the Quantity Theory of Money. Changes in the money supply will, in the long run, have a direct and proportional impact on the price level. Although the theory imposed a strong prior assumption on the cause and effect, notably the direction of travel from money to prices, it became the central tenet of monetarism, an influential theory that argued that increasing the amount of money in the economy led only to inflation and not real economic growth. It was with this in mind that Milton Friedman was to later say: 'Inflation is always and everywhere a monetary phenomenon.'[14]

The assumption in the Quantity Theory of Money that the economy is in a long-run equilibrium is crucial. Most economists would argue that the economy is predominately in a state of transition. Furthermore, empirically the velocity of circulation tends not to look that stable. Therefore, if V and Q are changeable, there is not necessarily a direct and stable relationship between money and prices.

However, this theory gave Fisher scope to see how money and prices might affect national output, and how these short-run fluctuations influenced the business cycle. He believed it was possible for the public to confuse rising prices as being driven by increased demand from a growing economy rather than an increase in the amount of money in circulation. In this instance, a rising price level might temporarily stimulate purchases if consumers believed the economy was doing well, a misconception he called 'money illusion'. In order to test this proposition, he looked for short-term correlations between prices and output. He introduced the distributive lag model, where current output movements are modelled on seven monthly lags of price changes. He concluded that 90 per cent of short-term output movements were accounted for by recent changes in prices. His findings convinced him he had dealt a blow to all other business-cycle theories, as only around 10 per cent of cyclical movements were not explained by fluctuations in prices. However, Fisher himself had made strong assertions, in particular the assumed causality between prices and output rather than vice versa. Mainstream economists thought his work interesting, but were less than accepting of the conclusions.

Fisher had a long-standing concern with how prices are set in the economy. In 1911 he published a book called *The Purchasing Power of Money*. He wanted to educate the general public about the consequences of money supply and inflation as he felt that people were unable to connect the two, and therefore could not protect themselves from the consequences of inflation. He later noted the European hyperinflation after the First World War, for which many causes were cited, but not the one Fisher believed to be paramount: an uncontrolled expansion in the money supply. He also wanted to make people understand the costs of inflation and why its control should matter. Inflation redistributes wealth from savers to borrowers since inflation reduces the quantity of goods those savings can buy while borrowers benefit from a reduction in the real value of what they owe. Also, workers on fixed incomes saw their real wages decline while companies tied to contracts agreed under the false premise of stable prices also suffered.

Fisher's Quantity Theory of Money argued that a stable money supply was the key to stable prices. By stable money he meant money that held a constant purchasing power over goods and services available in the economy. He used terms such as the 'constant dollar', 'standardizing the dollar', 'unshrinkable dollar' or the 'commodity dollar' to describe a dollar that could buy a constant amount of goods and services. His 'commodity dollar' would encourage the public to think about the purchasing power of a dollar when it came to setting prices and writing contracts.

Fisher's idea was in direct contrast to the gold standard, the de facto economic policy of the day. The gold standard required the dollar to be exchangeable for a fixed quantity of gold, but it had not always been successful at achieving price stability. His concept of the commodity dollar required a dollar to be fixed in value against a group of commodities (goods), and its gold content adjusted to maintain its purchasing power.

He had observed that, between 1873 and 1896, the dollar's value increased as American prices fell. Fisher argued that this led to a prolonged depression as the supply of money was determined by the amount of gold, so the money supply was growing at a slower pace than was needed for the number of transactions necessary to maintain growth in the economy. The obvious solution would have been to reduce the amount of gold in the US dollar to lower its value. If that resulted in too much inflation then the amount of gold backing the dollar could be increased. Practically speaking, Fisher's idea required gold coins to be removed from circulation and replaced with 'gold certificates', which would circulate with gold bullion backing. This way, the amount of gold in a dollar being circulated can be disconnected from a fixed quantity of gold. The idea was to vary the amount of gold backing the dollar, in order to maintain its purchasing power. Or, as Fisher put it, the weight of gold behind the dollar would vary with prices.

The book was very well received around the world. Keynes described it as a better exposition of monetary theory than was available elsewhere. However, in calling for the abandonment of the gold standard, Fisher had placed himself at odds with the consensus of political and business opinion. Those who opposed Fisher's idea at least saw the logic, but did not believe it would be easy or practical to implement. They were also worried about undermining confidence in the operation of the gold standard, which already had been exposed as a fallible system of price stability. Tinkering with the gold standard was not a preferred option. Any admission that it was not perfect, or that the value of the dollar might require adjustment, was considered subversive and liable to undermine confidence in both the operation of the system and the value of the dollar.

After failing to convince President Woodrow Wilson of the merits of his plan, Fisher believed that he had to garner public opinion. He attempted to do so in 1914 by publishing a non-technical and popularized version of his 1911 work, which he called *Why is the Dollar Shrinking?* Fisher also gave the Hitchcock Lectures in 1917 on 'Stabilizing the Dollar', which later became a book of the same title. In 1927 he gave the Geneva Lectures focusing on the problem of money illusion. The lectures were turned into a short book written in large text and with the general public in mind. The first part of the book focused on how money illusion created economic cycles. The second part was the policy prescription, outlining what a monetary authority should do and how individuals could avoid money illusion to protect their real living standards. His effort was to be fruitless. Despite a succession of publications and numerous speeches between 1912 and 1934, he was unable to persuade policymakers to adopt the principle of the commodity dollar.

Although the commodity dollar idea never took off, similar schemes such as index-linked wages and pensions have become widely adopted. The development of price and quantity indices in economics was largely due to Fisher, who argued that wartime inflation had called for the indexation of wages to protect real take-home pay. He had already applied the concept to his own staff.

In 1922 he published one of his most technical works, *The Making of Index Numbers*. He described how indices of price and output movements could be constructed. A year later he established the Index Number Institute. This was a business to prepare and issue economic index numbers for publications. In 1926 he added an economic analysis section to the INI, and by 1929 some of his statistics were reaching over 5 million newspaper readers.

The idea of indexation can also be applied to debt so investors' returns are protected from inflation. While a director of Remington Rand, Fisher pioneered the first inflation-indexed bond, where investors earned a set real return regardless of what the inflation rate was. It didn't catch on, simply because most investors at the time did not understand what they were being sold. Today most debt issuance is still in nominal terms that do not take inflation into account, but inflation-protected bonds have become part of the debt issued by governments around the world.

Although indexation schemes are now fairly widespread, perhaps the country which has come closest to embracing Fisher is Chile. The UF, or Unidad de Fomento (Development Unit), was introduced in 1967. The UF is nominally the Chilean currency, but corrected for inflation. It remains in use today for wage contracts, for instance, so pay rises are awarded in real terms. The UF made indexing to inflation transparent, and Chile is the most inflation-indexed country in the world.

The Nobel Prize-winning economist Robert Shiller, in the spirit of Irving Fisher, has proposed that contracts in the US be expressed in terms of baskets reflecting the real value of a consumer's need, or in Fisher's terminology, a set of commodities they buy. He also suggested that governments could issue debt, so sell government bonds, denominated in terms of shares of nominal GDP and proposed calling these shares Trills. Each would pay a quarterly dividend equal to one trillionth of a country's national output, in which case the dividend would automatically correct for movements in inflation.

The intellectual pursuit that dominated Fisher's work stemmed from his experience in losing his fortune in the Great Depression. As events overwhelmed him, he sought out explanations. He did not like to be proven wrong, and needed to understand what was happening. He remained convinced the market and the economy would recover, but first he felt a strong need to explain the drama of the Great Crash.

In his 1930 book *The Stock Market Crash – and After*, Fisher identified why the market had been pumped up excessively in the years preceding the crash. First, overeager shoestring investors had driven the market up beyond its fundamental worth and were overextending themselves using credit. There was also the influence of margin buying in certain stocks. (This was, of course, exactly what Fisher himself had been doing.)

By 1932 the US economy was far from being in recovery mode and the quick rebound to the 1929 crash predicted by Fisher looked increasingly unlikely. Unemployment had hit 25 per cent compared to around 4 per cent in 1929. GDP had fallen by over 40 per cent. Nearly 6,000 banks had failed since the crash. Despite the terrible news, Fisher still believed the depression was bottoming out, and that the economy would quickly move away from depression in 1933. It didn't.

After his experience of the 1930s, Fisher produced a theory of business cycles different from the monetarist version of his earlier work.

This was the debt-deflation theory of depression, which he laid out in his 1932 book *Booms and Depressions*, and summarized a year later in his famous 1933 article in *Econometrica* entitled 'The Debt-Deflation Theory of Great Depressions'. Fisher identified all great depressions as starting from a point of overindebtedness:

> The public psychology of going into debt for gain passes through several more or less distinct phases:
> (a) the lure of big prospective dividends or gains in income in the remote future;
> (b) the hope of selling at a profit, and realizing a capital gain in the immediate future;
> (c) the vogue of reckless promotions, taking advantage of the habituation of the public to great expectations;
> (d) the development of downright fraud, imposing on a public which had grown credulous and gullible.[15]

In the case of the Great Depression, the overindebtedness originated in reckless borrowing by corporations who had been encouraged by high-pressure salesmanship of investment bankers. The collapse of the debt bubble then led to a self-perpetuating vicious circle of falling asset prices, which, as Fisher knew from experience, made it hard to repay one's debt. It led to further distressed selling, rising bankruptcies and even bank runs as loans went bad on banks' balance sheets.

He then described the process of debt-deflation, where attempts to liquidate assets in order to reduce debts become self-defeating, as the ensuing fall in prices raises the real value of debts even more. In other words, the real cost of borrowing is the nominal interest rate minus inflation, so deflation increases the cost of debt while inflation would reduce it. Fisher observed:

> Each dollar of debt still unpaid becomes a bigger dollar, and if the over-indebtedness with which we started was great enough, the liquidation of debts cannot keep up with the fall of prices which it causes. In that case, liquidation defeats itself. While it diminishes the number of dollars owed, it may not do so as fast as it increases the value of

each dollar owed. Then, *the very effort of individuals to lessen their burden of debts increases it, because of the mass effect of the stampede to liquidate is swelling each dollar owed.*[16]

For Fisher, the simple way out of the crisis was reflation of the price level, which would reduce the real value of debt. Although Fisher's work was to come back into vogue later, his prognosis was generally ignored in favour of John Maynard Keynes, who in 1936 published *The General Theory of Employment, Interest and Money*. Keynes identified excessive saving and a lack of aggregate demand as the cause of the ongoing depression, and urged the government to restore full employment through deficit-financed government spending.

Ben Bernanke and financial accelerators

One of the criticisms of Fisher's debt-deflation explanation is that price changes simply have a redistributive effect between debtors and creditors. Falling prices result in an increase in the real value of debts, and a transfer of wealth from debtors to creditors. Therefore, creditors gain while debtors lose, but the overall impact on society should be closer to zero.

Ben Bernanke, who served two terms as the chairman of the Federal Reserve between 2006 and 2014, and oversaw the US central bank's response to the 2008 global financial crisis, was previously an academic economist and scholar of the Great Depression. In an article published in 1983 he claimed to have rescued the Fisher debt-deflation hypothesis by adding the idea of the credit crunch.[17] This would be the missing link between deflation and dramatic declines in nominal incomes.

As prices fall, the real debt burden of debtors rises; but, far from benefiting, it actually hurts creditors because falling asset prices, rising loan impairments and bankruptcies lead to a fall in the value of assets on bank balance sheets. These collateral effects lessen the incentive for creditors to lend, resulting in a credit crunch, which then hits aggregate demand in the economy through a fall in consumption and investment.

This idea goes to the heart of the 'financial accelerator' concept, which describes how financial conditions tend to propagate business cycles. It is predominately based on the idea of asymmetric information. Those wishing to borrow to invest have a much better understanding of the projects than the creditor. Therefore, debt contracts often require the posting of collateral, which is an asset that is pledged by the borrower to the project. For instance, a borrower may pledge his home as collateral for a loan. So, the collateral comes down to the net worth of the debtor. Falling asset prices reduce this net worth. Therefore, an economic downturn can lead to a tightening of financial conditions and less credit availability.

The Great Depression and ensuing debt-deflation led to wide-scale distress among borrowers, lowering their ability to pledge collateral. But this also increased the risk to lenders as the average financial health of borrowers deteriorated, which impeded the flow of credit to the economy. The banking panics of the 1930s caused banks to shut their doors to avoid facing the risk of a run on their deposits. This, however, shut them off from their customers and increased the asymmetric information problems between borrowers and lenders, which further dampened normal lending activities to households and businesses.

Fast forward seventy years and it is clear that financial accelerator effects played a key role in the run-up to, and the aftermath of, the 2008 global financial crisis. As mortgage lending is secured on the value of houses, rising house prices tend to improve the financial conditions of lenders as default risks fall. This encourages further mortgage lending, which has the effect of raising prices further. This lending may also be directed at riskier parts of the mortgage market, that is sub-prime, or less than prime creditworthiness, lending. As homes are worth more, the loan-to-value ratios increase, which also gives homeowners the opportunity to refinance their mortgages at lower rates of interest.

It is possible that the way banks finance themselves today has increased the impact of the financial accelerator on lending activity.

Historically, banks have been viewed as institutions that intermediate between savers (their depositors) and borrowers (those who take out loans). Banks today, though, are less dependent on deposits for money creation. Global money markets are substantial and provide a large source of wholesale funding to financial institutions.

What this means is that banks themselves may not be dissimilar to other borrowers. Banks that are well capitalized are likely to be able to raise wholesale funds at lower interest rates than those that are poorly capitalized. For banks, it is typically expensive to raise new capital on the open market, so their balance sheets are primarily determined by earnings and asset values. In turn, the level of bank capital relative to regulatory levels can be an important determinant of a bank's cost of financing. But banks' capital positions also tend to be strongly pro-cyclical since assets tend to increase in value in a boom and fall in a recession. This further enhances the potential potency of the financial accelerator, observed in the large build-up of mortgage debt and high leverage of the financial sector in the run-up to the financial crisis.

It also means that in the aftermath of a financial crisis, where the banking system finds itself overleveraged, burdened with non-performing loans and insufficient capital, there can be a sharp drop in the flow of credit to the economy. This was seen in Japan when the financial problems of its banks and corporations contributed to lost decades of growth.

During the 1980s, the Japanese economy had performed spectacularly. Japan grew at an average rate of 4.5 per cent per year, and there was a widespread belief that it might even overtake the US as the largest economy in the world. However, the Japanese boom had been fuelled by a colossal run-up in property and equity markets. Japan has struggled to recover from the sharp correction in these that occurred in 1991, ushering in over two lost decades of stagnant growth and falling prices.

Since 1992, the Japanese economy has grown at an average rate of just 0.9 per cent per year, less than a quarter of its pre-1991 growth rate. In money terms, it was only in 2016 that Japanese national output surpassed its 1997 level. This is because its weak real growth had been accompanied by falling prices. Its benchmark stock index has also failed to recover since the early 1990s crash. The Nikkei 225, which peaked at over 38,000 at the start of 1990, had fallen to 14,000 in August 1992. After the recent financial crisis, the market fell to a low of under 9,000 before recovering to around 20,000. Despite its recent good performance, the Japanese stock market is still only valued at about half of what it was before the crash.

Japan's recovery is hampered by a rapidly ageing population and strong competition from its Asian neighbours. However, it is expectations of a stubbornly weak economy, where prices are falling, that have created a deflationary mind-set that is hard to break out off. This can become self-fulfilling where low expectations cause households and businesses to hold back spending, which then delivers the deflation they feared.

Escaping a deflationary trap

Irving Fisher's debt-deflation theory about depressions was based on a small sample of just three short periods of deflation, 1837–41, 1873–79 and the Great Depression of the 1930s. While it is not uncommon for prices to be falling in certain sectors or product markets, a sustained deflation in the general or average price level was actually a rare event until it occurred in Japan.

In such an event, Fisher's solution, as he recommended repeatedly in letters to President Roosevelt and colleagues, was basically reflation. He proposed that the central bank should simply increase the price level to near its 1926 level by expanding the money supply in line with his formulation of the Quantity Theory of Money. He also suggested stabilizing the financial system by providing a government guarantee of bank deposits to curb harmful and destructive bank runs. He believed that membership of the gold standard prevented the necessary monetary expansion since the dollars in circulation were constrained by the amount of gold. Dropping the gold standard would free the dollar and allow it to fall in value during a depression, which could boost exports and therefore the economy.

He also proposed a gift or loan to employers who increase their labour force. Otherwise, he had no enthusiasm for fiscal policy or public works programmes, which Fisher saw as simply the swapping of private sector debt for public sector debt. A fiscal stimulus might support output and employment over a short horizon (around two years), but would not address the underlying causes of the depression. As such, it was simply a painkiller rather than a cure.

The US did devalue its currency and leave the gold standard but by 1933 the economy still wasn't recovering. Fisher had believed that confidence would return the economy to prosperity immediately, but it did not.

Nearly a century later, as Japan's experience shows, it is clear that reflating an economy is not as easy as Fisher thought. Japan has undertaken a number of periods of aggressive monetary policies with the central bank injecting cash through quantitative easing (QE) programmes. It seems that the war against deflation cannot be won simply through robust action from the central bank.

Combating deflation requires a change in consumer attitudes and firms' behaviour, so it's a more complex process than it appears. In a 2002 speech, Ben Bernanke argued that Japan should consider a 'helicopter money drop'.[18] It would inject money directly into the economy; in essence, a free gift of money to citizens. As a permanent gift, it could have a strong impact on consumer and producer expectations of inflation.

So far no major central banks or Treasury departments have taken up Bernanke's suggestion. It would certainly be unconventional, but radical solutions may need to be considered in economies hamstrung by high levels of debt.

Japan indeed faces a number of barriers to economic growth besides deflation. First, it has a large overhang of public debt which has made governments reluctant to use fiscal policy. Second, structural changes in the economy and financial reforms are required. Bernanke argued in 2002 that political constraints rather than a lack of policy instruments were the reason Japanese deflation has been so long-lasting.

In considering whether the US could suffer a similar deflationary episode to Japan's following the collapse of the dotcom bubble between 2000 and 2002, Bernanke had correctly predicted it to be unlikely. His primary argument was the relative structural stability of the American economy compared to Japan's, and its stronger ability to absorb shocks and grow. In particular, he mentioned the younger workforce, flexible markets, entrepreneurial spirit and openness to technological change all contributing to this resilience – and, by implication, that these were some of the factors absent in Japan. Bernanke would soon face a test of his theories with the 2009 Great Recession that followed the global financial crisis, and the prospect of repeating the 1930s loomed again.

Minsky meltdowns

Irving Fisher's insights were revived in the 1990s by Hyman Minsky, who had incorporated ideas from Fisher as well as others in formulating his theory that private corporate debt, largely ignored in macroeconomic models, would lead to a financial crisis. He warned against speculative bubbles arising in inflated asset prices which had economy-wide implications.

The financial instability hypothesis developed by Minsky describes how credit bubbles form,[19] while Fisher's debt-deflation described how they collapse and drag the economy into recession and depression. Minsky believed that, after prolonged prosperity, capitalist economies tend to move from a financial structure dominated by stable finance to one that increasingly emphasizes speculative and Ponzi finance, which are unstable. He viewed such cycles as endemic to a capitalist system, their severity depending on the dynamics of such a financial system and the regulations that govern the economy.[20]

When he passed away in 1996 at the age of seventy-seven, Minsky hadn't seen that the 2008 sub-prime mortgage bubble would cause *The Economist* to dub it 'Minsky's Moment'.[21] During his lifetime, his work attracted little notice, but the global financial crisis would elevate Minsky and his ideas.

Former Fed chair Janet Yellen, while vice-chair to Ben Bernanke during the 2009 recession, gave a speech entitled: 'A Minsky Meltdown: Lessons for Central Bankers'. She pointed out: 'As Minsky's financial instability hypothesis suggests, when optimism is high and ample funds are available for investment, investors tend to migrate . . . to the risky speculative and Ponzi end.' She added: 'In retrospect, it's not surprising that these developments led to unsustainable increases in bond prices and house prices. Once those prices started to go down, we were quickly in the midst of a Minsky meltdown.'[22]

Much like Fisher, Minsky's prescription would have entailed recognizing the importance of debt in causing the boom. Yellen agrees: 'Regardless of one's views on using monetary policy to reduce bubbles, it seems plain that supervisory and regulatory policies could help prevent the kinds of problems we now face. Indeed, this was one of Minsky's major prescriptions for mitigating financial instability.'[23]

It seems that interest in both Fisher and Minsky has been revived by the recent global financial crisis. However, the debt-deflation stage of the financial instability hypothesis so far remains a threat rather than a reality.

The global financial crisis

Just as the Great Recession offers parallels to the Great Depression, debt has once again returned as an issue for major economies after the 2008 global financial crisis. At the end of 2015, government debt as a share of GDP was 243 per cent in Japan, 105 per cent in the US, 92 per cent in the euro area, and 90 per cent in the UK. Adding private sector debt would more than double these debt levels.

A comparison with the 1930s gives a different picture. Debt-to-GDP ratios shot up in the 1930s because of deflation, when falling prices increased the value of debt to be repaid. Now they are high because there has been so much borrowing in the recent past.

Large debts are, of course, a necessary condition for debt-deflation, but even though inflation rates have fallen below the 2 per cent target set by many major central banks, actual deflation is still the dog that hasn't yet barked. But does this mean we have escaped debt-deflation? Did policymakers learn the lessons from the 1930s? And what might they still need to do?

According to Irving Fisher, when inflation is low and the economy collapses, the central bank should act more aggressively than normal to avoid the onset of deflation. Central banks have, indeed, done just this, slashing interest rates to near zero per cent. However, this has created an additional problem of the 'zero lower bound' for interest rates.

As Bernanke says, a central bank that sees its policy rate driven down to zero is not out of ammunition. In this instance, deflationary episodes may require the central bank to think in terms of unconventional policies to avoid outright price declines à la Japan. It is possible for the central bank to set a negative interest rate, charging commercial banks for depositing money with it in the hope that they will lend the money instead. This is the type of unconventional monetary policy that has been adopted by the European Central Bank, the Bank of Japan and others.

Even if interest rates are close to zero, there should still be a policy response. Simply running the printing press is always an option. Money could be injected into the economy through asset purchases such as quantitative easing, or even more aggressively via the equivalent of a 'helicopter drop'. This could work through fiscal policy, say through a tax cut or an increase in government spending funded not by borrowing but through the central bank printing money. Fisher thought that it should always be possible to reflate the economy back to where it ought to be. To him, central banks have not exhausted their armoury should they need to fight against deflation.

Fisher had also in the 1930s called for monetary policy to act as a lender of last resort to stabilize the financial system in order to stop the debt-deflation process and reinstate the credit system. He had highlighted the connections between violent financial crises and fire sales of assets accompanied by a general decline in both aggregate demand and the price level. He, therefore, would have probably approved of the bailout of the investment bank Bear Stearns in March 2008, which meant that a series of defaults and asset price falls were not initiated as the bank went into liquidation. Would a bailout of Lehman Brothers just a few months later have helped to avoid the global financial crisis altogether? Ben Bernanke, Fed chairman at the time, didn't believe that Lehman posed the same systemic risk as Bear Stearns. Fisher would probably have asked whether rescuing this bank would have prevented a series of defaults which could have served as a trigger for the financial crisis. But would the global financial crisis have been triggered by something else instead?

Fisher would have agreed that a well-regulated financial system would guard against debt-deflation by avoiding large and unsustainable build-ups of debt in the first place. Well-designed regulatory and supervisory powers play a role in preventing deflation by maintaining financial stability. They can act to rein in exuberant financing from dangerous financial innovations, practices and attitudes. Regulations and reforms are also needed alongside lender of last resort facilities to curb potential moral hazard problems. In other words, if the central bank is always there to bail a bank out, then a bank has less of an incentive to act prudently. Regulation can reduce this risk. In this respect, he would have welcomed the new macroprudential regulatory powers given to central banks after the 2008 financial crisis to target financial stability alongside their existing mandate of price stability.

Fisher's final years

The years 1933 to 1939 saw a period of frantic effort by Fisher to solve the country's problems and his own financial doldrums. He failed at both. The country wasn't following his recommendations, his own assets would never recover their value and his debts would never go away.

By 1945, when his sister-in-law died and his debt to her of more than $1 million was forgiven, his life was winding down. Margie had died suddenly in 1940, the year he lost his house at 460 Prospect Street because he could no longer afford to pay the rent. On his own, and now seventy-three years of age, he lived in a modest apartment when he was not on the road.

His death was in many ways a sad affair and reflective of Fisher's character traits. In September 1945, he believed that a blockage in his bowels was due to a kink in the lower intestines, something he had experienced fifteen years earlier. It then had caused some discomfort but eventually cleared up by itself. He believed his diet and exercise would be sufficient to bring about good health, and did not seek a second or specialist medical opinion.

When in the autumn of 1946 his health began to deteriorate, X-rays found an inoperable tumour in his colon that had spread to his liver. Had he acted the year before, his cancer may have been treatable and he could have lived several more years. In 1947, he passed away, and was buried next to his wife and daughter in New Haven, Connecticut, the home of Yale University.

After his death, the net value of his estate was estimated at around $60,000. He would have been disappointed that it amounted to so little, and it was certainly not enough to fund an Irving Fisher Institute he hoped would cement his legacy to both economics and health. Nevertheless, what he did leave was considerable – in intellectual if not financial terms. Between 1891 and 1942 he wrote thirty books, with more than 150 English and foreign-language editions.

Pictures show Irving Fisher to have been straight-laced, and throughout his life he was disciplined in all matters. Because of his seriousness, crusades and sometimes controversial beliefs, many people, including his economics colleagues, had thought Fisher odd and humourless.[24] Despite growing recognition, he is still under-appreciated and not quite as lauded as a Great Economist as is warranted by his work. Fisher was at the vanguard of modern economics, essentially inspiring the leading central bankers who were at the helm when the entire banking system was on the brink of collapse. There is no doubt his thinking continues to remain relevant today.

CHAPTER 6

John Maynard Keynes: To Invest or Not to Invest?

Few questions have been as prominent since the banking crash: should the British and European governments have cut public spending and adopted austere policies in the aftermath of the 2008 financial crisis?

In another parallel to the 1929 crash, this was also the question debated in Britain in the 1930s, which launched the Keynesian revolution in economics. John Maynard Keynes advocated government spending in a sharp break with neoclassical economics that eschewed the active use of fiscal policy in response to a downturn. Keynes gave an illustration:

> If the Treasury were to fill old bottles with banknotes, bury them at suitable depths in disused coalmines which are then filled up to the surface with town rubbish, and leave it to private enterprise on well-tried principles of *laissez-faire* to dig the notes up again . . . there need be no more unemployment and, with the help of the repercussions, the real income of the community, and its capital wealth also, would probably become a good deal greater than it actually is.[1]

Recognizing it's not ideal, but necessary, he adds: 'It would, indeed, be more sensible to build houses and the like; but if there are political and practical difficulties in the way of this, the above would be better than nothing.'[2]

Today the debate is again over the role of government spending while policymakers contend with high levels of public debt amidst a sluggish recovery in the aftermath of the worst financial crisis since the 1930s. Thus, Keynesian economics is back in the spotlight.

Keynes is not only influential because of his intellectual contributions. He was a compelling writer and known for his turns of phrase, including: '[Economics] should be a matter for specialists – like dentistry. If economists could manage to get themselves thought of as humble, competent people, on a level with dentists, that would be splendid!'[3] And: 'a speculator is one who runs risks of which he is aware and an investor is one who runs risks of which he is unaware'.[4]

John Maynard Keynes dominated British economics until the Second World War, but his influence extends globally. Across the Atlantic, America's first economics Nobel laureate, Paul Samuelson, was a standard bearer for Keynesian economics in the US. He helped to incorporate Keynesian thought into neoclassical economics, which became known as the 'neoclassical synthesis' – a term that he apparently coined – which underpins modern economics. Thus, without always being explicit, Keynes's ideas pervade the subject. They have certainly framed much of the fierce post-crisis debates over austerity and the best course of economic policy.

The life and times of John Maynard Keynes

Keynes was born in 1883, to the 'educated bourgeoisie', in his self-description of his social class.[5] As for his views of different social classes: 'Aristocrats were absurd; the proletariat was always "boorish". The good things in life sprang from the middle class.'[6]

He attended Eton College on a scholarship, followed by another scholarship to King's College, Cambridge. After working in the India Office of the British government, he returned to the University of Cambridge as a lecturer in 1909 and in 1911 was elected a fellow of King's, where he remained until his death in 1946.

His father was the Cambridge economist John Neville Keynes, which is why he is often referred to as Maynard Keynes. Describing John Neville Keynes, his son's noted biographer, Robert Skidelsky, wrote: 'the real barrier to a successful academic career was not lack of originality, but anxiety'.[7] Neville Keynes had turned down a professorship at the University of Chicago in 1894, perhaps reluctant to leave the familiarity of Cambridge, where he had a comfortable existence as Registry – the college's top and well-compensated administrator. He wrote two books in his career, the second of which accorded him a doctorate when he was thirty-eight. He lived another sixty years but rarely wrote again. Still, Alfred Marshall considered Neville Keynes his best student and asked him to edit the prestigious *Economic Journal*, founded in 1890. He declined, though his son Maynard Keynes took it on when he became a fellow at King's. Maynard Keynes exceeded his father's academic legacy in other respects too.

As his great-grandmother reminded him, 'You will be expected to be very clever, having lived always in Cambridge.' Maynard Keynes did not let her down, and excelled from a young age.[8] He has been described as standing 'head and shoulders above all the other boys' in his prep school, both physically and mentally.[9] At Eton, he won thirty-nine prizes, including the top awards for history and English, all of the main mathematical prizes, and even one in chemistry. He worked diligently and followed his father's habit of monitoring closely how his time was spent. In a letter to his parents he wrote: 'In a minute and a quarter my light has to be put out and I have many things to do before then.'[10]

After graduation, Keynes spent two years in the India Office as a civil servant. Keynes sat the civil service entrance exam and ironically did poorly in economics. He would have come top had it not been for the economics mark, but had to be content with second. This was important because the successful candidates could choose from the available posts in the different civil service departments in order of their rank in the exam. The Treasury was the plum job, but there was only one post available that year and the top candidate, a bright classicist from Oxford University called Otto Niemeyer, took it. Keynes, therefore, had to settle for the India Office. Had Keynes come top and got into the Treasury, he might have stayed. We might never have had the Keynesian revolution in economics.

Coming full circle, in the 1920s and 30s, when struggling to push his unorthodox policies arguing for government spending against the orthodox 'Treasury view', Keynes's principal opponent in the Treasury, and later in the Bank of England, was none other than Sir Otto Niemeyer, GBE, KCB. According to the *Oxford Dictionary of National Biography*, he was 'the outstanding Treasury official of the post-war years'. Keynes subsequently wrote in the Preface to his *General Theory*: 'The difficulty lies, not in the new ideas, but in escaping from the old ones, which ramify, for those brought up as most of us have been, into every corner of our minds.'[11]

During his time at the India Office, he did impress his immediate boss, Basil Blackett. Blackett later moved to the Treasury; and in the financial chaos of August 1914 remembered Keynes and called him in to help out temporarily. He ended up staying for the whole war. Thus, Keynes entered the Treasury in a rather more privileged and somewhat freelance position: he had a commanding role in the financing of the war, rubbed shoulders with all the top politicians and became the Treasury's chief representative at the Paris Peace Conference.

The aftermath of the First World War provided the context for some of Keynes's most lasting ideas. It led to *The Economic Consequences of the Peace*, and that conditioned the rest of his career. In the book, John Maynard Keynes argued that Germany could not afford the post-war reparations demanded in 1919. Sales broke records in England and the US; this book made Keynes's name.

Keynes found the work at the India Office easy but uninspiring, which is likely to have contributed to his decision to return to Cambridge after a short spell to become an academic. His time in government proved to be a valuable link, as he was to contribute actively to economic policy during both world wars.

He returned to Cambridge to take up a lectureship after being encouraged to do so by Alfred Marshall, with whom an earlier term of postgraduate work comprised Keynes's entire formal training in economics. Keynes had remarked at the time in a letter to his friend, the writer Lytton Strachey: 'Marshall is continually pestering me to turn professional Economist . . . Do you think there is anything in it? I doubt it.'[12]

Keynes had frequent occasion to return to London as he was part of the Bloomsbury Group, an intellectual collective who took their name from the district in London where many of them lived and whose membership included Strachey as well as Virginia Woolf and E. M. Forster. All enjoyed the arts, including ballet and after years of homosexual dalliances Keynes fell in love with the Russian ballerina Lydia Lopokova after watching her perform in 1921. They embarked on an affair and married four years later after she obtained a divorce from her husband, when Keynes was forty-two and she was thirty-three. It was a marriage that lasted for the rest of his life.

Rather unusually for an academic, Keynes – like Ricardo and Fisher before him – was also an investor. He made a fortune, but was nearly bankrupted several times. In 1936 he was worth over £500,000, or an eye-watering £27 million in today's money. Then he nearly lost it all in the 1937–38 recession when he was heavily leveraged, having borrowed to invest in the stock market. Still, at his death in 1946 he had an investment portfolio of £400,000 (£12 million today) and an art and book collection worth £80,000 (£2.5 million today).[13]

His experiences in the post-war boom and ensuing economic stagnation shaped his world-view. Unlike the classical economists, who believed that economies reacted quickly to shocks, Keynes believed the effect to be much more sluggish. For instance, savings were not used for investment, such as buying new equipment. Instead, Keynes saw at first hand that savings were used to fuel speculation. At that time investors had to deposit only 15 per cent when buying shares, and this high degree of leverage increased the speculative frenzy which prompted investors to keep betting.

This experience shaped his famous 'animal spirits' description of investment and the role of investors. He defined 'animal spirits' as 'a spontaneous urge to action rather than inaction, and not as the outcome of a weighted average of quantitative benefits multiplied by quantitative probabilities'.[14] It framed his view of investors:

> professional investment may be likened to those newspaper competitions in which the competitors have to pick out the six prettiest faces from a hundred photographs, the prize being awarded to the

competitor whose choice most nearly corresponds to the average
preferences of the competitors as a whole, so that each competitor has
to pick, not those faces which he himself finds prettiest, but those
which he thinks likeliest to catch the fancy of the other competitors,
all of whom are looking at the problem from the same point of view.
It is not a case of choosing those which, in the best of one's judgment,
are really the prettiest, nor even those which average opinion genu-
inely thinks the prettiest. We have reached the third degree, where
we devote our intelligences to anticipating what average opinion
expects average opinion to be. And there are some, I believe, who
practise the fourth, fifth and higher degrees.[15]

As Keynes once wryly observed, 'Worldly wisdom teaches that it
is better for reputation to fail conventionally than to succeed
unconventionally.'[16]

The Keynesian revolution

It was the time of the Great Depression and a sluggish economic
recovery between the two world wars that saw the launch of the
Keynesian revolution. Keynes's seminal work grew out of the Depression. It wasn't the first time that unemployment was an issue. The
economic woes of the late nineteenth century during the Long
Depression led to the term 'unemployment' appearing for the first
time in the *Oxford English Dictionary* in 1888. But it was of a different
magnitude in the Great Depression. From 1929–33, the US unemployment rate rose from 3 per cent to 25 per cent. Income in 1933
was lower than in 1922. The UK also entered a prolonged depression
and saw unemployment double to 20 per cent.

Keynes was critical of the Treasury's classical view, which was
to await the recovery passively, since they believed that economies
self-corrected in the long run. The long run for classical economists
was long indeed. Modern economists are inclined to think that the
long run is the amount of time needed for fixed capital to adjust,
whereas the classical economists of that time thought that population

had to adjust, so birth and death were also part of the long-run adjustment.

Undoubtedly, Keynes's legacy was to switch the focus from the long run to the short run, where adjustments were sluggish and governments could thus play a role. He famously observed: 'But this *long run* is a misleading guide to current affairs. *In the long run* we are all dead. Economists set themselves too easy, too useless a task if in tempestuous seasons they can only tell us that when the storm is long past the ocean is flat again.'[17]

In *The General Theory of Employment, Interest and Money*, published in 1936, Keynes focused on the short run. He homed in on deficient demand, which included weak household consumption and low firm investment, as determinants of the Great Depression. He argued that, even in normal times, the incentive to invest is too weak and the propensity to hoard cash is too strong. Without the necessary investment, the economy tends to operate at less than full employment, where all labour is deployed productively. If there were also a 'shock' to investment demand, such as a stock market crash, output and employment would decline, resulting in economic slumps. So, Keynes proposed that governments should incur debt to move the economy back to full employment. He stressed that government borrowing to spend need not be inflationary if the economy was operating below its potential, and advocated deficit spending, where the government borrowed to spend during downturns and repaid debt during the good times: 'The boom not the slump is the right time for austerity.'[18] A practical economist, he proposed a board of public investment to plan to have a stock of projects ready for when other types of investments started to decline.

Keynes saw some of his ideas put into action, albeit not entirely to his liking. He believed President Franklin D. Roosevelt's US National Industrial Recovery Act of 1933, commonly known as the New Deal, would improve the banking system and transport infrastructure of America, but the amount of government spending or fiscal stimulus injected under FDR's plan was much smaller than the 11 per cent of GDP or national output Keynes believed was needed. Thus, he was critical of the legislation for putting reform before recovery. Britain was even worse in Keynes's view. The UK government balanced the budget. Despite the lack of government support, a combination of exchange depreciation and low interest rates brought about a recovery. But it was temporary. In 1937–38, both economies once again fell into sharp recession.

Like now, there was a heated debate over what more spending would mean for the budget deficit and high levels of government debt. A budget deficit arises if the government spends more than it receives in a given year. Government debt is the total accumulated deficit over time. Keynes criticized the UK Treasury for confusing capital spending with government 'deficit finance'. Keynes argued that public investment was a tool for correcting an economy that was operating below its full potential but which his critics thought would lead to even bigger budget deficits.

Keynes was also concerned about uncertainty dampening investment and disagreed with neoclassical economists over the role of the interest rate.[19] They viewed the interest rate as the price which balanced savings and investment. Keynes argued instead that savings rose and fell with income. Keynes believed that uncertainty was why people held on to money, even if it was not the most sensible investment decision: 'For it is a recognized characteristic of money as a store of wealth that it is barren; whereas practically every other form of storing wealth yields some interest or profit. Why should anyone outside a lunatic asylum wish to use money as a store of wealth?'[20]

He continues: 'Because, partly on reasonable and partly on instinctive grounds, our desire to hold Money as a store of wealth is a barometer of the degree of our distrust of our own calculations and conventions concerning the future.'[21]

The implication was that deficit spending would lead to higher levels of national income, which would generate more savings that would in turn pay for the greater amounts of accumulated government debt.

It wasn't Keynes's only involvement in government policy. During the Second World War Keynes became involved in the Beveridge Report that was published in 1942 and which was the foundation of the British welfare state, introducing a comprehensive social insurance system covering individuals 'from cradle to grave'. It fitted into his theories of how fiscal policy can influence the economy. In other words, unemployment benefits act as 'automatic stabilizers' that increase government spending during downturns without the government having to choose to act.

In sum, the Keynesian revolution altered the face of economics in proposing that economies were frequently not at full employment and output. As demand could fall short, and not all of what was produced would be bought, there was a role for government spending in righting the economy.

Keynesian economics held sway until the 1970s, which was a decade of high inflation, propelled by two oil price shocks that led to dramatic price rises. The British economy was in the doldrums but suffered from inflation and a weak currency, which raised import prices of oil and other goods. By the autumn of 1976, the UK required bailing out by the International Monetary Fund (IMF), which lent it $4 billion and demanded deep cuts in government spending to reduce Britain's indebtedness. The demonstrable end of the Keynesian era in the UK was when the British prime minister, James Callaghan, in 1976 remarked that the country could no longer spend its way out of recession and even added that it had only worked before by 'injecting bigger and bigger doses of inflation into the economy'.[22]

Unusually, the 1970s was also a period of high unemployment. This combination of high inflation and high unemployment, known as stagflation, contradicted the standard relationships. That era saw the rise of New Classicists and monetarists like Milton Friedman, whose theories explained stagflation and propelled him onto the stage. Keynes's ideas fell out of favour. There is a parallel in that Keynes's ideas were in vogue during the 1930s because they could explain the pressing issue of the time, which was unemployment.

By 1980, *laissez-faire* had become the dominant theory in the US with the election of President Ronald Reagan. When he was the Republican candidate for the presidency against the incumbent Democrat, Jimmy Carter, he quipped: 'Recession is when your neighbour loses his job. Depression is when you lose your job. Recovery is when Jimmy Carter loses his job.' Reagan won.

Still, that decade also saw the emergence of the New Keynesians, such as Nobel laureate Joseph Stiglitz, because unemployment was once again an issue in the aftermath of the economic revolutions that took place under both Reagan and Callaghan's Tory successor, Margaret Thatcher. New Keynesians justified limited government intervention since unemployment can remain high for a long time, but incorporated New Classical theories about how people behave to explain why it takes time for economies to return to equilibrium.

By the end of the twentieth century, the New Neoclassical Synthesis emerged, which was similar to the movement in the 1950s during which the Neoclassical Synthesis approach had appeared. The New Neoclassical Synthesis incorporated the New Keynesians, New Classicists and monetarists into one framework that incorporated parts of each theory to explain how the economy works.

The New Neoclassical Synthesis thus includes New Classical theories of how consumers make decisions across time periods as well as incorporating 'rational expectations' theory. Rational expectations posits that consumers know that a tax cut today will mean tax rises in the future, so they don't change their behaviour, thus a tax cut would not raise consumption and boost growth. Intriguingly, only a surprise government policy would work. The concept of rational expectations has been challenged owing to its assumption that consumers behave completely rationally and can process huge amounts of information. Indeed, government fiscal policies such as those advocated by Keynes which are not 'surprises' have impact, though the evidence is that consumers behave somewhat, though not completely, rationally in response to tax cuts.

At the start of the twenty-first century, Keynes was back in the spotlight as deficits and public spending re-emerged as contentious issues after the 2009 Great Recession.

Budget deficits and austerity

Britain's budget deficit may have been halved since the 2008 financial crisis, but it was still around 5 per cent of GDP at the end of the 2014/15 Parliament. It's worth recalling that, when Britain was rescued by the IMF in 1976, its budget deficit was 6.9 per cent of GDP. But the deficit wasn't as much a concern this time, or indeed in 1993 when its previous post-war high of 7.8 per cent was reached. That's because Britain was affected by the global financial crisis that had increased the level of government debt in the world's major economies.

Following the 2008 crash, Britain's debt had increased to around 90 per cent of GDP, substantially above the 60 per cent level obliged by the EU Maastricht Treaty. Two of the three major credit rating agencies didn't see that level of debt as compatible with the AAA top credit rating. After the EU referendum vote to leave the European Union in 2016, Britain was downgraded from its last remaining AAA rating.

The UK government has cut the rate of increase in government spending in order to reduce the yearly deficits and stabilize the overall debt level. Was austerity the right thing to do? The IMF had urged Britain to reconsider imposing austerity before the economy had fully recovered. And not just Britain. The initial years of the recovery saw governments from Europe to America cutting public expenditure while private demand was weak. In the UK, the recovery was tepid and output even contracted at times. In fact, 2012 saw two non-consecutive quarters of negative GDP growth, although that's not a recession since the formal definition requires two such consecutive quarters.

In Britain, the pace of austerity had slowed alongside the economy, but was such a policy necessary? Part of the rationale for cutting government spending was that investors would not want to lend to the UK if it did not show that it was reducing its budget deficit. Otherwise the government's debt might increase to unsustainable levels. This view was exacerbated by the context of the euro crisis that erupted in early 2010. Britain was, of course, not party to that crisis and may even have benefited as investors sought safer investments in non-euro countries. But that backdrop drove some of the thinking about deficits and austerity.

At the end of 2009, during the midst of the Great Recession, Greece needed a bailout after admitting that its government accounting was at best unreliable. Investors sold off Greek government bonds and eventually other euro area countries with high levels of government debt also saw their borrowing costs rise. As fewer investors were willing to lend Greece money, it became more expensive and ultimately impossible for the Greek government to borrow to finance its normal operations. Portugal faced a similar problem. It was a different picture for Ireland and Spain as well as Cyprus, all of which rescued their own banks. But in doing so, their budget deficits shot up and they ended up also needing help from the 'troika' that oversaw the rescue programmes for countries which shared the single currency: the EU, the European Central Bank (ECB) and the IMF.

European governments believed that fiscal discipline was needed to restore investor confidence, so pushed ahead with austerity. Before the crisis, Greece borrowed at the same advantageous rates as Germany since bond markets seemed to view the euro area as one entity. That contributed to too much borrowing by the Greek government. Though that scenario is unlikely to be repeated, euro area leaders came up with additional reforms to try to enforce fiscal restraint. They stressed the need for member countries to adopt fiscal discipline if they are to share a single currency and a common monetary policy.

There is a move to create a fiscal union which would go beyond the budget deficit rules that are centrally enforced by the European Commission, which can set penalties for countries that miss their targets. There is even discussion of establishing a European Treasury as the central fiscal authority for the euro area. It certainly adds a political dimension to the austerity debate and also raises questions over whether the EU is heading towards a federal system, with fiscal powers split between nations and supranational institutions.

After the acute phase of the euro crisis subsided, concerns over economic weakness prompted the ECB to do something it declined to do during the Great Recession. For the first time, in 2015, the ECB undertook quantitative easing (QE) and made large-scale cash injections into the economy by buying government debt. This increase in the amount of money available to lend had, via the simple mechanics of supply and demand, the effect of driving down borrowing costs, which have since remained cheap. This is in the context of low government bond yields around the world, which would be expected in a slow-growth environment.

The combination of slow growth and low borrowing costs has added a new dimension to the austerity debate. Should governments be taking greater advantage of cheap rates to invest? Should budget deficits and debt be a secondary consideration when economic growth remains sluggish?

Investment and low interest rates

This question is being asked in both Europe and the US. In America, there is a push for more infrastructure investment, although the Republicans in Congress remain concerned about adding to the fiscal deficit. Of course, Republicans traditionally follow a non-interventionist philosophy, and are suspicious about the role of government in both investment and the economy in general. As former Republican President Ronald Reagan observed of government intervention: 'government's view of the economy could be summed up in a few short phrases: If it moves, tax it. If it keeps moving, regulate it. If it doesn't move, subsidize it,'[23] and remarked on a separate occasion, 'The nine most terrifying words in the English language are: I'm from the Government and I'm here to help.'[24]

This explains why the US plan is counting on private investors to help finance its projects.

On the other side of the Atlantic, the debate over investment has found more political common ground. Britain has moved into the spotlight when it comes to this debate since the vote to leave the European Union in June 2016 led the Bank of England to restart QE, which helps sustain low borrowing costs. Yields on ten-year government debt, known as gilts, fell to record lows of around just 1 per cent after the Brexit vote. Record lows had also been reached for twenty- and thirty-year debt. It meant that, for the first time, the British government could sell debt by paying around 1 per cent interest for a decade. Even with interest rates being raised in 2017 for the first time since the banking crisis, borrowing costs remain fairly low. So, do low interest rates affect the question of whether governments should borrow to invest now?

Keynes pointed out that there is no 'crowding out' of private investment when the economy is operating below its potential. 'Crowding out' refers to how governments borrowing to invest would make it harder for private firms to do so because their demand for loans would push up the interest rate and make it more expensive for others to borrow. However, since the British economy lost over 6 per cent of its output during the 2008 recession, and interest rates for loans are low, 'crowding out' would be unlikely, because the economy has lost so much output that there is a lot of scope for the public and private sectors to invest before their demand for funds pushed up borrowing costs. Moreover, increasing public investment can help economic growth, as it can have a 'crowding in' effect. In other words, government investment can make private investment more efficient, for example a good telecoms infrastructure increases the returns to a pound invested by a private company by giving them the fibre network to deliver faster services.

In Britain, public investment has been slashed deeply. It is easier to cut capital expenditure on projects such as highway repairs than to reduce the current budget dominated by public sector services. During the height of austerity, between 2008 and 2011, public invest- ment fell from 3.3 per cent of national output to 1.9 per cent, a staggering 40 per cent decline. Will that ground be made up and, more pertinently, will this trend of low investment be reversed? It would likely mean adopting Keynes's view that public investment should be separated out from what governments spend from day to day. Unlike such current spending, Keynes would argue that invest- ment generates future returns and should not be lumped in with daily payments for civil servants in assessing the budget of a government.

Indeed, with the establishment of a National Infrastructure Commission in 2015, and given this context of low borrowing costs, the British government now aims to invest and reverse the years of cuts to public investment.

The European Union has also acted on a large scale. The EU changed its focus to take advantage of low rates in a way that should not lead to ballooning budget deficits.

European Commission President Jean-Claude Juncker's infrastructure investment fund, the European Fund for Strategic Investments (EFSI), commonly referred to as the Juncker Plan, was established in 2015. It sought to raise the considerable sum of €315 billion over three years by working with the European Investment Bank (EIB), which issues bonds to finance projects that develop digital, transport, energy and other infrastructure, as well as improve funding for small and medium-sized enterprises (SMEs). This is indeed a way to leverage a relatively small sum into an ambitious pool of money. The EU has itself invested €16 billion and there was a further €5 billion put in by the EIB. The top AAA-rated EIB can then issue bonds, taking advantage of low interest rates, to leverage the initial €21 billion into a fund large enough to make a difference in jump-starting European growth. The European Commission plans to increase the size and duration of the EFSI. Bolstered by its initial success, European policymakers are keen to rejuvenate infrastructure, which needs to be updated in many countries in order to keep up with the needs of businesses, particular in a fast-changing digital era.

The EFSI ambitiously seeks to encourage private companies to invest, thereby largely reducing the impact of the infrastructure spending on government fiscal positions. But that means a reliance on public-private partnerships, which have a mixed record when it comes to maintaining long-term infrastructure projects, such as railways.

Still, the focus of the fund on small and medium-sized enterprises, which are Europe's best job creators but have suffered most from the low amounts of bank lending while the banking system rebuilds itself after the financial crisis, is pertinent.

These SMEs would also benefit from updated infrastructure.

During the last recession, it was public investment that was slashed as a part of austerity programmes in the EU, just as it was in Britain, much to the detriment of spending on infrastructure. Investment in the euro area has been around 15 per cent below its pre-crisis level. Thus, the OECD and others have argued that increases in public investment would boost economic growth and thus even reduce government debt.

Why, then, has it been so difficult to increase investment since the crisis? One constraint has been the imposition of fiscal austerity by governments whose main focus is on the budget deficit, which for the most part includes capital investment. It's only in the very recent past that economic growth has regained priority. That largely explains the public side, but private investment has also dropped sharply since the recession.

German companies, for instance, have doubled their retained cash in the past decade, and others have as well. American multinationals have amassed record amounts of cash on their balance sheets. Resolving why these companies don't invest is key to understanding why one of the pillars of growth, investment, hasn't delivered during the recovery.

Government and consumer spending were hit hard and slow to recover, leaving deficient demand, both public and private, which is a disincentive for companies to invest since future sales don't look strong. The sharpness and the duration of the Great Recession also created uncertainty over whether or not to commit funds for investment stretching well into the future. Plus, the time it took for decimated banking systems in Europe and America to recover forced some companies to retain their earnings in case they needed cash during a time when bank lending remained constrained. For investors there were also other, more enticing, places to put cash. Stocks, for instance, were pushed to sky-high levels by low interest rates across major markets. But global stock markets have since been descending from their heady heights. And there's uncertainty from the US, which has begun to normalize (i.e. raise) interest rates earlier than the rest of the world. This means that investments with fixed returns, such as in infrastructure, can be relatively more attractive. Traditionally, investing in roads or energy doesn't achieve a high return, though it does tend to be stable. Yields from infrastructure such as utilities and toll roads are usually set by regulators and range from 3 to 4 per cent. In a low-rate environment, that's not a bad return. Of course, one of the challenges is still the slowness with which major public projects are granted approval. Still, there's no shortage of such projects being proposed by EU member states. In any case, growth in the world's largest economic entity would help the world economy.

The renewed focus on growth by not just the European Commission but also national governments offers more opportunities to reconsider the investment and growth nexus pointed out by Keynes. The debate over whether governments should themselves be borrowing more to invest, and whether such capital expenditure should be separately considered in budgets as Keynes proposed, is unsettled. So, what would Keynes make of the current austerity debate, which has shifted to become more about a debate over government investment?

Keynes on the government's role in the economy

Keynes argued for government spending as a means to counteract slow economic growth. Especially during a recovery from a recession or depression, private demand is deficient, so extra spending by government is needed to ensure that aggregate demand remains sufficient to maintain full employment. But what would Keynes have made of the debate over governments borrowing to invest in times outside acute crises or recession?

The cash hoarding that he predicted is evident in the post-crisis economy. Even though interest rates are very low, not enough firms are borrowing to invest, which has contributed to the slow-growth environment. For the reasons noted earlier, when investment doesn't respond to interest rates, unlike in normal times, monetary policy is no longer enough to boost the economy, which means that fiscal policy is also needed to increase investment and generate more growth.[25]

Investment is one of the components identified by Keynes that make up the level of aggregate demand in the economy. Consumption is generally viewed as being more stable than investment. When income increases, consumption tends to rise but not as much and also declines by less. Since some income is saved while the rest is consumed, the gap between consumption and production must be filled by investment if full employment is to be maintained.

Classical economists had assumed that savings automatically became investment. Keynes's insight was to treat savings distinctly. He discovered the 'paradox of thrift' that arises when, as more people try to save, the aggregate amount of savings in an economy actually *falls*. This happens because, as savings increase, consumption falls, which reduces total output, which in turn reduces the income from which savings are made. The problem gets worse the richer societies become since wealthier people tend to save a higher fraction of their income. This is why he advocated 'heavy death duties', which would redistribute wealth, especially unearned wealth, towards those more inclined to consume than save.[26] So, some redistribution of wealth from the rich would help investment, but Keynes worried that too much redistribution would hurt growth.

As Keynes believed that the normal tendency was for the marginal propensity to save to be stronger than the incentive to invest, he was supportive of governments borrowing to invest since he believed the economy usually operated below its potential and public investment should therefore supplement private investment. His idea was to use fiscal policy to maintain a high level of public or semi-public investment. Investment should encourage consumption by raising the overall level of output and thus income to consume out of. The more consumption there was, the higher the national income, and therefore the greater the savings of the society that could be used to finance investment. A permanently high level of publicly directed investment would offset fluctuations in private investment, and contribute to the economy remaining in a 'quasi-boom'.[27] Keynes viewed the state as an investor in line with its role in providing a social safety net discussed earlier, though he worried about the costs of Beveridge's welfare state.

Keynes proposed government action to accelerate or delay

investment projects as necessary: 'I expect to see the State . . . taking an ever greater responsibility for directly organizing investment . . . I conceive, therefore, that a somewhat comprehensive socialization of investment will prove the only means of securing an approximation to full employment.'[28]

Keynes urged the government to take on a greater role in investment as the need became clearer. His notion of 'socializing investment' may well encompass a government-backed infrastructure bank or fund to help get projects off the ground. He might not have viewed private sector participation as necessary, but might have been willing to include private investors who would pool their money with the government to build infrastructure. This is in line with the EU investment fund described earlier that leverages public funds to attract private financing.

Would this policy lead to persistent budget deficits? This was one of the criticisms of Keynes. It's why governments have been reluctant to borrow to invest. They fear bond investors will ask for higher returns to lend them money, increasing the borrowing costs for a country that could jeopardize its economic growth.

The verdict is far from settled. The Chicago School of monetarists say that Keynes's counter-cyclical policies are bound to fail since their effects will be anticipated, either immediately or after a short lag. Harvard economist Robert Barro argues that future tax rises to pay for government deficit spending are figured into long-term interest rates by investors and savers. That will lead to higher rates in the future and make government borrowing more expensive and the budget deficit less affordable. This view can be traced to David Ricardo. Under Ricardian equivalence, rational people know that the government debt will have to be repaid at some point in the form of higher taxes so they save in anticipation and do not increase current consumption that boosts growth. Still, the perceived need to increase investment and economic growth has shifted the public debate closer to what Keynes advocated even during non-crisis times. There is also a growing inclination to separate capital from current spending in government accounts, so investment doesn't count the same as day-to-day public spending. Given the debate over low investment, low borrowing costs and concerns over growth, Keynes's relatively lesser-known views on public investment could have a greater impact on the structure of an economy than his better-known arguments about government deficit spending.

Keynes's legacy

Keynes passed away in 1946 after helping to construct the post-Second World War Bretton Woods System, which included the formation of the sister institutions of the IMF and the World Bank. His memorial service was held at Westminster Abbey, close to Parliament, where he had latterly become a member of the House of Lords. He was survived by his widow, Lydia Lopokova, who continued his work with the Arts Council of Britain and lived another thirty-six years.

She died at the beginning of the Thatcher era, which saw the rollback of Keynesianism. But despite being in and out of favour, Keynes has had an enduring impact on economics. It's something that Keynes himself had predicted. The final passage of *The General Theory* reads:

> The ideas of economists and political philosophers, both when they are right and when they are wrong, are more powerful than is commonly understood. Indeed the world is ruled by little else. Practical men, who believe themselves to be quite exempt from any intellectual influence, are usually the slaves of some defunct economist. Madmen in authority, who hear voices in the air, are distilling their frenzy from some academic scribbler of a few years back. I am sure that the power of vested interests is vastly exaggerated compared with the gradual encroachment of ideas . . . soon or late, it is ideas, not vested interests, which are dangerous for good or evil.[29]

Keynes believed that there are no intractable economic problems, and that well-run economies would produce prosperity. Writing in 1930, he predicted: 'the *economic problem* may be solved, or be at least within sight of solution, within a hundred years. This means that the economic problem is not – if we look into the future – *the permanent problem of the human race.*'[30]

It means that we can look forward to a fifteen-hour working week, as 'three hours a day is quite enough'.[31] But, it would lead to an even greater challenge:

> [M]ankind will be deprived of its traditional purpose . . . Thus for the first time since his creation man will be faced with his real, his permanent problem – how to use his freedom from pressing economic cares, how to occupy the leisure, which science and compound interest will have won for him, to live wisely and agreeably and well.[32]

CHAPTER 7

Joseph Schumpeter: What Drives Innovation?

Innovation is the engine of economic growth, or, as Joseph Schumpeter put it, innovation in a capitalist economy is the 'perennial gale of creative destruction'.[1] Schumpeter's view was that the economy undergoes long cycles as new technologies are adopted, while existing technologies become obsolescent. And those new technologies give a boost to economic growth.

Joseph Schumpeter was perhaps the first economist to define the 'capitalist engine', in his 1942 *Capitalism, Socialism and Democracy*, his most important work.[2] Contrary to popular belief, the term 'capitalism' was not devised by Adam Smith. It is thought to have first appeared in *The Newcomes*, an 1854 novel by the author of *Vanity Fair*, William Makepeace Thackeray. According to the *Oxford English Dictionary*, Thackeray used the term capitalist to denote an owner of capital. Of course, Karl Marx referred to capitalism in his 1867 *Capital*, after which it was often used as an antonym for Marxism.

According to Schumpeter, 'Creative Destruction is the essential fact about capitalism.'[3] He framed capitalism around his theories about how the capitalist engine powers the economy. The economy is in constant flux, affected by waves of technological innovation, which explains how countries become more productive and wealthier over time. In his view, 'Stabilized capitalism is a contradiction in terms.'[4]

For example the steam engine, electricity and, more recently, the computer have all transformed the way that we work. Such innovations raise productivity, which increases the growth potential of the economy. In contrast to Marx, Joseph Schumpeter aimed to be value-neutral and analytical, so that his research would not be affected by ideology. Instead of revolution, Schumpeter's work delved into the details of the businesses responsible for path-breaking inventions and then explored the relationships between those innovations and the manner in which the economy and our living standards were improved by them.

It helped that Schumpeter had experience in the business world as well as in economic policy. He was a lawyer and an academic in his twenties and Austria's finance minister in his thirties, then became a banker before returning to academia. Although he made a fortune, he lost it all in a stock-market crash, which perhaps was a blessing in disguise, since it forced his return to economics. He eventually became a professor at Harvard University, where he wrote some of the most influential texts in the field.

Based on his own career, Schumpeter saw bankruptcy and the obsolescence of some industries simply as part of the cycle of the economy whose growth had benefited millions of people. He observed on one occasion: 'Practically every enterprise [is] threatened and put on the defensive as soon as it comes into existence,'[5] and, on another: 'It is the cheap cloth, the cheap cotton and rayon fabric, boots, motorcars and so on that are the typical achievements of capitalist production . . . the capitalist process, not by coincidence but by virtue of its mechanism, progressively raises the standard of life of the masses.'[6]

But Schumpeter didn't take the capitalist system for granted. He believed capitalism required vibrant entrepreneurship and prudent regulation. It was indeed an engine in that sense. Like a physical engine, capitalism required fuel, or it could break down.

What would the creator of 'creative destruction' say about the innovation challenges that abound in the world's major economies today? What would Schumpeter make of the challenge of innovating in a predominantly services, and increasingly digital, economy? That is the state of the UK, the US and most post-industrial economies, including Germany and others that may have retained a larger manufacturing base but whose services sector is still the largest part of their economies. And what would he have made of China's innovation, which is an important factor in terms of whether it can join the ranks of prosperous nations?

The life and times of Joseph Schumpeter

Joseph Schumpeter was born in 1883 in Triesch, a small town to the south-east of Prague, in the Austro-Hungarian (or Habsburg) Empire. The empire was expansive, including today's Austria, Hungary, Czech Republic, Slovakia, Slovenia, Croatia and parts of Poland, Ukraine, Italy and Romania. Both Schumpeter's grandfather and great-grandfather were mayors as well as businessmen. In fact, the family textile business brought the first steam engine to the town.

Schumpeter grew up at a time when the engine of capitalism was transforming society. The electric motor and internal combustion engine were dramatically changing the economy, much as the steam engine had done before. Along with the telephone and railways, these inventions increased economic growth and rendered old businesses obsolete.

In 1901 the world's three largest industrial firms were United States Steel, American Tobacco and Standard Oil. German companies, such as Krupp and Thyssen in steel, Siemens in electrical equipment and chemical giants Bayer, Hoechst and BASF had all become industrial powerhouses. But, in the empire, most people still lived on farms, while small businesses were losing out to cheaper products from industrializing nations such as America, Germany and Britain.

German Austria's per capita income in 1913 was only about half that of Britain, though twice that of Hungary. Most people had no access to indoor plumbing, clean water or mass-produced shoes and clothing. Telephones and central heating were available only to the wealthy. Austrian bureaucrats still handwrote documents even though typewriters had been in use for twenty years.

Because Schumpeter had grown up during a time of vast change, his Harvard student and later economics Nobel laureate Paul

Samuelson described him as 'completely qualified to play the important sociological role of the alienated stranger'.[7]

After Schumpeter's father passed away when he was five, he moved
with his mother to Graz, where one of the few universities in the
Austro-Hungarian Empire was located. It was highly unusual for a
young widow to move to another town. While there, she married a
member of the Austrian nobility. He was a sixty-five-year-old retired
general who was more than three decades her senior. The move to
Graz and his mother's second marriage meant Schumpeter could
attend the best schools. He became fluent in six languages, including
Greek and Latin. The family later departed for Vienna, where
Schumpeter eventually attended the city's prestigious university.

At that time, German-speaking universities were among the best
in the world and the University of Vienna was among the top echelon
for economics.[8] Like other European universities at the time, Vienna's
economics professors were part of the Faculty of Law. Schumpeter's
degree, received in 1906, was not in economics but in civil and Roman
law, which gave him knowledge of history. Later on, he practised as
an attorney, which provided exposure to the business world.

Unlike those economists who were interested in reforming public
policy, the Austrian School strove to make economics more rigorous
and move it away from politics altogether. This shaped Schumpeter's
concept of the subject. He believed that economics should be 'neu-
tral' and free from politics, which compromised objective analysis.

While studying, Schumpeter encountered the three leading
approaches to economics. First, the Classical School, founded by
Adam Smith and promulgated by David Ricardo and John Stuart
Mill, among others. These largely English economists were actively
involved with public policy. Schumpeter, though, criticized them for
their lack of imagination: 'Those writers lived at the threshold of the
most spectacular economic developments ever witnessed. Vast possibilities matured into realities under their very eyes. Nevertheless,
they saw nothing but cramped economies, struggling with ever-
decreasing success for their daily bread.'[9]

Despite his rejection of capitalism, and belonging to a school of thought of his own, Karl Marx was the only one who stressed the dynamics of a capitalist system, which left a mark on Schumpeter.

The German Historical School, which detailed histories of various industries and institutions, also affected Schumpeter. Centred in Berlin, its leading economist was Gustav von Schmoller and its well-known sociologist was Max Weber, who wrote *The Protestant Ethic and the Spirit of Capitalism*. Schumpeter believed their school didn't give enough credence to economic theory. But he admired Weber, who was willing to theorize as long as it was based on data, so they occasionally worked together despite the fact that the German and Austrian schools conflicted. Their common ground was the new doctrine of marginalism, investigating how individuals optimize their decisions to work and consume. In the final part of the nineteenth century, marginalism changed the foundations of economics, which ushered in an early version of the neoclassical revolution. W. Stanley Jevons, Carl Menger and Leon Walras are often quoted as the leading lights.

The rise of the Austrian School cannot be separated from the particular history of the Austro-Hungarian Empire. The empire was vast, conservative and aristocratic. Its economic policy was *dirigiste*. It had been, and still viewed itself as, the most powerful state in Europe. It controlled almost all of central Europe and most of the important industries were kept in state hands or under tight regulation.

The good side of this was that it had a large and meritocratic civil service, and key positions were held not by politicians but by professionals like Eugen Böhm von Bawerk in the Ministry of Finance, who rotated in and out of academia and the civil service. (Schumpeter was to follow in his footsteps, becoming finance minister in the post-war republic.) Such policies made the empire an important centre for economics. The society was very well organized and apparently quite stable.

But the bad side, of course, was that everything was slow and sclerotic as well as resistant to change. There was no real economic freedom for entrepreneurs so the economy was failing to adapt and invest, falling seriously behind other European nations, particularly the upstart Prussians. Underneath the surface, there were growing social strains until the shock of the First World War destroyed the system.

The Austrian School was a reaction to all this, hence their defining characteristics: entrepreneurship, anti-equilibrium and anti-planning. It was, as with all economic theories, rooted in its time. Just as Adam Smith reacted to the inefficiencies of eighteenth-century British government, the Austrian School reacted to the weaknesses of the nineteenth-century Austrian government.

The Austrian School was led by Schumpeter's professors. In 1905 Schumpeter enrolled in a seminar led by Menger's former student Böhm von Bawerk, who was a three-time finance minister of imperial Austria. His classmates included Ludwig von Mises, who became one of the leading free-market economists of the twentieth century through his own writings and those of his pupil Friedrich Hayek.

During his five years as an undergraduate Schumpeter published three articles. They appeared when he was just twenty-two. He wanted to pursue a career as both a professor and a public servant like his mentor, Böhm von Bawerk. But a lack of money and his middle-class background were impediments.

His circumstances changed with marriage. In 1907, at the age of twenty-four, he wed Gladys Ricarde Seaver, the thirty-six-year-old daughter of a Church of England official. Gladys was upper class and their marriage propelled Schumpeter into the aristocracy, much as his mother's second marriage had done for her.[10]

Schumpeter discovered that he could work as a lawyer in Cairo, which was then effectively a protectorate of Britain, with no experience. It was not possible in Vienna or London to do so. The newlyweds moved there, and in ten months Schumpeter had earned enough to finance his family for years.

They returned to Vienna, and in 1908 he published *The Nature and Content of Theoretical Economics*. The manuscript was his effort to reconcile the German Historical School with the Austrian marginalists in order to end the battle of Continental economics. It was similar to what Marshall had done when he synthesized the new marginalism with the old classical tradition of Smith and Ricardo.

Although it didn't sell well, the book contributed to his qualifications at the University of Vienna. Along with his examinations and delivery of the standard series of lectures, Schumpeter gained the certification to teach at any university in the Austro-Hungarian Empire.

He had wished to stay in Vienna, but ended up at the University of Czernowitz in present-day Ukraine. Schumpeter hadn't wanted to relocate to a remote city at the extreme eastern border of the empire, but he wasn't there long. At the age of twenty-eight, he left to become the youngest professor of political economy in the empire at the University of Graz, which was second in size only to the University of Vienna.

Schumpeter's *Theory of Economic Development* was published soon after, in 1911. This was the book that made his name and it was to become one of the classics in economics. An English edition was later published by Harvard University Press in 1934 with the subtitle: *An Inquiry into Profits, Capital, Credit, Interest and the Business Cycle*. The ideas in this very early work formed the core of Schumpeterian economics, which were later developed in *Business Cycles* (1939) and the most popular of his books, *Capitalism, Socialism and Democracy* (1942).

Schumpeter spent five months lecturing in America, which raised his profile, but soon after his return home the First World War broke out. Gladys had returned to England so was cut off from her husband. By 1920 he began to describe himself as unmarried, though the couple had not divorced.

By the age of thirty-two, Schumpeter had written three significant books and twenty articles. His profile was further heightened by a lecture entitled 'The Crisis of the Tax State'. In it, he criticized the tax regime, which he argued had reduced innovation by causing entrepreneurs 'to migrate to countries of lower taxation'.[11] He also highlighted how excessive demands for social services could weaken the capitalist system. It was after that lecture that he became Minister of Finance in Austria's First Republic. It was rather unusual for a political novice to become a senior government official and at the age of thirty-six, but they were exceptional times. The First World War turned Austria almost overnight from the most historic, biggest and a stable state in Europe into one with dire economic prospects and on the brink of revolution.

After leaving government in 1919, he wanted to stay in Vienna and live comfortably, so he became a banker and professional investor. He received a licence to operate the Biedermann Bank, which he viewed as compensation for his brief and challenging stint as finance minister.[12] He even eventually resigned from the University of Graz in 1921.

In his new occupation, Schumpeter gained insight into the role of banks in creating credit that could fund entrepreneurs. Between 1920 and the end of 1922 there was hyperinflation in Austria, despite which Schumpeter had managed to accumulated a significant fortune by the age of forty. But a year later, in 1924, Vienna's stock market crashed, losing a staggering three-quarters of its value. Schumpeter suffered similarly, because he was reluctant to unload his stocks as their value fell. He remained loyal to even failing firms, especially the entrepreneurial ones. It seems even the creator of 'creative destruction' found it hard to let firms fail.

Although he still had his position at the Biedermann Bank, Schumpeter fell into debt and was forced to resign. He ended up paying back the bank by borrowing from friends. It would take a decade before he was able to repay his debts. Having failed in both business and politics, Schumpeter himself epitomized the entrepreneurship that he would later write about.

Not everything was dire. While all this was going on he had fallen in love with Anna Josefina Reisinger, whom he had known since she was a child. Anna was the daughter of the concierge of the apartment building in Vienna where he had grown up, and more than twenty years younger than Schumpeter. Her parents objected but when she turned eighteen, they reluctantly allowed her to accept Schumpeter's proposal.[13]

Schumpeter joined the prestigious University of Bonn, which meant that he had a stable source of income and they could marry. Neither set of parents were supportive, Schumpeter's mother objecting to Anna's working-class background while Anna's parents were concerned about his age and his reputation as a womanizer. And then there was his marriage to Gladys, from whom he secured a civil waiver without her knowledge.

They finally married on 5 November 1925, when he was forty-two and she was twenty-two and without their parents' attendance. A year later, Anna died in childbirth, as did their baby son. His mother passed away around this time too. Schumpeter never escaped from the emotional stress of that year and buried himself in work.[14] During his seven years in Bonn, he was prolific and published sixty-five articles. He also made money through penning popular pieces and lecturing to business audiences to pay his debts and send money to Anna's parents, which he did for the rest of his life. True to his beliefs, he disliked prescribing policy remedies because it might compromise his objectivity. But, it was hard not to be involved during the 1930s. So, he wrote a series of articles as the world and Germany suffered from the Great Depression. He criticized bailouts of old or low-growth industries, but supported government intervention to help companies with strong growth potential. As a condition of public assistance, though, Schumpeter argued that they must adopt innovative practices.

Despite these challenging times, Schumpeter witnessed the impressive wholesale reinvention of business, which fed into his theory of 'creative destruction' where the innovators flourish. Small and medium-sized German businesses, mostly family owned, upgraded their operations and became known globally for their quality. Many of these *Mittelstand* companies are still around today, for example Hohner harmonicas, Krones labelling machines and the Jil Sander fashion label.

Big businesses also reinvented themselves. Five of Germany's ten largest firms manufactured steel at the time of his move to Bonn. By the time he left, several had merged to become Vereinigte Stahl-werke (United Steelworks), which was the biggest steel and mining company in Europe.

As his prolific research raised his profile, Schumpeter received numerous academic offers, including one from Harvard University. A good salary at an elite economics department led Schumpeter to accept a one-year visiting appointment from 1927–28 while maintaining his position at Bonn. As is common among those taking up visiting positions, Schumpeter found that he liked Harvard better and eventually accepted a permanent post in 1932. Given his stature, Schumpeter received the maximum salary for Harvard professors, which allowed him to send money regularly to friends and former students in Europe and pay his remaining debts in Vienna.

It was during this time that Schumpeter established the Econometric Society in 1930, along with the Norwegian economist and co-recipient of the first Economics Nobel Prize Ragnar Frisch and Yale's Irving Fisher. They wanted to promote the use of mathematical and statistical methods in economics, which Frisch named 'econometrics'. Schumpeter wrote the lead article for the society's first issue of *Econometrica*, which began publication in 1933 and remains a leading journal today.

Not all professors enjoy both teaching and research, and arguably few are great at both. Schumpeter was one of the rare exceptions. He organized several small discussion groups, including the Schumpeter Group of Seven Wise Men, who were rising stars. This group included the best of the Harvard Economics Department: Douglas V. Brown, Edward Chamberlin, Gottfried Haberler, Seymour Harris, Edward Mason, Overton H. Taylor and, his favourite, the future Russian Nobel laureate Wassily Leontief.[15] His students included stars such as America's first Nobel laureate in economics Paul Samuelson, who would correct Schumpeter's mathematical errors.

An engaging figure in public, Schumpeter was a popular teacher. But in private, he suffered from anxiety and despondency, and made his research the focal point of his days. As Schumpeter himself proclaimed: 'My work is my only interest in life.'[16] He even graded himself daily on his productivity, for example 0, 4/6, 0, 0, 1/3, 5/6, 1 for a weekly mark of just 50 per cent.[17]

But not all aspects of academic life suited Schumpeter. He disliked departmental meetings and referred to his colleagues as the 'fools' (a play on the German pronunciation of 'full' professors) and 'asses' (associate and assistant professors).[18]

After Adolf Hitler became Chancellor of Germany in 1933, Schumpeter became an active recruiter for American universities, working to secure places for German, particularly Jewish, economists. By the inter-war period many had left Vienna and the university's economics faculty was in decline.

Around that time, Schumpeter met Romaine Elizabeth Boody Firuski, a thirty-five-year-old graduate student in economics at Harvard who came from a prosperous old New England family. In 1920 she had received the first *summa cum laude* degree from Radcliffe College, the all-women sister college to Harvard. After an unhappy marriage had ended, she returned to Cambridge, Massachusetts, and worked as a research assistant for Schumpeter and others, and resumed writing her dissertation on English trade. He became her co-supervisor and she received her PhD from Radcliffe in 1934. Though he was fifty in 1933, and she was fifteen years younger, she was an intellectual partner and soon she became more. They married in New York in August 1937; his third marriage and one that lasted until his death in 1950.

Schumpeter's trio of major works was completed at Harvard: *Business Cycles: A Theoretical, Historical, and Statistical Analysis of the Capitalist Process* in 1939, *Capitalism, Socialism and Democracy* in 1942 and *History of Economic Analysis*, which was published posthumously in 1954.

Although he had laboured over *Business Cycles*, it did not receive widespread acclaim. This was a disappointment to Schumpeter, since he had spent seven years writing what he thought would be his seminal work. To make matters worse, at a Harvard seminar that his students organized to discuss it, they ended up talking about John Maynard Keynes's recent *The General Theory of Employment, Interest and Money*. Schumpeter's wordiness contrasted with Keynes's succinct prose, which may have also contributed to the students' choice. Several remarked that it was the only time they ever saw Schumpeter so angry.[19]

Ever since the 1936 publication of Keynes's magnum opus, the English economist had outshone Schumpeter. Keynes did not make much mention of the business cycle research of Schumpeter or other Continental European economists. In return, Schumpeter disputed even the title of the book, specifically the 'general' part, since he believed that Keynes's theory applied only narrowly to an economy in depression.[20]

What the *General Theory* did was offer a new explanation of the

Great Depression that outlined a way forward for the world economy. By contrast, Schumpeter did not believe in prescribing economic policy, consistent with his long-standing view that politics compromised objective economic analysis. In the Preface to *Business Cycles* Schumpeter wrote: 'I recommend no policy and propose no plan.'[21] That hurt the appeal of the book at a time when the public was seeking answers to the worst economic downturn in history.

Schumpeter had been active in European economic policy before, so he was not without opinion. Although he was not a fan of FDR's New Deal and he opposed Keynes's fiscal activism funded by deficit spending, Schumpeter believed that America needed public investment. In 1933 unemployment rose to a staggering 25 per cent. After falling with the introduction of the New Deal, it rose again to over 17 per cent in 1939, after the second recession of that decade. It was then that he started writing the book that would leave his mark on the subject. *Capitalism, Socialism and Democracy* began as a series of essays, which reacted to a time of turmoil. It encompassed the Great Depression, the rise of Marxism that challenged capitalism and the Second World War.

It was published in 1942, but due to the Second World War it wasn't until the second (1947) and third (1950) editions that *Capitalism, Socialism and Democracy* became prominent. The book struck a popular nerve since it captured the great debate of the period. At that time, 40 per cent of the global population was living under communism and another quarter or so in at least partly socialized economies.

Schumpeterian economics

Joseph Schumpeter's most influential work addressed fundamental questions about how an economy operates. Schumpeter wondered if capitalism was doomed to fail, as argued by Marx. If socialism replaced capitalism, would the economy prosper? The third part of the title refers to whether there would be democracy alongside either capitalism or socialism.

Schumpeter makes the case emphatically for capitalism. He argues that people's lives had improved tremendously because of 'creative destruction':

> The opening up of new markets, foreign or domestic, and the organizational development from the craft shop and factory to such concerns as US Steel illustrate the same process of industrial mutation – if I may use that biological term – that incessantly revolutionizes the economic structure *from within*, incessantly destroying the old one, incessantly creating a new one. This process of Creative Destruction is the essential fact about capitalism.[22]

Schumpeter's firms were not powerless to influence the economic environment, in stark contrast to standard economic models. In using the term 'business strategy', Schumpeter challenged the assumption of 'perfect competition', where all firms are identical, and sell homogeneous products, so have no strategic decisions to take. He viewed firms as making decisions about employment, production and investment, which all affected the growth of the economy. He also disagreed with economic models where transactions happened seamlessly without lawyers, accountants or the numerous other operational aspects of real businesses.

He also argued against the anti-big-business sentiment then prevalent in America. The US was home to about half of the world's biggest companies and yet had a strong entrepreneurial culture. Schumpeter argued that such 'trustified' capitalism did not stifle innovation or prevent the growth of new businesses. Alongside US multinationals, thousands of new companies emerged. Through the process of 'creative destruction', the most innovative survived. Schumpeter notes that from 1897 to 1904, 4,227 American companies merged into 257 large corporations, including such well-known names as Goodyear, Pepsico, Kellogg, Gillette, Monsanto, 3M and Texaco.

In Schumpeter's view, few monopolies survived in the long term, owing to 'creative destruction'. The successful innovator might reap monopoly profits for a while, but others in the same industry will soon try to imitate the product. The entrepreneur will preserve his profit for as long as possible through patents, further innovation and advertising, which are all acts of 'aggression directed against actual and would-be competitors'.[23] But every entrepreneur's profit is temporary because competitors will eventually copy the innovation, causing market prices to fall. This sequence, which Schumpeter calls 'competing down', is observable in all industries except those protected by government. It may take several years and can be hard to see, but it is inevitable. For Schumpeter, because high profits are possible, even if temporary, big business contributes positively towards innovation and therefore economic growth.[24] So why are monopolists frequently in the spotlight? In Schumpeter's view: 'Why then all this talk about monopoly? . . . Economists, government agents, journalists and politicians in this country obviously love the word because it . . . is sure to rouse the public's hostility.'[25]

Schumpeter also believed that capitalism was a fragile system. The rise of big business undercut smaller ones who commanded greater loyalty from workers and also tended to have more political influence in their communities. In addition, society was likely to resist major innovations because they tend to destroy the status quo. He observed: 'Entrepreneurs were not necessarily strangled', but 'they were not infrequently in danger of their lives'.[26] For instance, craft guilds in Britain invoked medieval laws and petitioned for regulations outlawing factories and mechanical devices. In the early 1830s rural labourers smashed the new threshing machines which were threatening their livelihoods. In fact, 'the history of capitalism is studded with violent bursts and catastrophes'.[27] Schumpeter also thought that people might act against their economic interests because of their beliefs: 'Socialist bread may well taste sweeter to them than capitalist bread simply because it is socialist bread, and it would do so even if they found mice in it.'[28]

Thus, Schumpeter warned: 'I felt it my duty . . . to inflict upon the reader . . . my paradoxical conclusion: capitalism is being killed by its achievements.'[29] So, political oversight was needed. Schumpeter believed that the upheaval caused by entrepreneurs could engender social turmoil which may even lead the capitalist engine to stall. Thus, economic growth required a stable government, specifically the rule of law and protection of private property. The system that he most admired was the British one with its constitutional monarchy and bicameral Parliament comprising Commons and Lords. He held in high regard Britain's apolitical civil service, which gave that stability to a capitalist system. It is only within such a system that Schumpeter's 'creative destruction' could flourish.

In Schumpeter's system: 'The introduction of new production methods, the opening up of new markets – indeed, the successful carrying through of new business combinations in general – all these imply risk, trial and error, the overcoming of resistance, factors lacking in the treadmill of routine.'[30] These disruptions to the routine explain why economies expand and go through periods of 'destruction'. Schumpeter argued that innovations in specific industries affected other parts of the economy, such as their suppliers, distributors and, eventually, customers. In the nineteenth and early twentieth centuries, economic growth was driven by a series of breakthroughs. Specifically, five industries led economic development: cotton textiles, railroads, steel, automobiles and electricity. Such industry-specific innovation 'does not follow, but creates expansion'.[31]

Rather than an economic concept of an equilibrium that an economy returns to, Schumpeter's view of innovation involves continuous disequilibrium that is led by entrepreneurs transforming an industry with economy-wide effects.

To enable such entrepreneurial innovators, Schumpeter stressed the importance of credit in a capitalist system. He believed capitalism to be the only system that enables people to become entrepreneurs before they have the funds to found an enterprise: 'it is leadership rather than ownership that matters'.[32] It was not only a bank credit line to keep a business operating that was necessary, but money for new ventures, which can be lost if the start-up fails without jeopardizing the entire economic system. In his career as a banker and investor, Schumpeter underwrote precisely such firms, even though it cost him his personal fortune.

That is also why he believed that the economy benefited from the rise of big business because they could afford to gamble on innovation. They also had access to capital markets, such as raising money by issuing debt on bond markets, as well as retained earnings, so were less reliant on more conservative bank loans. For instance, in the early twentieth century, firms such as American Telephone and Telegraph (AT&T), General Electric (GE), Eastman Kodak and DuPont set up research departments to develop new products. They made innovation an integral part of their business. Later in the century, large firms worldwide followed suit.

Perhaps the best examples of the Schumpeterian notion of innovation and economic growth are found in the East Asian economies, which underwent their 'growth miracle' during the mid-twentieth century, namely Japan, Korea, Taiwan and Singapore.[33] Schumpeter even lectured to great acclaim across Japan in early 1931. He generated extensive media coverage that is hard to picture today for economic lectures. Japanese policymakers notably adopted a Schumpeterian approach. They stressed saving and investment, and actively promoted a broad range of innovation across numerous industries. A slew of new Japanese multinational companies such as Sony, Sanyo and Honda eventually became globally competitive. During that period of the 1960s to the 1980s, Japan achieved the highest sustained growth rate for a major economy and became the world's second biggest economy. Japan's innovative companies led the nation to such growth that Japan even threatened America's standing.

Schumpeter's work established the crucial role that entrepreneurs play in capitalist economies, even though entrepreneurship itself can't be simply modelled mathematically. In his view, innovation is 'a feat not of intellect, but of will . . . a special case of the social phenomenon of leadership'.[34] In Schumpeter's definition, the entrepreneur is not a business executive or even the owner or chief executive of a successful firm. He is 'the modern type of "captain of industry" – obsessively seeking an innovative edge'.[35] It can even be hard to identify the entrepreneur: 'nobody ever is an entrepreneur all the time, and nobody can ever be only an entrepreneur'.[36] Particularly in large firms, the entrepreneur often not only innovates but also carries out management. In short, Schumpeter saw entrepreneurship as a key factor to start the engine of growth: 'Without innovation, no entrepreneurs; without entrepreneurial achievement, no capitalist returns and no capitalist propulsion.'[37]

For Schumpeter, 'Capitalist evolution spells disturbance. Capitalism is essentially a process of economic change.'[38] This change comes from innovative entrepreneurs. He outlined five types of innovation that derive from entrepreneurs:[39]

- The introduction of a new good, for example one with which consumers are not yet familiar, or of a new version of a good that is of better quality.
- The introduction of a new method of production.
- The opening of a new market.
- The conquest of a new source of raw materials or half-manufactured goods.
- The creation of a new organization of any industry, like the creation of a monopoly position (for example, through trustification) or the breaking up of a monopoly.

In summary, Schumpeter sees entrepreneurship as 'essentially one and the same thing' as technological progress that raises the growth of the economy.[40]

The challenge of staying on top as innovators

Nokia and BlackBerry

In the process of 'creative destruction', innovative products will displace old ones. In aggregate, the efforts of companies to improve the level of technological innovation hold the key to the success of the economy. The transition from old to new, though, is rarely seamless and includes the rise and fall of not just individual businesses but entire industries.

Nokia and BlackBerry phones are good illustrations of Schumpeter's 'creative destruction'. Nokia was once worth $150 billion but was eventually sold for just $7 billion. How did all of this market value disappear?

For Finland's Nokia it was the culmination of a rapid rise and fall. It introduced its first mobile phone in 1987 and by 1998 had overtaken Motorola to become the global market leader in handset sales. In

2005 it sold its billionth phone. Its peak was probably in 2007. By then its share of the global handset market had reached 40 per cent, including nearly half the smartphone market at the time, and its market capitalization hit $150 billion. Before its sale, its global market share had fallen to just 15 per cent, and this was mainly accounted for by its range of cheaper phones. Its share of the global smartphone market had plummeted to just 3 per cent.

A similar story of boom and bust describes the Canadian firm Research in Motion (RIM). Back in 2003 it launched the BlackBerry. By allowing people to email easily from their phones, its popularity grew quickly and its secure network was favoured by businesses and governments. The addictive nature of the phone led to it being nicknamed 'CrackBerry'. By the middle of 2008, the company was valued at around $70 billion.

The subsequent decline was steep and the landing hard. Just a decade after its founding, RIM reported losses of $1 billion that meant cutting 40 per cent of its global workforce. Haemorrhaging cash and sitting on a stockpile of unsold handsets valued at $930 million, it was bought out by a consortium led by Toronto-based private equity group Fairfax Financial in 2013. The price was just $4.9 billion. Together, Nokia and RIM have seen roughly $200 billion evaporate. How?

In 2007 Steve Jobs walked onto the stage at the Moscone Center in San Francisco, pulled an iPhone from his pocket and talked of a revolutionary product that was going to change everything. The rest, as they say, is history. Apple's take-off, along with Google's Android system, has mirrored the decline at Nokia and RIM.

So where did Nokia and RIM go wrong? Were they just the latest victims of 'creative destruction' in the digital age?

They weren't the first. In January 2012, after over 130 years of operations, Kodak filed for bankruptcy. The American company had once sold over 90 per cent of all film in the US and its little yellow boxes could be seen all around the world. Its death knell sounded simply because it was out-innovated in the very technology it had pioneered for over a century.

Ironically, Kodak had developed a prototype for the digital camera in 1975. But by the time it became apparent that it would be a game changer, it was too late. Japan's Canon and Fuji had already established a decisive lead in the digital camera market.

Kodak's is not an atypical story. A large incumbent company, successful for decades, finds it difficult to adapt to new technologies while it makes good profits in the traditional business areas. It is then left adrift once the whole industry has shifted for good. The lesson is, adapt or die.

Is this also true of Nokia and RIM? Nokia was innovative in hardware and was the dominant force at the outset of the smartphone market. However, Apple, and then Android, saw the value of software. Touch-screen technology changed the way people used their phones and both had app stores that were easy to use.

Perhaps Nokia showed a lack of urgency. In the early days of the iPhone era, the drop-off in global market share was gradual rather than abrupt, and Nokia was able to retain its position as the market leader. BlackBerry's problem was that it catered primarily for business users and was left stranded when, with the advent of social media, innovation in the mobile phones market became strongly consumer-led. RIM failed to respond to the consumerization of IT.

In today's high-technology era, consumers expect constant innovation and are quick to punish the products that fall behind. The pace of creative destruction has quickened and brands are no longer as resilient as they once were.

This is evident from the increase in stock market churn over the past few decades. In 1958 the average tenure of the companies listed on the S&P 500 was sixty-one years. By 1980, this had fallen to twenty-five years, and is now down to eighteen years. If the trend continues, three-quarters of the firms currently listed on the S&P 500 will be replaced by 2027.[41]

Apple and Samsung

What about the disrupter Apple? Could US technology giant Apple's empire fall? Apple has made bumper profits from international sales. In 2017, it was the most valuable traded company in the world in history. And what about Korea's Samsung, the market leader in the global smartphone market?

Japan's Sony is a cautionary tale. During the 1980s and early 1990s, Sony was the Apple of its day. The company was synonymous with quality in the electronics industry. In 1979 it launched the iconic Walkman. Even when cheaper personal stereos flooded the market, the demand for Walkmans remained high because people trusted the brand. During the 1990s it teamed up with the Dutch electronics giant Philips to perfect the compact disc media format, but that was probably its peak.

When Apple launched its iPod in October 2001, Sony was criticized for being slow off the mark in the MP3 market. Since then its fortunes have been all downhill. The stock of the company had been downgraded to junk status due to its severe challenges to improve sales and profitability, while its core businesses are subject to obsolescence and rapid changes in technology.

It is very premature to forecast the eventual decline of Apple, but Sony, Kodak, Nokia and RIM exemplify the potential force of creative destruction. It's been over a decade since the first iPhones started flying off the shelves. Apple, along with Samsung, has been at the vanguard of the smartphone revolution. The two companies dominate the global smartphone market. But there are signs that worldwide growth in smartphone sales is beginning to slow, and new competitors are emerging, notably from China. What might that mean for these two smartphone giants?

There are indications of market saturation in the world's developed markets, while stronger growth has been found in developing and emerging economies such as China. According to the International Data Company, half of smartphone sales around the world are below $100, excluding sales taxes. Prices have fallen as smartphone technology becomes standardized and a swathe of manufacturers target the budget end of the market. In developed markets, customers are becoming more price-sensitive and a bit less brand-orientated. Wiko, a French start-up that is majority owned by a Chinese firm, sells some of its phones for less than that $100 benchmark. It has quickly claimed a share of the French market and has set its sights on the rest of Europe.

Consumers are also benefiting from rapid improvements in standard technology, so a cheap price does not necessarily mean low quality. In 2012 less than half of all smartphones priced at $80 or less had a processor faster than 1 gigahertz. A couple of years later, nine out of ten at this price did. Budget smartphones have also followed the trend of larger screen sizes.

Then there are the new competitors from China. After Samsung and Apple, the next three biggest smartphone makers are all from China. They are eating into Samsung's world market share, which has fallen from one-third to around one-fifth. For Apple, two-thirds of its sales are outside the US, and in those markets the iPhone is facing considerable competition from cheaper brands.

And there are many of them. There are 6,000 handset manufacturers in Shenzhen alone. Once a fishing village close to Hong Kong, it's now a massive tech hub rivalling Silicon Valley in California. This area produces the majority of the mobile phones in the country, and China produces more than half of the 2.5 billion phones sold around the world annually.

In light of this competition, what might happen to the smartphone pioneers Apple and Samsung in the coming years and how might they adapt to the maturing market and growth in manufacturers of cheaper smartphones?

The iPhone generates the biggest portion of Apple's total revenues. It's an expensive product. With Google's Android operating system used in nearly three-quarters of all smartphones, the iPhone is looking increasingly like a luxury and niche brand. Apple has never been an out-and-out hardware company and might respond by developing its complementary software and services. iTunes has about a billion subscribers, and with its acquisition of Beats Music, Apple has made a foray into the video and music streaming business. It has also developed a mobile wallet, working with MasterCard and Visa.

Samsung manufactures smartphones at a range of prices, but is coming under intense competition from manufacturers of cheap phones. It has started branching out into what it calls 'wearable tech' through a range of smartwatches. Apple too has launched a smartwatch. However, the uptake of wearables has been slow. It is perhaps too early to say whether smartclothing, smartglasses or smartwatches will come to challenge or even replace the smartphone.

There is also scope for smartphones to become even smarter. The recent trend to increase screen sizes could lead to flexible screens or built-in projectors. Augmented reality may encourage people to live their lives through their smartphone screens by allowing us to interact in real time with our surroundings.

Battery developments have so far failed to keep pace with the power demands of more sophisticated devices. It is ironic that as our mobile technology becomes more advanced, we need more regular access to a wall socket.

Figuring out the next innovation, though, will undoubtedly matter for these two, especially as there's immediate competition on their heels. The world's third largest mobile handset maker, Chinese firm Huawei, has launched a big screen smartphone, a phablet (phone + tablet), with an eye to challenging Samsung and Apple in the global smartphone market. In Schumpeter's theory, how these companies manage the 'creative destruction' process matters not just for them, but also for their home economies. Schumpeter viewed the rise and fall of companies as the source of economic growth. As entrepreneurs create new companies and innovative products, the economy prospers along with them. Whereas standard models of the economy assigned no role to individual firms except as homogeneous producers of widgets, Schumpeter gave entrepreneurs the biggest role in explaining how innovation comes about and boosts the growth of an economy.

China's innovation challenge

China is the major economy currently facing the considerable challenge of becoming an innovator. Is it possible for 'Made in China' to become 'Designed in China'? Japan made that transformation, but many more countries have failed than have succeeded.

In the 1980s movie *Back to the Future*, Michael J. Fox's character Marty McFly travelled back in time to the 1950s. He met a scientist who demanded proof that he was from the future. Even though Doc Brown scoffed at the idea of an actor (Ronald Reagan) as the US president, Marty managed to convince him. But Doc's incredulity was further stretched when Marty says that in the future Japan will make 'all the best stuff'. In Doc's time, 'Made in Japan' was synonymous with products that were cheap and of low quality.

In roughly thirty years, Japan came to rival the United States and was the world's second-largest economy. Japanese manufacturing was transformed from producing low-cost goods into launching world-beating companies such as Toyota. Now that China has overtaken Japan economically, could its companies become the next global competitors? Just as one company can overtake another, so one country can overtake another too.

Innovation, of course, takes many forms. But there's one thing in common: talent. It's what Joseph Schumpeter pointed out, which is that innovation comes from innovators. Can China produce the next Steve Jobs, for instance? Will there be innovators that transform the way that we live through their inventions and ingenuity? The answer to the question of Chinese innovativeness goes beyond manufacturing and into all areas of society, including the creative industries.

The Chinese government is actively investing in innovation. R&D spending has increased rapidly. China is predicted to surpass even US R&D spending in the coming years. Of course, it's not just what is spent or the number of patents filed that determines innovation. It's how useful these inventions are. And that data does not yet exist for China.

To complicate matters, much manufacturing now involves global supply chains. For instance, half of China's exports are made by foreign-invested enterprises, so it's multinational companies that are producing in China as well as domestic firms. Harvard economist Dani Rodrik estimated that the value of Chinese exports suggests that they come from a country with a much higher per capita income. Does that mean that China produces innovative exports or is it a place for global assembly?

A case study is Huawei. The giant telecoms equipment firm was founded in Shenzhen in 1987 by Ren Zhengfei. It imported telecoms equipment from nearby Hong Kong, just across the then Chinese border. It now makes the networks that power the internet and mobile phone networks around the world. Huawei products are used by companies such as Vodafone since they make the USB dongles that provide mobile internet connections. As mentioned above, it has also entered the smartphone market. Ren could be one of Schumpeter's entrepreneurs since he transformed his business from being just an importer of telecoms equipment into the world's largest telecommunications company, one that invests heavily in R&D and technological innovation.

Huawei faces specific challenges as telecoms and tech can engender suspicion of industrial espionage. Ren's stint in the Chinese army is a cause for concern in the US and other places such as Australia. It adds to suspicion that he works with the Chinese government. Huawei denies all the allegations made against the firm, but it is still banned from bidding for US government contracts.

Ren Zhengfei even based Huawei's sprawling campus on Silicon Valley. The green, open environment is designed to encourage innovation and collaboration, and there are on-site basketball courts and ping-pong tables, which is unusual in China. Graduates say that Huawei is a prestigious place to work. Ambitious young engineers want to be part of a global, innovative company and they even call themselves *Huawei-ren* or Huawei people, the Chinese version of Googlers.

However, there are numerous obstacles faced by Chinese non-state companies like Huawei. It was only in the late 1980s that consumer markets developed in China as the centrally planned economy was liberalized and private firms emerged. State-owned companies still dominate key sectors of the economy and bank credit. As a private firm, Huawei could not rely on government policy that promoted Chinese-foreign joint ventures to gain technology and know-how. Instead, the company innovated and undercut competitors to gain market share.

Another difference in the Chinese attitude towards innovation is that firms like Huawei innovate to serve a market need. In other words, they don't create something entirely new and then look for a market for it. For instance, Huawei developed an 'anechoic' chamber that eliminates echo so they can test for interference from their antennae or handsets. It's one of only a few such chambers in the world and it is designed to fill a need and where they have a competitive advantage from their massive amounts of data. As Huawei operates in 150 countries and over one-third of the world's population uses their products, they have a great deal of data with which to test and then fine-tune and improve their products.

But the next stage still needs to be invention, which is well recognized in China. Tech companies like Huawei spend around 10 per cent of their revenue on R&D, which is in the same league as the biggest global innovators. Half of Huawei's 150,000 employees work in R&D and it holds over 50,000 patents, making it one of the top five patent filers worldwide. Of course, spending on R&D doesn't necessarily translate into an innovative product. Around a quarter of Chinese patents are in product design, which is viewed as less innovative than a new product, but it is a category of innovation recognized by Schumpeter, who saw the value of improving the quality of an existing good. In the US, the figure is much lower, less than 10 per cent.

Huawei is also working on cutting-edge research. In competition with Silicon Valley, the company is developing a universal translator to enable people to converse in different languages using software that will translate context and not just words. Research is being undertaken on artificial intelligence that can even interpret jokes, which are among the hardest things to translate. For instance, how would the following joke be translated?

English: Why did the chicken cross the road? To get to the other side.

Chinese: How do you get an elephant into a refrigerator? You open the door, and put it in.

The Chinese elephant plays the same role as the chicken in the joke.

Huawei's next strategic move was to make its name known not just to industry insiders, but to the 7 billion people around the world. It became the first Chinese company to make it into Interbrand's top 100 global brands. Huawei believes it can take on the market leaders because its innovation is centred on customer needs. But can it get global customers to choose its smartphones over Samsung's and Apple's? If Huawei succeeds, that would point to whether China can make that difficult leap from imitator to innovator. And that could help China become a prosperous nation.

The thing about history is that it rarely repeats itself. One advantage that Chinese firms have over Japan is that their home market has more than a billion people, so they start with the advantage of scale. Scale gives Chinese companies a leg up because they have a billion consumers to sell to, so they can test new products and services without leaving Chinese borders and facing foreign competition. A downside, though, is that it is possible to become a very large Chinese firm without facing global competition. Although nothing is ever guaranteed, it is possible that China will be the source of the next global giants.

That is precisely the aim of the 'going global' policy. China's Alibaba Group is the world's largest online retailer. Few may have heard of it before its IPO on the New York Stock Exchange since the company operates predominantly in China. But, as with other Chinese companies that are coming of age, Alibaba has become a multinational company. If Alibaba truly breaks into overseas markets, that is precisely where China would like to see its firms succeed. If 'Made in China' continues to be viewed as low quality, then it will not sell well to consumers around the world. But if Chinese brands become synonymous with being the best in the world, that would also mark China's transition into a country that can produce innovation.

The correlation between the emergence of innovative companies and the growth prospects of their home countries fits Schumpeter's view of how innovation fuels the engine of economies. As a case study, China's experience exemplifies how even a fast-growing economy faces obstacles. For countries that do not benefit from Chinese growth rates, the challenge is even bigger.

Motivated to the end

What would Joseph Schumpeter think about how contemporary companies and countries should innovate?

Schumpeter's legacy is to show that capitalism depends on entrepreneurs who in turn require a supportive system. He rejected the simple assumptions made by economists about how producers and consumers operate.[42] He believed that what was needed was empirical analysis of actual businesses, such as the ones discussed earlier, to understand the innovative activities of entrepreneurs. With that understanding, we can then assess what propels the engine of economic growth.

The above companies largely rose and fell through competition over the past several decades. It's become evident that, in this digital era, start-up costs have dropped sharply, so in that sense entrepreneurship has become easier than before. The internet allows a business to be set up at virtually zero cost, which makes self-employment, particularly in the services sector, simpler and cheaper. Therefore, so long as countries were supportive of entrepreneurs in terms of providing a stable system with sources of funds for investment, Schumpeter would not see innovating in the services sector as harder than in manufacturing. So, in predominantly services economies like Britain, America and much of western Europe, Schumpeter would not view entrepreneurship as more challenging than when he witnessed the emergence of manufacturing powerhouses, which had much higher start-up costs, and yet succeeded.

As Schumpeter foresaw, innovative companies have helped to lead their home countries' economic growth. Apple's and Google's dominance mirrors America's reign at the top of the global economy. The challenger China's encroachment is reflected in the rise of its start-ups that are snapping at the established tech giants' positions. Unlike state-owned companies, a number of Chinese multinational firms, such as Alibaba and Huawei, have been founded by entrepreneurs. Such entrepreneurial innovators are those whom Schumpeter had in mind when he described companies shaping the growth of economies. So long as China continues to produce innovative companies, then he would expect the world's second biggest economy to transform itself into an innovative economy and 'Made in China' to be seen as a marker of quality.

Whether it's America or China or Japan, entrepreneurs will

determine the growth potential of the country, in Schumpeter's view. As described in *Capitalism*, entrepreneurial innovation is the dynamic element that drives how economies evolve through a process of 'creative destruction', which is as visible today as during his time.

But, due to the economy experiencing constant innovation and obsolescence as a result of entrepreneurship, the inventor of 'creative destruction' would be reluctant to predict how a capitalist system might evolve. Schumpeter would be unlikely to be found on a stage at a conference predicting the next technology to disrupt an established market!

He had ample opportunities to do so. By his mid-sixties, Joseph Schumpeter was one of the most famous economists in the world. There was no Nobel Prize in economics during his lifetime, but he was hugely acclaimed.

Schumpeter was elected as president of the American Economic Association in 1947, the most prestigious office in the country for an economist and one of the very few occasions in its history that a foreign-born economist had been chosen. In 1949 he was also selected as president of the new 5,300-member International Economic Association headquartered in Paris.

Acclaim only fuelled his work ambitions. During 1949 and the early part of 1950 he wrote twelve articles, the most in any comparable period since the 1920s. He died of a cerebral haemorrhage one month before his sixty-seventh birthday at the height of his fame. His final book, *History of Economic Analysis*, was published posthumously in 1954.

Motivated to the end, Schumpeter was similar to those he wrote about. He didn't believe that entrepreneurs, or indeed consumers, would ever be satisfied. He placed himself, with his penchant for reinvention during a varied career, among the ranks of those innovators, many of whom have changed the way that we live. Schumpeter believed that the innovator-entrepreneur had a 'will to conquer . . . Our type seeks out difficulties, changes in order to change, delights in ventures.'[43]

CHAPTER 8

Friedrich Hayek: What Can We Learn from Financial Crises?

On 15 October 2011 members of the Occupy movement attempted to set up a protest camp in Paternoster Square, outside the London Stock Exchange. They were foiled, as the area was privately owned, so any protesters would have been trespassing and the police were able to seal off the entrance before any could enter. However, the group of around 3,000 people simply gathered instead outside nearby St Paul's Cathedral, where an indefinite camp was established. A month earlier a similar encampment had been set up in New York's Wall Street, and soon protests of different sizes emerged in cities around the world.

Occupy's slogan, 'We are the 99 per cent', referred to the high proportion of global wealth accounted for by the top 1 per cent of the distribution. They reflected the widespread public anger in the aftermath of the 2008 global financial crisis. The protesters called for financial reform, a fairer distribution of income and wealth and a rejection of austerity.

The Occupy movement reflected the modern version of a struggle that had been ongoing since the previous century. The twentieth century had witnessed an ideological battle between socialism and welfare state capitalism, culminating in the triumph of the latter with the fall of the Berlin Wall and the lifting of the Iron Curtain in 1989, which led to the break-up of the Soviet Union in 1991. Economics Nobel laureate Milton Friedman had observed:

There is no figure who had more of an influence on the intellectuals behind the Iron Curtain than Friedrich Hayek. His books were translated and published by the underground and black market editions, read widely, and undoubtedly influenced the climate of opinion that ultimately brought about the collapse of the Soviet Union.[1]

In the aftermath of the global financial crisis, the future of capitalism was once again up for debate. Had he been alive, free-market proponent Friedrich Hayek would have challenged the view that capitalism's time was up. He believed that the prosperity of society was driven by creativity, entrepreneurship and innovation, which were possible only in a society with free markets.

Hayek was a leading voice of the Austrian School. In the 1940s he disavowed the Keynesian revolution that was sweeping through the economics establishment. He attacked socialism when the welfare state was being formed in most major economies. In Hayek's view, socialism would invariably lead to central planning. When it comes to technological development, no progress can be made unless people are allowed to move into unexpected areas and learn from their mistakes. In *The Road to Serfdom*, Hayek describes how totalitarian regimes are not just unproductive but also suppress these freedoms. (The title of his best-known book comes from a phrase used by the French writer Alexis de Tocqueville, 'the road to servitude'.[2]) Instead, markets create the price signals and incentives to orientate the economy most efficiently.

To the wrath of the Occupy protesters, he would also have been less concerned about inequality, as he strongly believed societal progress was driven by the ideas of a few. When it came to financial markets, he would have said that they were already overregulated instead of not regulated enough. There is no doubt that Hayek would have been a controversial figure in the post-crisis world. Certainly, having spent most of the twentieth century fighting socialism, he would have much to say on the future of capitalism in the twenty-first.

The life and times of Friedrich Hayek

Friedrich August von Hayek was born in 1899 in Vienna. His father was a doctor employed by the Municipal Ministry of Health, and his mother came from a wealthy landowning family.

From a young age, Friedrich, or Fritz, as his mother called him, was determined to become a scholar. His father's true passion was botany and he had become a part-time lecturer at the University of Vienna, but above all wanted to become a university professor. This rubbed off on the young Friedrich. He helped his father with his botanical collections and came to believe that professorship was the highest accolade.

Despite this, and unlike many of the Great Economists featured in this book, he was not a first-class pupil. In fact, he showed little interest in studying at school and was actually rather rebellious. At the age of fourteen he failed Latin, Greek and mathematics and had to repeat the grade. Even so, he was still considered bright.

By the time Hayek turned fifteen, his attention was captured by the political excitement stoked up by the events that would lead to the First World War and the collapse of the Austro-Hungarian Empire. His focus turned to political philosophy, including ethics, morals, politics and economics.

Two years later, in March 1917, with the war still continuing, Hayek joined the army. He was still two months short of his eighteenth birthday, and after seven months of training was sent as an officer to the Italian front. He nearly did not survive the war. A piece of his skull was stripped by shrapnel. He nearly died when jumping from an observation balloon without first detaching his headphones, and he was nearly shot down in a dog fight. He had decided he wanted to join the diplomatic service, but before doing so he ended up joining the air force to prove he was not a coward.

However, the war was to end sooner than Hayek expected. In late 1918 he returned from Italy and enrolled at the University of Vienna. He studied law, but became interested in psychology, and eventually chose to become an economist: 'I was about equally interested in economics and psychology. I finally had to choose between the things I was interested in. Economics at least had a formal legitimation by a degree, while in psychology you had nothing. And since there was no opportunity for a job, I decided for economics.'[3]

Economics was part of the law faculty and offered, Hayek believed, the best vocational and financial prospects.

Life in Vienna, the capital city of the new Republic of Austria, was tough immediately after the war. Over a million young men from the Austro-Hungarian Empire had perished in the fighting. There were chronic shortages of food and fuel. Hyperinflation, or dramatic price increases, plagued the economy.

As with much of Europe, the conditions were ripe for communism and socialism to take over. There was a sudden acceptance and respect for Marxism, the welfare state and the planned economy. Hayek, though, was never enamoured of Marxism. He considered it very doctrinaire, and although reform and revolution were the sentiment of the day, he did not believe socialism to be the answer.

Economics at the University of Vienna was firmly established in the liberal free-market tradition, where Carl Menger was the architect of what came to be known as the Austrian School of economics. This school of thought contrasted with the collectivism of Marxism sweeping through much of Europe, emphasizing the importance of individuals and their free actions. Menger had described the concept of spontaneous order, wherein it is possible for a peaceful society to arise simply as a result of the rule of law creating the societal structure in which people flourish. The role of government then is not to direct the economy, but to establish and enforce the laws of property and those governing exchange that enable individuals to interact with each other in a mutually beneficial way. Liberty is a reflection of the supremacy of law, not its absence. Spontaneous order would be the centrepiece of much of Hayek's later thinking.

In 1921 he started working in the Austrian Office of Accounts (set up to settle international debt claims) for the economist Ludwig von Mises, who was well known as a monetary theorist and part of the Austrian School of economic thought at the University of Vienna. A couple of years later Hayek moved to New York in order to broaden his economics training. While he was working as a research assistant at New York University, his fellow Austrian Joseph Schumpeter wrote letters of introduction for him to meet a range of American economists.[4] It was there that he started work on a theory of business cycles. He also began, but did not complete, a doctoral thesis. The post-war hyperinflation in Austria had destroyed his family's wealth and he could not afford to live in any way other than poorly. After only one year, he returned to Austria.

Hayek was back in Vienna in 1924, once again in the Office of Accounts. But his marriage to Hella Fritsch soon thereafter led him to seek a more permanent job. Hayek had been close friends with von Mises, who helped to establish the Austrian Institute for Business Cycle Research based in Vienna, and in 1927 Hayek became its director. Initially, he had just two clerical assistants. It was later funded more generously by the Rockefeller Foundation. Hayek wrote prolifically during this period. His brief tour of the US led him to realize how new economic and statistical techniques could be introduced into economic research.

In the late 1920s Hayek wrote a number of articles in which he began to articulate business cycle theory. He opposed the US central banking system, the Federal Reserve, which had been set up in 1913. Hayek disapproved of the Fed's role in economic ups and downs.

It was not just monetary policy. Hayek also disputed the use of fiscal policy in moderating business cycles. His work was an early attack on John Maynard Keynes's hypothesis of excess saving or the paradox of thrift, discussed in Chapter 6. One of these articles, the 'Paradox of Saving', published in 1929, had caught the attention of Lionel Robbins, a young economist who had been recently appointed head of the Economics Department at the London School of Economics and Political Science (LSE). Hayek was the same age as Robbins.

Robbins wanted to bring British economics more fully into the twentieth century, so he sought a qualified theorist and one who was familiar with the other traditions. He sought to make the LSE a leading institution in the internationalization of British economics, and also to help him in his argument with Cambridge's John Maynard Keynes. In particular, Robbins opposed Keynes's ideas of increased spending on public works to battle the Great Depression. Robbins and Keynes had repeatedly clashed, and Robbins saw Hayek as an ally. So, Hayek arrived at the LSE in 1931 to deliver a series of four lectures, after which he was invited to join the faculty.

Hayek versus Keynes

It is fair to say that watching economics videos is not always the most exciting pastime. However, it is worth viewing *Fear the Boom and Bust*, launched on YouTube in 2010, where two proxies of Hayek and Keynes engage in a rap battle. Their argument is over the cause of the business cycle, and so far it has been viewed in excess of 6 million times. A sequel, where the two characters proclaim their responses to the Great Recession, is also available to watch should the mood take you. Their debate, although focused on the Great Depression of the 1930s, has been resuscitated by the recent global financial crisis. There is all of a sudden new interest in what Keynes and Hayek have to say about booms and busts.

Hayek was seen by many as Robbins's bulwark against Keynesian domination of economics and policy. It was not just Hayek versus Keynes, but also the LSE versus Cambridge. Despite this, the relationship between Hayek and Keynes was mutually respectful, even though they disagreed on most things and were rather being pitted against each other. In fact, Hayek and Keynes grew closer during the Second World War. Hayek became a British citizen in 1938, but his Austrian birth prevented him from serving in the war. When the London School of Economics relocated to Cambridge to avoid the Luftwaffe's Blitz on London, it was Keynes who had arranged rooms at his college, King's, to serve as Hayek's base.[5] The two purported rivals even spent a night together on the roof of the college chapel on the watch for German bombers.[6] In 1944 Keynes nominated Hayek to become a fellow of the prestigious British Academy instead of his disciple, Joan Robinson.[7] Upon Keynes's death in 1946, Hayek wrote to his widow that Keynes was 'the one really great man I ever knew, and for whom I had unbounded admiration'.[8] In contrast, Hayek never spoke with such personal admiration about Milton Friedman, even though they were both strongly connected with the Chicago School brand of liberalism in the 1950s and 1960s.

Hayek had been an early fan of Keynes, especially for his outspoken views on the Treaty of Versailles wherein he criticized the huge reparations demanded of Germany because he believed they would lead only to default. Keynes's 1923 *A Tract on Monetary Reform* was even lauded by Hayek. Keynes was also very generous in return. In the 1920s, Keynes was an influential economist, well known and highly regarded around the world, while Hayek was young, not a native English speaker, and far from established. Yet Keynes had responded graciously to Hayek's letters – so graciously that Hayek probably overestimated Keynes's professional opinion of him.

Perhaps at Robbins's behest, given the LSE–Cambridge rivalry, Hayek would later frequently criticize Keynes. In his review of Keynes's 1931 *A Treatise on Money* he had been very critical, even though Keynes had positively acknowledged the emerging German and Austrian Schools. But Keynes replied in kind. He was terribly rude about Hayek's *Prices and Production* of the same year, describing it as: 'one of the most frightful muddles I have ever read . . . It is an extraordinary example of how, starting with a mistake, a remorseless logician can end up in Bedlam.'⁹ Throughout his life, and after Keynes's death, Hayek would give interviews in which he questioned Keynes's understanding of the most basic economic concepts. He tended to get annoyed by what he regarded as the inconsistencies in Keynes's work and his propensity to change his position on economic issues.

Hayek would say that he and Keynes differed on most aspects of economics. Keynes was a pragmatic English economist focused on the practicalities of the subject and had little time for the more systematic European modes of thought. Hayek was the exact opposite. So, on technical matters, they could hardly agree on the meaning of terms, let alone understand each other. Where the argument was most public was over the drivers of fluctuations in the economy or business cycles. Keynes believed that recessions were the consequence of weak aggregate demand. The economy was subject to bouts of optimism and pessimism known as 'animal spirits'. However, government policy could do much to offset the impact of these on national output and employment.

Hayek's model of the business cycle is far more nuanced and harder to understand. This may be one of the reasons it was not so widely accepted, both at the time and subsequently, by economists and policymakers. Hayek's model is as follows. First, there are many different stages of production in creating goods. Each final good reflects the processing of primary and intermediate goods. At each stage of production there is a requirement for businesses to install capital goods such as machines. These are not the same for different factories and cannot be easily transferred across sectors or stages of production. Therefore, once installed, the stock of capital can only be used to produce certain goods.

So, it is possible for capital to be allocated inefficiently in the economy if it is directed to areas where demand has been temporarily boosted and cannot be sustained. As capital investment is not reversible or transferable, capital is essentially stuck and abandoned if under-utilized. The savings that funded the investment have been wasted, and could have been more efficiently used elsewhere in the economy. Hayek believed this misallocation of capital could arise from monetary policy, specifically if interest rates had been held too low, as that leads to bad investments.

This, according to Hayek, accounted for the Great Depression. The US Federal Reserve had kept interest rates too low throughout the 1920s. As a result, much of the capital investment was inappropriate and unsustainable going into the 1930s. A recession ensued as this build-up in capital was abandoned.

In stark contrast to Keynes, Hayek believed the government should then resist the urge to interfere. He viewed recessions as a necessary evil, simply periods of liquidation resulting from the past overaccumulation of capital. This is similar to what Nobel laureate Paul Krugman calls the 'hangover theory' of recessions.[10] Any policy that stimulates the economy may relieve some short-term suffering, but would ultimately prevent recovery by helping to maintain inefficient capital stock levels. It is the economic equivalent of the 'hair of the dog'. After a hard night of excessive drinking, a shot of vodka might perk you up for an hour or so, but will eventually lead to an even worse hangover.

As a theory of business cycles, Hayek's approach in *Prices and Production* was largely rejected. A few years later, in 1936, Keynes's *General Theory* swept all before it on both sides of the Atlantic. Even the London School of Economics essentially became Keynesian. Later on, Milton Friedman and Anna Jacobson Schwartz, in their 1963 book *A Monetary History of the United States*, would provide a widely accepted explanation of the Great Depression linked with the tightening of the money supply as the banking system folded. By contrast, Hayek's views that low interest rates during the 1920s led to the depression received little credence.

Keynes was very much the showman, witty and articulate. Hayek, by contrast, lacked charisma and the power of communication. He spoke with a thick Austrian accent and was by several accounts a poor teacher. It is said that his students at the LSE asked him to lecture in German as it was more understandable. His writing was not always that easy to follow either. Milton Friedman was a staunch admirer of Hayek, but still described Hayek's 1941 *Pure Theory of Capital* as basically unreadable.[11]

Suffice it to say that Keynes was more interventionist in the economy than Hayek. He agreed with Hayek over the evils of communism and fascism, but believed the market economy was unable to always self-regulate efficiently. Keynes was not an advocate of government intervening in business activities, but thought it should provide the conditions under which such activities take place. But while Keynes was telling politicians they could make things better, Hayek was telling them they would just make things worse. It cannot be a total surprise that they were more readily drawn to the Keynesian view.

Hayek's path to fame

In the late 1930s Hayek simply became forgotten as an economist and his views were no longer a topic of academic discussion. Hayek himself also began to step away from technical economic theory and towards broader issues of social inquiry. He had not forgotten his background in the Austrian School, which was firmly at odds with social planning and excessive government intervention in the economy. His contemporary von Mises had questioned how it would be possible for any economic system, by which he meant communism, to exist without a price mechanism to allocate and incentivize economic activity. He believed that critics of capitalism, and, at the time of the inter-war years, there were many, failed to point out how a socialist system could be properly organized. Without prices, there would be no way for the baker to know how much to sell his bread for.

Collectivist Economic Planning, which Hayek edited in 1935, marked his transformation from economic theory to political philosophy. He argued that society is more efficient when rules or laws enable each individual to use their own knowledge and abilities for their own purpose rather than conform to the plan of a central authority. He was opposed to the idea that it was possible to manage a technologically advanced society from a central perch. The role of the government is to help individuals maximize their own talents, ideas and knowledge. Hayek's fundamental belief is that fragments of knowledge could not be brought together into a single brain. Given the complicated nature of technologies and production processes, it would require knowledge that no single person or a committee could possess. However, a pricing system with profit incentives could establish a market, provided it was backed with recognition of private property, contracts, laws, societal norms and the ability to exchange goods.

As the Second World War started to wind down, Hayek had become an increasingly obscure academic. However, that was to change abruptly with the publication of *The Road to Serfdom* in 1944. It would make him one of the world's best-known thinkers.

The Great Depression before the war had shaken belief in the capitalist system and people had become used to centrally planned wartime economies. Hayek wanted to warn the British public about the dangers resulting from government control of economic decision-making through continued central planning, whether communist or fascist. He argued that the abandonment of individualism led not only to a loss of freedom and the creation of an oppressive society but inevitably also to totalitarianism and effectively the serfdom of the individual. Centralized planning was undemocratic because the will of a small number was imposed on the people and the rule of law and individual freedoms were sacrificed.

The Road to Serfdom received positive reviews upon publication. The Second World War was not quite over, but by now it was simply a question of when, rather than if, the Axis powers would be defeated. Across Britain, the question 'what next?' was already being asked.

The book was to make Hayek famous, and not just in economic or academic circles. Keynes referred to it as a 'grand book',[12] and sales far exceeded Hayek's modest expectations for what he had earlier described to his publisher, Routledge, as a semi-popular work. The initial 2,000 print run sold out within days. Routledge ordered another 2,000 copies and over the next two years fought a generally losing battle to keep up with demand. Wartime rationing of paper did not help matters, and Hayek often referred to *The Road to Serfdom* as that 'unobtainable book'.[13]

However, it was in America where its success far exceeded expectations. The book was primarily written for a British audience and its academic tilt meant it wasn't expected to do well there. Furthermore, it was at odds with the post-war political climate of the day in America, and had already been rejected by a number of US publishers. However, the University of Chicago Press agreed to publish the book and the US edition was published in September, six months after the British version, again with an initial 2,000 print run.

It took off in a big way. A glowing review in *The New York Times*

promoted interest, and soon the publishers realized they had a success on their hands. Another 5,000 copies were released and, just days
later, 5,000 more. The book reached real prominence when *Reader's
Digest*, which followed the *NYT* in describing it as 'one of the most
important books of our generation', published a twenty-page precis.
In those pre-TV days, its readership of 6 million could launch
a blockbuster, and it made Hayek a household name in the US as
people looked to life after war.

In Britain it did not quite have the political influence Hayek had
hoped for. After the end of the Second World War, the welfare
state was established in the UK. Conservative Prime Minister
Winston Churchill had quoted and used Hayek's book heavily in
the 1945 election campaign against Clement Attlee and the Labour
Party as an anti-socialist text. It did not have much resonance with
the British public, though, as Labour won a landslide victory. It is
fair to say that Hayek was not a supporter of the new interventionist
government.

Hayek preferred most activities to stay in private hands, but did
see the need for a limited role of government in markets to perform
the tasks that markets were not capable of. These included outlawing
poisonous substances and preventing crime, but also providing a basic
safety net. He wrote:

> there can be no doubt that some minimum of food, shelter, and cloth-
> ing, sufficient to preserve health and the capacity to work, can be
> assured to everybody . . . Where, as in the case of sickness and acci-
> dent, neither the desire to avoid such calamities nor the efforts to
> overcome their consequences are as a rule weakened by the provision
> of assistance, where, in short, we deal with genuinely insurable risks,
> the case for the state's helping to organize a comprehensive system of
> social insurance is very strong.[14]

In many ways Friedrich Hayek was at his peak in terms of celebrity
and reputation after the publication of *The Road to Serfdom*. He had
conceived the idea of setting up a society to bring German scholars
back into mainstream classical thought after the Second World War,

and a couple of years later, between 1 and 10 April 1947, the first Mont Pelerin Society conference took place in Switzerland. Hayek invited intellectuals who supported classical liberalism – in all, thirty-nine individuals from ten countries. Hayek was the first president and stayed in post until 1961. It continues today in the same liberal tradition, and eight Nobel Prize winners have been members.

Hayek had always been interested in psychology and after the success of *The Road to Serfdom* he indulged himself working on his next project, *The Sensory Order*. Published in 1952, the book set out a division of knowledge within societies where each person's share of knowledge was infinitesimally minuscule, which limited the knowledge attainable for any individual.

By this time, Hayek was drifting away from the London School of Economics. It is fair to say that he was no longer producing technical work. Keynes's death in 1946 had made it impossible to engage with him, thus removing one of Hayek's motivations. A messy divorce from his wife, Hella, also caused him to lose friends in London, among them his one-time biggest supporter, LSE's Lionel Robbins, who was appalled at Hayek's treatment of his ex-wife. Hayek had always believed he had married the wrong person,[15] admitting he had been on the rebound after discovering that his childhood sweetheart and distant cousin, Helene Bitterlich, had married another. He left Hella and their two children in 1949 and filed for divorce. In the face of Hella's objections, it was granted in 1950 via a court in Arkansas, where he was a visiting lecturer at the time and where the divorce laws were permissive. Helene was recently widowed, and a few weeks later the couple were married in Vienna. Hayek resigned from the LSE and the newlyweds moved stateside to start a new life in Chicago.

The Chicago School of economics was a school of thought based on free-market economics and a libertarian philosophy. It was not quite the same thing as the actual economics faculty within the university. Although the Chicago School was happy to identify with Hayek, given how well he fitted with their approach, he was not coveted by the Economics Department itself. *The Road to Serfdom* was recognized as an important book, but still mainly treated as a popular rather than a scholarly text. In the department's view, Hayek was now off the beaten track of economic research and no longer at the forefront of the technical work done at the university.

Furthermore, life in America in the 1950s was much different from the Great Depression years of the 1930s, and there was less interest in business-cycle theory, where Hayek's main research interests had been situated. In fairness, the lack of enthusiasm between Hayek and the Economics Department was probably mutual, since Hayek himself no longer considered himself solely an economist.

Instead, Hayek joined the university's John U. Nef Committee on Social Thought as Professor of Social and Moral Science. This multidisciplinary faculty consisted of a range of social and natural scientists, including the writer T. S. Eliot and the 1938 Nobel laureate in Physics, Enrico Fermi, allowing Hayek to study interests outside mainstream economic theory.

His next major work was *The Constitution of Liberty*. Hayek set out to show how liberty drove wealth and growth rather than the other way round. The more government is restricted, the more likely to arise are the individual spontaneity and creativity so vital to the advance of knowledge and civilization. He also reiterated previous arguments about the division of knowledge, and how it would be practically impossible for one human mind to comprehend and make efficient use of all the knowledge that guides society. The implication is of a very limited role for government in not just the economy, but also society.

In this book, he also laid out his thoughts on global inequality across nations. He did not think it was wholly a bad thing, in that it reflected the progress made by advanced Western countries, which would allow other countries to catch up faster than the centuries it took for Western countries to become advanced. On the same basis, he was also comfortable with inequality within societies, believing diversity to be necessary for society to prosper. There would be no mutual progress without inequality. According to Hayek, this was not an ethical consideration but historically observable: 'Recent European experience strongly confirms this. The rapidity with which rich societies here have become static, if not stagnant, societies through egalitarian policies, while impoverished but highly competitive countries have become very dynamic and progressive, has been one of the most conspicuous features of the post-war period.'[16]

In Hayek's view, society evolves so that the behaviour of successful individuals is adopted and imitated. The evolution of society is shaped by the new ideas of a comparative few. People with the better ideas determine developments; thus the market is an evolutionary mechanism where the economically talented prosper. Society can choose between equality and productivity. However, he did not agree with entrenched status quos, and the power, wealth and privilege they bestowed.

It took four years for Hayek to finish *The Constitution of Liberty*, completing the manuscript in 1959 to mark his sixtieth birthday. The book was published in February 1960 and intended for a general readership. Hayek considered it his best work, his magnum opus, and had suitably high expectations. *The Road to Serfdom* he described as a semi-popular book, but *The Constitution of Liberty* was, he hoped, to be *The Wealth of Nations* for the twentieth century.[17]

Unfortunately for Hayek, it would not come close to reaching the popularity of *The Road to Serfdom*. This time the book was not reviewed in *Time* or *Life*, and the *Reader's Digest* did not consider it suitable for a condensed version. Perhaps *The Constitution of Liberty* just did not capture the mood of the time in the way that *The Road to Serfdom* had as people looked beyond the Second World War. In 1962 Milton Friedman published *Capitalism and Freedom*, which he also felt was underappreciated.

Friedrich Hayek left Chicago and America in 1962, citing financial reasons. His divorce from Hella and frequent trips to Europe had put some pressure on his finances. He decided to re-enter the German-speaking world at the University of Freiburg in West Germany. He stayed there until 1969, when he spent a year as visiting professor at UCLA before he returned to Austria and the University of Salzburg. He would make one final move, returning with Helene to Freiburg in 1977, where he spent his remaining days.

During this time, his effort was predominately dedicated to

writing *Law, Legislation and Liberty*, the follow-up to *The Constitution of Liberty*. It is fair to say that *Law, Legislation and Liberty* was far more abstract than his earlier books. He made no effort this time to write for a general audience, assuming readers were familiar with his previous work.

The book was published in three volumes: *Rules and Order* (1973), *The Mirage of Social Justice* (1976) and *The Political Order of a Free People* (1979). One of the reasons it took so long to write is that between 1969 and 1974 his progress had been interrupted by ill health and depression. However, two events were to revitalize him.

The Nobel Prize in economics had been established in 1969. It was rumoured that the committee were keen to award the prize to Gunnar Myrdal, one of the pioneers of the Swedish welfare state, but it had been specified at inception that no Swede could win in the first five years. The sixth year was 1974, and Myrdal duly received the award that year. However, the prize was shared with Hayek. Both economists were reportedly surprised, Hayek because he had won; Myrdal because he had to share the award.[18]

Hayek had not considered himself a contender because his work in technical economics was too far in the past. Many American economists had forgotten him altogether; it was over ten years since he had left Chicago. The highest prize in economics rejuvenated him, and helped to restore both his health and motivation.

The 1970s had seen the major economies hit by stagflation (a combination of high inflation and high unemployment) in the aftermath of the 1973 oil price spike. In line with his previous theory of the business cycle forty years earlier, Hayek felt that the high inflation of the 1970s would lead to an economic crisis on the same scale as the Great Depression. Inflation had to be stopped in its tracks, even at the expense of short-run output and employment.

In 1976, a couple of years after he won the Nobel Prize, Hayek published *The Denationalization of Money*, where he ventured his idea that money should be issued by private firms rather than the government. His reckoning was that competition between money providers would favour the most stable of the currencies in circulation. The same competition would also enforce self-regulation. The work was widely derided. Milton Friedman pointed out that there was nothing in current law to prevent bilateral trade using any medium of exchange accepted by all parties. Curiously, the recent rise of crypto-currencies, such as Bitcoin, which are digital currencies that can be used to make purchases on the internet, are an example of non-governmental money.

Nevertheless, Hayek's body of work had made an impression on the politicians who would introduce free-market economics into the British and American economies in the 1980s. Hayek had been associ-ated with a London-based think tank, the Institute of Economic Affairs (IEA) since its establishment in 1955. He had been contacted by the IEA's founder, the businessman Antony Fisher, after he had read *The Road to Serfdom*. The idea of the IEA was to promote free markets and the limitation of government intervention in the econ-omy. The IEA had been closely associated with the Conservative Party leader Margaret Thatcher, who became the British prime min-ister in 1979. She was greatly influenced by Hayek's thinking and regularly quoted him in Cabinet and other meetings. On one occa-sion she interrupted a speaker who was urging the Conservatives to take a middle way on a variety of policy issues by pulling out a copy of *The Constitution of Liberty*, banging it on the table and proclaiming: 'This is what we believe!'[19] Thatcher had made Hayek relevant again. On her tenth anniversary as prime minister, she wrote to Hayek thanking him for his contribution to ideology and policy.

The Fatal Conceit was Hayek's last major work. Published in 1988, it pointed out the flaws and errors in socialism. In many ways, it was designed to be the crowning summary of his life's work and an epi-logue to *Law, Legislation and Liberty*. The insight was that the price system is an instrument which enables millions of people to adjust their efforts to events and conditions of which they have no concrete, direct knowledge:

> It took me a long time to develop what is basically a simple idea . . . I gradually found that the basic function of economics was to explain the process of how human activity adapted itself to data about which it had no information. Thus the whole economic order rested on the

fact that by using prices as a guide, or as signals, we were led to serve the demands and enlist the powers and capacities of people of whom we knew nothing . . . Basically, the insight that prices were signals bringing about the unforeseen coordination of the efforts of thousands of individuals . . . became the leading idea behind my work.[20]

In essence, Hayek had built on Adam Smith's 'invisible hand' and specifically homed in on the role of prices in determining the value of goods and services in an economy. With a knowledge of prices, people can choose to produce certain goods or work in certain industries. The economy as a whole operates efficiently even though no one has coordinated their efforts. The book was seven years in the making, and not well received. It marked the end of his professional career.

A year later, it was tremendously fitting that Hayek would witness the fall of the Berlin Wall and the disintegration of the Soviet Union that followed it. He lived long enough to see the victory of capitalism over communism, but only just. In 1992 he died at the age of ninety-two.

Hayek and the global financial crisis

At the time of his passing, Hayek had seen the dominance of capitalism over communism at the end of the Cold War between the Soviet Union and the United States. Yet, just two decades later, the capitalist system would face another great challenge. The 2008 financial crisis led to disillusionment with capitalism's excesses.

What would Friedrich Hayek have made of the 2008 global financial crisis that incited the recent backlash against capitalism? Hayek had argued that the Federal Reserve played a role in precipitating the Great Depression by keeping interest rates too low through the 1920s so that bad investments culminated in the Great Crash of 1929. It is likely he would have made a similar argument about Fed policy in the run-up to the global financial crisis.

Hayek would have probably traced it back to the steep cuts in interest rates the Fed made when the US economy looked like it was faltering after the bursting of the dotcom bubble. Between 2000 and 2004, the US interest rate was cut from 6.5 per cent to just 1 per cent. Inflation was low and growth was weak, so the Fed acted to ease the economic slowdown by cutting interest rates to try to boost investment and consumption. But this led to too much and riskier borrowing in the housing market, which would lead to bigger problems in sub-prime mortgages just a few years later. Hayek would have objected to central banks believing that they can successfully intervene in the economic cycle.

What would Hayek have advised during the global financial crisis itself? Since, for him, recessions were not necessarily pleasant but better for long-term health, he would not have in principle opposed the liquidation of the investment banks Bear Stearns and Lehman Brothers, or the government-supported lenders Fannie Mae and Freddie Mac. In theory, his work through the years points to a ready acceptance that insolvent institutions, or those that lent badly, should be allowed to go bust. What is not clear is whether he would have felt the need to bail these institutions out in order to prevent the systemic failure of otherwise sound businesses that their collapse might instigate.

We can be more certain that Hayek would be strongly against the huge quantitative easing (QE) programmes whereby central banks injected large amounts of cash into the US, European and Japanese economies. In the 1970s, he favoured allowing the economy to right itself without government intervention, even at the cost of higher unemployment in the short run. He would have thought that QE was nothing more than a bailout of failed institutions, primarily used to shore up their balance sheets and provide liquidity to the banks that had acted irresponsibly before the crash. The flow of easy money would simply allow the liquidation and restructuring of bad investments to be prolonged. QE has been described by Stanford economist John Taylor as 'mondustrial policy' ('monetary-industrial policy') since it represents discretionary government involvement in the economy to support certain industries.[21]

Naturally, Hayek's starting position is that all of this should have been unnecessary in the first place. The pain of the recession could have been avoided had the boom in lending and vast credit expansion not occurred. The standard viewpoint as people survey the wreckage caused by financial markets was that they were not regulated enough. Followers of Hayek, though, would go the other way. It wasn't the case that financial markets were allowed too much freedom, but that they just were not free enough. Prior to the crisis, they would say there was an abundance of regulation already in place. Government regulations actually created a false expectation among investors that they were protected from risk and default. If financial markets were unregulated, Hayek would argue, they would naturally develop the institutions that ensure trust and their reputation.

This view has been aired in the annual Hayek Lecture hosted by the Institute of Economic Affairs since his death in 1992. For instance, the 2012 lecture, 'Why We Still Need to Read Hayek', was given by John Taylor, who reflected on the tumultuous events of the global financial crash and what Hayek might have made of the post-crisis problems in the US economy.

Taylor set out the free-market principles he believed that allowed America to prosper: 'people are free to decide what to produce, what to buy, where to work, how to help others'. These choices should be made 'within a predictable policy framework based on the rule of law, strong incentives from the market system and a limited role for government.'[22]

These principles have sometimes been abandoned, with unfortunate consequences. Leading up to the Great Depression, the Fed sharply reduced the growth of the money supply, the government raised tax rates and tariffs and went beyond market principles in the National Industrial Recovery Act. In the 1960s and 1970s there were short-term stimulus packages as well as wage and price controls. The financial crisis reflects the latest abandonment of Hayek's principles. Governments bailed out financial institutions and responded to the crisis with aggressive monetary policies.

Avoiding these interventions would allow economic growth, in Hayek's view, driven by the market and not by government policies, to resume. Once the foundations of a market economy were properly set, including appropriate regulation of the financial system, then economic prosperity would return. And that would mean that there was a chance of restoring faith in the capitalist system.

Hayek would probably have agreed with a paraphrased version that substituted 'capitalism' for 'democracy' in an observation by his supporter Winston Churchill: 'No one pretends that democracy is perfect or all-wise. Indeed, it has been said that democracy is the worst form of Government except all those other forms that have been tried from time to time.'[23]

Hayek's influence

In 1979 Friedrich Hayek remarked: 'I have arrived at the conviction that the neglect by economists to discuss seriously what is really the crucial problem of our time is due to a certain timidity about soiling their hands by going from purely scientific questions into value questions.'[24]

Hayek was not timid and robustly promoted the ideology of the capitalist system. This avid defender of capitalism would certainly stand up for the free market as being preferential to the alternatives. None other than former British prime minister Margaret Thatcher, whose ethos was based on free-market principles, was an admirer: 'Adam Smith, the greatest exponent of free enterprise economics till Hayek and Friedman . . .'[25] Thatcher also remarked: 'All the general propositions favouring freedom I had either imbibed at my father's knee or acquired by candle-end reading of [conservative politician Edmund] Burke and Hayek . . .'[26]

Friedrich Hayek, though, was concerned about the pedestal upon which economists can be placed. In his 1974 speech accepting the highest prize in economics, he said:

I must confess that if I had been consulted whether to establish a Nobel Prize in economics, I should have decidedly advised against it . . . It is that the Nobel Prize confers on an individual an authority which in economics no man ought to possess . . . [T]he influence of the economist that mainly matters is an influence over laymen:

politicians, journalists, civil servants and the public generally. There is no reason why a man who has made a distinctive contribution to economic science should be omnicompetent on all problems of society – as the press tends to treat him till in the end he may himself be persuaded to believe. One is even made to feel it a public duty to pronounce on problems to which one may not have devoted special attention.[27]

Hayek was certainly influential, and whether he was comfortable with it or not, his influence remains evident today. Former US Treasury Secretary and Harvard economist Lawrence Summers said of Hayek: 'What's the single most important thing to learn from an economics course today? What I tried to leave my students with is the view that the invisible hand is more powerful than the [un]hidden hand. Things will happen in well-organized efforts without direction, controls, plans. That's the consensus among economists. That's the Hayek legacy.'[28]

CHAPTER 9

Joan Robinson: Why are Wages so Low?

It is one of the most pressing questions in American economic policy. Jason Furman, chairman of former US President Obama's Council of Economic Advisers, told me that the question he was asked most often by the president was: 'What's going on with wage growth? And what does that mean for the future of the economy?'[1]

The leader of the most powerful country in the world was asking this question. And it's not just a problem for America. It's a big issue for Britain and other major economies, ranging from Germany to Japan. Wages, after accounting for inflation, for the average worker in America have been stagnant for forty years. In the UK, there's been an unprecedented fall in real earnings since the 2008 global financial crisis. In Germany and Japan, median wages earned by people in the middle of the distribution have been stagnant for about two decades.

With the economic recovery underway in the United States and Britain, unemployment has come down dramatically to long-term levels of less than 5 per cent. So, it looks like employment has recovered from the recession. A healthier labour market usually means jobs and also better wages. Yet, puzzlingly, wages are not growing well.

It's not what models of perfectly competitive labour markets would predict. In those theories, workers are paid the value of their output so their wages would not be low if the economy was grow-ing and more of what they produced was demanded. But as Joseph

Schumpeter said in Chapter 7, perfect competition is one of the unrealistic constructs of economics that helps with solving mathematical equations but isn't how the real world operates.

This is where the sole female among the Great Economists in this book made her seminal contribution. Joan Robinson rejected perfect competition and sought to explain how imperfections can lead to discrepancies in wages and employment that are actually observed in markets. Because of her path-breaking work, Joan Robinson is viewed as 'the most important woman in the history of economic thought'.[2] Her place among the Greats, particularly at a time when there were few female economists, is noteworthy. Even now, women are significantly under-represented in the economics profession. Of the over 50,000 academic economists in the world, less than one-fifth are women.

Robinson's first book, *The Economics of Imperfect Competition*, was published in 1933 and brought her international recognition. Her ground-breaking manuscript was finished just three years after she began her study of economic theory. It changed the way that we think about how prices and wages are determined. She analysed price determination under monopolistic conditions, where there is monopoly power and less than perfectly competitive markets. In other words, markets were not full of firms too weak to influence the industry, the prices of goods or the pay of workers. She argued that where there was imperfect competition, workers are paid less than the market value of their labour. Widely read on both sides of the Atlantic, the book quickly became a standard text in this new research field of imperfect competition. It was reprinted thirteen times between 1933 and 1965.

Robinson's work followed Keynesian thought, so it disputed the neoclassical economic notion of perfectly competitive markets. In other words, she sided with John Maynard Keynes against their Cambridge predecessor, Alfred Marshall. The year after Keynes's *The General Theory of Employment, Interest and Money* appeared in 1936, she published *Essays in the Theory of Employment*, which refined and extended Keynes's ideas specifically in the labour market. She followed that work with another book, *Introduction to the Theory of*

Employment, impressively in the same year. It was the first textbook that would ingrain Keynesian concepts into economics.

Although she had been a follower of Keynes, she later concluded that neither neoclassical nor Keynesian economics could account for long-term economic outcomes. But she thought that Keynesian economics had the best shot. So, her last major work attempted to explain how economies develop. Published in 1956, *The Accumulation of Capital* presented a theory of how capital accumulation in the economy, which consists of investment by firms and the government, changes over time in an attempt to better explain the long-run dynamics of growth.

Robinson was plied with honours throughout her long career. But she was also controversial. Although she was one of the most influential and prolific economists of the time, with a publication record stretching from 1932 to two years after her death in 1983, she was never awarded the highest prize in economics. Nobel laureate Paul Samuelson said: 'I was surprised that she never received the Nobel Prize.' He added: 'She has been a very contentious figure, but also a very important figure.'[3] Robinson was under consideration by the Swedish Academy in the mid-1970s and apparently short-listed but repeatedly passed over.

The possible reasons why she went from Keynes's inner circle to an outsider are varied. In addition to growing scepticism over Keynesian economics, Joan Robinson rejected even her own earlier work rooted in Keynesianism as she sought new answers to the long run. She also rejected the mathematical focus of economics that had gradually emerged, led by Irving Fisher and others discussed in earlier chapters. One of her favourite sayings was: 'I never learned mathematics, so I had to think.' When she was approached to serve on the board of the Econometric Society, she refused on the basis that she could not read the highly technical articles published by the leading in-house journal, *Econometrica*, which were about quantification and theory.[4]

Writing a book on Marxian economics as she moved beyond Keynesianism also contributed to her marginalization from mainstream economists. And her support of the communist regimes of

China and North Korea did not make her popular. She did not hide her beliefs; she even dressed up in Vietnamese peasant outfits to give lectures.[5] A part of it also probably reflected the challenges she faced in a male-dominated era and profession.

Yet Joan Robinson was a pioneer in introducing imperfect competition into economics, a concept that has fundamentally transformed the field. As Robinson once observed: 'The subject matter of economics is neither more nor less than its own technique.'[6] She has given economists the techniques and tools to help analyse the challenge of low pay, among others.

The life and times of Joan Robinson

Joan Robinson (née Maurice) was born into an elite family in Surrey in 1903. Her father was a baronet and a major general in the British army in the First World War. Her grandfather was a famous surgeon who taught at Cambridge University, where she studied and built her career.

She read economics at Girton College, graduating in 1925 without much distinction and with a Second Class degree. The following year she married Austin Robinson. He was to become a significant Cambridge economics professor and editor of the *Economic Journal*, but nevertheless was to be overshadowed by Joan. They moved to India for two years as he was to become the economics tutor to the young maharajah of the Indian state of Gwalior.

When her husband returned to Cambridge University, she began attending Piero Sraffa's lectures on the 'advanced theory of value', which was the standard term for what we would now describe as the theory of what determined prices in an economy. Sraffa's article in the *Economic Journal* in 1926 had radically abandoned the assumption of competitive markets and focused on monopolies. Before then, the theory of monopoly was used only to analyse firms with dominant market power, such as public utilities or railways. After his article, interest grew in analysing imperfectly competitive markets. His work stimulated research among Cambridge and other economists, including Robinson, who would go on to establish imperfect competition as a new branch of economics.

It wasn't an easy time for female economists. In 1881 students at Girton and Newnham, the two Cambridge colleges for women, received permission to sit for honours examinations and have their papers evaluated, which were the same as those set for men. But they would not receive degrees. Cambridge was the only British university where women were still excluded from lectureships and administrative positions. It wasn't until 1925, the year that Robinson graduated, that women could take up university posts. They remained excluded from college fellowships at men's colleges, which formed the core of Cambridge teaching and research.

In addition to the barriers faced by women at Cambridge, Robinson had earned less than a First Class degree. She had to publish research that would serve in place of a successful fellowship dissertation to establish herself as a serious economist. As an upper-middle-class woman, she had domestic help and thus she had research time. In the span of just a year and a half, between March 1931 and October 1932, she completed what would become a trail-blazing book, *The Economics of Imperfect Competition*.

In thinking about firms with monopoly power, Robinson recast the theory of what determines prices in less than perfectly competitive markets. In so doing, she was also able to reconcile the two sides of economics. On the one side were those who used diagrams to establish precise theoretical relationships, for example price and quantity. The other side were the empiricists who thought data trumped theory.[7] Robinson's diagrams were based on empirical observations about how markets actually operated, which was less than perfect, and resulted in wages that were lower than a worker's output warranted.

Another factor in Robinson's ascendancy to the core of Cambridge economics was her relationship with the Cambridge economist Richard Kahn. In 1930 they shared ideas. By 1931 they were having an affair. They were discovered by none other than John Maynard Keynes: 'Early in 1932 Keynes surprised them on the floor in Kahn's study, "though I expect", he told [his wife] Lydia, "the conversation was only on *The Pure Theory of Monopoly*".'[8]

Robinson's pregnancies in 1934 and 1937, which produced two daughters, did not seem to change their relationship. In 1938 Robinson suffered a psychiatric breakdown and she and her husband began leading separate lives.[9] In 1952 she suffered another breakdown, though less severe than the first one.

Richard Kahn could have been a potential competitor in developing a new theory of imperfect competition. Instead, he became a supporter. Kahn was a protégé of John Maynard Keynes. She joined him, her husband, Sraffa and James Meade in what was known as the 'circus'. In 1935 Robinson was one of these five economists Keynes entrusted for feedback on *The General Theory*.[10] This placed Joan Robinson at the centre of Cambridge economics. Keynes even wrote the Introduction to her *Introduction to the Theory of Employment*, which was the first textbook in Keynesian economics.

In 1934, Robinson had been appointed to a part-time probationary lectureship at Cambridge University. By 1937, she had a full-time probationary lectureship, which led to a permanent lectureship the following year. She was amidst some of the most influential economists of the time. In 1938 Cambridge economics was led by Keynes, Sraffa and Kahn. As well as those, there was J. R. Hicks and A. C. Pigou. John Hicks would later receive both a knighthood and, in 1972, the highest prize in economics. He shared the Nobel Prize with Kenneth J. Arrow for their work on introducing welfare concepts into economics, such as assessing how people's utility or happiness is affected by economic choices. Arthur Pigou more fully developed the idea of 'externalities', the costs or benefits to others that are not taken into account by, for example, a polluter or a person who plants trees. A Pigouvian tax is a tax that is imposed on the polluter to get them to internalize the social cost of their polluting activities.

Despite her distinguished perch, Joan Robinson faced competition in claiming to lead a new research field. Edward Chamberlin at Harvard University published *The Theory of Monopolistic Competition* three months before Robinson's *The Economics of Imperfect Competition*. But at a roundtable discussion held at the American Economic Association (AEA) meeting in December 1933 on the topic they adopted

Robinson's concept, and not Chamberlin's, to set the parameters of the new research area. She was helped by Kahn's visits to American universities, which broadened Robinson's references in her book as compared with Chamberlin's. Edward Chamberlin, though, would go on to develop the fruitful field of industrial organization, which researched questions such as oligopolistic interaction that analysed how a few companies can dominate an industry, for example the airline sector. Robinson would later develop her more theoretical approach in the field of labour economics rather than the theory of the firm. Curiously, one of the discussants of the papers presented was Chamberlin himself, and it was chaired by Joseph Schumpeter. Schumpeter would later recommend Robinson for honorary membership of the AEA: 'I know I shall be considered out of order if in this anti-feminist country, I suggest honoring a woman, but Mrs. Joan Robinson had a well-earned international success with her book *The Economics of Imperfect Competition* in 1933. By virtue of it she holds a leading position in one of the most popular lines of advance.'[11]

Robinson's next book complemented and extended Keynes's *General Theory*. In March 1936, only a month after Keynes's book appeared, she published an article titled 'The Long-Period Theory of Employment'. Since Keynes's assumptions focused on the short run, Robinson extended his work to analyse long-term conditions. In June of the same year, another article, 'Disguised Unemployment', appeared, which again extended Keynesian economics. Keynes argued that insufficient demand resulted in unemployed workers. Robinson posited that when workers are laid off, they take less productive jobs in order to survive even if they resort to selling matches on street corners. Although they are technically employed, such employment was really disguised unemployment, which meant the official unemployment rate was not telling the whole story. Robinson's *Essays in the Theory of Employment*, published in 1937, further explored the problems around employment that were raised in the *General Theory*.

Joan Robinson's emergence as a world-leading economist was impressively rapid. In 1930 she was the wife of a Cambridge faculty member. By the end of that decade she was an internationally respected economist at the heart of the Keynesian revolution. Yet she was only made a full professor at Cambridge University in 1965, the year her husband retired from his professorship.

Joan Robinson published her last major work in 1956. *The Accumulation of Capital* was a study of economic growth models that moved away from the standard Keynesian and neoclassical approaches to gain a deeper understanding as to why some countries prosper. Like her other research, this work is highly readable, especially as she makes her case using diagrams and figures rather than equations and complex mathematical models. Along these lines, her work in the 1960s increasingly moved towards economic development issues, especially in India, but also in China and North Korea.

That was not the sole new direction of research that she pursued. Robinson also examined the basis of economics, as in her 1962 book, *Economic Philosophy*, where she wryly observed: 'All along [economics] has been striving to escape from sentiment and to win for itself the status of a science.'[12] She added: 'lacking the experimental method, economists are not strictly enough compelled to reduce metaphysical concepts to falsifiable terms and cannot compel each other to agree as to what has been falsified. So economics limps along with one foot in untested hypotheses and the other in untestable slogans.'[13]

Still, Robinson saw the task of economists as 'sort[ing] out as best we may this mixture of ideology and science. We shall find no neat answers to the questions that it raises.'[14]

Robinson's imperfect markets

Joan Robinson's work on imperfect competition offers no neat answers but can help explain why wages have failed to keep pace with productivity, that is, output per worker, since markets are just not perfect in the real world. It might seem curious to many why it took so long to discover this! In fact, one would be hard pressed to give many examples of a perfectly competitive market. It goes to show how entrenched had become the idea that the market works perfectly efficiently, driven by the 'invisible hand'. It wasn't until

Keynes challenged the neoclassical view of quickly self-righting markets that the ground was laid for the work of Robinson and others to develop theories of imperfectly competitive markets.

Under perfect competition, a firm would choose to produce at the point where the volume it sells is warranted by the cost of producing it. Workers would be paid the value of the last unit of output they produced. Employers would not be able to pay less because exploitation (known as 'economic rents') would be eroded by competition, i.e., another firm would be able to pay a bit more until the point where the wage equalled what they could sell the last unit for. So, the last or 'marginal' unit reveals the value of what a worker has produced, which then sets the wage.

But Robinson points out that if markets are imperfectly competitive, then firms *can* earn economic rents because rents aren't entirely eroded by competition.[15] In that situation, firms have market power. This could be the result of accidents of history, in that some were first in the market, others held patents, and still others have influence over the market due to the entrepreneurship of their founders.

She developed a theory of 'monopsony' to refer to the market power that firms can wield in the labour market alongside the more familiar and established term, monopoly power, where firms have market power in the product market and can charge more for a good or service above their costs, earning them monopoly profits. Monopsony power allows employers to pay workers less than the value of their output, and keep more for themselves.

There has been an active debate over whether monopsony exists. Economists have been sceptical about firms being able to possess power over labour markets. The British National Health Service (NHS) is an example of an organization whose main employer, in this case the government, is pretty much the sole employer, so can set wages and employment conditions. Others include the local labour markets of many towns, which are often dominated by one or two major industries. (Robinson used coal mining as the most extreme example of her day.) Indeed, the classical economists made the somewhat surprising point that, almost by definition, there are always significantly fewer employers than workers. Employers are not usually worried about where their next pay cheque is coming from, unlike employees. Employers typically have a much stronger common interest than workers. The end result is that quasi-collusive cartels or monopsonies are not that uncommon, which is then somewhat balanced by workers unionizing.

These, though, are considered rarer than firms with monopoly power. Because workers can change industries, monopsonies are not as common as monopolies. Numerous examples of monopolistic industries come to mind. For instance, a few firms dominate the mobile phone market and a few search engines monopolize the internet. We've seen some of these firms become the subject of regulatory inquiries for anti-competitive practices due to their market power.

According to Robinson, if there are imperfections in the labour market that cause it to be less than perfectly competitive, then those imperfections can lead to different wage levels. This is plausible since workers are not homogeneous or perfectly interchangeable. For instance, workers have different willingness or ability to work, which is known as labour supply elasticity. Full-time versus part-time work is a good example of how much labour a worker wants to, or can, supply to the employment market. If a woman has childcare responsibilities, then she may only take on part-time work. It means that employers can offer different wages even to equally productive individuals. Employers 'exploit' these labour supply differences and earn 'rents' by offering wages that are less than the output produced. (Rents can also be gained in other contexts, such as when monopolists gain what would have gone to consumers.) If there are imperfections in both factor (labour) and product (for example rail) markets, then there are even greater potential 'rents'.

Wages also affect employment levels. If some groups have higher 'reservation wages', that is, a wage level that tips them into deciding to enter the labour force or not, and accept a job or not, then there will be different employment levels too. That is seen in the different labour force participation rates for men and women, which are usually lower for women, who may not choose to work if their wage barely covers their childcare or other familial costs such as taking care of elderly parents, for instance.

Robinson's theory shows that if there is not perfect competition, which is highly likely, then workers will receive lower wages than they should earn based on their productivity, and firms will earn 'rents'. Such 'exploitation' of workers will persist until the market structure changes so that competition leads firms to lose their market power. This market power is what enables firms to pay wages below what the workers produce.

Robinson's ideas paved the way for an examination of what determines wages. Her theories show how the problem of low pay goes beyond labour productivity and is related to the structure of markets.

The problem with pay

Low pay wasn't always a problem. After the Second World War in the 1950s and 1960s, wages grew strongly during what is known as the Golden Age of economic growth. Then, the oil crises of the 1970s struck. Wage growth slowed all over the world to some extent. In the United States in particular by the end of the 1970s, median wage growth – the wages of people in the middle of the income distribution – started to stagnate.

Still, the post-Second World War period saw wage growth of 4 per cent on average per annum even after the 1970s slowdown. But then the Great Recession hit in 2009 and there was a huge fall of economic output, as well as wages, after the financial crisis.

Some countries, mostly emerging economies, have done better, both before the crisis and afterwards. China in particular has done well. The growth of China since 1979 has led to double-digit annual increases in wages even after the crisis. India has also done relatively well. Many emerging economies are industrializing, so wage growth is less of a problem than in advanced economies.

By contrast, wages in the UK were affected badly. In Britain there was a more than 10 per cent fall in real wages (wages after adjusting for inflation) in the six years after 2008. Wages started picking up again around 2013, but that fall in real wages is unprecedented. The only other time this was seen was in the 1920s.

Since 2009 the pace of nominal wage growth in the UK has slowed to around 2 per cent. At 2 per cent, wage growth is about half the level it was 20–30 years before the Great Recession. When inflation is at 2 per cent, that means stagnant real wages since the pay increase is eroded by having to pay higher prices. Britain did experience real wage growth in 2014 for the first time since the crisis, but only due to negligible inflation. That lasted about two years until inflation started to pick up again in 2017, when real wages again declined.

The economy has recovered and unemployment has fallen back to below the long-term level of around 5 per cent in Britain and the US, but wage growth has lagged behind. It is peculiar because wages would usually improve along with the economy. Over the long run, the fundamental reason that wages grow is because of productivity growth driven by new technologies and ideas. It means that businesses can afford to pay workers higher wages.

But the International Labour Organization (ILO) finds that since the early 1980s, the productivity growth of workers exceeded that of their average wage growth in several large developed economies, including Germany, Japan and the United States. For France and Britain, productivity and wages grew at a similar pace. The UK suffers additionally from poor productivity growth (that is discussed in Chapter 12). So, productivity growth has outpaced wage growth in a number of advanced economies in recent decades.[16] Why has this relationship between what firms can afford to pay workers and what they do pay broken down?

Globalization is one explanation. There's no example of globalization that's closer to the West than the reunification of Germany in the early 1990s. Cheaper workers from East Germany, and less costly places to produce just a short distance away in eastern Europe, brought the challenge of globalization home. There was a vast wage differential between West and East Germany. With greater competition, workers in what had been West Germany experienced wage stagnation around the mid-1990s. That's when Germany gained the title 'the sick man of Europe'. Growth rates were between 0 and 1 per cent and economic prospects were looking poor. But Germany had a remarkable transformation just before the Great Recession hit.

At that time Germany was in a strong position because the export markets, in particular in Asia, but also in Europe, were buying Germany's manufactured products. China needed German capital goods to build its factories, in particular for the production of higher-end consumer goods to which China started to turn by the 2000s. So, when the recession hit, Germany was in a strong economic position.

This transformation was forced by globalization, specifically the accession of eastern European countries into the European Union in the early 2000s. There was the possibility that German industries could relocate production into these new EU countries, where wages were much lower, and German companies were threatening to do so unless unions or worker representatives agreed to wage restraint and became more flexible about employment terms.

In the face of the threat posed by globalization, the unions agreed. An important change was that wage negotiations were decentralized from the level of the industry and region down to the level of the firm. In that way, wage deals could reflect the needs of particular companies in a very competitive and fast-changing environment.

So, Germany gained competitiveness of output at the cost of wages, which, particularly at the lower end, started to fall. At the median, wage growth was essentially stagnant. And that's partly why German industry has become more competitive. Of course, there have also been improvements in productivity, but wage restraint has played a large role.

The flexible approach of both employers and unions helped to retain domestic production in many of Germany's core manufacturing sectors and kept employment in the country, albeit with workers earning less. This is in contrast to a number of its European neighbours such as France and Italy, who have seen some of their manufacturing leave the country. Germany was the first European country to come out of recession. Afterwards, it became something of an economic superstar, exporting a great deal not just to China and other developing countries but also to Europe and the US. As economic conditions improved, though, so did wage pressure, which led to a minimum wage being introduced for the first time in January 2015.

But global competition isn't the only reason wages in developed economies are low. Japan was successfully competing in the global economy while its workers had lifetime job security until it suffered a real estate bubble that burst in the early 1990s. Yet, now, it exemplifies another phenomenon that has contributed to low wages: the emergence of non-permanent or temporary workers.

Across rich countries, the proportion of temporary workers has increased. The OECD, which is a think tank centred on advanced economies, finds that the average wage of a temporary worker versus a permanent one is as much as 50 per cent lower in the worst case (Spain) and nearly 20 per cent lower even at the more equal end (Germany).

In Japan, the proportion of temporary workers in the labour force has doubled since 1999. A large portion of those on temporary contracts are women. Almost 40 per cent of the workforce has comprised casual and part-time employees, whose wages are often much less than half of those with permanent employment contracts. The lifetime employment system that was part of the Japanese miracle in the 1980s ended up with the collapse of that system a decade later.

After the crash, Japanese companies were looking for short-term profits so had to reduce labour costs. Replacing full-time with non-regular workers was one solution. These replacements are often *haken*, or temporary agency workers. Their employment lacks security, they earn less than half a regular worker's wage and, unlike permanent workers, receive no guaranteed wage increases.

Another factor keeping wages down is that it is difficult for Japanese workers to move to another company. The lifetime employment system created a labour market where few change employers after getting a permanent job. As a result, Japanese workers do not have a strong bargaining position. And competition from temporary workers restrains the wages of all workers.

This helps to explain why median wages in Japan have been stagnant for two decades and raising wages is a priority for a Japanese government desperate to get the economy going again through consumption growth fuelled by higher incomes. There are also social consequences that the government is keen to avoid. Men in temporary employment, for example, are less likely to settle down, because their earnings are not enough to support a family.

But it's not only Japan that's seen the rise of job insecurity, or only temporary workers that are a cause of low wages. There's another factor that's seen most acutely in the world's biggest economy: automation.

The number of robots used in manufacturing is increasing dramatically. It's most concentrated in sectors like automobile production, but it's spreading throughout the advanced economies. Over the last couple of decades in the US and across the industrialized countries, technology has improved in leaps and bounds. Computers have complemented and enhanced the skills of professionals, so jobs at the high end of the skill distribution are growing. But the same innovations have replaced the jobs of people in the middle of the skill spectrum, for example in automated factories. Jobs at the lower end of the skill distribution are less affected, since services jobs such as fast-food restaurants are still filled by people. So, jobs at either end of the skill distribution are growing, while those in the middle are declining.

The middle class (those earning between 50 per cent below and 50 per cent above the median income) has shrunk to less than half the US population for the first time since at least the early 1970s, according to the Pew Research Center. The data from the last recession show why: more than half of jobs created since 2010 are low wage. This process, which has been happening for over a quarter of a century, is known as the 'hollowing out' of the middle class.

So, technology has benefited some more than others. While technology helps to raise overall economic growth, it does not follow that the gains are shared equally by firms and workers, a development that would not surprise Joan Robinson. In 2015, the US produced around $18 trillion of GDP. About $10 trillion is paid to workers in wages and benefits, but the rest is largely company profits. Over the past few decades, the proportion of earnings that goes to workers in the form of wages has gone down, while the proportion going to businesses in the form of profits has gone up. This is another reason wages around the world are not rising as expected alongside productivity and economic growth. Thus, even if productivity increases, wages may not increase proportionately.

Trade union membership also plays a role. US data for the last hundred years show that when the proportion of workers in trade unions has dropped, the share of income going to the poorest Americans has also fallen. Trade union density is now less than 10 per cent and the share of income going to the bottom 90 per cent of households is also at a near century low.[17] In short, weaker worker bargaining power and technology have contributed to the shrinking middle class in America. Coupled with globalization and the growth of part-time jobs, these factors help explain low wages in the US and elsewhere.

Of course, wages in rich countries are not low in absolute terms. The level of wages even at the lower percentiles of the distribution in Germany is much higher than in many other European countries. Even so, wage growth is a problem, especially for those in the middle class who are experiencing earnings stagnation.

What would Joan Robinson make of the low-pay challenge?

Robinson's theory of wage determination

In Robinson's model of the labour market, firms determine how much labour to employ by comparing their output and cost. Taking into account how much revenue it produces, a firm sets its employment level at the point where the 'marginal product' of what is produced is just equal to the 'marginal cost' of employing the next unit of labour. This is regardless of whether the product or factor markets are perfect or imperfect. When markets are imperfect, then employers have market power and can 'exploit' workers by paying them less than what is earned from their output. Because such exploitation arises from the unequal bargaining strength of employers and employees, one way to reduce exploitation is to increase the bargaining power of workers, for example through trade unions or collective bargaining. Legislation to place workers on a more equal footing with employers is another avenue. Germany did that by giving workers statutory representation in the boardroom. The rights of non-unionized workers also require protection.

Bargaining strength is important in many cases, but raising wages through bargaining is not the sole solution to the problem of exploitation in Robinson's theory. That could result in unemployment and continued exploitation at the higher wage, since a firm with market power could demand a sub-optimal amount of labour. The remedy would be to remove the source of the market imperfection by increasing competition. This would erode a firm's monopoly or monopsony power. In a competitive market, a firm that exploited its workers would lose them to another firm that did not. Greater competition for workers would prevent their wages from falling too low. In Robinson's view, the remedy for low wages would be to fix the imperfections in the market itself by regulating to increase competition. That would provide a longer-lasting solution.

But Robinson also thought that greater competition might drive down wages, because prices fall as competition increases, and workers are paid the value of their marginal product; that might even be less than the former exploitative wage. She believed a minimum wage would help, and attached great importance to government intervention to improve exploitative outcomes as well as increasing competition in markets.

Accordingly, she would probably have been in favour of the OECD's recommendations to boost pay by reforming labour markets to make them more competitive. Regulating markets so there are fewer entry barriers increases competitiveness, and that has improved employment outcomes across advanced economies. Allowing the more productive firms to flourish means that they will attract workers away from less productive ones. This reallocation of jobs generates benefits for the economy as well as for the workers who have better job opportunities.

The OECD is also concerned about the growth of temporary contract workers. This would certainly worry Joan Robinson. The increase in temporary or part-time jobs would fall under her theory

of 'hidden' or 'disguised' unemployment. The United States measures not only the number of people who are officially unemployed,
but also those who want and are available for full-time employment
but have had to accept part-time work. When this number is added
to the official unemployment rate, along with those who are available
for work but not seeking employment, the US unemployment picture looks less rosy. This U-6 unemployment rate, as it is known, has
fallen alongside the official unemployment rate since the financial
crisis, but it hovers around 9 per cent. The U-6 unemployment rate
rose as high as 17 per cent during the Great Recession, more than
doubling from around 8 per cent before the crash.

Disguised unemployment contributes to low wages, as discussed
earlier when we examined the increase in part-time work in advanced
economies, and is another example of how Robinson's ideas have
shaped how we think about unemployment. Instead of being content
to take the official unemployment figures at face value, recognizing
underemployment as a form of unemployment helps to identify
another pressure driving down earnings. In Robinson's view, when
workers move from lower to higher productivity jobs, then those
workers should earn higher wages, provided the market is competitive. By utilizing Robinson's definition of unemployment, the United
States has a truer picture of its workforce with which to assess its
economic policies. It's a practice that some other countries such as
those in Europe are beginning to develop, which is unsurprising,
given the increase in part-time work and the challenge of low pay in
advanced economies.

Robinson believed that government policy can play a role in
addressing low wages, so long as policymakers examine the deeper
causes of pay. The exploitation of workers will continue so long as
firms wield market power. But, similarly to Joseph Schumpeter, she
believed that the monopoly power of firms would not survive. Any
firm that was earning 'rents' would attract other firms to the same
industry. Greater competition means that monopsonies will not
last. Still, like her one-time mentor, John Maynard Keynes, Robinson believed that addressing the short-run issues that workers
face during periods where there are monopolies exploiting them are

more important than waiting for the market structure to sort itself out in the long run. Given how long the problem of low pay has persisted, and the continuing fall in the share of income going to workers versus that going to the owners of capital, Robinson would say this issue requires urgent action. Her theories do not address all of the causes of low pay, but they can help to identify some of the ways in which slow wage growth can be remedied.

A remarkable life

There is no doubt that Robinson's research has helped economists sort out some of the answers to questions such as why pay does not behave as predicted by perfectly competitive markets. But, as she also stresses, without scientific proof like in natural science, economic analysis cannot offer definitive answers. The best that we can strive for is to be guided by more realistic models of the labour market. Robinson thus points out one of the reasons why we should all study economics: 'The purpose of studying economics is not to acquire a set of ready-made answers to economic questions, but to learn how to avoid being deceived by economists.'[18]

Joan Robinson passed away in 1983 after a long and influential life. Her work opened up a whole new way of looking at markets by rejecting the standard economic views of wages and others based on an unrealistic belief in perfect competition. Those markets don't really exist, but low wages do.

The solution to the problem of pay, unsurprisingly, is complex, as would be expected in Robinson's complicated world of imperfect competition, worker exploitation and the resultant low wages. Still, for workers who are in work, it's a problem that can be solved. As Robinson remarked: 'The misery of being exploited by capitalists is nothing compared to the misery of not being exploited at all.'[19]

CHAPTER 10

Milton Friedman: Are Central Banks Doing Too Much?

The 2008 financial crisis has introduced new economic terms into popular use, like central banks undertaking quantitative easing (QE or cash injections), forward guidance (central banks saying what they think interest rates might be in the future), negative interest rates (central banks charging commercial banks for depositing money with them) and macroprudential policy (central bank regulations aiming for financial stability), to name a few. These are in addition to using interest rates to target price stability or inflation, and are 'unconventional' or fairly new monetary policy tools.

All of which raises the question: Are central banks doing too much? And is what they are doing working to help the economy? It's untested ground. Bank of England Governor Mark Carney quipped that they're trying to get 'theory to catch up with practice', while former Fed Chairman Ben Bernanke reworked the classic economics joke: 'The problem with QE is that it works in practice, but it doesn't work in theory.'*

The main unconventional policy is QE. It has been restarted once again in Britain after the referendum vote in June 2016 to leave the European Union. QE is also being used by euro area countries and Japan even while the US central bank has ceased. Injecting cash to boost the economy because interest rates have been cut to zero or even into negative territory is one of the most controversial monetary policy tools in recent times. Cutting rates is one way of making

---

* The original was: 'It works in practice, but does it work in theory?'

lending cheaper, which can increase borrowing by households and firms who then respectively spend and invest and so aid the recovery. But because interest rates were at rock bottom, central banks needed another way to increase the amount of credit in the economy. QE was that policy. Simply put, central banks electronically 'printed' money and used it to buy bonds, which are government or corporate debt. This put money onto the balance sheets of companies that thus sold their bonds in exchange for cash, which central banks hoped would be invested and boost the recovery.

This represents a new era in monetary policy. The leading scholar in monetary economics is Milton Friedman. He made his name researching the causes of the Great Depression that followed the last systemic banking crash in 1929. His conclusion that the crisis was due to poor monetary policy fundamentally changed our understanding of that period and of post-crisis policies.

To this day Friedman remains a divisive figure in popular opinion, but that's largely a reflection of the very libertarian and pro free-market positions he was to take publicly later in life rather than the body of economic research that led to his 1976 Nobel Prize. He was viewed as one of the key influences behind the Reagan and Thatcher administrations in the 1980s, both of which were ideologically driven towards smaller government and more *laissez-faire* capitalism. Both leaders attracted criticism, some of which inevitably reflected on Friedman as a well-known conservative who was central to their economic thinking.

Like most academics, by the time he received his Nobel Prize he was really past the zenith of the research that propelled him to the award in the first place. This is generally true of grand prizes, but particularly true for the economics Nobel Prize in the years following its inception in 1969, when there was a lot of catching up to do to recognize the pioneers. Between the late 1930s and early 1960s, Friedman produced a remarkable body of work. His theories on monetary policy and other economic concepts, such as what drives people to consume, remain deeply engrained in the subject and in public policy today.

It was only in the 1960s that Friedman turned towards political writing. His involvement in public affairs then continued to the very end of his life in 2006. In 2003 he had publicly backed Hollywood actor Arnold Schwarzenegger for Governor of California. (The Terminator claimed, in fact, that Adam Smith and Friedman were among his influences.)

It's fair to say that Friedman had a career of two halves. The first as an academic economist; the second as a public figure and political influencer. To a certain extent, the second half has overshadowed the first and it has become increasingly necessary to recall just how large and long-standing his contribution to economics was.

Friedman's views on the Great Depression were game-changing. In the aftermath of the 2008 financial crisis, policymakers were at great pains to try to avoid the mistakes made in the 1930s, most of which had been identified by Friedman. Since the crisis, central banks around the world have thrown the kitchen sink at reviving their battered economies, keen to avoid accusations of repeating the mistakes pointed out by Friedman.

In 2005, one year before his death, he published an article in the *Journal of Economic Perspectives*. Here he reaffirmed his conjectures over the role of monetary policy in the Great Depression and the grave mistakes made by the Federal Reserve. Had he been alive, Friedman would undoubtedly have had a lot to say about the events that followed a few years later, the reaction of policymakers to them, and where we find ourselves today.

The life and times of Milton Friedman

Milton Friedman was born in 1912 in Brooklyn, his parents having emigrated separately to America in the late nineteenth century from Carpathian Ruthenia, part of the old Austro-Hungarian Empire located in Ukraine, Slovakia and Poland, leaving family and everything else behind. They met in New York's Jewish community. When Friedman was one year old they moved to the small commuter town of Rahway, New Jersey, twenty miles outside New York City. This is where he grew up with his three sisters. The family was not wealthy and lived modestly, running a shop from their home.

From an early age Friedman was marked out as an excellent student, and spent much of his free time in the local library. He entered the first grade a year early, skipping kindergarten altogether. In the middle of the sixth grade he was promoted into the seventh, making him two years younger than most of his peers. Although he was smaller than the other children, he was talkative and had a loud voice.[1]

Friedman graduated high school a month short of his sixteenth birthday in 1928. That same year he enrolled at Rutgers University in nearby New Brunswick, leaving the family home for the first time to live on campus. His strong exam performance and family circumstances saw him qualify for a scholarship.

He originally intended to major in mathematics. As a relatively young child, he had observed that 'individuals who have exceptional mathematical ability get early deferences and develop great confidence in their ability to solve problems'.[2] However, like many economists over the years, including several in this book, he was pulled away from the 'proper' sciences towards the social science of economics. One of the key influences on Friedman at this time was Arthur Burns, who was later to become America's central banker as chairman of the Federal Reserve. Friedman's father had died of a heart attack when he was fifteen and about to enter his final year of high school. Burns was Friedman's professor at Rutgers, and it was he who convinced the youngster that economics was a useful subject that could help end the depression in which America was then mired. Friedman described Burns as being like a 'surrogate father'.[3] He cited Burns and another Rutgers economics professor, Homer Jones, who would also become a central banker as senior vice-president of the regional Federal Reserve Bank of St Louis, as his reasons for becoming an economist.

When Friedman entered Rutgers, the Roaring Twenties were nearly over. By the time he graduated in 1932 with a Bachelor's degree in economics, achieving high but not exceptional honours, the Great Depression had set in. With a quarter of the workforce unemployed, the economy seemed to be the urgent problem.

Many people have gone through Friedman's life, looking for early influences in which his libertarian and monetarist thinking might be rooted. However, if there were any at this time, they were certainly well hidden. It appears that the Great Depression and the potential for economics to play a role in alleviating the crisis were as big a factor as any in piquing Friedman's interest.

After Rutgers, at the age of just twenty, Friedman headed to the University of Chicago, with which he was later to become so closely associated. The two big names at Chicago at this time were Jacob Viner and Frank Knight. Viner was a leading trade economist and economic historian, while Knight was renowned for his work on the impact of uncertainty on markets. During much of their time at Chicago, Viner and Knight jointly edited the *Journal of Political Economy*, published by the university's own press; it remains one of the leading economics journals to this day.

It was there that Friedman met his wife Rose (née Director). Both were postgraduate students and they sat next to each other in Viner's class. He arranged his students alphabetically, and there was no one between them. Friedman and Rose had much in common. She was born in Russia in 1911, and had moved to the US with her family in 1914 before the outbreak of the First World War. She was also Jewish, but her family was more strictly orthodox. (In fact, Friedman had effectively been agnostic since the age of thirteen.) Rose had completed her undergraduate studies at Chicago. Like Friedman she was good at mathematics and had graduated high school just after her sixteenth birthday, meaning she also skipped at least one year.

Their courtship was slow. Having started dating in 1932, they spent long periods apart as Friedman's career took him elsewhere. They were finally married in 1938, when they were both twenty-six years old. They had two children: Janet, born in 1943, and David, born two years later. One of the biggest upheavals once they started a family was that Friedman had to change his work habits. His preferred time to work in his youth was from midnight to 4 a.m.

He gained an intellectual partner in Rose, who played a significant role in Friedman's research, and they would later write books together. He recalls 'many a pleasant summer evening discussing consumption data and theory in front of a blazing fire'.[4]

★

After graduating in 1933 from Chicago with a Master's degree in economics, Friedman was to spend a year at Columbia University in New York before returning to Chicago. But as the academic year came to a close, he needed a job. America was in the midst of the Great Depression and President Franklin D. Roosevelt's New Deal programme had been attracting the brightest minds to Washington, DC. Friedman's friend from Chicago, Allen Wallis, had gone to work for the National Resources Committee. He followed. Between 1935 and 1937 he worked on developing a cost of living index. His work there contributed towards the PhD he earned from Columbia and was the basis for *A Theory of the Consumption Function*, which he would publish twenty years later while a professor at Chicago. Friedman considered this his most technical piece of research, for which he was to later win the Nobel Prize, along with his work on monetary economics and business cycles.[5]

After two years in Washington, Friedman moved back to New York to work at the National Bureau of Economic Research (NBER). One of his professors from Columbia, Wesley Mitchell, was director. He also taught part-time at Columbia and worked as a research assistant for Simon Kuznets, who was to go on and win the 1971 Nobel Prize in economics. He had encouraged Friedman to work with empirical data, which at the time was a field in its formative stage, and became an important part of Friedman's approach to economics.

In September 1939 war broke out in Europe, but with little immediate effect on either Friedman or America generally, which was not to enter the war for another two years. So life continued fairly normally for Friedman. During the 1940–41 academic year, he moved to the University of Wisconsin as a visiting professor. By now he was twenty-eight, and it was his first proper academic appointment. Although he was then offered a non-tenured position at the university, he turned it down in order to head back to Washington to work as an aide to Secretary of the Treasury Henry Morgenthau, who had played a key role in developing and financing the New Deal under Roosevelt.

In 1943 he relocated again to New York to join the Statistical Research Group at Columbia University. This was a prolific research period, during which he spent time developing techniques for improving the measurement of war materials. It was a formidable department run by his friend Allen Wallis. In May 1945 the war in Europe was winding down and Friedman returned to teaching. His good friend from Chicago, George Stigler, who would go on to win the 1982 Nobel Prize, was at the University of Minnesota teaching microeconomics and put in a good word for him. Friedman joined to teach macroeconomics and through the academic year 1945–46, they shared an office, becoming known as 'Mr Micro' and 'Mr Macro'.[6]

Towards the end of the academic year, an opportunity arose at the University of Chicago. Ironically, it was Stigler who was targeted, but he failed his interview with the president of the university. Chicago was the then home to the Cowles Commission for Research in Economics, which was a centre focused on linking economics to mathematics. Stigler was not deemed mathematical enough. He was in good company. Friedrich Hayek also claimed he was rejected on similar grounds. But this meant that opportunity knocked for Friedman. Stigler was generous, saying that his own rejection was to be a great service to Chicago.[7]

Friedman started teaching at the University of Chicago in 1946. It was then, and still is, one of the world's leading departments for economics. Its faculty was full of eminence: twenty-nine winners of the Nobel Prize in Economic Sciences since its inception in 1969 have had some connection with Chicago's Department of Economics. But things had changed significantly since Friedman attended as a student a decade earlier. Its two leading lights had faded. Viner had moved to Princeton University, and Knight's influence in economics had waned as he moved into political philosophy.

The department had been the home of the Cowles Commission since 1939. Friedman certainly acknowledged the scholarship Cowles brought to the university, but ultimately saw the world differently. His background at the National Resources Committee, the Statistical Research Group and the NBER steered him towards a statistical presentation of economic data rather than the formulaic presentation of theory favoured by the commission. Friedman believed strongly that economic theory should be subject to empirical corroboration to test its relevance to the real world. Prediction was the key factor;

theories and policies should be evaluated not on the basis of the realism of their assumptions but solely on the basis of the accuracy of their predictions. He considered Cowles as excessively formal and too concerned with tautological mathematics rather than explaining the world.

Friedman was able to push Cowles out of Chicago as his own power in the faculty grew. In 1951 he was awarded the third ever John Bates Clark Medal, the then-biennial (since 2009, annual) award for the best American economist under the age of forty, and probably the most prestigious prize in economics at the time since the Nobel Prize in economics didn't yet exist. He was now where Viner had been previously as the dominant figure in the department. In fact, he was teaching Viner's old course on price theory.

He was a popular teacher, but at the same time a tough grader who demanded high standards. It was not uncommon for him to award no 'A' grades in an entire academic year, and often he would only read and grade the first 500–1,000 words of his students' essays to encourage them to write more clearly and concisely. If a student were late to class, he would usually stop teaching until the student had taken his seat. Students had to present their work in order to participate at his workshops. Despite these pressures and the risk of low grades, students flocked to his classes because of his insight and his explanatory powers. Outside the classroom he was regarded as kind and generous. When he and Rose spent a year travelling the world in the early 1960s, they were hosted by many of his former students.

The notion of the 'Chicago School' has become associated with monetarism (a belief that the total amount of money in an economy could not permanently alter the economy) and *laissez-faire* capitalism. It coincided with Friedman's tenure at the university, which was to span three decades between 1946 and 1976. Perhaps it should really be referred to as the 'Friedman School'?

In 1976, Friedman was awarded the Nobel Prize in economics. At the time, the award was then only in its seventh year, but it was still a big deal and, without any doubt, the biggest prize available in economics. His award raised eyebrows due to his perceived closeness to the Chilean junta led by General Augusto Pinochet which was then in government.

It was a controversial topic, particularly in Scandinavia with its strong social democratic tradition and home to many Chilean refugees.

Since the 1950s, a number of students from Chile had studied economics at the University of Chicago. Friedman had little direct contact with them unless they had either taken his course or attended his workshops. Before the military coup that brought Pinochet to power in 1973, free-market policy ideas held little sway in Chile. In March 1975 Friedman had visited Chile as part of the Chicago–Chilean studies programme. He met Pinochet for forty-five minutes. This trip was seen by many in the context of the growing influence of the 'Chicago Boys' in Chilean economic policy. As a result, Friedman was perceived to be closely associated with the regime, *The New York Times* going so far as to identify him personally as the guiding light of the junta's economic policy. There were protests at the University of Chicago and for the next decade Friedman often entered public debates through side entrances. As he stood to make his laureate speech, a member of the audience shouted: 'Down with capitalism. Freedom for Chile.' Friedman is so far the only recipient of a Nobel Prize to be heckled at his acceptance presentation.

Although he was an advocate of the economic reforms introduced in Chile, he never publicly endorsed or supported the regime. In fact, as a libertarian, the suppression of freedoms would have run counter to his beliefs. He himself viewed the protests as hypocritical and baseless. In a speech in Chile, Friedman had criticized the regime as being too restrictive and argued that freedom was the best way of achieving prosperity for the country. He turned down honorary degrees from Chilean universities since he did not want acceptance to be conveyed as support for the regime politically.

It should be said that the majority of the media was supportive of his award, including the *Wall Street Journal*, *The Financial Times* and *Newsweek*. He had, after all, been awarded the prize for his contribution to economics rather than politics.

In terms of his political leanings, Milton Friedman is closely associated with strong libertarian views. He once wrote:

Fortunately, we are waking up. We are again recognizing the dangers of an overgoverned society, coming to understand that good objectives can be perverted by bad means . . . Fortunately, also, we are as a people still free to choose which way we should go – whether to continue along the road we have been following to ever bigger government, or to call a halt and change direction.[8]

He also had some pithy sayings to encapsulate his views: 'If you put the federal government in charge of the Sahara Desert, in five years there'd be a shortage of sand.' And, in an echo of Adam Smith: 'With some notable exceptions, businessmen favor free enterprise in general but are opposed to it when it comes to themselves.'[9]

His views were set out in his best-selling *Capitalism and Freedom* (1962), which sold over a million copies. Despite its success, Friedman felt a little frustrated that it was not more widely acclaimed. Perhaps because Friedman was, as yet, little known outside economic and academic circles, it had largely been ignored by the main US publications. It was reviewed only by top-ranked economics journals such as the *American Economic Review*.

Capitalism and Freedom was largely collated from his Volker Lectures given between 1956 and 1961, organized by the William Volker Fund to promote libertarian views, and was strongly influenced by John Stuart Mill's *On Liberty*. The book argued for a limited role for government in a free society with more to be done by the market. He highlighted a number of unjustified activities of government. The list included unnecessary intervention in markets. Friedman opposed price support for agriculture, tariffs, rent control, minimum wages, maximum ceiling prices and fixed exchange rates. He also opposed direct government involvement in the economy, highlighting the detailed regulation of industry, the control of radio and television, toll roads, public housing and national parks, and the legal prohibition of carrying mail for profit as examples of taking government too far. Friedman was also in favour of the legalization of drugs, school vouchers, health saving accounts and an end to conscription in peacetime.

In short, Friedman advocated a limited role for government, countering objections with: 'Underlying most arguments against the free market is a lack of belief in freedom itself.'[10] For Friedman, each government policy needed to be carefully analysed for its impact on the economy. In his view: 'One of the great mistakes is to judge policies and programs by their intentions rather than their results.'[11]

He also argued for a negative income tax to replace the plethora of social security and welfare schemes and to guarantee a minimum income. This was first proposed in the 1950s, but became a serious policy prospect when in 1969 President Richard Nixon proposed the Family Assistance Program. It bears some resemblance to the universal basic income (UBI) now being debated, whereby the government gives a basic level of income to every citizen. Friedman's concept of a negative income tax would return income to those earning below a threshold. It is somewhat more complex than UBI, but would still have been simpler than the welfare system at the time. The original idea was to make sure that work paid more than state benefits. However, the work provision was eventually removed, much to the annoyance of Friedman. The idea dominated welfare reform discussions until failing in the Senate Finance Committee in 1970. Friedman also advocated a flat tax, which removed entirely any progressiveness in the tax system (when those with higher income levels pay a higher proportion of their earnings in tax). This was not just about incentivizing work but also about improving the simplicity of the system and lowering the high costs of compiling tax returns. In the end, he settled for a significant reduction in the top rate of tax from 70 per cent to 28 per cent, which President Ronald Reagan delivered in the 1980s.

A few years earlier, in 1977, Friedman had retired from the University of Chicago at the age of sixty-five. He took a role at the conservative Hoover Institution at Stanford University as a senior research fellow, where his wife also had an office. His intention was to do academic work at a more leisurely pace, and he and Rose collaborated on a number of papers, essays and books in the years that followed.

In 1980 the Friedmans published *Free to Choose*, which was the best-selling non-fiction title in the US that year, shifting some 400,000 copies. It was based on two principles. The first was the political freedom inherent in Thomas Jefferson's Declaration of Independence: the preservation of life, and liberty, and the pursuit of happiness. The second was Adam Smith's notion of economic freedom, where free exchange is to the benefit of the economy and was largely free from government intervention.

At the time, his old friend Allen Wallis had become chairman of the Corporation for Public Broadcasting (PBS) and had recommended Friedman for a programme. The Harvard economist John Kenneth Galbraith had recently filmed a series on the history of economic thought, and Friedman was thought to offer an ideological balance to Galbraith's more Keynesian views. So, $2.5 million was raised to film a documentary series consisting of ten episodes. Each show consisted of a half-hour presentation by Friedman on a specific topic followed by a discussion for the same period of time. *Free to Choose* earned Friedman more in royalties than all his other books combined, and the television series it accompanied made him a household name.

Friedman's political influence

After the publication of *A Monetary History* in 1963, Friedman stepped back from academic economics to pursue more political writing. In his early life, Friedman had never really exhibited any strong political leanings, but by then his teaching load had been much reduced and his academic endeavour was less intense than before. He felt the US was heading in a more libertarian direction, and compulsory conscription to fight in the Vietnam War had made his ideas popular among college graduates. It was also the time of libertarian thinkers such as Ayn Rand and Friedrich Hayek.

Milton Friedman was also becoming increasingly well known as a leading conservative economist. He became involved in Arizona Republican Senator Barry Goldwater's presidential campaign in 1964. A *Newsweek* article had suggested he could do for Goldwater what J. K. Galbraith had done for John F. Kennedy. Although Goldwater lost by a landslide to incumbent President Lyndon B. Johnson, the campaign gave Friedman exposure and a huge boost to his public profile. It led to a regular column in *Newsweek*, for which he wrote over 300 pieces between 1966 and 1984.

In the 1968 presidential race he was once again brought into the fray on the Republican side. His former mentor Arthur Burns, now a presidential counsellor and chairman-in-waiting of the Federal Reserve, had been asked to set up an advisory committee on the economy to provide recommendations to Richard Nixon, should he win. He did, and between 1970 and 1971 Friedman and the president met on several occasions, but the relationship was becoming fraught. Nixon had tried to persuade Friedman to use his relationship with Burns to put pressure on the Fed to lower interest rates but he refused. The 1971 wage and price controls introduced by Nixon were anathema to Friedman's free-market orthodoxy. In his memoirs, Friedman described this as the most damaging thing Nixon had done to the US, including the Watergate scandal that led to his resignation in 1974. His initial strong support for Nixon had become rather tepid as early as 1972.

In 1976 Friedman threw his support behind Ronald Reagan. He had first met Reagan in 1967 while he was a visiting professor at UCLA and Reagan had just been elected governor of California. They shared similar views on the funding of higher education. Reagan was ideologically close to Friedman. He had read some of the most free market of economists, including Ludwig von Mises and Friedrich Hayek. It was said he read *Capitalism and Freedom* while running for governor. In 1975 Reagan vacated that office, and a short while later Friedman indicated he would support his presidential campaign.

Reagan failed to win his party's nomination that year, but in 1980 became the Republican presidential candidate. Reagan made clear his economic convictions: control federal spending and rein back regulation, reduce personal income tax rates and introduce predictably sound and stable monetary policy. All of these could have come from Friedman. Reagan won a landslide victory over the Democratic incumbent, Jimmy Carter. Although Friedman did not serve in the Reagan administration, he was widely seen as the guru behind the scenes through the Economic Policy Advisory Board.

Despite his outspoken views, it was never thought that Friedman wanted a full-time political position. He turned down a seat on the

Council of Economic Advisers, the highest body advising the US president, on numerous occasions. He would almost certainly have accepted the post of Chairman of the Federal Reserve,[12] though it seems he was never offered it. He enjoyed, with Rose, a lifestyle that saw them spend various parts of the year in Chicago, Vermont, California and, of course, Washington, DC. Perhaps he also thought it would be better for his longer-term influence to not be hamstrung by having always to toe the party line as a government official.

Across the Atlantic, Friedman's thinking had found an additional home in the UK. Prime Minister Margaret Thatcher was ideologically similar to Reagan, and Britain was set for a radical change in direction. In the 1970s the economic policy debate in Britain was essentially Friedman versus Keynes. Friedman had even debated with well-known Keynesians on British TV, which revealed him to be an effective communicator. Friedman's style was to have a very simple, punchy message and stick to it. His opponents pointed to all the complexities and difficulties, and probably lost the audience as a result. After one such debate a journalist asked a Keynesian who would win if Friedman had debated Keynes himself. The answer was: Friedman would win, but Keynes would be right!

In addition, much of Friedman's thinking had been disseminated through the right-wing think tank, the Institute of Economic Affairs, where his views on the inadequacy of Keynesian stabilization policy and the benefits of a low-tax, low-regulation economy and monetary stability had enjoyed an enthusiastic audience. In Reagan and Thatcher, Milton Friedman had found two world leaders who were acolytes of the free-market capitalism and monetarist ideologies he had championed over the previous two decades.

Friedman's influence didn't end there. His seminal work in economics was no less influential in shaping how modern central banking still works today. *A Monetary History of the United States, 1867–1960* was perhaps Milton Friedman's magnum opus in terms of economic ideas. It was jointly authored with Anna Jacobson Schwartz, with whom he began work in 1948, but it wasn't until 1963 that their 884-page treatise was published. The work had initially been commissioned by the National Bureau of Economic Research. Arthur Burns had replaced Wesley Mitchell as director and he asked Friedman to study monetary factors in economic activity, especially in the business cycle.

The research was to question the Keynesian view of the Great Depression. Keynes had identified the weakness of aggregate demand stemming from an excess of saving and a dearth of investment in the aftermath of the stock market crash of 1929 as the main cause. This gave credence to the idea that the New Deal programmes of President Franklin D. Roosevelt helped to resolve the crisis. The Keynesian view gave little weight to monetary factors. With interest rates having fallen close to zero, an active monetary policy which sought to stimulate the economy through changing rates would be like 'pushing on a piece of string'. Just as pushing on a piece of string does nothing of substance, interest rates that low likewise cannot move the economy in any direction. So, the Keynesians concluded that the Fed had done everything it could and that monetary policy had simply run out of bite.

Friedman and Schwartz categorically disagreed and placed monetary forces at the heart of the crisis. The project was very data intensive, mainly because much of the necessary information on the stock of money had not yet been collected. Until Friedman and Schwartz developed the M1 and M2 metrics of measuring the money supply, the Federal Reserve had no way of gauging the amount of money in the economy. They were to conclude that, had the Federal Reserve been publishing these statistics between 1929 and 1933, the Great Crash may have never become the Great Depression, or at least the magnitude and persistence of the downturn would have been mitigated because the negative impact of monetary policy would have been evident.

In fact, they said the stock market crash of 1929 was partly the result of the Federal Reserve's actions in 1928. The stock market had risen sharply at the back end of the 1920s, causing the Fed to implement a deliberate tightening of policy in the spring of 1928 to curb speculation on Wall Street. The governor of the influential New York Fed, Benjamin Strong, had strong reservations about using monetary policy to constrain the boom, but died in October 1928. His death created a leadership vacuum at one of the twelve regional banks that feed into the US central bank's decisions. Friedman and Schwartz argued that, had it not been for the premature death of Strong, many of the subsequent mistakes made by the Fed might have been avoided. His successor, George Harrison, was more in line with the rest of the thinking of the central bank in pushing for an interest rate hike. Rates subsequently rose to 5 per cent, the highest since 1921. This was sufficient to slow the growth of the US economy, which hit its cyclical peak in August 1929. The downturn in the economy was a precursor to the stock market crash in October.

Friedman and Schwartz, though, did not see the Great Depression as the inevitable conclusion of the crash of 1929. The stock market did lose half its value between September and November, including a big drop on Black Tuesday, 29 October. However, the market had doubled in the previous eighteen months and stocks actually recovered 20 per cent in the six months after the crash. There had also been plenty of other significant falls in the stock market in recent history that had not resulted in depression. The US economy had experienced bigger shocks that were not followed by a protracted downturn.

In the first year of the Great Depression, US GDP dropped by a massive 12 per cent and unemployment increased to 9 per cent. However, falling prices or deflation in 1920–21 had seen a decline in national output of some 7 per cent and a rise in unemployment to between 9 and 12 per cent. Despite this, the rest of the 1920s had been a rip-roaring time for the American economy.

One of the key findings in *A Monetary History* was what Friedman and Schwartz described as the 'Great Contraction' between 1929 and 1933. They were referring not to a large drop in GDP or prices, but to a decline in the amount of money available in the economy as a consequence of widespread bank failures. In the year following the crash, the US money supply fell by a relatively small 2.6 per cent as the Federal Reserve cut interest rates and lent heavily to the banking sector. Injecting a great deal of cash into banks gave them some much-needed liquidity and prevented the stock market collapse from precipitating an immediate banking crisis. However, the Fed believed that further loosening of monetary policy might pump up the stock market bubble and lead to inflation.

Between 1930 and 1933 the US money supply contracted by over a third, coinciding with a raft of bank failures. Between October 1930 and March 1933 there were four major bank runs. Most of these occurred between August 1931 and January 1932, when there were 1,860 bank failures and the money supply fell at an annual rate of 31 per cent. As deposits were withdrawn for fear of failure, banks had less money to lend, so the supply of credit to the economy evaporated, which led to downward pressure on output and prices.

It was not just fear of encouraging a further run-up in prices of assets such as stocks that had made the Federal Reserve reluctant to pump money into the economy, where it was especially needed by a banking sector which was haemorrhaging deposits. The US had maintained its membership of the gold standard, an international system of fixed exchange rates. In September 1931 a wave of speculative attacks on sterling had forced Great Britain out of the standard. Speculators thought the economy was weak, so the currency should weaken too, which was not possible since it was fixed to a set amount against gold. They sold off sterling, which meant the British government needed to use its gold reserves to maintain the value of the currency. That was considered too expensive, so Britain abandoned the gold standard. As speculators turned their attack towards the US, the Fed was forced to raise interest rates to make buying the dollar more attractive. They tightened monetary policy between August 1931 and January 1932 to stem the outflow of gold as international investors liquidated their dollar deposits.

Friedman was not an advocate of fixed exchange rates. Continued membership of the gold standard, he believed, had held the Fed back from a more convincing monetary stimulus. He observed that the best performing countries through the early 1930s were those that were not in the gold standard, those that had abandoned the system and those that were in the standard but had large gold reserves. In each of these three cases, the countries involved could exercise more flexibility in monetary policy in response to the economic depression.

Friedman and Schwartz argued that this might have prevented the Federal Reserve from being more active and forceful. To emphasize the point, they cited the events of April to August 1932, when the Fed, under pressure from Congress, made a $1 billion open-market purchase (a monetary injection equivalent to about 2 per cent of national income) which was successful in stemming the drop in the money supply and stimulating a small rise in GDP and industrial production. But when Congress broke for recess and the economy looked like it was on the turn, the loosening of policy ended. Friedman and Schwartz argued that, had it not done so, the economy may well have continued to improve.

The Fed was also a poor lender of last resort to the banking system. There was little coordination between the Federal Reserve Board of Governors based in Washington and the Regional Reserve Banks. There was also a stigma attached to accessing the Federal Reserve's discount window facilities, which allowed financial institutions access to emergency funding from the central bank in times of stress as banks did not want to advertise their vulnerability in case it might ignite a run on their deposits. In any case, access to the window was limited and only associated banks were eligible. The liquidity support for the banking system was severely flawed.

In November 1932, Franklin D. Roosevelt won a landslide victory against Herbert Hoover, with the Democrats also taking large majorities in both Houses of Congress. However, FDR didn't assume office until March 1933 and in the meantime, bank failures continued. It was widely believed that FDR would devalue the dollar or leave the gold standard altogether. It was costly to maintain a currency peg to gold, especially when the economy was in serious trouble. This encouraged the large-scale conversion of dollars into gold, putting further pressure on the banking system as dollar deposits were withdrawn.

One of FDR's first acts on taking office was a week-long banking holiday from which 5,000 banks never reopened their doors. However, this allowed the insolvent banks to be weeded out. The New Deal programme that significantly increased government spending to boost the economy was also in force, but Friedman and Schwartz pointed to the dollar devaluation of 60 per cent and its exit from the gold standard as the more important factors in halting the Great Contraction. It returned monetary freedom to US policymakers.

Between 1933 and 1936 there was a strong recovery and reflation in the US economy. The 1933 and 1935 Banking Acts introduced changes to the Federal Reserve System to enhance the ability of the Fed to stabilize the banking system. The measures included extending the ability of the Federal Reserve to more easily lend money based on receiving collateral, including to non-financial firms; the Glass–Steagall Act, resulting in the separation of commercial and investment banking functions; regulation of deposit interest rates; and strict limits on entry to the market. Also important was the creation of the Federal Deposit Insurance Corporation (FDIC) in 1933 to stem the problem of ruinous bank runs. The FDIC remains in place today and guarantees that depositors won't lose their money (currently up to $250,000) if a bank goes under.

The bottom line from *A Monetary History* was that the Fed caused the crisis, turning a stock market crash into a full-blown depression by failing to pump sufficient liquidity into the economy to support the banks. Instead, they allowed runs on bank deposits to proceed relatively unchecked, resulting in bank failures and a severe deflation in output and prices. In a speech given in 2002 to commemorate Milton Friedman's ninetieth birthday, then Fed chairman Ben Bernanke apologized on behalf of his organization. He said: 'You're right, we did it. We're very sorry. But thanks to you, we won't do it again.'[13]

Little did he know that soon, he would be given the opportunity to live up to these words.

Friedman and the 2008 financial crisis

The global financial crisis occurred in 2008 with repercussions across the world economy. Financial deregulation since the 1980s meant that financial markets and global linkages across national borders became much more diverse. Then, in 1999, the Gramm–Leach–Bliley Act repealed the Glass–Steagall Act of 1933 that had previously separated retail from investment banking. More of the risks undertaken by investment banks could be transmitted to retail (deposit-holding) banks. In the 2008 crisis, we were at the cusp of the first potential systemic banking failure since the 1929 crash that had led to the passage of Glass–Steagall in the first place.

European banks were exposed to US sub-prime mortgages and some had also borrowed from US wholesale money markets. It meant that European bank lending became less reliant on deposits since they could access the same cheap money as the Americans. When Northern Rock failed in 2007, it was the first bank run in Britain in more than a century. The UK is closely linked to US financial markets and also faced the prospect of a systemic banking collapse during the 2008 crisis.

So, did central banks act sufficiently to avoid repeating the mistakes of the 1929 crash? Have central banks learned the lessons from the Great Depression, including those set out by Milton Friedman, whose seminal research changed our view of the 1930s?

Ben Bernanke, like Friedman, was also a scholar of the Great Depression. Therefore, when the global financial crisis struck in 2008, he was well placed as Fed chair to prevent the same mistakes from happening again.

Like the Great Depression, the recent financial crisis was preceded by an asset price boom, but this time centred in the housing market rather than the stock exchange. According to the Case-Shiller repeat sales index, US house prices doubled between 1999 and 2007. This was largely due to a huge expansion in housing credit. The quasi-government enterprises Fannie Mae and Freddie Mac strongly supported government policy to extend home ownership to lower income households by effectively underwriting mortgages requiring smaller down payments and allowing higher price-to-income ratios. The result was an increase in mortgage lending to less financially secure households. NINJA (no income, no job, no assets) and NO-DOC (no documentations) were acronyms that became commonplace in the mortgage market. There was rapid growth in the two riskiest components of the market, sub-prime and Alt-A mortgages, which are both below 'prime' or the standard measure of creditworthiness.

Despite this, the banking sector had, or so it thought, found a way to mitigate the increased riskiness of lending. Riskier mortgages could be repackaged with others into mortgage-backed securities (MBS) and given the highest (AAA) credit ratings for the creditworthiness of the debt, while still offering a higher rate of return than other safe assets such as Treasury bills. Credit default swaps (CDS) could be purchased to provide insurance against any losses should there be a default. Bankers created funds, such as special purpose vehicles (SPVs) and structured investment vehicles (SIVs), to hoover up these financially engineered securities offering better returns than safe assets like government debt, and sell the SPVs and SIVs to clients. These special funds often borrowed heavily in the money markets and, being based offshore, avoided the capital requirements and regulatory oversight of other financial institutions. Between 2001 and 2005 there was a lending boom in America like no other.

The collapse in house prices in 2007 triggered massive defaults in the US mortgage market. Homeowners with negative equity walked away from their properties. It meant that the originators of mortgages, or those that had bought mortgage-backed securities, found themselves with assets worth less than their liabilities. The banks were in trouble.

It is true that this financial crisis, though, differed from the Great Depression in several important ways, thus the lessons from the 1930s may not have carried over exactly, but it is still useful to compare the two. The Great Depression analysed by Friedman and Schwartz in *A Monetary History* was essentially a liquidity crisis. Banks facing runs on their deposits needed a forceful and competent lender of last resort to stem the flow. Here, the Federal Reserve failed.

In the global financial crisis, the biggest problem was solvency rather than liquidity. It became difficult to price complicated and opaque securities backed by a pool of assets where the value, quality and riskiness of each were difficult to ascertain. So the credit market could not determine which firms were solvent and which were not. Naturally, lenders were unwilling to extend loans without being able to determine the creditworthiness of the borrower. Most of these problems lay with the investment banks.

The Fed reacted quickly to the crisis. It cut interest rates sharply and extended discount window facilities. Learning the lessons from the previous crisis, the TAF (term auction facility) enabled banks to bid anonymously for funds from the Fed and avoid the stigma of being seen as an institution in trouble. Transparency in policymaking is usually considered preferable, but in crisis mode opacity might be the better option.

The Federal Reserve also made a number of large-scale asset purchases in a process known as quantitative easing (QE). Between November 2008 and June 2010 it purchased around $175 billion of long-term securities, thus injecting that amount of cash into the economy. In November 2010, as the economy wobbled, it made further purchases of long-term Treasury bonds amounting to $600 billion in its QEII programme. Finally, a third dose of QE was initiated in September 2012 when the Fed announced the purchase of $40 billion in mortgage-backed securities each month for an indefinite period. This was dubbed 'QE infinity' by investors. The final QE programme was raised to $85 billion in December, before being tapered back to $65 billion per month in June 2013. By the time QE was halted in October 2014, the three QE programmes had seen the Federal Reserve accumulate a staggering $4.5 trillion in assets.

As a result, the M2 measure of money supply, which had tanked during the Great Depression, had increased sharply in the global financial crisis following the large expansion of the Federal Reserve's balance sheet. A repeat of the bank panics and runs seen between 1930 and 1933 was also avoided.

Would Friedman have approved of the QE and other policies used in dealing with the 2008 crisis?

In terms of purchasing government debt such as Treasury bonds in order to drive down long-term interest rates and inject liquidity into the banking system, he would have been undoubtedly in favour. However, the purchase of mortgage-backed securities in his mind might have been conceived as a bailout of a troubled asset. His prescription for the Great Depression was for the Fed to provide liquidity, not bailouts.

The Fed's response to the crisis also involved the direct rescue of certain financial institutions deemed too systemically important to fail. The investment bank Bear Stearns was particularly exposed to the US mortgage market and in 2008 was rescued by JPMorgan in a move strongly backed by the Federal Reserve. This was justified by the risk posed by Bear, the collapse of which could have brought down the entire banking system. In July 2008 the US Treasury bailed out and part-nationalized the government-supported enterprises at the heart of the crisis, Fannie Mae and Freddie Mac.

However, a couple of months later, Lehman Brothers was allowed to go bust. The fallout was to turn a US mortgage market crisis into a global financial crisis. Bernanke was later to argue in a 2012 speech that because Lehman was insolvent and posed less of a systemic risk than Bear Stearns, the Federal Reserve had no legal standing to make a bailout using public funds. The next day, however, the giant insurance firm AIG was rescued as the Fed was concerned about the impact on the credit default swap market if it were allowed to fail.

In the global financial crisis, the Federal Reserve provided direct credit to specific markets and businesses in need of liquidity. Friedman's recommended approach in the Great Depression was simply to flood the economy with general liquidity and allow solvency issues to sort themselves out. He might have viewed the targeted interventions made by the Fed, i.e. to save Bear Stearns and AIG but allow Lehman Brothers to go under, as undermining its independence and credibility and getting involved in specific cases.

However, the world in 2008 was different from 1929. There were now players in the financial sector that were literally too big to fail, in the sense that they might bring down the entire system with them. This was not such a problem in the Great Depression, when the systemic risks of any specific bank failure were quite low. With this in mind, Friedman might have grudgingly accepted Bernanke's approach as the best way forward. Of course, he would have been against the involvement of government-supported enterprises in the US housing market in the first place, and would have viewed the crisis as largely a result of the government's unsuccessful intervention in the mortgage market.

There is no doubt that Friedman's scholarship changed perceptions of the Great Depression. By focusing on the role of monetary policy, it greatly aided the response to the more recent crisis. But what about the unconventional monetary policies used afterwards to support the recovery?

The effectiveness of QE still relies to some extent on an ill-functioning banking system. It's all very well to create money; but that money still has to get out into the economy so small firms in particular can borrow and invest. There has been some evidence of positive impact from these unconventional monetary policies along those lines, but some worry about the side effects of increasing the supply of money so dramatically, especially since some of the money has flowed into stock markets which had reached heady heights around the world. It's fair to say the jury is largely still out.

Milton Friedman, though, was generally supportive of QE, which he witnessed in action in Japan. Japan was the first country to adopt QE after its real-estate bubble burst in the early 1990s, so this policy was initially used nearly two decades before the global financial crisis. Friedman approved of what the Japanese central bank did, commenting on their policy: 'The surest road to a healthy economic recovery is to increase the rate of monetary growth.'[14] He argued that the Bank of Japan should undertake QE since interest rates had been cut to rock bottom and the economy was still in dire straits:

> Defenders of the Bank of Japan will say, 'How? The bank has already cut its discount rate to 0.5 per cent. What more can it do to increase the quantity of money?' The answer is straightforward: The Bank of Japan can buy government bonds on the open market, paying for them with either currency or deposits at the Bank of Japan, what economists call high-powered money. Most of the proceeds will end up in commercial banks, adding to their reserves and enabling them to expand their liabilities by loans and open market purchases. But whether they do so or not, the money supply will increase . . . There is no limit to the extent to which the Bank of Japan can increase the money supply if it wishes to do so.[15]

Since he supported QE in Japan, Friedman would have viewed the use of unconventional policies such as cash injections by the US, the UK, the euro area and elsewhere as just as necessary to get lending going in these economies. Central banks in Japan and Europe setting negative interest rates would fall under the same canopy of using a novel tool to try to increase the flow of money into the economy.

But Friedman would have viewed more cautiously the grant of macroprudential policy which gives central banks more direct power to regulate markets to further their monetary policy aims. However, the financial system is much more complex and global today, so Friedmanites may well support the notion that targeting credit and debt levels has become an important area for central banks to manage as part of keeping the monetary system stable. Working out how these policies of targeting inflation and financial stability should work together would surely have been up Friedman's street as economists are now devising a framework for a new monetary policy era.

Finally, for those who question the effectiveness of unconventional tools, particularly QE, Friedman would probably point to the successful winding down of this policy as the American economy has recovered. Even if these policies generated some adverse consequences such as pushing up stock prices, the priority would be to keep monetary policies supportive until the economy was on a sound footing.

Friedman would say that not acting to keep money flowing in the system was the reason why the Great Depression was 'Great'. In response to critics of Japan's loose money policy, Friedman wrote in the *Wall Street Journal*: 'After the US experience during the Great Depression, and after inflation and rising interest rates in the 1970s and disinflation and falling interest rates in the 1980s, I thought the fallacy of identifying tight money with high interest rates and easy money with low interest rates was dead. Apparently, old fallacies never die.'[16]

He warned that this mistake should not be repeated. After all, it was four years after the US economy was thought to have recovered in 1933 that the country was plunged back into recession in 1937. As policymakers contemplate potential parallels to the 1930s, Friedman would have urged them to heed this lesson and not rein back monetary policy prematurely.

Two Lucky People

Milton and Rose Friedman's long marriage and partnership extended beyond family life. They formed a prolific pair, especially in their later years at the Hoover Institution, when Friedman had stepped back from academic economics to focus on his popular writing. It was during this collaborative time that they co-authored the best-selling *Free to Choose* in 1980 as well as *Tyranny of the Status Quo*, published in 1984. They also co-wrote *Two Lucky People: Memoirs*, published in 1998.

Friedman himself regarded *Capitalism and Freedom*, published in 1962, to be 'a better book' than the very commercially successful *Free to Choose*, published two decades later.[17] He thought it was 'more philosophical and abstract, and hence more fundamental'.[18] In his view, the latter book complements the former. Friedman even named his Vermont hilltop home, situated in 120 acres, 'Capitaf' after *Capitalism and Freedom*.[19] However, most economists would regard his *A Monetary History of the United States, 1867–1960*, written with Anna Jacobson Schwartz, as his finest work.

Rose outlived Friedman by three years, passing away at the ripe age of ninety-eight in 2009. She would have witnessed her husband's work being invoked and applied to the first systemic banking crisis since the one of their formative years in the 1930s.

Milton Friedman would have relished that his widow saw his research being applied: 'The true test of any scholar's work is not what his contemporaries say, but what happens to his work in the next twenty-five or fifty years. And the thing that I will really be proud of is if some of the work I have done is still cited in the textbooks long after I am gone.'[20]

CHAPTER 11

Douglass North: Why are so Few Countries Prosperous?

It's one of the enduring conundrums of our time: why so few countries are prosperous. But will it remain one? There has been tremendous progress, so much so that the World Bank has stopped categorizing countries as 'developed' or 'developing' and now uses regional classifications instead. Are we really about to witness the end of poverty and find the solution to the decades-old question of why so few countries are rich?

How few is few? Well, of the just under two hundred countries in the world that produce economic data, only about fifty are classified as high income. It is a difficult club to join. The World Bank estimates that of the 101 countries that were classified as middle-income in 1960, just a baker's dozen had become prosperous by 2008.[1] Those whose per capita GDP or average income have approached the level of the United States are: Equatorial Guinea, Greece, Hong Kong SAR (China), Ireland, Israel, Japan, Mauritius, Portugal, Puerto Rico, Singapore, South Korea, Spain and Taiwan.

The answer to why only thirteen countries have become rich in the past half-century should include an analysis of the types of institutions that underpin their economies. Possessing good institutions is what economists have come to focus on after standard economic factors, such as capital, labour (including human capital that accounts for education and skills) and technological progress specified in neoclassical growth models, have been unable to explain in full why some nations prosper while many do not.

The seminal research on institutions and economic development was pioneered by Douglass North. He, and those who followed him, systematically analysed how some countries adopted good institutions and what might be done to reform the bad ones. North observed:

> The evolution of government from its medieval, mafia-like character to that embodying modern legal institutions and instruments is a major part of the history of freedom. It is a part that tends to be obscured or ignored because of the myopic vision of many economists, who persist in modeling government as nothing more than a gigantic form of theft and income redistribution.[2]

In North's view, the existing models were unable to answer the essential question as to why economic growth varies across nations:

> What accounts for their widely disparate performance characteristics? This divergence is even more perplexing in terms of standard neoclassical and international trade theory, which implies that over time economies, as they traded goods, services, and productive factors, would gradually converge. Although we do observe some convergence among leading industrial nations that trade with each other, an overwhelming feature of the last ten millennia is that we have evolved into radically different religious, ethnic, cultural, political, and economic societies, and the gap between rich and poor nations, between developed and undeveloped nations, is as wide today as it ever was and perhaps a great deal wider than ever before.[3]

It seems hardly radical, but North took economics out of its comfort zone, which consisted of examining more easily measured inputs like labour and capital and instead brought in politics, sociology and history in order to understand why some countries succeed and others fail.

North won the Nobel Prize in economics in 1993. Along with his fellow laureates Ronald Coase (who won in 1991) and Oliver Williamson (who won more than a decade later in 2009), North founded the field of New Institutional Economics. This work was later expanded upon by MIT economist Daron Acemoglu and University of Chicago political scientist James Robinson, notably in their book *Why Nations Fail: The Origins of Power, Prosperity, and Poverty*, and by many others who have built on North's work on the role of institutions in economic development.

North spent his career trying to find the reasons behind economic disparity, which he formalized as: 'What accounts for societies experiencing long-run stagnation or an absolute decline in economic well-being?'[4] This is the question posed in this chapter, and is also, perhaps, the key economic challenge of our time.

The life and times of Douglass North

Douglass North was born in 1920 in Cambridge, Massachusetts. His father's job as an insurance executive meant that the family moved frequently during North's childhood. He lived in both Canada and Switzerland as well as in several US states. For his first degree, North pursued a triple major in philosophy, political science and economics at the University of California at Berkeley. His recollection of his studies will give many hope: 'My record at the University of California as an undergraduate was mediocre to say the best.'[5]

He became a navigator in the Merchant Marine in the Second World War after graduation. He had hoped to go to law school, but the war intervened and he ended up serving. North explained: 'I was a conscientious objector. I didn't want to kill anybody. I picked something where other people would shoot at me but I wouldn't shoot back.'[6]

It was during these three years, which North said gave him time to read, that led him to relinquish his plans for a career in law. Instead, he thought that he should become an economist or a photographer. They were certainly diverse choices. The former won out because, as he recalled: 'what I wanted to do with my life was to improve societies, and the way to do that was to find out what made economies work the way they did or fail to work'.[7]

Towards the end of the Second World War, North married for the first time and subsequently fathered three sons. His second marriage was in 1972, to Elisabeth Case. They met when she was an editor at Cambridge University Press, having previously worked at Michigan University Press. After their marriage, she was credited with editing some of his articles.

After the war, North returned to the University of California at Berkeley to earn a PhD in economics. His first academic job, which he took up in 1951, was at the University of Washington. He remained there for 32 years until he joined Washington University in St Louis, where he spent the rest of his career. He also held visiting professorships at Cambridge, Stanford and Rice Universities, though none of North's permanent appointments were at top-ranked universities. This illustrates not only that it is possible to succeed outside of the top universities, but also how difficult it is to gain acceptance from them for unorthodox ideas.

As noted, after four decades of research he won the highest prize in the discipline, receiving the Nobel Prize in economics in 1993 for his pioneering work on institutions and how they influence economic development. This was a question that interested North from the very start of his career. Even his PhD dissertation focused on explaining differential regional growth rates within the US, and was the basis of his first book, *The Economic Growth of the United States from 1790 to 1860*, published in 1961.

In 1966–67 came a change of focus as North decided to study European economies after he received a grant to live in Geneva for a year. It was an intellectual turning point:

> I quickly became convinced that the tools of neo-classical economic theory were not up to the task of explaining the kind of fundamental societal change that had characterized European economies from medieval times onward. We needed new tools, but they simply did not exist . . . it was not possible to explain long-run poor economic performance in a neo-classical framework. So I began to explore what was wrong.[8]

It was a long road, and one that eventually led him to work with political scientists in the 1980s. That research culminated in his seminal work, *Institutions, Institutional Change and Economic Perform-ance*, published in 1990. His research filled a gap in economics, offering an explanation of why so many countries remain poor:

> The disparity in the performance of economies and the persistence of disparate economies through time have not been satisfactorily explained by development economists, despite forty years of immense effort. The simple fact is that the theory employed is not up to the task.
>
> . . . Put simply, what has been missing is an understanding of the nature of human coordination and cooperation. Now, that certainly should not surprise a disciple of Adam Smith. Smith was concerned not only with those forms of cooperation that produced collusive and monopolistic outcomes, but also with those forms of cooperation that would permit realization of the gains from trade.[9]

North created a new way of thinking about economics, which put human behaviour at the core. It led to a long career of not just research but also policy engagement. North was advising countries around the world on applying institutional analysis to their growth policies while in his eighties![10]

Douglass North believed that institutions are the key to understand-ing the development of an economy. In the Preface to *Institutions, Institutional Change and Economic Performance* he wrote: 'History mat-ters. It matters not just because we can learn from the past, but because the present and the future are connected to the past by the continuity of a society's institutions.'[11]

He was not the first scholar to deploy history in economic argument, but he pioneered the incorporation of institutions into economic ana-lysis. North defined institutions as: 'the rules of the game in a society . . . Institutions reduce uncertainty by providing a structure to everyday life.'[12] So, institutions can be formal, such as laws, or informal, such as those that police societal norms of behaviour. North believes both can evolve over time, which is why history matters a great deal in under-standing how development occurs. His work rejected the separation of political and social institutions from the workings of the economy.

North argued: 'Institutions affect the performance of the economy by their effect on the costs of exchange and production.'[13] In other words, poor institutions are costly. At a minimum, excessive regulations are burdensome and add cost to doing business. At the extreme, economies cannot grow if there are unstable political institutions that lead to war or conflict.

Understanding this link between institutions and development points the way to the necessary reforms. For instance, North attributes the success of the United States to its institutions: 'US economic history has been characterized by a federal political system, checks and balances, and a basic structure of property rights that have encouraged the long-term contracting essential to the creation of capital markets and economic growth,' and contrasts that with its southern neighbours that have struggled to develop beyond middle-income status: 'Latin American economic history, in contrast, has perpetuated the centralized, bureaucratic traditions carried over from its Spanish/Portuguese heritage.'[14]

Through studying these economies, North concludes that the institutions that have been good for development include the rule of law as well as openness to globalization. Those institutions provide positive incentives for people to engage in business and productive activities, which generate economic growth. Specifically, he points to market-supporting institutions as important: 'the underlying institutional framework persistently reinforced incentives for organizations to engage in productive activity'.[15] In particular, North believed that institutions mattered for technological progress, a key element of economic growth. North found this was common among prosperous economies, such as the United Kingdom: 'The security of property rights and the development of the public and private capital market were instrumental factors not only in England's subsequent rapid economic development, but in its political hegemony and ultimate dominance of the world.'[16]

He believed that the lack of such good institutions is why some developing countries have lagged behind. In his view, many of their institutions do not provide the sort of positive incentives that exist in the US and UK: 'The opportunities for political and economic entrepreneurs are still a mixed bag, but they overwhelmingly favor activities that promote redistributive rather than productive activity, that create monopolies rather than competitive conditions, and that restrict opportunities rather than expand them. They seldom induce investment in education that increases productivity.'[17]

He also believed that institutions perpetuate themselves. This view that good and bad institutions tend to self-perpetuate implies there is 'path dependence' in economic development. Path dependence was used by North to explain vicious circles of poverty and virtuous circles of growth. In a virtuous circle, the government invested in education and technological improvements that reinforced the good institutions, which generated growth that helped such good institutions to persist. In other words, path dependence means that good or bad institutions lead to persistently good or bad institutions, which reinforce an economy's growth path – either positively or negatively. What comes next depends on what has come before.

For North, path dependence helps to explain differential long-run economic outcomes. It's also why he posited that it's hard to reform economies to change their course, which will require political and social change that can be slow to bring about: 'Reversal of paths (from stagnation to growth or vice versa) . . . will typically occur through changes in the polity.'[18]

Before we look at what North would say about how to address the current development challenge, let's first examine in more detail why so many countries remain poor.

The development challenge

One aspect of the development challenge may not exist for long. The United Nations, with the support of all countries around the world, and the World Bank have set an ambitious target of ending extreme poverty by 2030. It would mean that, for the first time, there would be no one who lives on less than $1.90 per day, adjusted for what a dollar buys in the country or 'purchasing power parity'. What would it take? Could we really see the end of poverty?

First, there has been a great deal of progress already. The poverty rate in the developing world has fallen dramatically since 1981. Back then, more than half (52 per cent) of the global population lived on less than $1.25 per day. That's dropped to around 10 per cent under the comparable measure of $1.90 per day.

One of the UN's Millennium Development Goals (MDGs) was to halve poverty by 2015 from 1990 levels. In fact, this was achieved five years early. In 1990, more than one-third (36 per cent) of the world's population lived in abject poverty. That was halved to 18 per cent in 2010, due largely to China's rapid economic growth, and progress in the East Asian region. Four out of five people lived in poverty in 1981 and that has fallen to 8 per cent. On current trends, the fastest growing region in the world could see the end of poverty within a generation.

Sub-Saharan Africa is the only region where the number of people living in extreme poverty has increased during the past three decades. Even though the percentage of the African population living in extreme poverty is slightly lower than in 1981, population growth means that there is a greater number of people living in poverty. They account for more than half of the extreme poor in the world, despite Africa making up only 11 per cent of the global population.

In all, over a billion people have been lifted out of poverty worldwide since 1990, which is an extraordinary achievement. For the first time in history, just one in ten people live in extreme poverty around the world, and both the United Nations and the World Bank believe we are moving towards the historic goal of ending extreme poverty by 2030, so achieving the first of the Sustainable Development Goals (SDGs) adopted in 2015.*

Could we really be the first generation in history to succeed in eradicating global poverty? What precisely does the end of poverty look like? It doesn't mean that no one lives on less than $1.90 per day.

---

* The other sixteen Sustainable Development Goals are: zero hunger; good health and well-being; quality education; gender equality; clean water and sanitation; affordable and clean energy; decent work and economic growth; industry, innovation and infrastructure; reduced inequalities; sustainable cities and communities; responsible consumption and production; climate change; life below water; life on land; peace, justice and strong institutions; partnerships for the goals.

The World Bank assumes that a 3 per cent poverty rate is equivalent to the end of poverty since there will be some who move into poverty only temporarily, perhaps when they lose their jobs. This is known as 'frictional' poverty.

To get to that point would take a heroic effort. The number of poor people will have to decrease by 50 million every year until 2030. That is the equivalent of a million people per week. That pace is daunting. If met, it would mean lifting all but a quarter of a billion people out of an estimated 8.6 billion people on the planet then out of abject poverty.

Which policies might get us to that outcome? A country that we can perhaps learn from is fast-growing China. It had a higher poverty rate in 1990 than Africa, yet it has accounted for the bulk of global poverty reduction in the past few decades. But growth alone is clearly not enough, since Africa, the second fastest growing region in the world after Asia, has failed to make similar progress.

Drawing lessons from one country or region to another always needs to be done carefully and the Chinese economy is in transition from central planning under the governance of a one-party state, as discussed in the Marx chapter. That means, for instance, that land is effectively owned by the government and leased from the state. It doesn't mean that some haven't become very wealthy developing land gained through government favour, but most people have been lifted out of poverty through self-employment and not by exploiting the land and its resources. This is in contrast to Africa, where, as Oxford economist Paul Collier points out, unlike China, income growth has been based on natural resources and the gains have not been widely shared.[19]

In China, policies were designed to raise the productivity of agriculture, which lifted hundreds of millions out of poverty in rural areas. The World Bank has proposed similar targeted growth policies, such as supporting agricultural productivity, in developing countries.

Unlike Africa, China did not rely much on overseas aid, a standard tool in poverty alleviation policies. This has contributed to the mixed evidence about the impact of aid on reducing poverty, which has led to a fiery debate. Still, the UK-based Overseas Development

Institute (ODI) believes that there is a role for aid, but that there needs to be an overhaul of the way it is used.

So, it is tricky to apply lessons drawn from the past to the remaining stubborn pockets of poverty. Around half of the extreme poor live in Africa and another third in South Asia. For instance, Tanzania, which has grown well and been devoid of conflict, has seen the number of poor increase from 9 million two decades ago to 15 million. South Asia also lags in terms of the progress made in East Asia despite its growth, so again it is not possible to count on growth alone to lift the remaining 767 million people out of poverty.

Doubtless, the circumstances of individual countries matter a great deal in terms of what works, as North would stress. But if the progress made in the past couple of decades can be replicated in some fashion and tailored to individual countries, then it's possible that the remaining poor could be lifted out of abject poverty. That would imply that the 36 per cent poverty rate in 1990, which had dropped to 18 per cent in 2010, would fall by a comparable magnitude by 2030. It would indeed mean the end of poverty in our lifetimes. As Nobel laureate Robert Lucas, Jr, remarked:

> Is there some action a government of India could take that would lead the Indian economy to grow like Indonesia's . . . ? If so, *what*, exactly? If not, what is it about the 'nature of India' that makes it so? The consequences for human welfare involved in questions like these are simply staggering: Once one starts to think about them, it is hard to think about anything else.[20]

There is also the prospect of a crisis derailing economic growth. That has been a feature of developing countries in the post-war period. Once prone to crisis, Douglass North's theory of path dependence would suggest that it is not surprising that it occurs time and again.

A history of crises

Even among emerging economies or emerging markets, which are alternative terms for developing countries that have a track record of economic reform and good growth prospects, the past few decades have been characterized by a series of financial crises that has prevented sustained growth spells. China may have had a four decade-long growth spell that has not been interrupted by crisis and it has nearly eradicated extreme poverty, but that is not the case for many other developing countries.

What is known as the first-generation currency crisis refers to the Latin American crisis of 1981–82. Countries such as Brazil, Mexico, Argentina and Chile had three traits that made them vulnerable: a large budget deficit, so their governments were borrowing to spend, a large trade or current account deficit, so they were importing more than they were exporting, and high inflation, so prices were rising fast. These traits put pressure on their fixed exchange rate against the US dollar, known collectively for those four countries as the *tablitas*. Large deficits and inflation in a country often cause investors to sell their holdings of its currency and buy others that are more stable, usually the dollar, which is what happened in Latin America. The 'twin deficits' (budget and trade) and high inflation are why emerging economies are viewed as vulnerable to growth-derailing crises.

The second-generation currency crisis refers to the collapse of the European exchange rate mechanism (ERM) in 1992. Even though that was a crisis involving developed economies, there are similar features to the Latin American episode. Many Britons still recall Black Wednesday, when sterling and other currencies, such as the Italian lira, left the peg to the Deutschmark (DM) that they had signed up to two years earlier. A loss of market confidence meant that to keep their currencies pegged would have meant raising interest rates to unacceptable levels if investors were to be persuaded to buy sterling and maintain the exchange-rate peg. UK interest rates had reached 15 per cent, and the impact on economic growth of staying in the ERM would simply have been too detrimental during a recession. High interest rates made borrowing more expensive and depressed investment, so worsening growth. Unlike the Latin American economies, the troubled European nations did fairly well after the crisis. Weaker currencies made what they sold abroad cheaper, so exports became more competitive and Britain, for instance, grew well during the 1990s. One difference between Latin America and Europe is that the latter had more stable institutions such as well-regarded central banks, which emerged from the debacle with their reputations more or less intact, whereas in Latin America the crisis led to a loss of confidence in their economic systems and investors pulled out for the long term. This is in line with North's theory that good institutions persist and breed prosperity even through crises.

The third-generation financial and currency crisis took place in Asia in 1997–98. What distinguishes the Asian financial crisis from the first two is that it was a financial crisis that led to a currency crisis. When foreign investors suddenly pulled their money from Thailand after years of capital inflows into the country, it led the Thai baht to collapse. There was a 'sudden stop' of cash inflows that had been lent to Thai businesses. The crisis spread to Malaysia, Indonesia, Hong Kong and South Korea. To try to retain the foreign money to which their businesses had grown accustomed, these economies had to raise interest rates, which hurt growth. (It was similar in that sense to the ERM crisis.) When money flowed out of these countries, their currencies collapsed as investors had no need to keep hold of them any longer. That is why it is known as a financial crisis first and foremost.

What was surprising about the third-generation crisis was that it affected Asian economies, which, unlike Latin America in the early 1980s, were viewed as growing well and did not have huge trade or fiscal deficits. Yet the five economies initially involved were mired in crises that hurt their growth for years. The other worrying trait of the third-generation crisis was contagion, the impact of the Asian financial crisis also being felt in emerging economies around the world. It affected Russia in 1998, Turkey in 1999 and Brazil and Argentina by the early 2000s. This was not because these economies traded much with or invested a great deal in the affected Asian nations, but probably because investors became indiscriminately wary of all developing markets, plunging those economies into crisis too. Argentina, on the other side of the world from where the crisis began, ended up with the largest sovereign default in modern times until Greece took that title a decade later.

This history highlights that the most vulnerable to crises are those emerging economies with the greatest exposure to foreigners owning their debt. When creditors no longer want to hold that debt, it is more expensive for countries to borrow on debt markets because they have to pay a higher interest rate to attract lenders. The reason foreign debt is in focus is because when their loans and other investments, dubbed 'hot money', leave the country, those investors will sell that nation's currency too. A weaker currency then makes it more expensive to repay debt that is denominated in US dollars, which worsens the debt problem. Borrowing in US dollars is referred to as the 'original sin' of developing countries for this reason. This is why there is so much focus on a country's foreign exchange reserves, so that vulnerable economies can show that they possess foreign currency sufficient to pay for their imports and debt and are less affected by currency and capital movements.

Such crises can derail economic growth for years. A currency or financial crisis can and has prevented emerging economies from becoming rich, since an extended period of growth is a necessary trait of the countries that have overcome the middle-income trap discussed earlier. South Korea and Taiwan both grew strongly for over two decades, for example. If developing countries can grow for sustained periods, not only would poverty end in those countries, but also they might even be propelled into the ranks of the rich.

When it comes to sustained high growth rates, there is another concern. Economic growth of emerging markets has slowed in the 2010s. Among the large emerging economies, the so-called BRIC economies owing to their initials, Brazil and Russia have struggled to grow while India and China continue to develop but at a more moderate pace. It's a trend mirrored in the smaller emerging economies. And that raises the question as to whether the emerging market growth story may be over before they have ended poverty and become prosperous.

But their slowing growth should not be unexpected since many of them have become middle-income countries in recent years after a couple of decades of strong growth. For the first time, emerging economies account for more than half of the world's GDP, but, as the rich countries know from experience, richer nations grow more slowly than poorer ones. It's not surprising that the fast-growth spell of emerging economies has slowed down.

After China, India and the former Soviet Union opened up in the early 1990s their economies immediately benefited from access to world markets. Their integration with the global economy helped launch an era of globalization where terms like offshoring came into vogue and globalization surged: exports of goods and services increased from 20 per cent of world GDP to around 30 per cent by the 2010s. Foreign investment poured into cheaper and fast-growing emerging economies as they opened up, which helped their companies to learn from more established multinationals and contributed to a growing new middle class in those countries.

As countries become richer, their pace of growth inevitably slows. Developing ones grow quickly because they are starting the process of industrializing and trading from scratch, so the gains are relatively larger and arrive quickly. Richer nations grow more slowly since they have to innovate and upgrade their industries in order to raise their productivity. For China, 4 per cent growth would be a cause for disappointment; for the USA it would be magnificent.

According to Douglass North, what determines how much an economy will slow down, and thus its long-term growth prospects, is the quality of its institutions. Vietnam and Myanmar, a pair of newly globalized economies, offer useful case studies. They both hold huge promise, but also face significant obstacles. South Africa is another notable case. Let's consider each in turn.

Vietnam's institutional challenge

In 1986 the Vietnamese government launched a series of market-oriented reforms known as *doi moi*. Since then the country has been in transition from central planning to a 'socialist market economy' with the Communist Party remaining in charge. Vietnam is a sizeable country, not quite China's 1.3 billion, but at over 90 million people its population is among the twenty largest in the world. So, Vietnam is a potentially significant economy, given its population. Like China, Vietnam instituted economic reforms in a lagging economy while retaining the communist political regime.

One leftover from the old system is that its state-owned companies dominate bank lending and account for more than half of the country's bad debt. Vietnam is sometimes viewed as the 'next China' owing to its stable transition and communist rule, but there are concerns about a looming debt crisis. The creation of market-oriented institutions and the dismantling of the centrally planned apparatus that had governed the market will attempt the challenging task of altering the path of the economy, the sort of difficult 'path dependence' described by Douglass North.

Among the hardest institutions to reform are state-owned enterprises. For Vietnam, the dominance of such firms, and their associated bad debt, remains a problem years after the launch of *doi moi*. In common with other nations, Vietnam created 'bad banks' or asset management companies to take the bad debts off the books of the state-owned banks. This is what China did in 1999, when it created four such companies to try to clean up the balance sheets of its big state-owned banks prior to opening up the sector when it joined the World Trade Organization in 2001. But the problem with bad debt is not just the stock, but the flow. In other words, the continued accumulation of debts from inefficient state-owned enterprises cannot be ignored.

China in the mid-1990s took a huge step forward in privatizing or restructuring most of the state-owned firms. The number of large state-owned enterprises dropped from about 10 million to less than 300,000 by the end of that decade. It still has a sizeable state-owned sector, but a notable attempt was made to cut the flow of bad debt by increasing the efficiency of the remaining state-owned firms. This was by partially privatizing or selling shares in even the largest state-owned firms, including banks. Of course, China created other problems for itself when it used the banking system to provide most of the finance behind its large fiscal stimulus to boost the economy during the 2008 global financial crisis, discussed in Chapter 3.

Vietnam has pledged to reform its state-owned enterprises, but it has progressed slowly. It wasn't until 2011 that Vietnam started to reduce the number of state-owned enterprises significantly, from 1,309 to 958 in the five years to 2015. And it has a lot more to privatize to get to its target of 190 by 2020. So, it has taken around three decades to reform state firms.

Again like China, Vietnam decided not to follow the 'shock therapy' route taken by the former Soviet Union when it quickly transitioned from a centrally planned economy during the early 1990s. Instead it gradually introduced market forces, including allowing non-state firms to operate, so that the government could slowly reform the state-owned sector.

Looking at the decade-long recession that the former Eastern Bloc nations experienced after their rapid transition, it probably isn't surprising that China and Vietnam seem to have done the smart thing. However, there is an important impediment to both of their reforms, namely that undertaking a more rapid transition removes the inefficient 'hand' of the state. Quickly dismantling the old system prevents the build-up of vested interests and the creation of new power bases in the marketized economy by those who benefit most from the ongoing reforms and can forestall further progress. (Of course, there were numerous problems with the transition of Russia and others, including the unrealistic expectation that a private economy could just fill the vacuum if the old state one was dismantled.)

China undertook what has been described as an 'easy-to-hard' reform sequence in that politically easier reforms like incentivizing agricultural output were done first, while leaving the harder reforms of the state-owned sector for later. As the theory predicted, those new power bases have made it more difficult to implement further reform. Similarly, Vietnam's reforms seem to be mired in the inability of those who run the state-owned firms to allow them to become at least partly if not wholly privatized. In other words, those who benefited from the reforms of the economy are now hanging on to their inefficient firms, which are a drag on the banking system.

There are consequences for the Vietnamese economy. Vietnam's government debt is half of GDP and, importantly, over one-third is owed to foreign creditors. When the debt of state-owned enterprises is added in, the figure doubles to a sizeable 100 per cent of GDP. When the total debt owed by the government is the same magnitude of a country's annual national output, concern over a potential debt crisis grows. To avert it would require cutting off the flow of bad debts from state-owned firms as well as pushing ahead with some degree of privatization. To achieve this will require overcoming a raft of vested interests.

The lesson for countries tackling reforms is, as North had warned, that the power of vested interests in keeping institutions unchanged must be considered as well as the efficiency of the proposed measures. For Vietnam, it is a warning worth heeding.

Myanmar's fast changing institutions

Myanmar, formerly known as Burma, has also recently opened up. It faces a different sort of challenge than Vietnam does, but is similarly reforming the very structure of its economy and its institutions in order to alter its economic path.

Investors call the country the 'final frontier'. The *Star Trek* reference aside, there is a sense of the yet to be explored about Myanmar. It is the last large Asian economy to become globally connected, and opened up only in 2011 after half a century of military rule and the release from house arrest of Nobel Peace laureate Aung San Suu Kyi.

The statistics tell the story: in 2011 just 6 per cent of the population had access to a mobile device and only about 10 per cent had a bank account. Decades of military rule have left Myanmar underdeveloped and one of the poorest countries in Asia. But that also means that, with the right sorts of institutional reforms, it has significant potential to grow quickly. It sits in the world's fastest-growing region with well-established global supply chains, which can help an economy industrialize and grow rapidly if it is part of the worldwide manufacturing network. Unlike many smaller countries in developing Asia, Myanmar, with a population similar in size to that of South Korea, can utilize a significant home market to promote growth as well as expand its exports. This explains the interest of many multinational corporations who eye an under-served market. Plus, it is well endowed with oil, gas and minerals. Thus, Myanmar is one of the countries that can attract foreign investment for all three reasons that typically motivate multinational companies: natural resources, lower costs and new markets.

Myanmar's potential has certainly caught the attention of the world's largest companies looking for the next double-digit growth economy. But opening up too quickly to investment flows has pitfalls, as seen in the numerous crises plaguing emerging economies outlined earlier. This was avoided by China, which has led to talk of the so-called Beijing Consensus serving as an alternative model for newly marketizing nations.

In vogue after the success of China's growth and the critiques levelled at the Washington Consensus, could the Chinese model be a model for Myanmar as it embarks on a historical opening to the global economy?

Of course, there may not even be a consensus about the Beijing Consensus, as the Chinese growth experience cannot be easily modelled. And there are many elements of China's marketization process that are similar to the Washington version. The Washington Consensus was a model of economic development promulgated during the 1980s and 1990s that stemmed from the IMF and US Treasury, both located in Washington, DC. The model was premised on privatization and financial and trade liberalization. As a number of developing countries failed to benefit from following these prescriptions, which was seen both in the decade-long recession of the former Soviet Union during the 1990s and in the 1980s Latin American crisis, the Washington Consensus fell out of favour and developing countries sought an alternative. Some turned to China, whose market-oriented reforms proceeded at a more gradual pace and with sequencing of key reforms. For instance, state-owned enterprises were slowly reformed and were not subject to mass privatization until a couple of decades into the reform process. China also established a non-state sector that absorbed the laid-off workers, so preventing persistent large-scale unemployment. But as discussed earlier, one consequence is that reforms are incomplete and state ownership persists.

China is not alone in growing rapidly in the region. South Korea, Taiwan, Singapore and Hong Kong did the same, serving as a partial model for China as it enacted targeted reforms to boost global integration into production and supply chains that allowed these economies to industrialize through plugging into worldwide manufacturing. State-directed credit also helped to avoid specialization in less desirable areas such as primary (agricultural, resource) products.

As a model of development, the Beijing Consensus in emphasizing gradual and managed opening to the world economy and slower reforms of the existing economic institutions could be more appealing than a more rapid marketization model. Key to the Beijing Consensus is industrialization, which in China's case involved reindustrialization as existing and new industrial firms were reformed and encouraged to enter into higher tech industries. For Myanmar, which is not a transition economy, so it does not have state-owned enterprises like China to restructure, the more standard Lewis model would apply. Crafted by the Nobel laureate Arthur Lewis, this model sees economic growth occurring when workers move out of low-productivity agriculture and into more productive factories and the services economy. Although with a different stress, the end result is the same: industrialization supports economic development. That shift to industry could launch Myanmar into the rapid-growth phase experienced by other Asian countries.

So, the Beijing Consensus perhaps offers a better set of guidelines for Myanmar than the Washington Consensus as it is derived from the experience of its East Asian neighbours. About 70 per cent of Myanmar's population are employed in the agriculture and resources sector, which accounts for over half of the country's economic output. It means that there is a lot of scope to industrialize, which can launch a country into fast growth as it 'catches up', as occurred in the East Asian 'miracle' economies of South Korea, Taiwan, Singapore and Hong Kong, which are among the few that have become rich in the post-war period.

However, as a latecomer and a richly endowed country, plugging into regional production chains will be key or else Myanmar risks specializing in resources and being crowded out by more competitive foreign firms. It is in the right region to exploit that potential, since about half of the world's consumer electronics are produced in Asia. It means Myanmar has the potential to grow in a diversified manner and could develop rapidly if it industrializes. But the bumpier road travelled by some of its Southeast Asian neighbours suggests that success cannot be taken for granted. And it will depend on government policies, also including in the crucial area of social stability. The East Asian 'tiger' economies of Hong Kong, Singapore, South Korea and Taiwan had also enacted land reform and other forms of redistribution that allowed their growth to be accompanied by greater equity. By contrast, China's lack of such policies contributes to it having levels of inequality that are causing social resentment. That is another lesson to note from the growth experience of its neighbours. Institutional reforms, such as adopting redistributive policies to promote income equality alongside industrialization, can allow Myanmar to develop economically without the high levels of income inequality seen in China. These are the very sorts of reforms that Douglass North would propose. Myanmar has already begun to alter the path of its economy and, if successful, then the once bright economy in Southeast Asia can re-emerge and take its place in the fastest growing region in the world.

Exemplified by Vietnam and Myanmar, Asia is progressing with institutional reforms and its growth has led to expectations that extreme global poverty might be eradicated. But Africa remains the big question mark, where so many of the world's poor still reside. Still, South Africa's transformation, led by another path-altering political change, offers a glimpse as to what is possible.

Africa's progress and challenges

When apartheid finally ended in South Africa in the early 1990s, the phrase 'Africa rising' was often heard. Over the past couple of decades, Africa was the second fastest growing region in the world after only Asia. This is a far cry from the years when the region's dominant issues were discussions about debt forgiveness. But poverty rates remain stubbornly high.

This is despite the fact that on the back of the extraordinary commodity boom of the 2000s, African nations have grown well, many quite rapidly, averaging 5 per cent a year in the past decade. This was the longest expansion of incomes in the region in thirty years.

Whether these countries can sustain that economic growth, and do more for poverty reduction, depends on a number of factors, including whether they have managed to industrialize and mechanize agriculture using the proceeds from the commodity boom. That would make growth more inclusive in that the benefits from it are widely shared, which would matter a great deal to poverty reduction. Whether they have done enough to adjust to the end of that extraordinary period will soon be evident in their economies.

For the dominant economy in the region, the transformation post-apartheid has been notable and serves as a case study of effective institutional change. At one stage, South Africa accounted for one-third of the entire output of the nearly fifty countries in sub-Saharan Africa. Its average income during the 1980s was less than $3,000 per capita, which ranked it as a lower middle-income country. By the 2010s, a couple of decades after the end of apartheid, incomes had doubled and propelled South Africa to become an upper-middle-income country. And it became part of the BRICS, the 'S' to Brazil, Russia, India and China. South Africa is one of the five large emerging economies highlighted by financial markets. Its popularity with investors seeking higher returns signalled its arrival as one of the new players in the global economy.

This is not to suggest that South Africa doesn't have challenges. To name just a few, income inequality and joblessness remain tough issues. The average income of black Africans in the country is one-tenth to one-fifth of that of whites. Work is another persistent problem. With the unemployment rate at over 25 per cent, the lack of jobs, particularly for the black population, is a recurrent concern. Some of these economic woes are legacies of apartheid, which was a system of racial segregation in place between 1948 and the early 1990s. It was ended after the release from prison in 1990 of Nelson Mandela, who was later elected president. Mandela had worked for decades to end the unfair system that designated the majority of the South African population second-class citizens. Even though official discrimination against blacks has ended, they remain less well off economically more than two decades later. It's an example of Douglass North's path dependence and why institutions are slow to change, even with the will to do so. And how it takes time for a disadvantaged group to advance even after the formal barriers have been removed since they start from a weaker economic position. It's one of the challenges holding back the country's growth potential decades after Nelson Mandela led the nation into a new era.

This jars with the perception that South Africa is an attractive destination for investors. This is why the country has been described as having a First World financial market within a Third World economic system. Further reform of its economic and political institutions is needed to close that gap, as South Africa has been a beacon for the sub-Saharan region but also epitomizes the development challenges the region still faces. For other African nations, South Africa demonstrates how far a country can advance when institutions are reformed to be more equitable. This is in line with the work of Douglass North: economic development that focuses a great deal on understanding the institutional impediments to growth. Every African nation has its own history and institutions to grapple with, but there is no question that their success will determine whether global poverty will be eradicated in the coming years.

Taking stock

So, what would Douglass North make of the development challenges in the years ahead? What would he say about why some nations remain poor while others have become rich? Is the sharp divide in the world's economies set to continue? After all, current trends point not only to the end of the need to distinguish between developed and developing countries, but also to a concern that the emerging economy growth story could be over before those countries have overcome poverty.

North would certainly recognize that economic growth does not necessarily mean poverty reduction. He believed that poor institutions can persist and enrich some without any resultant economic growth benefiting the country as a whole: 'Rulers devised property rights in their own interests.'[21] So, North believed that institutions can be corrupt, particularly when it comes to who owns such assets as natural resources and land, which have been a source of conflict in Africa.

But North would argue that countries can learn from successful cases such as those in Asia where institutions have worked to bolster economic development and reduce poverty: 'Clearly the existence of relatively productive institutions somewhere in the world and low-cost information about the resultant performance characteristics of those institutions is a powerful incentive to change for poorly performing economies.'[22]

Notably in East Asian nations such as South Korea and Singapore, good governance seems to have played a role in their growth. Their government policies were geared at promoting manufacturing and exporting. They also focused on expanding education to the entire society. These sorts of institutions are ones that North would describe as good for economic growth.

But good institutions are not easy to come by. Simply transplanting a well-crafted set of rules or even an entire legal system into a developing country doesn't work. That's evident from the countries of the former Soviet Union's unsuccessful attempt to adopt Western legal systems during its transition from communism to capitalism. After the collapse of the USSR in the early 1990s, those newly independent countries in eastern and central Europe adopted the Western rule of law and regulations. But decades later, legal protections and rights are still not effectively enforced in many of those nations. Laws that are imposed artificially rather than develop organically do not necessarily fit. The challenge for economies is how to build good institutions suitable to their domestic contexts. As North observed:

> Although formal rules may change overnight as the result of political or judicial decisions, informal constraints embodied in customs,

traditions, and codes of conduct are much more impervious to deliberate policies. These cultural constraints not only connect the past
with the present and future, but provide us with a key to explaining
the path of historical change.[23]

Thus, North would say that bolstering the rule of law will take
time as culture changes gradually, but developing rules-based institutions that provide for good governance will eventually determine
how such countries will develop down the line. Of course, political
stability and a lack of conflict are also essential or good institutions
will struggle to take hold. North was well aware of the challenges of
developing beneficial institutions within often messy political and
economic backdrops in the world's poorest countries. It's why he
advocated paying attention to informal institutions, which includes
doing business with those you trust while the legal system improves.
Social networks or social capital help to explain how countries with
poor legal systems do business as the moral pressure, often from their
own communities, constrains bad behaviour; for instance, if your
neighbour absconds with your money, then his family will be ostra-
cized in the village. How societies interact is crucial in understanding
how institutions evolve. North stressed: 'Informal constraints matter. We need to know much more about culturally derived norms
of behavior and how they interact with formal rules to get better
answers to such issues.'[24]

To get those answers about how norms of behaviour will influence
the reform of formal institutions such as the rule of law will require
economics to broaden its perspective to include the messier aspects
of how societies operate. As North put it in one of his last
contributions:

> My pet peeve all through the last twenty years or thirty years has
> been the narrowness of economists, in fact of all social scientists, in
> not opening up whole new areas . . . I think the biggest thing I want
> to leave with you is how we've got to study more about how the
> mind and brain work and how the structure is evolving over time as
> we get more information, more knowledge, and when it's going in
> directions that are creative.[25]

North's research has certainly opened up the subject. As a result of his path-breaking work and legacy, economists have considered institutions much more carefully as an essential part of understanding economic development. For instance, building on North's work, Daron Acemoglu and James Robinson, whose book was mentioned earlier as an exemplar of the current thinking in economics, examined in detail instances from around the world in which bad institutions led to dire outcomes. They concluded that the issue is when the institutions that underpin the economy are extractive and encourage exploitation rather than productive effort:

> Nations fail today because their extractive economic institutions do not create the incentives needed for people to save, invest, and innovate. Extractive political institutions support these economic institutions by cementing the power of those who benefit from the extraction. Extractive economic and political institutions, though their details vary under different circumstances, are always at the root of this failure . . . The result is economic stagnation and − as the recent history of Angola, Cameroon, Chad, the Democratic Republic of Congo, Haiti, Liberia, Nepal, Sierra Leone, Sudan, and Zimbabwe illustrates − civil wars, mass displacements, famines, and epidemics, making many of these countries poorer today than they were in the 1960s.[26]

They agree with North that path dependence leads to a vicious circle of persistently poor development, and also that it is possible to break the cycle: 'The solution to the economic and political failure of nations today is to transform their extractive institutions toward inclusive ones. The vicious circle means that this is not easy. But it is not impossible.'[27]

Acemoglu and Robinson point to successes, including Botswana, China and the American South, which are 'vivid illustrations that history is not destiny'.[28] But it will require a broad-based political and social coalition to push for reforms, as proposed by North, and a bit of luck 'because history always unfolds in a contingent way'.[29]

There are more successes now than ever before. Research by the OECD estimates that by 2030, for the first time in history, more than half of the world's population will be considered middle class. That's 4.9 billion out of an estimated 8.6 billion people. In 2009 1.8 billion (out of around 7 billion) people earned between $10 and $100 per day, a measure of the income that defines the new global middle class. That's enough to buy a refrigerator, adjusted for what a dollar buys in their countries.

In 2030, nearly two-thirds of the middle class worldwide – 3 billion people – will be in Asia on current trends. The United Nations describes it as a historic shift not seen for 150 years. The European and North American middle class will fall from more than half of that class's world total to one-third.

Because of Douglass North's insights, we are closer than ever before to understanding how to end poverty. Following his precepts, a number of countries have developed successfully in the past few decades, leading to an unprecedented expansion of the middle class around the world. Even if economics doesn't have all of the solutions, looking more broadly at institutions holds the promise that one day we will learn why some nations are rich and others are poor, and, most importantly, why some nations fail and why some ultimately prosper.

North would agree: 'We are just beginning the serious study of institutions. The promise is there. We may never have definitive answers to all our questions. But we can do better.'[30]

CHAPTER 12

Robert Solow: Do We Face a
Slow-Growth Future?

Economic growth across major economies is slower today than before the 2008 global financial crisis, but not just as a result of the crash. Economies such as the United States, the euro area, Japan and the UK had been experiencing a marked slowdown in productivity growth since the mid 2000s.

Some economists are warning about permanently slower growth in advanced economies, in part because their ageing populations will be less productive. Could these economies be facing what the former US Treasury Secretary and Harvard economist Lawrence Summers describes as 'secular stagnation'? If so, then those countries face a worrying economic future. Fewer workers require fewer office buildings and less equipment, which also depresses investment and therefore the economic outlook. That point seems to be approaching: US labour force growth slowed to just 0.2 per cent in 2015, down from 2.1 per cent from the 1960s to 1980s; for the UK, the annual average rate of labour force growth is somewhat better, but it is still down to around 0.6 per cent.

An overwhelming concern is that the situation in Japan in the early 1990s will be repeated in the West. When the real estate bubble burst, the ensuing economic collapse revealed an underlying stagnation that had been masked by the crisis. Japan's problems have been compounded by a population that has been shrinking since 2010. A smaller workforce makes it harder to improve productivity and raise output growth. Slow productivity growth in particular is an issue for

Britain, which is facing its weakest recovery in modern memory. This is a lesson to heed, since national output has recovered to pre-crisis levels, but productivity continues to lag behind the overall recovery.

So, the new normal growth rate may be lower than before. Or, worse, be stagnant. How worried should we be?

The author of the workhorse of economic growth models, Robert Solow, might provide some answers. The Solow model shows that economic growth occurs when workers and capital are added to the economy, but that it is sustained only when there is also technological progress. Better technology improves labour productivity, which increases capital accumulation by slowing down the diminishing returns to capital. Diminishing returns happen when a worker is given more than, say, two computers; that worker won't produce as much with the third computer as compared with the first two unless there is better software that allows computing to be done without the person using it all the time. Technological progress allows the existing inputs of workers and capital to be used more efficiently. An increase in output due to technology is referred to as total factor productivity (TFP) in economic growth models. Physical capital as well as human capital — the skills and education of workers — are central to this model. It's especially pressing for rich countries, where the working-age population is ageing or even shrinking and having better-skilled workers is even more important. How to raise productivity lies at the heart of whether or not we're doomed to a stagnant future.

What would Robert Solow, whose pioneering work has helped us to understand what generates economic growth, make of the prospect of low productivity and a slow-growth future for major economies?

The life and times of Robert Solow

Robert Solow was born in 1924 in Brooklyn. The son of Jewish immigrants, his was the first generation of the family to go to college. He attributes his intellectual awakening to the New York City public school system, where a teacher got him interested in nineteenth-century French and Russian novelists. That wasn't the only trigger that Solow describes: 'Like many children of the Depression I was curious about what made society tick.'[1]

That curiosity led to him obtaining a scholarship to attend Harvard University in 1940. After serving in the US army from 1942 to 1945, he returned to Harvard and his fiancée, Barbara Lewis, known as Bobby. They had met before he was deployed and wrote to each other daily while he was serving in North Africa and Italy. After the end of the war, Bobby graduated from Radcliffe College, the all-women sister college to Harvard. In 1945 they married and both embarked on their doctoral studies in economics at Harvard. Bobby completed her dissertation after a thirteen-year interruption to raise their three children and later taught at Brandeis and Boston universities, where she focused on Irish and Caribbean economic history. They were married for nearly seventy years until her death in 2014 at the age of ninety.

Bobby may have been the reason that Solow became an economist. He asked his wife whether the economic courses that she had taken were worthwhile. Solow was persuaded and pursued economics, which brought him under the tutelage of Wassily Leontief and others.[2] Leontief was a Nobel laureate who won the top prize in economics in 1973 for his work on measuring inputs such as labour and capital and their relationship to national output, presented in 'input–output tables'. As his research assistant, Solow produced the first set of measurements of how much capital investments added to output in the American economy.

As Solow's interests turned to statistics and probabilistic models, he spent 1949–50 studying these subjects at Columbia University, which had more experienced teachers in that area. It helped him finish his doctoral dissertation, which modelled changes in wage distributions and unemployment. His thesis won the Wells Prize at Harvard, which offered not just publication as a book but also $500, which was a considerable sum in 1951. But upon rereading the thesis, Solow thought he could improve upon it, so it remains unpublished and the cheque is still uncashed.

After he received his PhD in economics that year, he joined the Massachusetts Institute of Technology, where he became a professor in 1958. Solow spent his academic career at this leading economics faculty, though he was also visiting professor at Cambridge and Oxford universities in the 1960s.

Solow was active in public policy from the start. After obtaining his PhD, he took on consulting assignments for the RAND Corporation in 1952. During his time working with the President's Council of Economic Advisers from 1962–68, Solow helped draft the Keynesian-influenced economic policies that were the hallmark of the John F. Kennedy and Lyndon B. Johnson administrations. In 1965–69, he served on President Johnson's Committee on Technology, Automation and Economic Progress, and then on President Richard Nixon's Commission on Income Maintenance from 1969–70. Solow even spent a spell as a central banker when he was director and later chairman of the board of the Federal Reserve Bank of Boston from 1975 to 1980. In recognition of his long public service, Solow was awarded the Presidential Medal of Freedom in 2014, the highest honour granted to civilians by the United States government.

Solow had received accolades from the start of his career. In 1961 he received the prestigious John Bates Clark Medal, awarded to the best US economist under the age of forty. It is now often viewed as a precursor to the Nobel Prize. He was well regarded throughout his career, which included serving as president of the American Economic Association in 1979. He is also a past president of the Econometric Society, member of the National Science Board, Fellow of the British Academy and recipient of the National Medal of Science. Perhaps unsurprisingly, Solow was awarded the highest prize in economics in 1987 for his work on economic growth. Before the award he had been mentioned regularly as a possible Nobel laureate, which led him to quip: 'My friends have been telling me that I would get it if I lived long enough.'[3]

Yet, economic growth was not his first interest. Solow had intended to focus on statistics and econometrics in his academic career. He attributes his switch to macroeconomics to chance. He was allocated an office next to Nobel laureate Paul Samuelson at MIT. In his 1987

Nobel Prize autobiography, he commented: 'Thus began what is now almost forty years of almost daily conversations about economics, politics, our children, cabbages and kings.'[4]

Solow retired in 1995 to make room for younger scholars, though he remains active in numerous scholarly projects, and still occupies an office that was next to Samuelson's until the latter's death in 2009.

The Solow growth model.

In influential articles in 1956 and 1957,[5] Robert Solow laid the foundations for understanding economic growth. The Solow growth model is the standard neoclassical model that is taught in every textbook, including mine. The best-known result from growth models is the Solow residual. The Solow residual refers to the unexplained portion of economic growth which isn't attributed to adding inputs such as workers and capital. The residual captures technological progress, which generates more output from a set of inputs. Of course, it also captures anything else not related to inputs of labour and investment, so temporary rises in government spending and monetary easing also get included. It means that some, but not all, of what is captured in the Solow residual is the productivity advancing technology needed to sustain economic growth over the longer term. This is the TFP (total factor productivity) mentioned earlier.

Across countries, there is a clear association between periods of high output growth and significant technological progress. Developed nations all grew well between 1950 and 1973, and then slowed together during 1974–87. There seems to be a connection with the adoption of similar technologies. For instance, the strong period of growth in the 1950s and 60s is associated with post-war technological advances, such as widespread air travel and industrial robots.

Curiously, recent technological improvements, centred on computing, information and communication technologies (ICT) and the internet, do not seem to have raised productivity across the economy. Solow's 1987 observation that 'You can see the computer age everywhere but in the productivity statistics' is known as the Solow paradox.[6] He revisited this question decades later, but concluded that we still do not know, as the role of computing is still evolving. Solow points out that since our lives and work have been transformed by computers, this technology should have improved our productivity. But productivity growth was slow from around 1970 to 1995, which is the period when computing took off. In a shorter period, from 1995 to 2000, productivity growth was faster, which may be attributed to the lagging effects of adopting computing. Solow believes it takes time for businesses to learn to use computers productively, so the early years were not a good indicator. In a 2002 interview he doubted that productivity growth would revert to the fast pace seen previously because 'Comparing the computer with electricity or the internal combustion engine just doesn't seem to me to be justified yet.' Solow also revealed: 'I always thought that the main difference the computer made in my office was that before the computer my secretary used to work for me, and afterward I worked for my secretary.'[7]

Solow's scepticism reflects one view that the ICT revolution would not generate as much economy-wide productivity improvement as the earlier Industrial Revolution that introduced general purpose technologies such as the steam engine during Adam Smith's era, or the Second Industrial Revolution that saw the introduction of railways and electrification during the period lasting from the late nineteenth century until the First World War. Others disagree and expect that productivity will improve once these new ICT and digital technologies become truly embedded into work practices and businesses. A major challenge to Solow's view is related to technology. The developers of endogenous growth models from the 1960s onwards criticized Solow for not explaining where technology came from.

Endogenous growth models treat technology as determined within the model; in other words, 'endogenously' generated by the capital and labour within an economy. The neoclassical Solow model was alleged to treat technological progress as if it were 'manna from heaven'. By contrast, endogenous growth theories attempt to explain how technological advances come about, raising the productivity of an economy. Those models say that educated researchers and investment in R&D are what generates technological improvements, which in turn boosts economic growth.

Solow was unconvinced by some of the assumptions of endogenous growth, particularly in its simplest form, known as the AK model. (The 'A' in the title of the model refers to the economics shorthand for technology, while 'K' refers to capital.) This theory says that the rate of technical improvement in an economy is proportional to its growth rate; in other words, technology and the economy grow at the same rate. Solow thought that process seemed too neat to be plausible. Although they differ in terms of how growth comes about, these models follow the implications set out by the Solow model. Endogenous growth theories extend Solow's neoclassical model in spelling out how innovators produce technological progress.

Another criticism relates to the work of Douglass North discussed in the previous chapter. A difficulty of the Solow model is that it can account for differences in growth rates across countries only by appealing to technological progress. So, institutions such as those favoured by North play little role in explaining why some countries are wealthy while most are not.

On the other hand, the Solow model can explain why countries have different levels of per capita income, and indicate whether we are converging to a slow-growth future. Growth should speed up if an economy is operating below its steady state, or the level of output that it is capable of producing. So, if an economy is starting to develop and has low levels of capital stock, then it should realize higher returns to its capital than a country which is developed and has had a lot of capital accumulation. If these economies have the same levels of technology, investment rate and population growth, then the developing country will grow faster than the developed one because of diminishing returns to capital discussed earlier. The output per worker gap between these countries will narrow over time as both economies approach the steady state. This important prediction of the neoclassical model is known as the convergence hypothesis: developing countries will grow faster than developed countries if they have the same steady state until they converge to the same income level.

Does this bear out empirically? If there is convergence, then there should be an inverse relationship between a nation's starting level of income and subsequent growth. Japan, which started at a much lower level of development in the post-war period, grew more quickly than other more developed economies. From 1950 to 1990, Japan experienced growth that was on average much faster than that of the US. For rich countries there was an inverse relationship between their initial level of per capita income and growth rate between 1880 and 1973. However, there is no clear relationship in more recent periods for either rich countries or all countries in the world. So, there is limited evidence of convergence.

Some poorer and middle-income countries (particularly China) have grown faster, and begun to catch up with wealthier nations, which is what the model predicts. But there are many poor countries that have grown slowly. In terms of the world income distribution, instead of seeing convergence, there have been signs of polarization between rich and poor nations.

What about those nations that are developed and experiencing a slowdown in growth? What can be done to raise productivity in advanced economies? It is a question that other nations may also eventually face.

The productivity challenge

The Organisation for Economic Co-operation and Development (OECD) highlights the productivity challenge as one of the biggest issues since the 2008 banking crisis.[8]

Britain is among the worst affected. By any number of metrics, UK productivity (output per hour) is lower than it should be based on pre-crisis trends, which is a puzzle. In other words, productivity growth has slowed down considerably since the crash.

One way to think about the immediate post-crash period is that it has been a job-rich recession. Employment recovered a year earlier than output, and unemployment never hit the 3-million mark reached during the recessions of the early 1980s and 1990s. But output per worker was lower during this period since less output was demanded in a recession than in normal times. Since the 2008 crisis, output per worker grew at just 0.2 per cent per year, which is a fraction of the 2.1 per cent average growth rate between 1972 and 2007. Wage flexibility helped to maintain jobs during the latest recession, a decline in real wages making it possible to keep people in work.[9]

Employers hoarding workers instead of laying them off doesn't explain the entire productivity puzzle.[10] Part of the answer may be that the British economy has a large services sector in which it is difficult to measure either investment or output accurately.[11] But the US also has a large services sector and doesn't suffer from the productivity problem to the same extent, so mismeasurement is unlikely to be the whole story either.

The Bank of England has concluded that output per hour is around 16 per cent lower than expected.[12] Unlike previous recessions, productivity hadn't picked up during the recovery. This is the essence of the 'productivity puzzle'.

That said, productivity growth was already slowing down before the crisis. The OECD points to low investment as an explanation. As a share of GDP, UK investment began to trail that of the US, Canada, France and Switzerland in the 1990s. Investment fell from around a quarter of GDP in the late 1980s to just over 15 per cent. Low investment means there's less productive capital for employees to work with, and thus lower output per worker.

This was also one of the conclusions of the Bank of England. They can explain between half to three-quarters of the productivity puzzle. Mismeasurement accounts for around a quarter. They then looked at cyclical factors related to the business cycle and also at the possible structural reasons behind lagging productivity, i.e. how the economy is structured as opposed to cyclical variations. Some of the cyclical factors concern hoarding workers and doing work that doesn't immediately add to output. Structural reasons include low capital investment and inefficient resource allocation, where workers are not moving from low- to high-productivity sectors. That can happen when there are high firm survival rates resulting in so-called zombie firms that have survived only due to the extraordinarily low interest rate environment.

This is not just a UK problem, however. The term 'secular stagnation' has been revived as a concern for all developed economies and requires revisiting our models of growth. The slow recovery of the United States was what led Harvard economist Lawrence Summers to warn about a slow-growth future for advanced economies. At the forefront of this issue is Japan. Since its early 1990s crash it has experienced several 'lost decades' of growth, not helped by the survival of zombie firms in its initial recovery, which contributed to those unproductive years. Since then, Japan has launched the most aggressive economic policy in the world in an attempt to end decades of stagnation. As the rich economy with the most aged population, which is an important factor contributing to secular stagnation, how Japan fares will hold lessons for others.

Japan's 'lost decades'

Japan's growth since the early 1990s has hovered around 0–1 per cent and productivity growth has been poor. The three major economic policy 'arrows' introduced by Japanese prime minister Shinzo Abe at the end of 2012 with the aim of revitalizing the world's third largest economy have been dubbed 'Abenomics'.

The first arrow – aggressive expansion of the money supply in an attempt to end deflation or price declines – has failed to hit the target consistently. There have been positive signs, but the challenge of ending years of stagnant prices is immense. Stock markets have hit multi-year highs but the real economy hasn't benefited sufficiently. Higher market valuations alone have not been enough for firms to raise wages that are fundamental to sustaining price rises. They are instead looking for more output per worker in order to justify higher pay. Average real wages were hit by the 2008 crisis and are yet to recover fully.

The second arrow, fiscal policy, hasn't quite hit the mark either. In one instance, a 2014 government decision to raise the sales tax from 5 per cent to 8 per cent, the first such increase in seventeen years, squeezed spending and tipped the economy back into recession. In its immediate aftermath, GDP contracted at an annualized pace of 7.3 per cent in the April–June quarter, the worst contraction since the economy shrank by 15 per cent in the 2008 global financial crisis. This mirrored 1997, when a sales tax increase had sent the economy into recession, revealing an underlying weakness of demand. Raising taxes was intended to reduce Japan's indebtedness. It was always the case that any attempt to address the country's staggering debt, which at around 240 per cent of GDP is the highest in the world, would be an economic drag, but the scale of it is a reminder of the fragility of the revival of the Japanese economy.

The hardest arrow to score with was always going to be the third – the structural reforms that target the way that the economy is constituted and run. How can Japan raise productivity when its population and labour force are shrinking? Can firms be enticed to invest in a country where consumption demand is low after years of stagnation have taken their toll and people are concerned about taking on debt? Abe's structural reforms include over 240 initiatives to raise productivity. Such reforms take time, and ministers warn that it could take a decade for Abenomics to work. So it may be years before the positive impact of any structural reforms are felt. Abe is Japan's sixth prime minister in ten years. Time is seemingly a luxury for Japan's leaders, yet it's the very thing that they need to turn around an economy that's been struggling for decades, during which Japan has fallen from the world's second largest economy to its third.

The country that overtook it also faces slower growth and an ageing population. For a middle-income country, China has a demographic profile that is similar to rich nations. Its working-age population is shrinking, though it has ended its 'one child policy' to counter the ageing demography. Also, if Britain and America as well as Japan are counting on innovation to keep them rich, China needs to get there before its growth slows down, as discussed in previous chapters.

For Europe, the focus is also growth, and a lot is hanging on the governments' ability to deliver. German Chancellor Angela Merkel has said that the legitimacy of the European project depends on people becoming better off. So the European Union is also focused on raising growth through investment, as discussed in the chapter on John Maynard Keynes.

Raising growth and productivity to counteract a stagnant future is, then, a common challenge for major economies. And it is one that has been increasingly recognized by policymakers. Turning to Great Britain, the government has begun to focus on economic growth, particularly with respect to its particularly worrying low-productivity challenge.

The UK government's renewed focus on growth

During the 2008 banking crash, 'benign neglect' of the productivity issue by successive governments who were focused on the immediate crisis meant there was insufficient attention paid to economic growth. As the country worst affected by the global productivity slowdown, Britain has since placed this issue at the centre of its economic growth agenda. For one thing, following research by the Bank of England and others, the government has focused on raising investment.

For instance, it has established a National Infrastructure Commission. The UK needs investments in 'hard' infrastructure (such as transport links) as well as 'soft' (such as digital networks), which can be just as important to induce business investment. Britain's track record on this issue has been somewhat mixed. Development of the digital economy has been impressive in some respects. For instance, Silicon Roundabout in London has attracted more venture capital than other European cities. But there are also areas of the country where even getting a mobile phone signal is challenging. The other significant area where investment is needed is skills. Business surveys routinely point to a skills shortage cramping their growth. It seems that investment is needed in physical and also digital infrastructure as well as in human capital.

Greater devolution of taxation powers to local governments decentralizes decision-making authority, which can boost investment. It has worked in Germany and China, where local banks and authorities have better knowledge of their regions. But it can also create inefficient competition among localities and generate duplicative activities that are protected by local vested interests.

Increasing private investment is needed, so clarity about policies and transparent regulations matter. As one example, some companies are deterred from making sizeable infrastructure investments, which can otherwise be attractive owing to their fixed returns, by regulatory changes. Others worry about Brexit, which adds to uncertainty over Britain's future economic relationship with the European Union.

Increasing public investment can help to boost private investment, as government expenditure in infrastructure can have a 'crowding in' effect. In other words, government investment can make private investment more efficient, for example good telecoms infrastructure increases the returns to a pound invested by a private company. Yet, public investment since 1997 has averaged just 2.4 per cent of GDP, which is 1.1 percentage points below the average for the G7 advanced economies.

As mentioned before in the Keynes chapter, the debate concerns whether the government should take advantage of very low interest rates to borrow and increase public investment. Keynesians would support separating government investment from current budgetary spending because investing today will generate greater returns in the future.

It's not just government policy, of course, that matters for investment. The Bank of England also identified misallocation of capital as a related issue. To invest, businesses need financing. It's less of a problem for large firms, but the vast majority of the country's businesses are small. A financial system dominated by banks that have been focused more on repairing their balance sheets than on lending is an impediment. Turning to capital markets is less easy because of the small size of Britain's debt markets for companies. It's an issue that the US does not face since most lending comes not from banks but from bond or stock markets, where companies issue debt or shares to raise funds. It's also an issue for the EU, which is trying to reduce reliance on bank lending through the creation of a new Capital Markets Union that aims to promote a larger and more integrated debt market in the European Union.

There's no question that investment is important, and it's related to the structural issues that underpin the productivity puzzle in the UK. The topic of low wages was discussed in the Joan Robinson chapter. Lower pay means that some companies hire workers instead of installing more units of capital, which depresses investment.[13]

The OECD has looked at this issue and finds that weak output growth is a drag on productivity. That brings us full circle in that output per worker or machine can't increase strongly if overall economic growth remains subdued. Importantly, wages are related to productivity. The OECD says that, because labour productivity has been 'exceptionally weak' since the crisis, real wages and per capita GDP or average incomes have largely been flat. So it's not just the economy as a whole that suffers, but individuals too.

Even if concern about the recent decline in output per worker is less of one because jobs have been preserved, the longer-term trend is still a great source of worry since productivity matters for economic growth. For instance, the sustainable way for us all to enjoy higher incomes requires increasing productivity. The causes of low productivity are not entirely unknown, and the consequences affect our future standards of living. So, if the productivity puzzle has become more prominent on the policy agenda, then that helps the government to focus on what really matters for the long-term standard of living in the UK.

Solow on the slow-growth dilemma

What would Robert Solow have suggested as a solution to the slow-growth dilemma?

Ensuring that investment stays buoyant is particularly urgent after a financial crisis and recession. Solow has argued that long-run growth prospects can be affected by an economic downturn. This has been an issue for Europe for many years. He observed:

> as suggested for instance by the history of the large European economies since 1979, it is impossible to believe that the equilibrium growth path itself is unaffected by the short- to medium-run experience. In particular the amount and directions of capital formation is bound to be affected by the business cycle, whether through gross investment in new equipment or through the accelerated scrapping of old equipment.[14]

Low investment tends to follow a financial crisis in which banks were not lending and firms were not keen to invest. This can have lasting effects on the growth potential of an economy. So, business cycles, which are considered to be short- or medium-run events, can alter the long-term prospects of an economy. This was seen in Japan after its early 1990s crash and is now a worry in the aftermath of the 2008 financial crisis for the US, UK, the euro area and other developed economies.

Solow also points out that related high unemployment, which is an issue for the euro area after the 2010 crisis that erupted with a bailout for Greece, can have an impact on an economy's future as joblessness could cause it to be stuck on a lower growth path for a long time: 'I am also inclined to believe that the segmentation of the labor market by occupation, industry and region, with varying amounts of unemployment from one segment to another, will also react back on the equilibrium path.'[15]

This is the well-known concept of hysteresis, whereby long stints in unemployment render workers' skills obsolete. It impedes them from rejoining the labour market and thus reduces the number of productive workers, meaning that unemployment will remain higher than before the crisis and hurt the country's growth potential. The lingering high rates of unemployment in the euro area, particularly youth unemployment, which has been in double digits in some countries for nearly a decade, highlight this concern of Solow's. Workers are crucially important in economic growth models, as they are not just the labourers but also the innovators.

Thus, Solow would most likely agree that more investment to boost growth is needed. In his model, technological progress, the crucial ingredient in economic growth, could be impeded through low investment: 'much technological progress, maybe most of it, could find its way into actual production only with the use of new and different capital equipment. Therefore the effectiveness of innovation in increasing output would be paced by the rate of gross investment.'[16]

Reversing the decline in investment, especially since the 2008 crisis, takes on a new urgency, since as Solow observed: 'the way remains open for a reasonable person to believe that the stimulation of investment will favor faster intermediate-run growth through its effect on the transfer of technology from laboratory to factory'.[17]

In short, whether we face a slow-growth future depends on increasing investment and decreasing unemployment, because both of these factors affect the innovation and technology improvements that underpin economic growth, as per Solow's model. Since technology determines the prospects of an economy, how much is invested in capital and people matters a great deal. Those productive factors determine how innovative an economy can be, and thus its economic future, or its new equilibrium path. In Solow's view:

> The new equilibrium path will depend on the amount of capital accumulation that has taken place during the period of disequilibrium, and probably also on the amount of unemployment, especially long-term unemployment, that has been experienced. Even the level of technology may be different, if technological change is endogenous [determined by the amount of capital and workers in the economy] rather than arbitrary [where innovations happen from time to time in a less deterministic way].[18]

The new path of economic growth, whether it is fast or slow, is within the control of the government and shaped by the decisions of firms and workers, so it is not just the inevitable outcome of an ageing society or other factors. Some of Japan's economic stagnation is thought to be related to its demographics since its population is the oldest and fastest ageing in the world. Its heavy investment in robotics is perhaps one way of using technology to supplement a shrinking workforce. Instead of workers producing output, they may be substituted by robots producing that output. But that also raises the prospect that robots will lead to unemployment in certain sectors. Automated production of goods and services might just be used to replace retiring workers, but it could force some out of a job too.

Solow would view the possibility that we face a slow-growth future as depending on how investment and workers fare, since they determine the productivity growth of the economy. Investment by governments (which hinges on the austerity debate from the earlier chapter on Keynes) or private firms can help restore the capital stock that has plummeted since the crisis which would help to reduce the likelihood of a slow-growth future. Government can make it more attractive to invest by providing tax incentives to promote innovation or improve infrastructure. So long as investment can be increased, then Solow would not view a slow-growth future as inevitable. His model is based on growth deriving from capital accumulated through investment and productive workers, so policies to support both of those factors of production would generate more output.

It's challenging, as seen in Japan, and some factors like demographics are difficult to alter, but the above suggestions can help and the advent of new technologies could be game changing. Solow would probably view the debate over whether the technologies of the digital era are as productive as the steam engine or electrification of the earlier industrial revolutions as being related to investment. If the computer age is to increase productivity and so lead to a stronger phase of economic growth, it will require investment in not just R&D but also people's skills and firms' practices to embed those technologies into how businesses operate.

The basic tenets of Robert Solow's model of economic growth point the way forward. As the saying goes, demography is not destiny. After all, as I write this, Solow is an active economist working well into his nineties.

*

Robert Solow is not only a scholar but also understands the importance of contributing to public discussions of economic issues. He once wrote an essay entitled 'How Economic Ideas Turn to Mush'. He observed that it was challenging to convey complicated ideas outside one's profession. Once an economic idea reaches the public, it has been changed in one way or another.[19] Solow offers this advice to economists:

> Try to formulate an economic problem in a very clear, focused way. Try to answer one question at a time, and insist on that. And above all – this is really what's difficult – at least I know that I tend to forget it: Don't omit qualifications. Never claim more than you actually believe or can justify. What makes that hard is that what people want – especially if they're being fed it in sound bites on a television program or in a two-sentence quotation in *The Wall Street Journal* – what they want is something very definite. They don't ever want those qualifications. And you must never let them off that hook. The interesting thing is that I think it's useful. An economist trying to talk to the general public gains respect by insisting on the qualifications, by not appearing as a pundit, as someone who knows all the answers.[20]

Solow may also be one of the few academics who appreciates the importance of work–life balance. Each summer he decamps to Martha's Vineyard, a popular seaside retreat for those living in Massachusetts, where he works on his research and also sails.[21] He had spent some of his million-dollar Nobel Prize money on a jib for his boat. Even in his leisurely pursuits, Solow sees parallels with the life of an economist:

> Apart from the activity itself, the main thing I like about sailing is that it teaches you that the water and the wind out there don't give a damn about you. They're doing whatever the laws of physics tell them to do and your problem is to adjust as best you can. And learning to adjust, to adapt, is not a bad thing for economists to learn either: Adapt to changes in the world . . . You've got to fit your model to the world, not the world to your model.[22]

Epilogue: The Future of Globalization

Economic prosperity has been linked to globalization. The rapid global economic growth of the post-war period was accompanied by the fast expansion of international trade and investment. As we buy goods and access information, often without regard to national borders, it's unlikely that globalization will be rolled back. But trade expansion and the opening up of markets are stalling. The global trade system covering nearly all nations' exports and imports under the World Trade Organization (WTO) is fragmenting into a set of accompanying regional and bilateral free trade agreements. This colossal challenge to the future of globalization and the growth of the world economy would benefit from the ideas of the Great Economists.

A couple of dramatic events in the past few years have highlighted a backlash against the uneven gains from globalization. Although there are numerous differences between Britain's decision to leave the European Union and the ascendancy of political outsider Donald Trump to the White House, the two events reveal a number of things about the electorate's discontent with the status quo, including globalization.

In a historic referendum in June 2016, Britain became the first sovereign nation to vote to leave the European Union. Some of the surveys of voters suggest that a backlash against globalization played a role in Brexit, alongside dominant themes such as sovereignty and immigration. The UK government has insisted that Britain will maintain its global outlook, which will constitute a different set of policies than its current trading relationships with EU and non-EU countries, and will certainly be important to future prosperity.

Across the Atlantic, in the closely fought 2016 US presidential election, Republican candidate Trump had identified international trade as one of the problems confronting America that he would fix in order to 'Make America Great Again'. In his inauguration speech, Trump made it clear that, in his administration, economic policy would be driven by the principle of 'America First'. He said it means there are two rules: 'Buy American, Hire American'. Of course, as in Britain, the disaffection of the US electorate is not just with trade. But the targeting of globalization in response to economic challenges reflects an underlying discontent with the uneven benefits from opening up to the global economy. Populism fuelling anti-establishment sentiment poses a challenge to current economic policies.

Trump's predecessor, Barack Obama, attributes some of the discontent to globalization:

> Globalization combined with technology combined with social media and constant information have disrupted people's lives in very concrete ways – a manufacturing plant closes and suddenly an entire town no longer has what was the primary source of employment – and people are less certain of their national identities or their place in the world . . . There is no doubt [this] has produced populist movements both from the left and the right in many countries in Europe . . . When you see a Donald Trump and a Bernie Sanders – very unconventional candidates who had considerable success – then obviously there is something there that is being tapped into: a suspicion of globalization, a desire to rein in its excesses, a suspicion of elites and governing institutions that people feel may not be responsive to their immediate needs.[1]

So, is globalization in trouble? What would the Great Economists make of this backlash against it? And, most importantly, what would they advise to best help the losers from it?

The changing face of free trade

There has been a shift away from multilateral trade deals that apply to all WTO members, which encompass the near totality of trading nations. There is still a push for free trade agreements that reduce tariffs, and to adopt other measures to ease trade and investment, but these are increasingly in the form of regional and bilateral trade agreements. Europe has trade and customs agreements either agreed or pending with some eighty countries, all but a handful of them with other WTO members, which reflects the importance of continued liberalization and opening up of overseas markets for trade beyond the current coverage of the WTO.

Let's remind ourselves what tariffs encompass and why they are economically inefficient. Tariffs are the charges that governments impose on imports and exports. They are effectively a tax, so can distort prices. Because tariffs add a cost, and thus reduce economic efficiency, they can be a drag on growth. Free trade agreements (FTAs) such as the EU's single market, aim to eliminate most of them. But, a number of governments use tariffs to protect their industries from competition from bigger global rivals until they are more mature. Labour groups also want protection for domestic jobs. So, tariffs are more than just an economic decision to impose a tax. There are often political motives behind their imposition.

There are also non-tariff barriers (NTBs) to add to the mix. These are the other ways to be protectionist without imposing tariffs, such as through insisting on standards for certain industries that can restrict imports. For instance, Thai prawn exporters found it hard to meet American standards for the type of net that allowed them to sell to the US. Regulations matter even more for the services sector, which is the biggest part of the British, American and most other major economies. This is the main reason for the push by the EU for an international agreement on services. The Trade in Services Agreement (TiSA) has the potential of opening up the biggest part of the global economy and becoming a major element of the next big round of multilateral trade liberalization under the WTO. TiSA was launched in 2013 and attempts to open up the services market, which comprises 70 per cent of global and EU GDP but only 25 per cent of world and EU exports. In other words, trade in goods may have been liberalized under the current WTO regime, but for major economies the biggest part of their national output, which is services, faces barriers in global markets.

Countries want to reduce trade barriers, and are increasingly seeking to do so via regional FTAs that are in addition to their WTO membership. Had President Trump not pulled the US out, the

Trans-Pacific Partnership (TPP) would have been the world's biggest free trade area, linking North America with Pacific Rim countries encompassing parts of Latin America and Asia. The US under the Obama administration had hoped to gain from this new trade agreement since 61 per cent of US goods exports and 75 per cent of US agricultural exports go to the Asia Pacific region. The European Union has also been pursuing an equally ambitious free trade agreement with America. The Transatlantic Trade and Investment Partnership (TTIP) would be a FTA that would link the US with the EU.

The pursuit of massive regional FTAs is a reaction to the World Trade Organization expansion stalling. It has been a long time since the last big WTO initiative, the Doha Round of 2001, where countries launched negotiations to open global markets up further. So, instead of trying to wrangle a deal with almost the entire world, regional trade agreements have sprung up and bilateral agreements have expanded, though it would be better for all countries to trade on the same terms with all others.

The problem with this approach is that if a country hasn't signed up to the rules of the new free trade areas (or hasn't even been invited to join), it's excluded and can't share the benefits. Being left out of TPP and the TTIP means China is striking its own deals. China is negotiating with ASEAN (Association of Southeast Asian Nations) and other Asian nations to form a regional free trade agreement, the Regional Comprehensive Economic Partnership (RCEP). China had also offered to set up a Free Trade Area of the Asia Pacific (FTAAP) as an alternative to the TPP.

These regional FTAs are not the best outcome relative to a multilateral agreement under the WTO, but perhaps they're better than not having any new trade deals at all. The creation of sizeable free trade areas where domestic companies can gain economies of scale by selling to a much larger customer base than would otherwise be possible is one of the motivations, especially for smaller economies.

That's why Southeast Asia is also pursuing an ambitious free trade area. The single market that ASEAN launched at the end of 2015, known as the ASEAN Economic Community (AEC), is comparable to the EU in terms of population. With over 600 million people, the

AEC links the ten nations of Southeast Asia ranging from rich Singapore to poor Laos into a bloc aiming for the removal of tariffs and sharing common standards. The AEC intends to rival the EU and perhaps even eventually overtake it, based on the 5 per cent plus economic growth rate of ASEAN as compared to the 1–2 per cent growth of the EU. The AEC is also considering a single visa regime, akin to an Asian version of Europe's Schengen Agreement.

ASEAN policymakers emphasize that the impetus behind the AEC is to compete with the sizeable markets of the EU and the US as well as neighbouring China and India. With twice the population of the United States and one that is similar to the scale of the EU, the AEC has the potential to become one of the largest economic entities in the world. If, like the EU, the AEC becomes a common reference point for the rest of the world and, like the US, a market that global businesses feel obliged to be in, then it will have succeeded. It seems that Southeast Asians certainly have that ambition.

The US is adding uncertainty by focusing on bilateral trade agreements, which is a significant change from its previous agenda of multilateral and regional free trade. For President Donald Trump, the reason is that he is putting 'America First'. With the shift in the world's biggest economy, the question of how to address the backlash against globalization will be even more important.

Trumpism

The rise of Donald Trump is perhaps the most striking example of how those who have lost out economically in the past few decades sought a political outlet to convey their frustrations. An exit poll of voters conducted by *The New York Times* revealed that his voters thought the economy was performing poorly and their families' financial situation was worse as compared to those who voted for Democratic candidate Hillary Clinton.[2] There are other causes of disaffection. But globalization is in Trump's sights. This has worrying ramifications.

As discussed in the Joan Robinson chapter, median wages have been stagnant in America for forty years. The picture hasn't improved with the 2009 Great Recession. Jobs occupied by those in the middle of the wage spectrum, earning roughly $13.83–21.13 per hour, made up about 60 per cent of those lost during the last recession, but just 27 per cent of those created in the recovery. And it's not just in this recession. I recall attending a lecture by then President Bill Clinton who spoke about how many jobs had been created in the recovery after the early 1990s recession. A woman raised her hand and said, 'Yes, Mr. President, I have three of those jobs and still can't make ends meet.'

Economists attribute the stagnation of living standards to two main factors: globalization and 'skill-biased technical change'. The latter refers to technological progress benefiting skilled workers. In the US and across the industrialized countries, innovations such as computerization and automation have complemented and enhanced the skills of professionals. But the same innovations have replaced jobs that used to be done by people in the middle of the skill spectrum. The growth of automation especially has dramatically changed manufacturing. The number of robots has been increasing and, although presently concentrated in sectors like automobile production, their use is spreading throughout the economy. Hence jobs at either end of the skill distribution are growing, while those in the middle are declining.

This is intertwined with globalization. As discussed in the Ricardo chapter, trade creates 'losers' when an economy imports what was previously made domestically. The 'winners' are those who work in the industries that are expanding because a country is specializing in that sector and exporting from it. As US imports of manufactured goods have increased, mid-skilled jobs in that sector have been disappearing. After growing from 13 million jobs in 1950 to peak at nearly 20 million in 1980, 2010 saw a drop to a historic low of about 11.5 million. A rebound since the recession has taken manufacturing employment up to around 12.3 million, although this is still lower than in 1950. It's a similar pattern in the UK. Around 2.6 million people work in manufacturing, a figure that has halved since the late 1970s. Manufacturing accounts for 8 per cent of all jobs, down from a quarter in 1978.

This combination of factors has resulted in a lack of improvement in living standards for many Americans in the middle of the income distribution, and it's a big part of the dissatisfaction with the status quo expressed in the last election.

I had my own experience of the rise of Trump when I presented a documentary for the BBC titled *Linda for Congress*. I went on the road to take the pulse of the electorate before the 2016 elections by embarking on a hypothetical campaign to run to become a United States congresswoman. We 'hired' a campaign manager, a pollster, a fundraiser, a speech writer, etc. – the whole set of political campaign staff. As an economist and broadcaster, I am familiar with politicians but it never occurred to me to want to become one.

In order to remain impartial, I ran as an Independent. That worsened my chances straight away because I didn't have the support, financial and otherwise, or the voter base of the Democratic or Republican party. John Whitbeck, the head of the Republican Party in Virginia, said that he would 'crush' me if I ran against his guy.

Jokingly, I hope, because that's where my hypothetical district was. We chose Virginia because it's one of the handful of super-swing states in the US presidential election. It's purple in complexion (a blend of Democrats and Republicans, so blue and red), and that was reflected in the fact that it had a Democratic governor but was represented by predominately Republican Congress members. We focused on the 5th District, since the incumbent was a Republican while the previous one had been a Democrat.

I travelled through the state to meet voters. I met a tobacco farmer in Keysville who ran a global business selling his crops, including soybeans, to Russia, Vietnam and Brazil, among others. I met him in his impressive house on ten acres of land with its own lake and horses. As an exporter, he was supportive of open global markets, but he did not think that globalization worked for Americans. For instance, he told me that he was opposed to President Obama's trade and immigration policies, which promoted greater openness. But, when I asked him about how he ran his farm, he told me that he wrote to his congressman to help get permission to employ his Mexican farmhands.

I experienced similar reactions at a Methodist church in Farmville and a Christmas Parade in Cumberland. The voters I met were a mix of Republicans and Democrats, among whom was a grandmother who was watching the parade on the back of a pick-up truck with her extended family. This housekeeper told me that it seemed wrong for a family of six to live on just $12 an hour. She, like most of the others I had met, were blue-collar workers whose livelihoods had been squeezed by globalization and technological change that has shrunk the number of mid-skilled, well-paid factory jobs.

And, like others, she was voting for Trump, though they were nice about my hypothetical campaign. What stuck with me was the support that Trump had, especially among those who believed that they had lost out in the past few decades. Now that Trump is president, his supporters want a bigger piece of the economic pie.

Helping the losers from globalization

The question is how best to do so. This challenge isn't just for America but for any nation where the benefits of globalization have not been shared fairly.

The impressive growth of emerging economies in the past few decades has led to less inequality between nations as more poor countries 'catch up' to rich ones during an era where markets around the world have become increasingly connected through trade and investment. Globalization has helped emerging economies to grow well since they have been able to export to America and Europe while benefiting from Western investment.

So, because of the relatively faster growth of emerging economies, inequality has fallen across nations as the income gap has narrowed between developed and developing countries. Yet, global income inequality has stayed largely unchanged. That's because *within* countries, inequality on average has either failed to improve significantly or, in some cases, even become worse.

Recall from the Alfred Marshall chapter how sharp the rise in inequality has been in America. Inequality in America has risen so much that the current era has been dubbed a Second Gilded Age.

Although not always so stark, inequality is a problem for many nations, including Britain, where economic disparity has contributed to a backlash against globalization and even against capitalism itself. The term 'inclusive growth', which refers to economic growth that benefits everyone in a society, has been touted in the United Kingdom. It's also been heard in America, which has suffered from a 'squeezed' middle class and stagnant wages.

Though the rise in income inequality can be partly traced to globalization, that does not suggest the remedy is to be found in trade policy alone. As detailed in the David Ricardo chapter, there are certainly distributional effects from trade – some groups will win, others will lose – even if the overall economy gains. But there are other factors at play too. It's difficult to disentangle the effects on inequality stemming from trade from those that arise due to technological change that rewards the highly skilled more than those workers in the middle of the skill spectrum; the latter has a larger impact. Even though there are measures that can be included in trade agreements to ensure that appropriate standards for labour and environment protection are met, domestic policy measures such as redistribution and government spending on skills are more likely to be able to address directly growing inequality.

An example of a fiscal policy that can aid redistribution and economic growth is government-backed investment in both hard and soft infrastructure, as noted in the Keynes chapter. With low borrowing costs after the financial crisis, the US, British, European, Japanese and other governments don't have to pay much to raise capital on bond markets, so it may be a good time to invest, as discussed in that chapter. Infrastructure investment could generate well-paid, middle-skilled jobs, since the sector spans manufacturing as well as the digital economy. Such targeted fiscal policy could raise incomes for certain segments of the population instead of general policies that redistribute income. Improving infrastructure and raising the income of the middle class who comprise the bulk of consumers are both likely to increase growth.

Helping the losers from globalization and addressing inequality should, then, be primarily a domestic rather than a trade issue for governments. Yet, the backlash against globalization focuses policymakers' attention on trade agreements, which means that further opening up is under strain. But the burst of foreign direct investment that accompanied the rapid growth of international trade since the early 1990s was one of the reasons developing countries grew so well that a billion people were lifted out of extreme poverty and reduced the gap between them and rich nations.

What would our Great Economists make of all of this? Would they say globalization is in trouble?

Great Economists on the backlash against globalization

For Adam Smith and David Ricardo, pursuing free trade would be at the top of their priorities. During the era of the classical economists, which included the repeal of the Corn Laws, being an open economy helped the UK punch above its weight in the world. They would undoubtedly urge countries to focus on the benefits of globalization.

For Karl Marx, the election of Trump may be read as a populist revolt against the capitalists who have gained from globalization while the working classes have lost out. Joan Robinson, who latterly supported communist regimes in China and North Korea, may well share that sentiment. Their aims would include wanting to see a radical change in institutions, particularly around employment, to address inequities.

Consistent with his policies to reduce inequality, Alfred Marshall would urge using moderate redistribution in terms of taxes and transfers to help the losers from globalization. Given his later conversion to redistributive policies, he would probably agree that the focus should be on domestic and not mainly trade policies to address the distributional impact from globalization.

Irving Fisher would be watching for signs of major economies turning inward, which would add to the risk of repeating the 1930s. That's when protectionist measures such as the Smoot–Hawley Act imposed high tariffs on imports into the United States, which worsened the Great Depression. Fisher would also be monitoring the impact of heightened economic uncertainty stemming from growing anti-globalization sentiment on international investors who buy government debt and determine the borrowing cost for all of us. The less well-off would be hit hardest as they are more likely to rely on loans to fund their homes, for instance.

For John Maynard Keynes, an active government which spent to help the losers from globalization would be an answer. He would advocate increasing public investment to create those middle-skilled jobs that have been hollowed out by the globalization process. He would certainly not shy away from deploying an array of domestic policies to address the backlash against globalization and boost economic growth at the same time.

His contemporary Joseph Schumpeter would concur with the need for all nations to maintain their global outlook. More open and competitive markets speed up the process of creative destruction, which is good for growth in the long run. He wrote during the depths of the Great Depression and subsequent world war, so unsurprisingly, he would value openness to the world and say that it was essential for strongly growing nations.

Friedrich Hayek and Milton Friedman would agree. They would advocate for free markets, in particular, ensuring that political events such as Trump's America First policy and Brexit did not mean that the US and Britain turned inward and compromised the operation of markets. Hayek viewed globalization as enabling path-breaking nations to move ahead, which then allowed other countries to benefit from catch-up growth by imitating successful nations. They would applaud both the openness of many markets around the world and the greater interconnectedness of nations that followed.

Douglass North would urge an examination of where the current trade deals have failed to address the concerns of losers and reform them where appropriate. He may also embody the most pertinent views as to how to manage Brexit in particular. Britain leaving the EU presents a circumstance entirely different from that of a country seeking a trade agreement afresh. North's work stresses how path dependence and history matter. For him, building on existing institutions would be vital to formulating a future relationship between the UK and the EU.

Robert Solow would stress that investment is key to stronger growth and better jobs. But international agreements on investments are few (the EU and China intend to agree one), so he would presumably support a push to set common standards on investment and liberalize or open up the services sector, for which rules and regulations are more important than tariffs.

Undoubtedly, most of the Great Economists would strongly advocate for a continuing process of liberalization and not a turn inward, given how important globalization has been for economic growth. The sentiment would be even stronger for their intellectual followers who have lived through the extraordinary period of globalization since the end of the Cold War in the early 1990s and incorporated such insights into their research. There are many who have benefited from the pioneering research of the Great Economists, but MIT's Paul Samuelson stands out. His theories embody the synthesis of Keynesian and neoclassical ideas that characterize economics today. Samuelson helped develop the 'neoclassical synthesis' approach, which is the basic framework for modern macroeconomics, discussed in the Keynes chapter.

In addition, Paul Samuelson's seminal work furthered David Ricardo's model and has become the standard set of theories for analysing the impact of international trade on the economies of trading nations. Samuelson's research explained how trade boosted growth, but at the same time unevenly affected workers. His work can help us think about the 'losers' from international trade. So, the ideas of this great economist can point to how to address the backlash against globalization.

Paul Samuelson, 'the last of the great general economists'

Paul Samuelson was born in 1915 and came of age in the 1930s, when the rise of protectionism worsened the US economy. Samuelson was the leading Keynesian in America after the Second World War, although he described himself as a 'cafeteria Keynesian' as he merely selected the parts that he liked.[3] He adopted Keynesianism after being taught by top neoclassical economists at the University of Chicago, where he enrolled at the age of sixteen, after which he obtained his PhD at Harvard University and joined MIT in 1940.

Regarding his approach to economics, Samuelson remarked: 'I did not throw out my education lightly, but what I was being taught was of no use in explaining what I saw around me. It was the Great Depression . . . Keynesianism really fitted what was going on pretty well.'[4]

But he changed his mind after 1967: 'I had distrust . . . of American Keynesianism. For better or worse, US Keynesianism was so far ahead of where it started.'[5]

Samuelson had by then joined together neoclassical economic thought with John Maynard Keynes's approach, a consensus view that had starting emerging in the post-war period, into a framework known as 'neoclassical synthesis'. Samuelson's textbook *Economics* helped to popularize this approach. It has been in continuous print since 1948. Later editions were revised by Yale economist William Nordhaus; the nineteenth edition was published in 2009, the year of his death. *Economics* was the best-selling economics textbook for decades; millions of copies were sold worldwide. Samuelson was quoted as saying: 'Let those who will, write the nation's laws if I can write its textbooks.'[6] As a sign of his stature, he was awarded the Nobel Prize in 1970, the first American to be recognized, in the second year of the annual award.

So, this great economist's work, including his ideas on trade, embodies the legacy of the dominant mainstream strands of economics that we have covered in this book. When he passed away at age ninety-four, *The Economist* described him as the 'last of the great general economists'.[7] Samuelson was a generalist who worked on a wide range of issues concerning the economy, such as trade and public finance. He didn't specialize in any one area, as later economists tended to do.

It's fitting that this final chapter includes what this 'last of the great general economists' would have made of the backlash against globalization. Paul Samuelson just missed the recovery from the global financial crisis that has heightened the debate over the impact of globalization. His work on the welfare effects of trade, building on the Ricardian model, can help assess how globalization policies can be reshaped, given the political discontent revealed by Brexit and Trumpism.

His research has helped to explain how people's livelihoods are affected by trade; specifically, he has shown how trade affects wages and incomes within a country. His factor price equalization theorem says that, when nations trade, prices of traded goods will converge, and so would the wages of those producing those products. That means that wages in America will decline and move towards those of its trading partner, for example China, over time in the traded sectors. It helps to explain the stagnant median wages of particularly blue-collar workers, especially in manufacturing.

Trade, therefore, has a direct impact on incomes and standards of living. Having helped to identify this effect, Samuelson, whose approximate lineage is Keynesian, would be likely to have looked to domestic fiscal policy to help the 'losers' from globalization. Based on his work on social welfare or welfare for a society, he would have recommended that all such redistributive policies be judged through the lens of an ethical observer to decide which policy was better than another. The challenging practicalities of implementing such an approach also helps explain why good policies are not always adopted.

But leaving the distributional consequences of globalization unaddressed would allow the negative attitudes against globalization to continue and doubts could even be raised over whether it is beneficial to trade. That is worrying for the future of global economic growth itself. The challenge would be getting leaders to act. An adviser to US presidents, Paul Samuelson once remarked: 'I can't think of a President who has been overburdened by a knowledge of economics.'[8]

At least the right questions are now being asked, even though the solutions are not straightforward. Samuelson would have approved. He once quipped: 'Good questions outrank easy answers.'[9]

The way forward

Brexit and Trumpism are among the most prominent political expressions of discontent with the status quo. Globalization's unequal impact, creating winners and losers, is part of that status quo. But there are other factors, such as robotics and automation, at play too.

Still, it can be easier to be unhappy with globalization because it is more discernible than the impact of encroaching technological change. If trade did not improve welfare and benefit a nation, then Samuelson believed that countries wouldn't engage in it and would revert to a state of 'autarky' in which there was no international trade.[10] Yet there has been trade among nations for centuries; it is a question of addressing where and why trade doesn't work for everyone.

That would be precisely the sort of challenge that the Great Economists would relish. For them, the chance to redefine how globalization is managed so that the benefits can be spread more widely would be viewed as an opportunity to rethink some fundamental concepts. They would surely embrace as intellectually stimulating the challenge of re-examining how to raise the quality of economic growth and not just its speed. Explaining how the economy optimally operates, and analysing what hasn't worked and how that can be improved, is how they made their collective mark on the world.

The Great Economists in this book set the foundations of economics and crafted the models that underpin the field to this day. They formulated the general models to explain how the economy works. From Adam Smith's 'invisible hand' to the Solow model of economic growth, we have, respectively, the general model of how an efficient market operates and what generates prosperity. The Great Economists also shared a propensity to push the boundaries of economics to come up with models that better explained the real world; for example Joan Robinson was not content with the assumption that markets operated perfectly all the time so she developed a theory of imperfect competition.

And the Great Economists were all drawn to the most pressing economic issues of the day, for which they offered analyses and ways forward. Recall that David Ricardo's theory of international trade contributed to the repeal of the protectionist Corn Laws, while John Maynard Keynes played a part in the recovery after the 1930s Great Depression. Milton Friedman tackled the cause of that depression, which helped the central bankers in charge of the 2009 Great Recession to avoid repeating the mistakes of the last systemic banking crisis. Thus, the insights of the Great Economists, which have been gleaned from over two centuries of studying the world's economic problems, can help us shape the future of globalization and confront today's challenges.

Although they were very different characters, and sometimes disagreed fiercely about how the economy works, the Great Economists were similar in a number of respects. The key one is that they formulated general models to tackle the biggest economic challenges. That is why their thinking remains relevant today. The legacy of their lives and work demonstrates that ideas have always had a lasting impact on society – both then and now.

Acknowledgements

I am hugely indebted to Graeme Chamberlin for his steadfast support of this project. His many contributions to the book, including numerous insightful additions, based on his impressive economic knowledge, were invaluable.

I am also extremely grateful to Martin Slater. His encyclopaedic knowledge of economics, and of economists, added so much to the book. He injected colour and helpful historical context, which were greatly appreciated.

This book would not have been possible without the support and encouragement of my brilliant publisher, Daniel Crewe, at Viking. His insightful edits and keen interest have improved the text and he has been a delight to work with throughout. I feel lucky that he came up with the idea for this book that suits my interests so well.

Another key person is my agent, Will Francis, of Janklow and Nesbit UK. He is, simply put, terrific in every respect. I am very fortunate to have him in my corner as a long-standing supporter.

I would like to thank my US publisher, Pronoy Sarkar, at Picador, an imprint of Macmillan. His enthusiasm for this book is infectious! I feel fortunate to have his support and encouragement.

I would also like to acknowledge the many wonderful journalists with whom I have worked over the years. Their dedication to telling stories of relevance to people's lives made it possible for me to present a wide variety of TV and radio programmes that cover some of the most important economic and business issues of our time. I am delighted to include some of those adventures here.

A special thanks goes to Hannah Ludbrook for her enthusiastic promotion of my book, and to Connor Brown for all of his help throughout the enjoyable process. I also appreciate all of the work of Sarah Scarlett at Penguin Random House, who has looked after the international rights so well. And I thank Trevor Horwood for his diligent copy-editing of the manuscript, as well as Dave Cradduck for his thoughtful compilation of the index. Indeed, a huge thanks goes out to the helpful Ellie Smith and the entire team at Viking/Penguin Random House for their energetic support of this book.

The contributions of my students, colleagues and members of the public are also evident throughout this work, since they have helped me identify the economic issues that matter most. Our interactions in the classroom, at conferences and in public forums have left an indelible imprint on me as to how economics affects our lives. I am immensely grateful to have had so many opportunities to hear and discuss the impact of economic policies.

Finally, I would like to thank all of you – the readers of this book – for being interested in the big economic challenges of our time. It is only through your engagement that we can go about crafting a better economic future for us all.

Glossary

BRIC economies The acronym stands for Brazil, Russia, India and China, a term coined by investment bank Goldman Sachs to identify the large emerging markets with good growth potential.

current account deficit/surplus The difference between the value of traded goods and services, and portfolio capital, flowing into and out of the country.

first-generation currency crisis The Latin American crisis of 1981–82.

forward guidance Central banks giving guidance as to where interest rates might be in the future.

G7 A group comprising seven of the world's major economies – Canada, France, Germany, Italy, Japan, the United Kingdom and the United States – formed with the intention of shaping global economic policy.

global financial crisis The failure of many of the world's leading financial institutions precipitated in 2008 by the collapse of the US sub-prime mortgage market.

gold standard Exchange rate system operational in the nineteenth and early twentieth centuries in which participating countries fixed their currencies to be exchanged for a specified amount of gold.

Great Crash The collapse of the US stock market in October 1929. Also known as the Wall Street Crash.

Great Depression The worldwide economic downturn that followed the *Great Crash* and lasted for most of the 1930s.

Great Recession The recession that followed the *global financial crisis* in 2009.

IMF (International Monetary Fund) A Bretton Woods institution focused on global economic stability.

inclusive growth Economic growth that benefits everyone in a society.

laissez-faire Literally 'let (people) do'. Used to describe a policy of non-intervention by the state or government.

Long Depression The global recession that occurred during the last quarter of the nineteenth century.

macroprudential policy Central bank regulations aiming for financial stability.

median income The level of income of the person at the midpoint of the distribution.

monopoly A firm that has market power in the product market.

monopsony A firm that has market power in the labour market.

OECD (Organisation for Economic Co-operation and Development) A think-tank for advanced economies, based in Paris.

negative interest rates Central banks charging commercial banks for depositing money with them.

purchasing power parity (PPP) A theory of exchange rate determination, which argues that the exchange rate will change so that the price of a particular good or service will be the same regardless of where you buy it.

quantitative easing (QE) Cash injections into the economy by a central bank.

Ricardian equivalence David Ricardo's theory that rational people know that the government debt will have to be repaid at some point in the form of higher taxes so they save in anticipation and do not increase current consumption that boosts growth.

second-generation currency crisis The collapse of the European exchange rate mechanism (ERM) in 1992.

STEM Science, technology, engineering and mathematics.

third-generation financial and currency crisis The Asian financial crisis of 1997–98.

Wall Street Crash See *Great Crash*.

World Bank A Bretton Woods institution focused on alleviating poverty.

WTO (World Trade Organization) An intergovernmental organization formed in 1995 that regulates international trade, which was preceded by the General Agreement on Tariffs and Trade (GATT), in force since 1947.

Bibliography

Acemoglu, Daron and James A. Robinson, 2012, *Why Nations Fail: The Origins of Power, Prosperity, and Poverty*, London: Profile Books

Agénor, Pierre-Richard, Otaviano Canuto and Michael Jelenic, 2012, 'Avoiding Middle-Income Growth Traps', *Economic Premise*, 98, World Bank, Washington, DC

Allen, Robert Loring, 1993, *Irving Fisher: A Biography*, Cambridge, MA and Oxford: Blackwell

Aslanbeigui, Nahid and Guy Oakes, 2009, *The Provocative Joan Robinson: The Making of a Cambridge Economist*, Durham, NC: Duke University Press

Bagehot, Walter, 1895, 'Ricardo', in Walter Bagehot, *Economic Studies*, ed. Richard Holt Hutton, London: Longmans, Green & Co., pp. 197–208

Barnett, Alina, Sandra Batten, Adrian Chiu, Jeremy Franklin and María Sebastiá-Barriel, 2014, 'The UK Productivity Puzzle', *Bank of England Quarterly Bulletin*, Q2, pp. 114–28

Behrens, Kristian, Giordano Mion, Yasusada Murata and Jens Südekum, 2014, 'Trade, Wages, and Productivity', *International Economic Review*, 55(4), pp. 1305–48

Bernanke, Ben, 1983, 'Nonmonetary Effects of the Financial Crisis in the Propagation of the Great Depression', *American Economic Review*, 73(3), pp. 257–76

——, 2002, 'Deflation: Making Sure "It" Doesn't Happen Here', remarks by Governor Ben S. Bernanke before the National Economists Club, Washington, DC, 21 November; www.federalreserve.gov/boarddocs/speeches/2002/20021121/

Blaug, Mark, 1956, 'The Empirical Content of Ricardian Economics', *Journal of Political Economy*, 64(1), pp. 41–58

——, 1985, *Economic Theory in Retrospect*, Cambridge: Cambridge University Press

Buchholz, Todd, 2007, *New Ideas from Dead Economists: An Introduction to Modern Economic Thought*, New York: Penguin

Burns, J. H. and H. L. A. Hart, eds., 1977, *A Comment on the Commentaries and A Fragment on Government*, The Collected Works of Jeremy Bentham, Oxford: Clarendon Press

Cairncross, Alec, 1993, *Austin Robinson: The Life of an Economic Adviser*, Basingstoke: Palgrave Macmillan

Caldwell, Bruce, 1998, 'Why Didn't Hayek Review Keynes's *General Theory?*', *History of Political Economy*, 30(4), pp. 545–69

———, 2004, *Hayek's Challenge: An Intellectual Biography of F. A. Hayek*, Chicago: University of Chicago Press

Campbell, John, 2008, *Margaret Thatcher*, vol. II: *The Iron Lady*. London: Vintage

Chamberlin, Graeme and Linda Yueh, 2006, *Macroeconomics*, London: Cengage

Churchill, Winston, 1974, 'Speech, House of Commons, November 11, 1947', in *Winston S. Churchill: His Complete Speeches, 1897–1963*, ed. Robert Rhodes James, vol. VII, London: R. R. Bowker, p. 7566

Clement, Douglas, 2002, 'Interview with Robert Solow', *The Region*, Federal Reserve Bank of Minneapolis, 1 September; www.minneapolisfed. org/publications/the-region/interview-with-robert-solow

Colander, David C. and Harry Landreth, 1996, *The Coming of Keynesianism to America: Conversations with the Founders of Keynesian Economics*, Cheltenham: Edward Elgar

Collier, Paul, 2007, *The Bottom Billion: Why the Poorest Countries are Failing and What Can Be Done About It*, Oxford: Oxford University Press

Cooper, Douglas P., 1973, 'Dr. Paul Samuelson', *The Douglas P. Cooper Distinguished Contemporaries Collection*, 1 September; www.wnyc.org/story/paul-samuelson/

Crafts, Nicholas, 2005, 'The First Industrial Revolution: Resolving the Slow Growth/Rapid Industrialization Paradox', *Journal of the European Economic Association*, 3(2/3), pp. 525–34

David, Paul A., 1990, 'The Dynamo and the Computer: A Historical Perspective on the Modern Productivity Paradox', *American Economic Review*, 80(2), pp. 355–61

De Vecchi, Nicolò, 2006, 'Hayek and the *General Theory*', *European Journal of the History of Economic Thought*, 13(2), pp. 233–58

Dworkin, Ronald W., 2015, *How Karl Marx Can Save American Capitalism*, Lanham, MD: Lexington Books

Ebenstein, Alan, 2001, *Friedrich Hayek: A Biography*, New York: St. Martin's Press

Ebenstein, Lanny, 2007, *Milton Friedman: A Biography*, New York: Palgrave Macmillan

Fisher, Irving, 1892, 'Mathematical Investigations in the Theory of Value and Prices', *Transactions of the Connecticut Academy*, 9, p. 119

———, 1919, 'Economists in Public Service: Annual Address of the President', *American Economic Review*, 9(1), Supplement: Papers and Proceedings of the

Thirty-First Annual Meeting of the American Economic Association, pp. 5–21

——, 1930, *The Stock Market Crash – and After*, New York: The Macmillan Company

——, 1933, 'The Debt-Deflation Theory of Great Depressions', *Econometrica*, 1(4), pp. 337–57

——, 1997, *The Works of Irving Fisher*, 14 volumes, ed. William J. Barber, assisted by Robert W. Dimand and Kevin Foster, London: Pickering & Chatto

Fisher, Irving and H. Bruce Brougham, 1928, *Prohibition Still at its Worst*, New York: Alcohol Information Committee

Fisher, Irving Norton, 1956, *My Father: Irving Fisher*, New York: Comet Press Books

Fitzgibbons, Athol, 1988, *Keynes's Vision: A New Political Economy*, Oxford: Oxford University Press

Flatau, Paul, 2001, 'Some Reflections on the "Pigou-Robinson" Theory of Exploitation', *History of Economics Review*, 33, pp. 1–16

Foster, Richard, 2012, 'Creative Destruction Whips Through Corporate America', *Innosight Executive Briefing*; www.innosight.com/wp-content/uploads/2016/08/creative-destruction-whips-through-corporate-america-final2015.pdf

Friedman, Milton, 1963, *Inflation: Causes and Consequences*, Bombay: Asia Publishing House

——, 1991, 'Economic Freedom, Human Freedom, Political Freedom', address by Milton Friedman, The Smith Center, Seattle Central College, 1 November; http://seattlecentral.edu/faculty/jhubert/friedmanspeech.html

——, 1999, 'Transcript for: Friedrich Hayek', Think Tank with Ben Wattenberg, pbs.org; www.pbs.org/thinktank/transcript726.html

——, 2002 [1962], *Capitalism and Freedom: Fortieth Anniversary Edition*, Chicago: University of Chicago Press

——, 2012, 'Milton Friedman in His Own Words', Becker Friedman Institute for Research in Economics, University of Chicago; https://bfi.uchicago.edu/news/post/milton-friedman-his-own-words

Friedman, Milton and Rose Friedman, 1980, *Free to Choose*, San Diego: Harcourt

——, 1998, *Two Lucky People: Memoirs*, Chicago: University of Chicago Press

Friedman, Milton and Anna Jacobson Schwartz, 1971 [1963], *A Monetary History of the United States, 1867–1960*, Princeton: Princeton University Press

Goodridge, Peter, Jonathan Haskel and Gavin Wallis, 2013, 'Can Intangible Investment Explain the UK Productivity Puzzle?', *National Institute Economic Review*, 224, pp. R48–R58

Groenewegen, Peter, 1995, *A Soaring Eagle: Alfred Marshall 1842–1924*, Aldershot: Edward Elgar

Hansen, Alvin H., 1939, 'Economic Progress and Declining Population Growth', *American Economic Review*, 29(1), pt I, pp. 1–15

Hausmann, Ricardo and Federico Sturzenegger, 2007, 'The Missing Dark Matter in the *Wealth of Nations* and Its Implications for Global Imbalances', *Economic Policy*, 22(51), pp. 470–518

Hayek, Friedrich A., 1979, *A Conversation with Friedrich A. von Hayek: Science and Socialism,* Washington, DC: American Enterprise Institute for Public Policy Research

———, 1986, 'The Moral Imperative of the Market', in *The Unfinished Agenda: Essays on the Political Economy of Government Policy in Honour of Arthur Seldon*, London: Institute of Economic Affairs

———, 1994, *Hayek on Hayek: An Autobiographical Dialogue*, ed. Stephen Kresge and Leif Wenar, Chicago: University of Chicago Press

———, 2001 [1944], *The Road to Serfdom*, London and New York: Routledge Classics

———, 2006 [1960], *The Constitution of Liberty*, London and New York: Routledge

International Labour Organization, 2014, *Global Wage Report 2014/15*, Geneva: International Labour Office

———, 2016, *Global Wage Report 2016/17*, Geneva: International Labour Office

International Labour Organization and Organisation for Economic Co-operation and Development, with contributions from the International Monetary Fund and World Bank Group, 2015, 'The Labour Share in G20 Economies', report prepared for the G20 Employment Working Group, Antalya, Turkey, 26–27 February

Jörberg, Lennart, 1997, 'Robert W. Fogel and Douglass C. North', in *Nobel Lectures in Economic Sciences, 1991–1995*, ed. Torsten Persson, Singapore: World Scientific, pp. 61–126

Keynes, John Maynard, 1924, 'Alfred Marshall, 1842–1924', *Economic Journal*, 34(135), pp. 311–72

———, 1931, 'The Pure Theory of Money: A Reply to Dr Hayek', *Economica*, 34, pp. 387–97

———, 1936, *The General Theory of Employment, Interest and Money*, London: Palgrave Macmillan

———, 1937, 'The General Theory of Employment', *Quarterly Journal of Economics*, 51(2), pp. 209–23

———, 1963 [1931], 'Economic Possibilities for Our Grandchildren', in *Essays in Persuasion*, New York: W. W. Norton

————, 1971–89, *The Collected Writings of John Maynard Keynes*, 30 vols., ed. Elizabeth Johnson and Donald Moggridge, Cambridge: Cambridge University Press

King, John E., 2013, *David Ricardo*, Basingstoke: Palgrave Macmillan

Krugman, Paul, 1998, 'The Hangover Theory', *Slate*, 4 December; www.slate.com/articles/business/the_dismal_science/1998/12/the_hangover_theory.html

Lucas, Robert E., Jr., 1988, 'On the Mechanics of Economic Development', *Journal of Monetary Economics*, 22(1), pp. 3–42

Marshall, Alfred, 1890, *Principles of Economics*, vol. I, London: Macmillan

————, 1961, *Principles of Economics*, vol. II, London: Macmillan for the Royal Economic Society

Marx, Karl, 1978 [1853], 'The Future Results of British Rule in India', *New York Daily Tribune*, 8 August 1853, in Robert Tucker, ed., 1978, *The Marx-Engels Reader*, 2nd revised edn, New York: W. W. Norton

————, 1990–92 [1881–83], *Capital*, ed. Frederick Engels, trans. Ben Fowkes (vol. I) and David Fernbach (vols. II and III), London: Penguin Classics

————, 2008 [1852], *The Eighteenth Brumaire of Louis Bonaparte*, Rockville, MD: Wildside Press

Marx, Karl and Friedrich Engels, 2015 [1848], *The Communist Manifesto*, London: Penguin Classics

McCraw, Thomas K., 2007, *Prophet of Innovation: Joseph Schumpeter and Creative Destruction*, Cambridge, MA: Harvard University Press

McCulla, Stephanie H., Alyssa E. Holdren and Shelly Smith, 2013, 'Improved Estimates of the National Income and Product Accounts: Results of the 2013 Comprehensive Revision', US Bureau of Economic Analysis, Washington, DC

Milanovic, Branko, 2016, *Global Inequality: A New Approach for the Age of Globalization*, Cambridge, MA: Harvard University Press

Milgate, Murray and Shannon Stimson, 1991, *Ricardian Politics*, Princeton: Princeton University Press

Mill, John Stuart, 1848, *Principles of Political Economy*, London: John W. Parker

Minsky, Hyman P., 1992, 'The Financial Instability Hypothesis', The Jerome Levy Economics Institute of Bard College, Working Paper No. 74

Mitchell, Brian R., 1988, *Abstract of British Historical Statistics*, Cambridge: Cambridge University Press

Muro, Mark, Jonathan Rothwell, Scott Andes, Kenan Fikri and Siddharth Kulkarni, 2015, 'America's Advanced Industries', Brookings Institution,

Washington, DC; www.brookings.edu/wp-content/uploads/2015/02/ AdvancedIndustry_FinalFeb2lores-1.pdf

Nasar, Sylvia, 2011, *Grand Pursuit: The Story of the People Who Made Modern Economics*, New York: Simon & Schuster

Newcomb, Simon, 1885, *Principles of Political Economy*, New York: Harper

Nobelprize.org, 1974, 'Friedrich August von Hayek – Banquet Speech', Nobel Media AB 2014; www.nobelprize.org/nobel_prizes/economic-sciences/laureates/1974/hayek-speech.html

——, 1987, 'Robert M. Solow – Biographical', Nobel Media AB 2014; www.nobelprize.org/nobel_prizes/economic-sciences/laureates/1987/ solow-bio.html

——, 1987, 'Robert M. Solow – Prize Lecture: Growth Theory and After', Nobel Media AB 2014; www.nobelprize.org/nobel_prizes/ economic-sciences/laureates/1987/solow-lecture.html

——, 1993, 'Douglass C. North – Biographical', Nobel Media AB 2014; www.nobelprize.org/nobel_prizes/economic-sciences/laureates/1993/ north-bio.html

North, Douglass C., 1988, 'Institutions, Economic Growth and Freedom', in *Freedom, Democracy, and Economic Welfare: Proceedings of an International Symposium*, ed. Michael A. Walker, Vancouver: Fraser Institute

——, 1990, *Institutions, Institutional Change and Economic Performance*, Cambridge: Cambridge University Press

North, Douglass C., Gardner Brown and Dean Lueck, 2015, 'A Conversation with Douglass North', *Annual Review of Resource Economics*, 7, pp. 1–10

OECD, 2012, 'Income Inequality and Growth: The Role of Taxes and Transfers', OECD Economics Department Policy Notes, No. 9

——, 2013, 'New Sources of Growth: Intangible Assets', Paris: OECD; www.oecd.org/sti/inno/46349020.pdf

——, 2015, *Economic Surveys: United Kingdom*, Paris: OECD

Ostry, Jonathan D., Andrew Berg and Charalambos G. Tsangarides, 2014, 'Redistribution, Inequality, and Growth', International Monetary Fund Staff Discussion Note SDN/14/02; www.imf.org/external/pubs/ft/ sdn/2014/sdn1402.pdf

Parsons, Talcott, 1931, 'Wants and Activities in Marshall', *Quarterly Journal of Economics*, 46(1), pp. 101–40

Pessoa, João Paulo and John Van Reenen, 2013, 'Decoupling of Wage Growth and Productivity Growth? Myth and Reality', Centre for Economic Performance, London School of Economics and Political Science Discussion Paper No. 1246; http://cep.lse.ac.uk/pubs/download/ dp1246.pdf

Pigou, A. C., 1953, *Alfred Marshall and Current Thought*, London: Macmillan

Pigou, A. C., ed., 1925, *Memorials of Alfred Marshall*, London: Macmillan

Piketty, Thomas, 2014, *Capital in the Twenty-First Century*, Cambridge, MA: Harvard University Press

Ranelagh, John, 1991, *Thatcher's People: An Insider's Account of the Politics, the Power and the Personalities*, London: HarperCollins

Reagan, Ronald, 1986, 'The President's News Conference', 12 August; www.presidency.ucsb.edu/ws/?pid=37733

———, 1986, 'Remarks to State Chairpersons of the National White House Conference on Small Business', 15 August; www.reaganlibrary.gov/archives/speeches/1986/081586e.html

Reich, Robert, 2012, *Beyond Outrage: What Has Gone Wrong with Our Economy and Our Democracy, and How to Fix It*, New York: Vintage Books

Ricardo, David, 2011 [1817], *On the Principles of Political Economy and Taxation*, London: John Murray

Robinson, Joan, 1932, *Economics is a Serious Subject: The Apologia of an Economist to the Mathematician, the Scientist and the Plain Man*, Cambridge: Heffer

———, 1962, *Economic Philosophy*, Harmondsworth: Pelican Books

———, 1969 [1933], *The Economics of Imperfect Competition*, London: Palgrave Macmillan

———, 1974, *Reflections on the Theory of International Trade: Lectures Given in the University of Manchester*, Manchester: Manchester University Press

———, 1980, 'Marx, Marshall, and Keynes', *Collected Economic Papers*, vols. II–V, Cambridge, MA: MIT Press

Ross, Ian Simpson, 2010, *The Life of Adam Smith*, 2nd edn, Oxford: Oxford University Press

Samuelson, Paul A., 1969, 'The Way of an Economist', in *International Economic Relations*, ed. Paul A. Samuelson, International Economic Association Series, London: Macmillan, pp. 1–11

———, 1977, 'Joseph A. Schumpeter', *Dictionary of American Biography*, New York: Scribner

———, 1986, 'Gold and Common Stocks', in *The Collected Scientific Papers of Paul Samuelson*, vol. V, ed. Kate Crowley, Cambridge, MA: MIT Press

———, 2005, *On Being an Economist*, New York: Jorge Pinto Books Inc.

Schumpeter, Joseph, 1928, 'The Instability of Capitalism', *Economic Journal*, 38, pp. 361–86

———, 1934, *The Theory of Economic Development*, Cambridge, MA: Harvard University Press

———, 1939, *Business Cycles: A Theoretical, Historical and Statistical Analysis of the Capitalist Process*, 2 vols., New York: McGraw-Hill

———, 1942, *Capitalism, Socialism and Democracy*, New York: Harper & Brothers

————, 1951, *Ten Great Economists from Marx to Keynes*, New York and Oxford: Oxford University Press

————, 1954, *History of Economic Analysis*, New York: Oxford University Press

————, 1955, 'Social Classes in an Ethnically Homogeneous Environment', trans. Heinz Norden, in *Imperialism, Social Classes: Two Essays by Joseph Schumpeter*, New York: Meridian Books

————, 1991 [1918], 'The Crisis of the Tax State', in *The Economics and Sociology of Capitalism*, ed. Richard Swedberg, Princeton: Princeton University Press

————, 1997 [1954], *History of Economic Analysis*, London: Routledge

Shove, Gerald F., 1942, 'The Place of Marshall's *Principles* in the Development of Economic Theory', *Economic Journal*, 52(208), pp. 294–329

Skidelsky, Robert, 1995, *John Maynard Keynes*, vol. II: *The Economist as Saviour, 1920–1937*, London: Penguin

————, 2003, *John Maynard Keynes 1883–1946: Economist, Philosopher, Statesman*, New York: Penguin

————, 2010, *Keynes: The Return of the Master*, London: Penguin

Skousen, Mark, 2001, *The Making of Modern Economics*, Armonk, NY and London: M. E. Sharpe

Smith, Adam, 1759, *The Theory of Moral Sentiments*, London: A. Millar; Edinburgh: A. Kincaid & J. Bell

————, 1978 [1763], *Lectures on Jurisprudence* (alternative title for the *Lectures on Justice, Police, Revenue and Arms*), ed. Ronald E. Meek, David D. Raphael and Peter G. Stein, Oxford: Clarendon Press

————, 1979 [1776], *An Inquiry into the Nature and Causes of the Wealth of Nations by Adam Smith*, eds. R. H. Campbell, A. S. Skinner and W. B. Todd, Oxford: Clarendon Press

Solow, Robert, 1956, 'A Contribution to the Theory of Economic Growth', *Quarterly Journal of Economics*, 70(1), pp. 65–94

————, 1957, 'Technical Change and the Aggregate Production Function', *Review of Economics and Statistics*, 39(3), pp. 312–20

Sperber, Jonathan, 2013, *Karl Marx: A Nineteenth-Century Life*, New York: Liveright

Stewart, Dugald, 1793, 'Account of the Life and Writings of Adam Smith', read to the Royal Society of Edinburgh and published in Adam Smith's posthumous *Essays on Philosophical Subjects* of 1795, London and Edinburgh: T. Cadell Jun and W. Davies

Stiglitz, Joseph, 2012, *The Price of Inequality: How Today's Divided Society Endangers Our Future*, New York: W. W. Norton

Sutter, Robert G., 2013, *Foreign Relations of the PRC: The Legacies and Constraints of China's International Politics Since 1949*, Lanham, MD: Rowman & Littlefield

Taylor, John B., 1993, 'Discretion Versus Policy Rules in Practice', *Carnegie-Rochester Conference Series on Public Policy*, 39, pp. 195–214

————, 1999, 'A Historical Analysis of Monetary Policy Rules', in *Monetary Policy Rules*, ed. John B. Taylor, Chicago: University of Chicago Press, pp. 319–48

————, 2009, 'The Need to Return to a Monetary Framework', *Business Economics*, 44(2), pp. 63–72

————, 2012, 'Why We Still Need to Read Hayek', The Hayek Lecture, The Manhattan Institute for Policy Research, New York City; www. hoover.org/sites/default/files/hayek-lecture.pdf

Thatcher, Margaret, 1993, *The Downing Street Years*, London: HarperPress

Thompson, Derek, 2009, 'An Interview with Paul Samuelson, Part One', *The Atlantic*, 17 June; www.theatlantic.com/business/archive/2009/06/an-interview-with-paul-samuelson-part-one/19586/

Turner, Michael J., 1994, 'Before the Manchester School: Economic Theory in Early Nineteenth-Century Manchester', *History*, 79(256), pp. 216–41

Wapshott, Nicholas, 2011, *Keynes Hayek: The Clash That Defined Modern Economics*, New York: W. W. Norton

Wood, John Cunningham, ed., 1993, *Alfred Marshall: Critical Assessments, Volume IV*, London: Routledge

World Bank, 1993, *The East Asian Miracle: Economic Growth and Public Policy*, Washington, DC: World Bank

World Bank and Development Research Center of the State Council of China, 2013, 'China 2030: Building a Modern, Harmonious, and Creative Society', Washington, DC; http://documents.worldbank. org/curated/en/781101468239669951/China-2030-building-a-modern-harmonious-and-creative-society

Yellen, Janet, 2009, 'A Minsky Meltdown: Lessons for Central Bankers', presentation to the 18th Annual Hyman P. Minsky Conference on the State of the US and World Economies – 'Meeting the Challenges of the Financial Crisis'; www.frbsf.org/our-district/press/presidents-speeches/yellen-speeches/2009/april/yellen-minsky-meltdown-central-bankers/

Yergin, Daniel and Joseph Stanislaw, 1998, *The Commanding Heights: The Battle Between Government and the Marketplace that is Remaking the Modern World*, New York: Free Press

Yueh, Linda, 2010, *The Economy of China*, Cheltenham: Edward Elgar

————, 2011, *Enterprising China: Business, Economic, and Legal Developments Since 1979*, Oxford: Oxford University Press

————, 2013, *China's Economic Growth: The Making of an Economic Superpower*, Oxford: Oxford University Press

Notes

Introduction: Great Economists on Our Economic Challenges

1. Adam Smith, 1979 [1776], *An Inquiry into the Nature and Causes of the Wealth of Nations*, eds. R. H. Campbell, A. S. Skinner and W. B. Todd, Oxford: Clarendon Press, bk II, ch. 3, para 2.
2. Alvin H. Hansen, 1939, 'Economic Progress and Declining Population Growth', *American Economic Review*, 29(1), pt I, pp. 1–15.

Chapter 1 – Adam Smith: Should the Government Rebalance the Economy?

1. Adam Smith, 1979 [1776], *An Inquiry into the Nature and Causes of the Wealth of Nations*, ed. R. H. Campbell, A. S. Skinner and W. B. Todd, Oxford: Clarendon Press, bk IV, ch. 2, para. 10.
2. Ibid., bk V, ch. 2, pt II, appendix to arts. I & II, para. 12.
3. Ibid., bk V, ch. 1, pt III, art. II, para. 15.
4. Ibid., bk V, ch. 1, pt III, art. II, para. 8.
5. Dugald Stewart, 1793, 'Account of the Life and Writings of Adam Smith, LL. D.', read to the Royal Society of Edinburgh and published in Adam Smith's posthumous *Essays on Philosophical Subjects* of 1795, London and Edinburgh: T. Cadell Jun and W. Davies, pp. lxxx, lxxxi.
6. Ian Simpson Ross, 2010, *The Life of Adam Smith*, 2nd edn, Oxford: Oxford University Press, p. xxxi.
7. Smith, *Wealth of Nations*, bk V, ch. 3, para. 92.
8. Ross, *Life of Adam Smith*, p. xxxi.
9. Brian R. Mitchell, 1988, *Abstract of British Historical Statistics*, Cambridge: Cambridge University Press, pp. 869–73.

10. Stephanie H. McCulla, Alyssa E. Holdren and Shelly Smith, 2013, 'Improved Estimates of the National Income and Product Accounts: Results of the 2013 Comprehensive Revision', US Bureau of Economic Analysis, Washington, DC

11. OECD, 2013, 'New Sources of Growth: Intangible Assets', Paris: OECD; www.oecd.org/sti/inno/46349020.pdf

12. Adam Smith, 1978 [1763], *Lectures on Jurisprudence* (alternative title for the *Lectures on Justice, Police, Revenue and Arms*), ed. Ronald E. Meek, David D. Raphael and Peter G. Stein, Oxford: Clarendon Press, p. 499.

13. Smith, *Wealth of Nations*, bk I, ch. 2, para. 12.

14. Adam Smith, 1759, *The Theory of Moral Sentiments*, London: A. Millar; Edinburgh: A. Kincaid and J. Bell, pt IV, s. 1, para. 10.

15. Ibid.

16. Smith, *Wealth of Nations*, bk IV, ch. 2, para. 9.

17. Ibid., bk II, ch. 2, para. 106.

18. Ibid., bk II, ch. 4, paras. 14–15.

19. Ibid., bk I, ch. 11, pt 1, para. 5.

20. Ibid., bk V, ch. 1, pt 3, art. II, para. 50.

21. Ibid., bk V, ch. 1, pt 3, art. III, para. 14.

22. Ibid., bk IV, ch. 7, pt 2, para. 44.

23. Smith, *Lectures on Jurisprudence*, p. 514.

24. Ibid., bk V, ch. 3, para. 92.; Ross, *Life of Adam Smith*, p. 315.

25. Ross, *Life of Adam Smith*, p. 302.

26. Smith, *Wealth of Nations*, bk IV, ch. 5, Digression concerning the Corn Trade and Corn Laws, para. 43.

Chapter 2 – David Ricardo: Do Trade Deficits Matter?

1. John E. King, 2013, *David Ricardo*, Basingstoke: Macmillan, p. 5.

2. Ibid., pp. 15–16.

3. Thomas Piketty, 2014, *Capital in the Twenty-First Century*, Cambridge, MA: Harvard University Press, pp. 314–15.

4. Nicholas Crafts, 2005, 'The First Industrial Revolution: Resolving the Slow Growth/Rapid Industrialization Paradox', *Journal of the European Economic Association*, 3(2/3), pp. 525–34.

5. David Ricardo, 2011 [1817], *The Works and Correspondence of David Ricardo*, vol. IV, ed. Piero Sraffa, Cambridge: Cambridge University Press, p. 21.

6. Murray Milgate and Shannon Stimson, 1991, *Ricardian Politics*, Princeton: Princeton University Press, p. 144.

7. King, *David Ricardo*, p. 36.

8. Mark Blaug, 1956, 'The Empirical Content of Ricardian Economics', *Journal of Political Economy*, 64(1), pp. 41–58.

9. Walter Bagehot, 1895, 'Ricardo', in Walter Bagehot, *Economic Studies*, ed. Richard Holt Hutton, London: Longman, Green & Co., pp. 197–208.

10. Mark Blaug, 1985, *Economic Theory in Retrospect*, Cambridge: Cambridge University Press, p. 136.

11. Joseph Schumpeter, 1997 [1954], *History of Economic Analysis*, London: Routledge, pp. 472–3.

12. Adam Smith, 1979 [1776], *An Inquiry into the Nature and Causes of the Wealth of Nations*, eds. R. H. Campbell, A. S. Skinner and W. B. Todd, Oxford: Clarendon Press, bk IV, ch. 2, para 12.

13. Ricardo, *Works and Correspondence*, IV, p. 23.

14. Ibid., p. 21.

15. King, *David Ricardo*, p. 88.

16. Ricardo, *Works and Correspondence*, IV, pp. 28, 32.

17. Ibid., p. 35.

18. Ibid., p. 33.

19. Ibid., p. 41.

20. Ricardo Hausmann and Federico Sturzenegger, 2007, 'The Missing Dark Matter in the *Wealth of Nations* and Its Implications for Global Imbalances', *Economic Policy*, 22(51), pp. 470–518.

21. Mark Muro, Jonathan Rothwell, Scott Andes, Kenan Fikri and Siddharth Kulkarni, 2015, 'America's Advanced Industries', Brookings Institution, Washington, DC; www.brookings.edu/wp-content/uploads/2015/02/AdvancedIndustry_FinalFeb2lores-1.pdf

22. Paul A. Samuelson, 1969, 'The Way of an Economist', in *International Economic Relations*, ed. Paul A. Samuelson, International Economic Association Series, London: Macmillan, pp. 1–11, at p. 9.

23. Joan Robinson, 1974, *Reflections on the Theory of International Trade: Lectures Given in the University of Manchester*, Manchester: Manchester University Press, p. 1.

24. Ibid., pp. 1, 6.
25. Mark Skousen, 2001, *The Making of Modern Economics*, Armonk, NY and London: M. E. Sharpe, p. 18.
26. Smith, *Wealth of Nations*, bk IV, ch. 2, para 43.
27. Skousen, *The Making of Modern Economics*, p. 103.

Chapter 3 – Karl Marx: Can China Become Rich?

1. Karl Marx and Friedrich Engels, 2015 [1848], *The Communist Manifesto*, London: Penguin Classics, p. 9.
2. Todd Buchholz, 2007, *New Ideas from Dead Economists: An Introduction to Modern Economic Thought*, New York: Penguin, p. 129.
3. Ibid., p. 116.
4. Jonathan Sperber, 2013, *Karl Marx: A Nineteenth-Century Life*, New York: Liveright, p. 4.
5. Ibid., p. 5.
6. Ibid., p. 24.
7. Ibid., p. 72.
8. Ibid., p. 99.
9. Marx and Engels, *Communist Manifesto*, p. 39.
10. Ibid.
11. Sperber, *Karl Marx*, p. 255.
12. Karl Marx, 2008 [1852], *The Eighteenth Brumaire of Louis Bonaparte*, Rockville, MD: Wildside Press, p. 1.
13. Karl Marx, 1978 [1853], 'The Future Results of British Rule in India', *New York Daily Tribune*, 8 August 1853, in Robert Tucker, ed., 1978, *The Marx-Engels Reader*, 2nd revised edn, New York: W. W. Norton, p. 662.
14. Sperber, *Karl Marx*, p. 450.
15. Ibid., p. 431.
16. Linda Yueh, 2013, *China's Growth: The Making of an Economic Superpower*, Oxford: Oxford University Press, chapter 5.
17. World Bank and Development Research Center of the State Council of China, 2013, 'China 2030: Building a Modern, Harmonious, and Creative Society', Washington, DC; http://documents.worldbank.

org/curated/en/781101468239669951/China-2030-building-a-modern-harmonious-and-creative-society

18. Karl Marx, 1991 [1883], *Capital: Volume III*, ed. Frederick Engels, trans. David Fernbach, London: Penguin Classics, p. 678.

19. Marx and Engels, *Communist Manifesto*, p. 27.

20. Robert G. Sutter, 2013, *Foreign Relations of the PRC: The Legacies and Constraints of China's International Politics Since 1949*, Lanham, MD: Rowman & Littlefield, p. 23.

21. Linda Yueh, 2010, *The Economy of China*, Cheltenham: Edward Elgar, chapter 4.

22. Buchholz, *New Ideas from Dead Economists*, p. 136.

23. Ronald W. Dworkin, 2015, *How Karl Marx Can Save American Capitalism*, Lanham, MD: Lexington Books, p. 72.

24. Ibid.

25. Sperber, *Karl Marx*, p. 65.

Chapter 4 – Alfred Marshall: Is Inequality Inevitable?

1. Joseph Stiglitz, 2012, *The Price of Inequality: How Today's Divided Society Endangers Our Future*, New York: W. W. Norton.

2. Peter Groenewegen, 1995, *A Soaring Eagle: Alfred Marshall 1842–1924*, Aldershot: Edward Elgar, p. 227.

3. Ibid., p. 294.

4. Michael J. Turner, 1994, 'Before the Manchester School: Economic Theory in Early Nineteenth-Century Manchester', *History*, 79(256), pp. 216–41.

5. John Maynard Keynes, 1924, 'Alfred Marshall, 1842–1924', *Economic Journal*, 34(135), pp. 311–72.

6. Gerald F. Shove, 1942, 'The Place of Marshall's *Principles* in the Development of Economic Theory', *Economic Journal*, 52(208), pp. 294–329.

7. A. C. Pigou, ed., 1925, *Memorials of Alfred Marshall*, London: Macmillan, p. 334.

8. Alfred Marshall, 1961, *Principles of Economics*, vol. II, London: Macmillan for the Royal Economic Society, pp. 598–614.

9. J. H. Burns and H. L. A. Hart, eds., 1977, *A Comment on the Commentaries and A Fragment on Government, The Collected Works of Jeremy Bentham*, Oxford: Clarendon Press, p. 393.

10. John Cunningham Wood, ed., 1993, *Alfred Marshall: Critical Assessments, Volume IV*, London: Routledge, p. 290.

11. Branko Milanovic, 2016, *Global Inequality: A New Approach for the Age of Globalization*, Cambridge, MA: Harvard University Press, p. 166.

12. Pew Research Center, 2015, 'The American Middle Class is Losing Ground: No Longer the Majority and Falling Behind Financially', 9 December; www.pewsocialtrends.org/2015/12/09/the-american-middle-class-is-losing-ground/

13. Robert Reich, 2012, *Beyond Outrage: What Has Gone Wrong with Our Economy and Our Democracy, and How to Fix It*, New York: Vintage Books, p. 142.

14. OECD, 2012, 'Income Inequality and Growth: The Role of Taxes and Transfers', OECD Economics Department Policy Notes, No. 9, Paris: OECD.

15. Alfred Marshall, 1890, *Principles of Economics*, vol. I, London: Macmillan, pp. 96–7.

16. Talcott Parsons, 1931, 'Wants and Activities in Marshall', *Quarterly Journal of Economics*, 46(1), pp. 101–40, at p. 128, n. 7, citing Alfred Marshall's letter to the editor of *The Times*, 'The Post Office and Private Enterprise', 24 March 1891.

17. John Stuart Mill, 1848, *Principles of Political Economy*, London: John W. Parker, pp. 13–14.

18. Pigou, *Memorials of Alfred Marshall*, p. 363.

19. A. C. Pigou, 1953, *Alfred Marshall and Current Thought*, London: Macmillan, p. 56.

20. Jonathan D. Ostry, Andrew Berg and Charalambos G. Tsangarides, 2014, 'Redistribution, Inequality, and Growth', International Monetary Fund Staff Discussion Note SDN/14/02; www.imf.org/external/pubs/ft/sdn/2014/sdn1402.pdf

21. Groenewegen, *A Soaring Eagle*, p. 737.

22. Pigou, ed., *Memorials of Alfred Marshall*, p. 427.

Chapter 5 – *Irving Fisher: Are We at Risk of Repeating the 1930s?*

1. 'Fisher Sees Stocks Permanently High', *The New York Times*, 16 October 1929, p. 8.

2. Ibid.

3. Joseph Schumpeter, 1951, *Ten Great Economists from Marx to Keynes*, New York and Oxford: Oxford University Press, p. 223.

4. Irving Fisher, 1892, 'Mathematical Investigations in the Theory of Value and Prices', *Transactions of the Connecticut Academy*, 9, p. 119.

5. Robert Loring Allen, 1993, *Irving Fisher: A Biography*, Cambridge, MA and Oxford: Blackwell, p. 229.

6. Ibid., p. 17.

7. Irving Norton Fisher, 1956, *My Father: Irving Fisher*, New York: Comet Press Books, p. 26.

8. Irving Fisher, 1997, *The Works of Irving Fisher*, 14 vols., ed. William J. Barber, assisted by Robert W. Dimand and Kevin Foster, London: Pickering & Chatto, vol. I, p. 4.

9. Allen, *Irving Fisher*, pp. 147–8.

10. Irving Fisher and H. Bruce Brougham, 1928, *Prohibition Still at its Worst*, New York: Alcohol Information Committee.

11. Irving Fisher, 1919, 'Economists in Public Service: Annual Address of the President', *American Economic Review*, 9(1), Supplement: Papers and Proceedings of the Thirty-First Annual Meeting of the American Economic Association, pp. 5–21, at p. 16.

12. Ibid., p. 10.

13. Simon Newcomb, 1885, *Principles of Political Economy*, New York: Harper, p. 346.

14. Milton Friedman, 1963, *Inflation: Causes and Consequences*, Bombay: Asia Publishing House, p. 17.

15. Irving Fisher, 1933, 'The Debt-Deflation Theory of Great Depressions', *Econometrica*, 1(4), pp. 337–57, at p. 349.

16. Ibid., p. 344.

17. Ben Bernanke, 1983, 'Nonmonetary Effects of the Financial Crisis in the Propagation of the Great Depression', *American Economic Review*, 73(3), pp. 257–76.

18. Ben Bernanke, 2002, 'Deflation: Making Sure "It" Doesn't Happen Here', remarks by Governor Ben S. Bernanke before the National Economists Club, Washington, DC, 21 November; www.federal-reserve.gov/boarddocs/speeches/2002/20021121/

19. Hyman P. Minsky, 1992, 'The Financial Instability Hypothesis', The Jerome Levy Economics Institute of Bard College, Working Paper No. 74.

20. Ibid.

21. 'Minsky's Moment', *The Economist*, 30 July 2016; www.economist.com/news/economics-brief/21702740-second-article-our-series-seminal-economic-ideas-looks-hyman-minskys

22. Janet Yellen, 2009, 'A Minsky Meltdown: Lessons for Central Bankers', presentation to the 18th Annual Hyman P. Minsky Conference on the State of the US and World Economies – 'Meeting the Challenges of the Financial Crisis'; www.frbsf.org/our-district/press/presidents-speeches/yellen-speeches/2009/april/yellen-minsky-meltdown-central-bankers/

23. Ibid.

24. Allen, *Irving Fisher*, p. 9.

Chapter 6 – John Maynard Keynes: To Invest or Not to Invest?

1. John Maynard Keynes, 1936, *The General Theory of Employment, Interest and Money*, London: Palgrave Macmillan, p. 129.

2. Ibid.

3. John Maynard Keynes, 1963 [1931], 'Economic Possibilities for Our Grandchildren', in *Essays in Persuasion*, New York: W. W. Norton, p. 373.

4. John Maynard Keynes, 1971–89, *The Collected Writings of John Maynard Keynes*, 30 vols., ed. Elizabeth Johnson and Donald Moggridge, vol. XII, *Economic Articles and Correspondence: Investment and Editorial*, Cambridge: Cambridge University Press, p. 109.

5. Robert Skidelsky, 2003, *John Maynard Keynes 1883–1946: Economist, Philosopher, Statesman*, New York: Penguin, p. 53.

6. Ibid., p. 53.

7. Ibid., p. 36.

8. Ibid., p. 43.

9. Ibid., p. 45.

10. Ibid., p. 60.

11. Keynes, *General Theory*, p. 5.

12. Todd G. Buchholz, 2007, *New Ideas from Dead Economists: An Introduction to Modern Economic Thought*, New York: Penguin, p. 210.

13. Robert Skidelsky, 2010, *Keynes: The Return of the Master*, London: Penguin, p. 62.

14. Keynes, *General Theory*, p. 103.

15. Ibid., p. 158.

16. Ibid.

17. Keynes, *Collected Writings*, vol. IV: *A Tract on Monetary Reform*, p. 65.

18. Keynes, *Collected Writings*, vol. XXI: *Activities 1931–1939: World Crises and Policies in Britain and America*, p. 390.

19. John Maynard Keynes, 1937, 'The General Theory of Employment', *Quarterly Journal of Economics*, 51(2), pp. 209–23.

20. Ibid., pp. 215–16.

21. Ibid., p. 216.

22. Skidelsky, *Keynes: The Return of the Master*, p. 107.

23. Ronald Reagan, 1986, 'Remarks to State Chairpersons of the National White House Conference on Small Business', 15 August; www.reaganlibrary.archives.gov/archives/speeches/1986/081586e.html

24. Ronald Reagan, 1986, 'The President's News Conference', 12 August; www.presidency.ucsb.edu/ws/?pid=37733

25. Graeme Chamberlin and Linda Yueh, 2006, *Macroeconomics*, London: Cengage, ch. 4.

26. Keynes, *General Theory*, p. 373.

27. Ibid., p. 322.

28. Ibid., pp. 164, 378.

29. Ibid., pp. 383–4.

30. Keynes, *Essays in Persuasion*, p. 366.

31. Ibid., p. 369.

32. Ibid., p. 366.

Chapter 7 – Joseph Schumpeter: What Drives Innovation?

1. Joseph Schumpeter, 1942, *Capitalism, Socialism and Democracy*, New York: Harper & Brothers, p. 84.
2. Thomas K. McCraw, 2007, *Prophet of Innovation: Joseph Schumpeter and Creative Destruction*, Cambridge, MA: Harvard University Press, p. x.
3. Schumpeter, *Capitalism*, p. 83.
4. Joseph Schumpeter, 1939, *Business Cycles: A Theoretical, Historical and Statistical Analysis of the Capitalist Process*, vol. II, New York: McGraw-Hill, p. 1033.
5. Schumpeter, *Business Cycles*, vol. I, p. 107.
6. Schumpeter, *Capitalism*, pp. 67–8.
7. Paul A. Samuelson, 1977, 'Joseph A. Schumpeter', *Dictionary of American Biography*, New York: Scribner, Supplement Four, p. 722.
8. McCraw, *Prophet of Innovation*, p. 40.
9. Joseph Schumpeter, 1954, *History of Economic Analysis*, New York: Oxford University Press, p. 571.
10. McCraw, *Prophet of Innovation*, p. 60.
11. Joseph Schumpeter, 1991 [1918], 'The Crisis of the Tax State', in *The Economics and Sociology of Capitalism*, ed. Richard Swedberg, Princeton: Princeton University Press, pp. 114–16.
12. McCraw, *Prophet of Innovation*, pp. 104–5.
13. Ibid., pp. 117–19.
14. Ibid., p. 165.
15. Ibid., p. 213.
16. Ibid., p. 223.
17. Ibid, p. 225.
18. Ibid.
19. Ibid., p. 271.
20. Nicolò De Vecchi, 2006, 'Hayek and the *General Theory*', *European Journal of the History of Economic Thought*, 13(2), pp. 233–58.
21. Schumpeter, *Business Cycles*, vol. I, p. vi.
22. Schumpeter, *Capitalism*, p. 83.
23. Schumpeter, *Business Cycles*, vol. I, pp. 104–7.
24. Schumpeter, *Capitalism*, pp. 93, 99–100.

25. Ibid., pp. 99–100.

26. Schumpeter, *Business Cycles*, vol. I, pp. 243–4.

27. Ibid., pp. 100–102.

28. Schumpeter, *Capitalism*, pp. 167, 170, 190–91.

29. Ibid., p. xiv.

30. Joseph Schumpeter, 1955, 'Social Classes in an Ethnically Homogeneous Environment', trans. Heinz Norden, in *Imperialism, Social Classes: Two Essays by Joseph Schumpeter*, New York: Meridian Books, pp. 120–22.

31. Joseph Schumpeter, 1928, 'The Instability of Capitalism', *Economic Journal*, 38, pp. 361–86.

32. Schumpeter, *Business Cycles*, vol. I, pp. 103–4.

33. World Bank, 1993, *The East Asian Miracle: Economic Growth and Public Policy*, Washington, DC: World Bank.

34. Schumpeter, 'The Instability of Capitalism', pp. 364–6.

35. Joseph Schumpeter, 1934, *The Theory of Economic Development*, Cambridge, MA: Harvard University Press, pp. 75–8.

36. Schumpeter, *Business Cycles*, vol. I, pp. 102–3.

37. Schumpeter, *Business Cycles*, vol. II, pp. 907–1033.

38. Schumpeter, *Economic Development*, pp. 75–8.

39. Ibid., p. 66.

40. Schumpeter, *Capitalism*, pp. 101–2, 110.

41. Richard Foster, 2012, 'Creative Destruction Whips Through Corporate America', *Innosight Executive Briefing*; https://www.innosight.com/wp-content/uploads/2016/08/creative-destruction-whips-through-corporate-america_final2015.pdf

42. Schumpeter, *History of Economic Analysis*, pp. 19, 27.

43. McCraw, *Prophet of Innovation*, p. 500.

Chapter 8 – Friedrich Hayek: What Can We Learn from Financial Crises?

1. Milton Friedman, 1999, 'Transcript for: Friedrich Hayek', Think Tank with Ben Wattenberg, pbs.org; www.pbs.org/thinktank/transcript726.html

2. Bruce Caldwell, 2004, *Hayek's Challenge: An Intellectual Biography of F. A. Hayek*, Chicago: University of Chicago Press, p. 2.

3. Friedrich A. Hayek, 1994, *Hayek on Hayek: An Autobiographical Dialogue*, ed. Stephen Kresge and Leif Wenar, Chicago: University of Chicago Press, p. 40.

4. Caldwell, *Hayek's Challenge*, p. 150.

5. Bruce Caldwell, 1998, 'Why Didn't Hayek Review Keynes's *General Theory*?', *History of Political Economy*, 30(4), pp. 545–69, at p. 556.

6. Nicholas Wapshott, 2011, *Keynes Hayek: The Clash That Defined Modern Economics*, New York: W. W. Norton, p. xi.

7. Sylvia Nasar, 2011, *Grand Pursuit: The Story of the People Who Made Modern Economics*, New York: Simon & Schuster, p. 402.

8. Ibid.

9. John Maynard Keynes, 1931, 'The Pure Theory of Money: A Reply to Dr Hayek', *Economica*, 34, pp. 387–97, at p. 394.

10. Paul Krugman, 1998, 'The Hangover Theory', *Slate*, 4 December; www.slate.com/articles/business/the_dismal_science/1998/12/the_hangover_theory.html

11. Alan Ebenstein, 2001, *Friedrich Hayek: A Biography*, New York: St. Martin's Press, p. 81.

12. Athol Fitzgibbons, 1988, *Keynes's Vision: A New Political Economy*, Oxford: Oxford University Press, p. 178.

13. Ebenstein, *Friedrich Hayek*, p. 128.

14. Friedrich A. Hayek, 2001 [1944], *The Road to Serfdom*, London and New York: Routledge Classics, pp. 124–5.

15. Caldwell, *Hayek's Challenge*, p. 133.

16. Friedrich A. Hayek, 2006 [1960], *The Constitution of Liberty*, London and New York: Routledge, p. 44.

17. Ebenstein, *Friedrich Hayek*, pp. 196, 238.

18. Ibid., p. 261.

19. John Ranelagh, 1991, *Thatcher's People: An Insider's Account of the Politics, the Power and the Personalities*, London: HarperCollins, p. ix.

20. Friedrich A. Hayek, 1986, 'The Moral Imperative of the Market', in *The Unfinished Agenda: Essays on the Political Economy of Government Policy in Honour of Arthur Seldon*, London: Institute of Economic Affairs.

21. John B. Taylor, 2009, 'The Need to Return to a Monetary Framework', *Business Economics*, 44(2), pp. 63–72.

22. John B. Taylor, 2012, 'Why We Still Need to Read Hayek', The Hayek Lecture, The Manhattan Institute for Policy Research, New York City, 31 May; www.hoover.org/sites/default/files/hayek-lecture.pdf

23. Winston Churchill, 1974, 'Speech, House of Commons, November 11, 1947', in *Winston S. Churchill: His Complete Speeches, 1897–1963*, ed. Robert Rhodes James, London: R. R. Bowker, vol. VII, p. 7566.

24. Friedrich A. Hayek, 1979, *A Conversation with Friedrich A. von Hayek: Science and Socialism*, Washington, DC: American Enterprise Institute for Public Policy Research, p. 6.

25. Margaret Thatcher, 1993, *The Downing Street Years*, London: Harper-Press, p. 618.

26. John Campbell, 2008, *Margaret Thatcher*, vol. II: *The Iron Lady*, London: Vintage, p. 628.

27. Nobelprize.org, 1974, 'Friedrich August von Hayek – Banquet Speech', Nobel Media AB 2014; www.nobelprize.org/nobel_prizes/economic-sciences/laureates/1974/hayek-speech.html

28. Daniel Yergin and Joseph Stanislaw, 1998, *The Commanding Heights: The Battle Between Government and the Marketplace that is Remaking the Modern World*, New York: Free Press, p. 150.

Chapter 9 – Joan Robinson: Why are Wages so Low?

1. 'The Inquiry', presented by Linda Yueh, BBC World Service, 8 March 2016.

2. Nahid Aslanbeigui and Guy Oakes, 2009, *The Provocative Joan Robinson: The Making of a Cambridge Economist*, Durham, NC: Duke University Press, p. 1.

3. 'Prof. Joan Robinson Dies at 79; Cambridge', *The New York Times*, 11 August 1983.

4. Paul Flatau, 2001, 'Some Reflections on the "Pigou-Robinson" Theory of Exploitation', *History of Economics Review*, 33, pp. 1–16.

5. Aslanbeigui and Oakes, *The Provocative Joan Robinson*, pp. 2–3.

6. Joan Robinson, 1932, *Economics is a Serious Subject: The Apologia of an Economist to the Mathematician, the Scientist and the Plain Man*, Cambridge: Heffer, p. 4.

7. Aslanbeigui and Oakes, *The Provocative Joan Robinson*, pp. 48–9.

8. Robert Skidelsky, 1995, *John Maynard Keynes*, vol. II: *The Economist as Saviour, 1920–1937*, London: Penguin, pp. 448–9.

9. Alec Cairncross, 1993, *Austin Robinson: The Life of an Economic Adviser*, Basingstoke: Macmillan, p. 172.

10. Aslanbeigui and Oakes, *The Provocative Joan Robinson*, p. 9.

11. Ibid., p. 133.

12. Joan Robinson, 1962, *Economic Philosophy*, Harmondsworth: Pelican Books, p. 25.

13. Ibid., p. 28.

14. Ibid.

15. Joan Robinson, 1969 [1933], *The Economics of Imperfect Competition*, 2nd edn, London: Macmillan, ch. 18 on monopsony.

16. International Labour Organization, 2014, *Global Wage Report 2014/15*, Geneva: International Labour Office, p. 10.

17. International Labour Organization and Organisation for Economic Co-operation and Development, with contributions from the International Monetary Fund and World Bank Group, 2015, 'The Labour Share in G20 Economies', report prepared for the G20 Employment Working Group, Antalya, Turkey, 26–27 February.

18. Joan Robinson, 1980, 'Marx, Marshall and Keynes', *Collected Economic Papers*, vol. II, Cambridge, MA: MIT Press, p. 17.

19. Robinson, *Economic Philosophy*, p. 45.

Chapter 10 – Milton Friedman: Are Central Banks Doing Too Much?

1. Milton and Rose Friedman, 1998, *Two Lucky People: Memoirs*, Chicago: University of Chicago Press, p. 22.

2. Ibid., p. 262.

3. Ibid., p. xi.

4. Ibid., p. 165.

5. Lanny Ebenstein, 2007, *Milton Friedman: A Biography*, New York: Palgrave Macmillan, p. 100.

6. Ibid., p. 47.

7. Ibid., p. 52.

8. Milton and Rose Friedman, 1980, *Free to Choose*, San Diego: Harcourt, p. 310.

9. 'Milton Friedman in His Own Words', 2012, Becker Friedman Institute for Research in Economics, University of Chicago; https://bfi. uchicago.edu/news/post/milton-friedman-his-own-words.

10. Ibid.

11. Ibid.

12. Ebenstein, *Milton Friedman*, p. 187.

13. Ben Bernanke, 2002, 'On Milton Friedman's Ninetieth Birthday', Remarks by Governor Ben S. Bernanke: At the Conference to Honor Milton Friedman, University of Chicago, 8 November; www.federalreserve.gov/boarddocs/speeches/2002/20021108/default. htm

14. Milton Friedman, 1997, 'Rx for Japan: Back to the Future', *Wall Street Journal*, 17 December.

15. Ibid.

16. Ibid.

17. Milton Friedman, 1991, 'Economic Freedom, Human Freedom, Political Freedom', address by Milton Friedman, The Smith Center, Seattle Central College, 1 November; http://seattlecentral.edu/faculty/jhubert/ friedmanspeech.html

18. Milton Fricdman, 2002 [1962], *Capitalism and Freedom: Fortieth Anniversary Edition*, Chicago: University of Chicago Press, p. xii.

19. Ebenstein, *Milton Friedman*, p. 182.

20. 'Milton Friedman in His Own Words'.

Chapter 11 – Douglass North: Why are so Few Countries Prosperous?

1. Pierre-Richard Agénor, Otaviano Canuto and Michael Jelenic, 2012, 'Avoiding Middle-Income Growth Traps', *Economic Premise*, 98, Washington, DC, World Bank, p. 1.

2. Douglass C. North, 1988, 'Institutions, Economic Growth and Freedom', in *Freedom, Democracy and Economic Welfare: Proceedings of an*

International Symposium, ed. Michael A. Walker, Vancouver: Fraser Institute, p. 7.

3. Douglass C. North, 1990, *Institutions, Institutional Change and Economic Performance*, Cambridge: Cambridge University Press, p. 6.

4. Ibid., p. 7.

5. Lennart Jörberg, 1997, 'Robert W. Fogel and Douglass C. North', in *Nobel Lectures in Economic Sciences, 1991–1995*, ed. Torsten Persson, Singapore: World Scientific, pp. 107-8.

6. Douglass C. North, Gardner Brown and Dean Lueck, 2015, 'A Conversation with Douglass North', *Annual Review of Resource Economics*, 7, pp. 1–10, at p. 6.

7. Nobelprize.org, 1993, 'Douglass C. North – Biographical', Nobel Media AB 2014; www.nobelprize.org/nobel_prizes/economic-sciences/laureates/1993/north-bio.html

8. Ibid.

9. North, *Institutions, Institutional Change and Economic Performance*, pp. 11, 12.

10. Nobelprize.org, 'Douglass C. North – Biographical'.

11. North, *Institutions, Institutional Change and Economic Performance*, p. vii.

12. Ibid., p. 3.

13. Ibid., p. 5.

14. Ibid., p. 116.

15. Ibid., p. 9.

16. Ibid., p. 139.

17. Ibid., p. 9.

18. Ibid., p. 112.

19. Paul Collier, 2007, *The Bottom Billion: Why the Poorest Countries are Failing and What Can Be Done About It*, Oxford: Oxford University Press.

20. Robert E. Lucas, Jr., 1988, 'On the Mechanics of Economic Development', *Journal of Monetary Economics*, 22(1), pp. 3–42, at p. 5.

21. North, *Institutions, Institutional Change and Economic Performance*, p. 7.

22. Ibid., p. 137.

23. Ibid., p. 6.

24. Ibid., p. 140.

25. North, Brown and Lueck, 'A Conversation with Douglass North', pp. 8, 9.

26. Daron Acemoglu and James A. Robinson, 2012, *Why Nations Fail*, London: Profile Books, pp. 372–3.

27. Ibid., p. 402.

28. Ibid., p. 426.

29. Ibid., p. 427.

30. North, *Institutions, Institutional Change and Economic Performance*, p. 140.

Chapter 12 – Robert Solow: Do We Face a Slow-Growth Future?

1. Nobelprize.org, 1987, 'Robert M. Solow – Biographical', Nobel Media AB 2014; www.nobelprize.org/nobel_prizes/economic-sciences/laureates/1987/solow-bio.html

2. Barnaby J. Feder, 1987, 'Man in the News: Robert Merton Solow; Tackling Everyday Economic Problems', *The New York Times*, 22 October.

3. Ibid.

4. Nobelprize.org, 'Robert M. Solow – Biographical'.

5. Robert Solow, 1956, 'A Contribution to the Theory of Economic Growth', *Quarterly Journal of Economics*, 70(1), pp. 65–94; Robert Solow, 1957, 'Technical Change and the Aggregate Production Function', *Review of Economics and Statistics*, 39(3), pp. 312–20.

6. Paul A. David, 1990, 'The Dynamo and the Computer: A Historical Perspective on the Modern Productivity Paradox', *American Economic Review*, 80(2), pp. 355–61.

7. Douglas Clement, 2002, 'Interview with Robert Solow', *The Region*, Federal Reserve Bank of Minneapolis, 1 September; www.minneapolisfed.org/publications/the-region/interview-with-robert-solow

8. OECD, 2015, *Economic Surveys: United Kingdom*, Paris: OECD.

9. João Paulo Pessoa and John Van Reenen, 2013, 'Decoupling of Wage Growth and Productivity Growth? Myth and Reality', Centre for Economic Performance, London School of Economics and Political Science, Discussion Paper No. 1246; http://cep.lse.ac.uk/pubs/download/dp1246.pdf

10. Alina Barnett, Sandra Batten, Adrian Chiu, Jeremy Franklin and María Sebastiá-Barriel, 2014, 'The UK Productivity Puzzle', *Bank of England Quarterly Bulletin*, Q2, pp. 114–28.

11. Peter Goodridge, Jonathan Haskel and Gavin Wallis, 2013, 'Can Intangible Investment Explain the UK Productivity Puzzle?', *National Institute Economic Review*, 224, pp. R48–R58.

12. Barnett et al., 'The UK Productivity Puzzle'.

13. Kristian Behrens, Giordano Mion, Yasusada Murata and Jens Südekum, 2014, 'Trade, Wages, and Productivity', *International Economic Review*, 55(4), pp. 1305–49.

14. Nobelprize.org, 1987, 'Robert M. Solow – Prize Lecture: Growth Theory and After', Nobel Media AB 2014; www.nobelprize.org/nobel_prizes/economic-sciences/laureates/1987/solow-lecture.html

15. Ibid.

16. Ibid.

17. Ibid.

18. Ibid.

19. Robert Solow, 1989, 'How Economic Ideas Turn to Mush', in *The Spread of Economic Ideas*, eds. David Colander and A. W. Coats, Cambridge: Cambridge University Press, pp. 75–84.

20. Clement, 'Interview with Robert Solow'.

21. Feder, 'Man in the News'.

22. Clement, 'Interview with Robert Solow'.

Epilogue: The Future of Globalization

1. 'Globalization and Rapid Change Sparked Backlash, Says Obama', *Financial Times*, 15 November 2016.

2. Jon Huang, Samuel Jacoby, Michael Strickland and K. K. Rebecca Lai, 2016, 'Election 2016: Exit Polls', *The New York Times*, 8 November; www.nytimes.com/interactive/2016/11/08/us/politics/election-exit-polls.html

3. Derek Thompson, 2009, 'An Interview with Paul Samuelson, Part One', *The Atlantic*, 17 June; www.theatlantic.com/business/archive/2009/06/an-interview-with-paul-samuelson-part-one/19586/

4. John Cassidy, 2009, 'Postscript: Paul Samuelson', *The New Yorker*, 14 December.

5. Thompson, 'An Interview with Paul Samuelson'.

6. David C. Colander and Harry Landreth, 1996, *The Coming of Keynesianism to America: Conversations with the Founders of Keynesian Economics*, Cheltenham: Edward Elgar, p. 28.

7. 'Paul A. Samuelson obituary', *The Economist*, 17 December 2009; www.economist.com/node/15127616

8. Douglas P. Cooper, 1973, The Douglas P. Cooper Distinguished Contemporaries Collection, 1 September; www.wnyc.org/story/paul-samuelson/

9. Paul A. Samuelson, 1986, 'Gold and Common Stocks', in *The Collected Scientific Papers of Paul Samuelson*, vol. V, ed. Kate Crowley, Cambridge, MA: MIT Press, p. 561.

10. Paul A. Samuelson, 2005, *On Being an Economist*, New York: Jorge Pinto Books Inc.

Index

Page references in **bold** refer to a complete chapter devoted to an economist.

Abe, Shinzo 274, 275
Acemoglu, Daron 240–41, 263
aerospace industry 20, 45
Africa 1, 246, 247, 248, 261
    Botswana 263
    South Africa 258–60
    sub-Saharan 246, 258–60, 263
    Tanzania 248
agriculture 26, 28, 39, 222, 257
    China 74, 247
    and industrialization 13, 14
    and Marx 70, 71
    mechanization 259
    and the Physiocrats 16, 26
    protectionism 35, 38
AIG 235
alcoholic beverages 20, 29
    Portuguese wine 46–7
    Prohibition 97, 101
Alibaba Group 169, 170
American Economic Association
    (AEA) 171, 199–200, 268
American Economic Review 222
American Telephone and Telegraph
    (AT&T) 159
apartheid 258, 259–60
Apple 161, 162–3, 164, 170
Argentina 249, 250
Arrow, Kenneth J. 199
artificial intelligence 168
Arts Council, British 142
ASEAN (Association of Southeast
    Asian Nations) 286

ASEAN Economic Community
    (AEC) 286–7
Asia 1, 206, 248, 258
    financial crisis (1997–98) 250
    see also specific countries
asset management companies 253
Aung San Suu Kyi 255
austerity 6, 124, 133–5, 137–8
Austrian School of economics 6–7,
    147, 148–9, 173, 175, 181
    see also Hayek, Friedrich
Austro-Hungarian Empire 146,
    148–9, 150, 174, 175, 215
automation 46, 208, 288, 296
    see also artificial intelligence;
    robotics

BAE Systems 20
Bagehot, Walter 37, 49
banks/banking 13, 20, 113–15
    'bad banks' 253
    bail-outs 121, 134
    Bank Charter Act of 1844 (Peel
        Banking Act) 40
    central banks *see* central banks
    China 68–9, 72, 253
    competition 26–7
    constrained lending 137, 138
    European Investment
        Bank 137
    financial crises *see* financial crises
    government guarantees on
        deposits 116

banks/banking – *(cont.)*
  and the Great Crash (1929) and Great
    Depression 104, 227–31
  and the Great Recession 13,
    231–3, 298
  interest rates *see* interest rates
  investment banking 113, 121, 137,
    190, 231–5
  mortgage lending *see* mortgage
    lending
  regulation 13, 27, 121, 225
  and Schumpeter 151
  shadow banking 68–9
  US Banking Acts (1933
    and 1935) 231
  World Bank *see* World Bank
Barro, Robert 141
Bear Stearns 121, 190, 235
Beijing Consensus 256, 257
Bentham, Jeremy 27, 34, 37, 81
Bernanke, Ben 113, 117–18, 119, 120,
    121, 213, 231, 232, 235
Beveridge Report 130–31
'Big Bang' (1986) 12
Bitcoin 188
Bitterlich, Helene 184, 186
Blackberry 160, 161, 162
Blackett, Basil 126
Blaug, Mark 37
Bloomsbury Group 127
Böhm von Bawerk, Eugen 148, 149
Bolshevik Party 62
Bonaparte, Louis-Napoleon 58
Bonaparte, Napoleon 57
Boody Firuski, Romaine Elizabeth 154
Botswana 263
Brazil 18, 249, 250, 251
Bretton Woods System 142
Brexit 133, 135–6, 283, 293, 295, 296
  foreign investment after 32
BRIC economies 18, 251, 259
  see also Brazil; China; India; Russia

Britain/UK
  and the 2008 financial crisis 1, 5, 12
  aerospace industry 20
  banking sector difficulties 20
  Black Wednesday 249
  budget deficits *see* budget deficits
  credit rating 133
  current account deficit 18, 32, 41
  deindustrialization 12, 13, 14, 42
  ERM exit of pound 18, 249
  EU referendum 1, 133, 135–6, 283,
    293, 295
  exports (general) 11–31 *passim*, 45
  exports of services 19, 41, 42
  foreign investment after Brexit 32
  GDP 18, 22, 41, 63–4, 133, 272
  and the gold standard 229
  gold supply 34
  government administration 20
  government's renewed focus on
    growth 276–8
  and the Great Depression 130
  IMF bail out (1976) 131, 133
  industrialization/Industrial
    Revolution 11, 12, 26, 30, 35, 36,
    39, 55–6
  inequality 291
  information technology industries 21
  investment as share of GDP 273
  labour force growth 265
  as largest world trader 35
  low wages 7, 194, 204–5
  manufacturing 13, 19, 28, 35, 45,
    49, 146
  national debt 37, 38, 119,
    130–31, 133
  National Infrastructure
    Commission 137, 276
  oil and gas industry 20
  productivity and wage growth
    272–4
  productivity puzzle 22–3, 273, 278

rebalancing the economy 13, 17–30, 49

reindustrialization 12–14

services sector 12, 13–14, 17–19, 20–23, 41, 42, 49, 145–6, 273

slow productivity growth 265–6

telecommunications industry 21

trade-to-GDP ratio 63–4

trade deficit 4, 18, 23, 32–3, 40–42, 50

trade with US 30

Treasury 125–6, 128, 130

unemployment 128, 205

wages and productivity 205, 273

welfare state 6, 130–31, 140

as 'workshop of the world' 40

Brookings Institution 43, 44

Brown, Douglas V. 153

Buccleuch, Henry Scott, 3rd Duke of 16

budget deficits 6, 130, 133–5, 138, 141, 249
and austerity 133–5

Burns, Arthur 216, 225

Burns, Mary 55

business cycle theory
Fisher 107, 110, 112–14
Hayek 7, 176, 177, 179–80
Schumpeter 150, 154

Callaghan, James 131

Cambridge School 93, 178, 197–8, 199
see also Keynes, John Maynard; Marshall, Alfred; Robinson, Joan

Cambridge University 77, 78, 197, 199–201, 242, 268
Girton College 197, 198
Kings College 124
Newnham College 77, 198
St Johns 77
and women 198

Canon 162

capital accumulation 36, 48, 64, 180, 196, 266, 271, 280, 281

capital investment 138, 179–80, 267, 273

capitalism 144–6, 155–60
in aftermath of 2008 financial crisis 173–4, 190–92
and communism 5, 74, 172, 173, 189
derivation of term 144
and Engels 55–6, 57
and the financial crisis of 2008 75
free-market 226
and Hayek 173–4, 192
inequality and capitalist economies 5, 76
laissez-faire see *laissez-faire*
and Marx 57, 61, 74, 148, 155, 292
and the Occupy movement 7
and Schumpeterian 'creative destruction' 144–6, 156–71
socialism vs welfare state capitalism 172, 173

car industry 43, 44, 158, 208, 288

Carney, Mark 213

Carter, Jimmy 132, 225

Case, Elizabeth 242

central banks 8, 113, 116, 120, 121, 122, 134, 190, 215, 232, 237
Bank of England 32, 34, 58, 126, 135, 250, 273, 276, 277
Bank of Japan 236
European Central Bank 134–5
Fed see Federal Reserve
forward guidance 213
macroprudential policy 121, 213, 237
monetary policy tools 213 see also quantitative easing (QE)

Chamberlin, Edward 153, 199–200

Chicago School 8, 141, 178, 184–5, 217, 219–21
see also Friedman, Milton

Chile 110–11, 220–21, 249

China 1, 13, 18, 46, 62–3, 201, 239, 249,
  253, 263, 275
  1949 revolution 70
  asset management companies 253
  banking system 68–9, 72, 253
  Beijing Consensus 256, 257
  Communist Party 62, 64, 85, 196–7
  corporate debt 68
  Cultural Revolution 84, 85
  domestic innovation 66
  economic transformation 52, 62,
    63–70, 247
  'effect'/'price' 66
  employment system 72
  entrepreneurs 67, 84–6
  exports 166
  Five Year Plan (1953) 71
  foreign direct investment
    (FDI) 65–6
  and Germany 206
  industrialization and
    reindustrialization 64, 257
  inequality 82, 84–7, 92, 258
  innovation challenge 165–9
  legal institutions 66–7
  manufacturing 68
  Maoism 62, 72–3
  and Marx 52, 62–3, 70–75
  national debt 12, 68, 69, 253
  openness 65–6
  'paradox' 64
  poverty reduction 63, 247, 249
  privatization 253
  R&D investment 64, 66, 166,
    167, 168
  regional free trade agreement 286
  renminbi (RMB) 32, 68
  as second largest economy 4, 75, 170
  services sector 13, 67–8
  shadow banking 68–9
  smartphones 163, 164, 165
  social networks 67

  trade-to GDP ratio 63–4
  and the USSR 62, 71–2
  wage increases 204
  women 72
Churchill, Winston 76, 183, 192
class
  Engels' *The Condition of the Working
    Class in England* 56
  and Marx 51, 56–7, 61, 70, 292
  middle *see* middle class
  and Ricardo 36, 40
  wage earner class 36
Classical School of economics 147
  see also Mill, John Stuart; Ricardo,
    David; Smith, Adam
Clinton, Bill 288
Clinton, Hillary 287
cloth 46–7
clothing 26
Coase, Ronald 240
Cold War 51–2, 75
Collectivist Economic Planning 181
collectivization 4
Collier, Paul 247
Columbia University 218–19, 267
communism 4, 51–75, 155
  Bolshevik Party 62
  and capitalism 5, 74, 172, 173, 189
  Chinese 62–75, 85, 196–7
  Communist League 56–8
  First International 59–60
  Marxism *see* Marxism
  and Robinson 196–7
  Socialist/Second International 60
  Third International 60
  USSR *see* Soviet Union
  Vietnamese 252
  vs welfare state capitalism 172, 173
Communist League 56–8
comparative advantage theory 4,
  46–9, 297
competition 26–7

'competing down' (Schumpeter) 157
imperfect 195, 197–8, 201–4, 209
between money providers 187–8
perfect 156, 195, 202
and Robinson 195, 197,
    198, 201–4, 209
wages and competitiveness 206
computers 208, 266, 269–70, 288
Conard, Ed 88
construction 3, 20
consultancy firms 22
consumerism 85, 162
consumption 36, 67, 74, 79, 140, 141
and comparative advantage theory 46
consumer spending 138
and marginal utility analysis 79
convergence hypothesis 271–2
corn, free trade in 40
Corn Laws 28, 33, 49–50
repeal 40, 49–50, 78
and Ricardo 34–5, 36, 39–40, 297
corporate debt 68, 85, 118, 214
Cowles Commission 219, 220
Crafts, Nicholas 19
crafts 35
credit crunch 113–14
credit default swaps (CDS) 233
credit rating 133
Crimean War 59
crypto-currencies 188
currency crises 249–51, 256
first-generation 249, 256
second-generation 249–50
third-generation 250
currency stability 38
Cyprus 134

death duties 140
debt
Chinese corporate 68
debt-deflation spiral 5, 97–8,
    112–16, 120

and government bonds 111
indexation and protection from
    110–11
and Minsky's financial instability
    hypothesis 118–19
mortgage debt 114
national *see* national debt
private corporate 118
as share of GDP 119, 133
decentralization 90,
    206, 277
defence 29
deflation 61, 97, 120, 228, 231
debt-deflation spiral 5, 97–8,
    112–16, 120
Fisher and combating deflation
    116–17, 120–21
Japan 115–16, 117–18
self-fulfilling 116
deindustrialization 12–14, 42
and globalization 14, 42
premature 14
reversing/reindustrialization 12, 14,
    19, 43, 44, 45–6, 64, 257
and trade 18, 32
US 12, 14, 42
Deng Xiaoping 52
depression *see* Great Depression (1930s);
    Long Depression (1880s);
    recession/depression
diminishing returns to capital 39,
    266, 271
distributive lag model 107
Douglas, David, Lord Reston 17
Douglas, Janet 17
DuPont 159

East Asian 'tiger' economies 258
    see also Hong Kong; Singapore;
        South Korea; Taiwan
eastern Europe 1, 205, 206
Eastman Kodak 159, 161–2, 163

Econometric Society 96, 153, 196, 268
Econometrica 112, 153, 196
economic development challenges
        239–41, 245–64
    and Beijing Consensus 256, 257
    financial/currency crises 248–52
    and institutions 8–9, 239–41, 243–5,
        252–8
    and Lewis model 257
    Myanmar 255–8
    and North 240–41, 244–5, 260–64
    and path dependence 245, 248, 253,
        260, 263, 293
    poverty eradication/reduction 2, 63,
        245–8, 260–61
    South Africa 258–60
    Sustainable Development
        Goals 246
    Vietnam 252–5
    and Washington Consensus 256
economic equilibrium 4–5, 24, 25, 79,
        107, 132, 149, 173, 279, 280
economic freedom 29, 224
economic growth
    and austerity 6
    barriers 73, 117–18
    convergence hypothesis 271–2
    development challenges *see*
        economic development challenges
    drivers of 2, 8–9, 18, 74, 144–5,
        157–9, 293 *see also* innovation;
        institutions; public investment;
        technology
    endogenous growth theories 270–71
    inclusive growth 291
    through investment 129, 136–9,
        276, 280
    Japan's growth 272
    and Japan's 'lost decades' 274–6
    Lewis model 257
    mercantilist doctrine of 38

    and new technologies 144–5,
        269–71, 280–81
    policy debates on raising 3
    and poverty reduction 63, 247, 249,
        260–61
    and productivity debate/challenge
        6, 265–6, 272–4
    slow growth and the future 265–82
    Solow model 266, 269–72, 278–81
    UK government's renewed focus on
        276–8
    and unemployment 279
Economic Journal 125, 197
economic rent 202, 203, 204, 211
    Ricardo's theory of 37–8
economies
    'animal spirits' of 179
    crises *see* financial crises
    deflation *see* deflation
    emerging *see* emerging economies
    equilibrium in 4–5, 24, 25, 79, 107,
        132, 149, 173, 279, 280
    GDP *see* gross domestic product
    global macroeconomic
        imbalances 66
    growth of *see* economic growth
    inequality and capitalist
        economies 5, 61
    inflation *see* inflation
    and international trade 9, 18
    and investment *see* investment;
        public investment
    national debt *see* national debt
    QE *see* quantitative easing
    rebalancing of 3, 13, 17–30, 49, 67–8
    recession *see* recession/depression
    services economy *see* services sector
    and stagnant wages 1, 7, 194,
        204, 206
    state intervention 2, 4–5, 12, 16,
        24–5, 27–8, 88–9, 140–41, 222

Economist 49, 118, 295
education 22, 23, 27, 41, 42, 71, 91, 239,
    245, 246n, 261, 266
  higher 19, 225
  role in reducing inequality 81, 91
  universal 27, 81
Eliot, T. S. 185
emerging economies 1, 2, 14, 163, 204
  BRICs 18, 251, 259
  convergence hypothesis 271–2
  financial/currency crises 248–52
  and globalization 288
  and world GDP 251
  see also economic development
    challenges
employment 46, 91, 273
  and automation 208
  China's post-1949 system 72
  exploitation of workers 56, 61, 70,
    202, 203–4, 209–10, 211–12
  and government spending 139
  and imperfect competition 195,
    203, 209
  losses with imports 288
  and Robinson 195–6
  and skill-biased technical
    change 87, 288
  temporary workers 207, 210–11
  wages and levels of 203–4
  work incentive 72–3
endogenous growth theories 270–71
Engels, Friedrich 51, 55–6, 59
  *The Condition of the Working Class in
    England* 56
  and Marx 51, 55, 56–7, 60 *see also*
    Marx, Karl: *Communist Manifesto*
    (with Engels)
Enlightenment
  European 16, 53
  Scottish 15, 27
entrepreneurs/entrepreneurship 149, 173

in China 67, 84–6
and Schumpeter 6, 145, 148, 150, 151,
    156–7, 159–60, 165, 170–71
Equation of Exchange 106–7
Equatorial Guinea 239
Ermen & Engels 55, 61
eugenics 101
euro area 1, 134, 213, 237, 279
euro crisis 133–4, 279
European Central Bank (ECB) 134–5
European Commission 134, 137, 139
European Fund for Strategic
    Investments (EFSI) 137
European Investment
    Bank (EIB) 137
European Union 1, 134, 137, 206
  austerity 137–8
  Capital Markets Union 278
  growth through investment 276
  Juncker Plan 137
  services sector 13
  single market 285
  Transatlantic Trade and Investment
    Partnership 286
  UK membership referendum 1, 133,
    135–6, 283, 293, 295
exchange rates
  exchange rate mechanism
    (ERM) 18, 249
  fixed 223
  see also gold: standard
exploitation of workers 56, 61, 70,
    203–4, 209–10, 211–12
  'economic rents' 37–8, 202,
    203, 204, 211
exports 18, 250
  China 166
  duties 29
  UK 19, 41, 42
  US 286
externalities 199

factor-price equalization theorem 296
factor reallocation 64–5
Fairfax Financial 161
Fannie Mae 190, 232, 235
Fear the Boom and Bust 177
Federal Deposit Insurance Corporation
    (FDIC) 231
Federal Reserve 8, 176, 180, 189–90,
    191, 218, 225, 227
  and the 2008 financial crisis 233–5
  and Friedman 225, 226, 227–31
  and the Great
    Depression 227–31, 233
Fermi, Enrico 185
financial accelerators 113–15
financial crises
    1857 crisis 59, 60, 61
    1929 Great Crash 95, 97, 104, 111,
      189, 227
    1990s real estate crash in Japan 5,
      116, 207, 236, 265, 274, 279
    2008 crisis 1, 2, 5–6, 9, 12, 13, 14, 18,
      30, 32, 68–9, 75, 76, 82, 114, 118,
      119–21, 136, 172, 189–92, 213, 231–7
  banking panics 59, 114
  currency crises *see* currency crises
  and development in emerging
    economies 248–52
  euro crisis 133–4, 279
  and financial stability 68
  leading to low investment 279
  and Marx 57, 59, 60, 61, 68
  see also recession/depression
financial services 3, 13, 18, 19, 20, 27
  see also banks/banking
financial stability 68, 118–19, 121, 192,
    213, 237
  Minsky's hypothesis 118–19
  see also central banks;
    macroprudential policy
Financial Times 162–3, 221

fiscal policy 8, 69, 90, 91–2, 94, 117,
    121, 131, 132, 134, 176, 253, 275,
    291, 296
  austerity *see* austerity
  government spending *see*
    government spending
  Keynes' fiscal activism 6, 7, 123,
    129–30, 132, 139, 140, 155, 179
  and public debt 117
  redistribution *see* redistribution
Fisher, Antony 188
Fisher, Ella 98
Fisher, George Whitefield 98, 99, 100
Fisher, Herbert 98
Fisher, Irving 2, 5, **95–123**, 196
  and the backlash against
    globalization 292–3
  Booms and Depressions 112
  business cycle theory 107, 110,
    112–14
  and central banks 117, 120, 121, 122
  on combating deflation 116–17,
    120–21
  debt-deflation theory of depression
    5, 97–8, 112–16
  distributive lag model 107
  doctoral thesis 99
  and the dollar 108–10
  and the Econometric Society 96, 153
  and eugenics 101
  Fisher equation 106–7
  and gold 108–9, 116–17
  How to Live 101
  imprint on economics 106–13
  and the Index Number Institute
    104, 110
  and the Index Visible Company 103
  life and times of 95, 97, 98–105,
    121–2
  and the Life Extension Institute 101
  The Making of Index Numbers 110

mathematical economics 99, 100
and Minsky 118–19
and the 'money illusion' 107–8
The Nature of Capital and Income 106
as presidential adviser 97, 116
and Prohibition 97, 101
The Purchasing Power of Money 108
Quantity Theory of
    Money 106–8, 116
The Rate of Interest 106
and Remington Rand 103, 110
*The Stock Market Crash –
    and After* 111
and stocks 95, 103–4, 105, 111
The Theory of Interest 96, 106
wealth 100, 103, 104, 105, 122
Why is the Dollar Shrinking? 109
Fisher, Margaret (Margie), née Hazard
    99, 105, 122
Fisher equation 106–7
Fitzgerald, F. Scott 84
foreign (direct) investment (FDI)
    65–6, 256, 292
Forster, E. M. 127
France 39, 40, 57
    French Revolution 53
    inequality 82
    Physiocrats 16, 25, 70
    and Trier 53
Freddie Mac 190, 232, 235
free market 8, 173, 188, 222–3
    capitalism 226 *see also* capitalism
    competition *see* competition
    see also free trade
free trade 284–7, 292
    and competition *see* competition
    in corn 40 *see also* Corn Laws
    regional and bilateral agreements
        10, 284–7
    and theory of comparative
        advantage 4, 46–9, 297

free trade agreements (FTAs) 10,
    283–7, 291–2
Friedman, David 217
Friedman, Janet 217
Friedman, Milton 8, 107, 172–3, 178,
    180, 188, **213–38**, 293
    and the 2008 financial
        crisis 231–7
    Capitalism and Freedom 186, 222–3,
        225, 238
    and the Federal Reserve 225, 226,
        227–31
    Free to Choose 223–4, 238
    and Goldwater 224
    and the Great Depression 214, 215,
        216–17, 227–31, 234, 235–6, 237,
        297–8
    John Bates Clark Medal 220
    and Keynes 226, 227
    libertarian views 221–2
    life and times of 215–31, 238
    *A Monetary History of the United
        States, 1867–1960* (with Schwartz)
        8, 224, 226–31, 238
    and monetary policy 214, 215
    and Nixon 225
    Nobel Prize 214, 218, 220, 221
    and Pinochet/Chile 220–21
    political influence 224–31
    and prediction 219–20
    and quantitative easing 236–7
    and Reagan 225
    and Stigler 219
    and Thatcher 226
    *A Theory of the Consumption
        Function* 218
    Two Lucky People 238
    Tyranny of the Status Quo 238
    Volker Lectures 222
Friedman, Rose, née Director 217,
    220, 223, 226, 238

Frisch, Ragnar 153
Fuji 162
Furman, Jason 88, 194

Galbraith, John Kenneth 224
gas industry 20
General Electric (GE) 159
German Historical School of
    economics 100, 148, 149
Germany
    and China 206
    competitiveness and wages 206–7
    and the Great Depression 152
    industrialization/Industrial
        Revolution 12, 52
    inequality 82
    manufacturing 13, 152
    and Marshall 80
    and Marx 52–5, 57
    productivity and wage growth 205
    retained cash of companies 138
    reunification and wages 205–6
    trade 206–7
    and the Treaty of Versailles 178
    wage stagnation 7, 194, 205–7
    worker representation 210
gilts 135–6
Glass–Steagall Act 231
global macroeconomic imbalances 66
globalization 9–10, 49, 252, 283–98
    backlash 10, 283–4, 291–6
    and deindustrialization 14, 42
    and emerging economies 288
    future of 283–98
    and inequality 88, 290–92
    losers from 9, 10, 49, 288,
        290–92, 296
    and low wages 205–6
    and prosperity 9–10, 283
    and specialization 28
    and trade 9–10, 283, 284–7

gold 34, 106
    and the dollar 108–10, 116–17,
        229, 230
    standard 108–9, 116–17, 229, 230
Goldwater, Barry 224
Google 170
    Android 161, 164
government administration 20
government bonds 111, 135
    see also gilts
government regulation 27, 30, 191, 225
government spending 3, 6, 123–4, 249
    deficit spending 129, 130, 141, 155
    and employment 139
    and Keynes 6, 123–4, 125–6, 129,
        130, 131, 136, 139–42 *see also* fiscal
        policy: Keynes' fiscal activism
    public investment/spending *see*
        public investment; public
        spending
Gramm–Leach–Bliley Act 231, 232
Great Britain *see* Britain/UK
Great Depression (1930s) 97, 105–6,
    111–13, 114, 116, 152, 179, 182,
    189–90, 191, 218
    Black Thursday 95
    Black Tuesday 95, 104, 228
    and the Federal
        Reserve 227–31, 233
    Fisher and risk of repeating the
        1930s 95–123
    and Friedman 214, 215, 216–17,
        227–31, 234, 235–6, 237, 297–8
    and 'Great Contraction' 228–30
    and Keynesian revolution/
        economics 128–31, 177,
        227, 297
    as a liquidity crisis 228, 230, 231, 233,
        234, 235
    and unemployment 6, 111, 128, 155,
        216, 228

and US GDP 228
Greece 134, 239, 250, 279
  see also euro crisis
gross domestic product (GDP) 9, 13,
    18, 41, 45, 50, 228, 230, 272
  debt-to-GDP ratio 119, 133
  emerging economies and world
    GDP 251
  and government spending 129
  investment as share of 273
  Japan 275
  per capita 83, 239
  trade-to GDP ratios 63–4
  US 2015 GDP 208
  US decline with Great Depression
    111, 228
  world GDP 50, 251, 252
growth of economies *see* economic
    growth
Guillebaud, Claude 94

Haberler, Gottfried 153
Hansen, Alvin 9
Hardenberg, Karl August von 53
Harris, Seymour 153
Harrison, George 228
Hausmann, Ricardo 41
Hayek, Friedrich 6–7, 149, **172–94**,
    219, 224, 225
  and the 2008 global financial crisis
    189–92
  and the backlash against
    globalization 293
  business cycle theory 7, 176, 177,
    179–80
  and capitalism 173–4, 192
  in *Collectivist Economic Planning* 181
  The Constitution of Liberty 185–6, 188
  *The Denationalization of
    Money* 187–8
  The Fatal Conceit 188–9

and the IEA 188
  influence 192–3
  and Keynes 173, 177–80, 182, 184
  Law, Legislation and Liberty 187
  life and times of 174–89
  Nobel Prize 187, 192–3
  'Paradox of Saving' 176
  path to fame 181–9
  political philosophy 181–4
  presidency of Mont Pelerin
    Society 184
  Prices and Production 180
  Pure Theory of Capital 180
  The Road to Serfdom 173, 182–5, 186
  and Schumpeter 176
  The Sensory Order 184
  and spontaneous order 175
  and Thatcher 188, 192
Hayek, Hella 184, 186
Hazard, Caroline 105, 121–2
Hazard, Margaret *see* Fisher, Margaret
Hazard, Rowland 99
Hegel, Georg Wilhelm 54
Hicks, John R. 199
higher education 19
Holland 40
Hong Kong 86, 239, 250, 257
Hoover, Herbert 97, 230
housing market 20, 190, 232–3, 235
Huawei 165, 166–9, 170
human capital 22–3, 239, 266, 276
Hume, David 15, 16, 31
hyperinflation 108, 151, 175
hysteresis 279

imports 29, 35, 50, 223, 249, 288
inclusive growth 291
income inequality 76, 81–4, 86–90,
    259, 290–91
Index Number Institute
    (INI) 104, 110

Index Visible Company 103
indexation schemes 110–11
India 18, 197, 201, 204, 252
individualism 182
Indonesia 250
industrialization 12–13, 55–6,
    64, 259, 270
  and agriculture 13, 14
  in China 64, 257
  Industrial Revolution 4, 11, 26, 30,
    35, 36, 39, 52, 55
  reindustrialization 14, 43, 44,
    45–6, 64
  Second Industrial Revolution 270
  and the workers'
    movement 61–2
  see also deindustrialization
inequality 5, 61, 76, 81–92
  and capitalism 5, 76
  in China 82, 84–7, 92, 258
  drivers of 87–8
  and globalization 88, 290–92
  growing 81–9
  Hayek and global inequality 185–6
  income inequality 76, 81–4, 86–90,
    259, 290–91
  and Marshall 81, 89–92
  reasons for rising inequality over
    past century 87–9
  and skill-biased technical
    change 87, 288
  in South Africa 259–60
  and tax 88, 291
  and technological change 291
  US 82, 87, 92, 290
  and welfare systems 87
inflation 8, 106, 107, 131, 187, 249
  and central bank regimes 228
  and debt indexation 110–11
  hyperinflation 108, 151, 175
  and savings 108
  stagflation 131, 187

and wages 205
information and communications
    technology (ICT) 14, 21, 269, 270
  smartphones and improvements in
    technology 164, 165 *see also*
    smartphones/mobile phones
Information Technology and
    Innovation Foundation (US) 45
infrastructure investment 69, 129, 135,
    136–9, 141, 276–7, 281, 291
innovation 6, 21, 66, 173, 288
  and challenge of staying on top
    160–65
  China's challenge 165–9
  as engine of economic growth 144–5
  industry-specific 158
  Schumpeterian 'creative destruction'
    and 144–6, 152, 156–71
Institute of Economic Affairs (IEA)
    188, 191, 226
institutions
  and economic development 8–9,
    239–41, 243–5, 252–8
  Myanmar 255–8
  and North 8–9, 240–41, 243–5, 250,
    261–3
  self-perpetuation of 245
  and technological progress 244
  Vietnam's institutional challenge
    252–5
intangible investments 22–3
interest rates 27, 120, 130, 176, 189,
    213–14, 249
  and the 2008 financial crisis 233–4
  and the Great Depression 189,
    227, 228
  investment and low rates 135–9,
    180, 277
  negative 213, 237
  and stocks 82, 138
International Labour
    Organization (ILO) 205

International Monetary Fund (IMF)
92, 131, 133, 134, 142, 256
International Working Men's
Association (IWMA) 59–60
internet 167, 170, 188, 203, 269
investment
and aggregate demand in
economy 139–40
capital investment 138, 179–80,
267, 273
with fixed returns 138
foreign (direct) 65–6, 256, 292
growth through 129, 136–9, 276, 280
in human capital 22–3, 276
infrastructure *see* infrastructure
investment
investment banks/banking 112, 121,
137, 190, 231–5
Keynes' view of investors 127–8
and low interest rates 135–9, 180, 277
low investment following financial
crises 279
private 135, 136, 138, 140, 141, 277
and productivity 281
public *see* public investment
R&D *see* research and development
investment
Robinson on capital accumulation
from 196
as share of GDP 273
'socializing investment' 141
and tax 277, 281
UK foreign investment after
Brexit 32
Ireland 134, 239
UK exports to 18
Israel 239
iTunes 164

Japan 1, 5, 115–16, 117–18, 159, 166,
207, 236, 237, 239, 265
'Abenomics' 274–5

economic growth 272
economic stagnation 274–5, 280–81
GDP 275
'lost decades' 274–6
manufacturing 166
national debt 117, 119, 275
productivity 205, 275
real estate crash in 1990s 5, 116, 207,
236, 265, 274, 279
robotics 281
as second largest economy 166
stagnant median wages 7, 194,
207–8
temporary workers 207, 208
wage growth 205
Jevons, W. Stanley 148
Jobs, Steve 161
Johnson, Lyndon B. 224
joint-stock companies 14
Jones, Homer 216
Journal of Economic Perspectives 215
Journal of Political Economy 217
JPMorgan 235
Juncker Plan 137

Kahn, Richard 198, 199, 200
Kant, Immanuel 80
Keynes, John Maynard 5–6, 83, 93,
123–71, 296
and the backlash against
globalization 293
and the Bloomsbury Group 127
and Bretton Woods System 142
and budget deficits 130, 141
counter-cyclical policies 141
and crowding out 136
on depression/recession 113, 179,
227
The Economic Consequences of the Peace
126
fiscal activism 6, 7, 123, 129–30, 132,
139, 140, 155, 179

Keynes, John Maynard – *(cont.)*
    and Friedman 226, 227
    The General Theory of Employment,
        Interest and Money 96, 113, 126,
        129, 142, 154–5, 180, 199, 200
    and government spending 6, 123–4,
        125–6, 129, 130, 131, 136, 139–42
    on government's role in economy
        139–42
    and Hayek 173, 177–80, 182, 184
    and investors 127–8
    Keynesian revolution 128–32
    legacy 124, 129, 142–3
    life and times of 124–8
    and Marshall 126
    and Niemeyer 126
    and paradox of thrift 140, 176
    at Paris Peace Conference 126
    Prices and Production 178
    and public investment 129, 130,
        136–7, 140–42, 277, 293
    and Robbins 176–7
    Robinson and Keynes/Keynesian
        economics 195–6, 198, 199,
        200–201
    and Schumpeter 154–5
    and 'socializing investment' 141
    A Tract on Monetary Reform 178
    and the Treasury 125–6, 128, 130
    A Treatise on Money 178
    wealth 127
Keynes, John Neville 78, 124–5
Khrushchev, Nikita 71–2
Knight, Frank 217, 219
Kodak 159, 161–2, 163
Korea
    North 46, 196–7, 201
    South 159, 239, 250, 251, 257, 261
Krugman, Paul 47, 82, 83, 88, 179
Krupp 146, 152
Kuznets, Simon 218

labour force growth 265
labour productivity 45, 266, 278
    and work incentive 72–3
laissez-faire 4–5, 11, 25, 77, 107, 131–2,
    214, 220
landowners 34, 36, 38, 39, 70
Lassalle, Ferdinand 80
Latin America 1, 244, 250, 256, 286
    currency crisis (1981–82) 249, 256
    see also specific countries
League of Nations 97
Lehman Brothers 121, 190, 235
Lenin, Vladimir 62
Leontief, Wassily 153, 267
Lewis, Arthur 257
Lewis, Barbara ('Bobby') 267
Life Extension Institute 101
Linda for Congress BBC documentary
    289–90
London 58–9, 127
London School of Economics and
    Political Science 7, 93, 177,
    180, 184
London Stock Exchange 33, 58
Long Depression (1880s) 6, 8, 61–2, 78
Lopokova, Lydia 127, 142
Louis XIV 25
LSE *see* London School of Economics
    and Political Science
Lucas, Jr, Robert 248

Ma, Jack (Ma Yun) 85
Maastricht Treaty 133
macroprudential policy 121, 213, 237
    see also central banks; financial
        stability
Malaysia 250
Malthus, Thomas 34, 35, 60, 70
Manchester 55, 59
Mandela, Nelson 259–60
manufacturing 3, 13, 28, 35, 49, 146

additive (3D printing) 43–4
automation in 208
China 68
and deindustrialization 13–14
GDP contribution in UK 18, 45
German 13, 152
high-tech 12, 19, 44–6
and industrialization 13 *see also*
    industrialization
Japan 166
'manu-services' 22, 41–2
'March of the Makers' 12, 18
mass-manufactured goods 26
and national statistics 14–15
reshoring 43, 44, 45–6
rolling back deindustrialization
    process 12
and Smith 16
trade patterns changed by advanced
    manufacturing 44–6
US 12–13, 18, 42–3, 146, 288
Mao Zedong 71, 72
Maoism 62, 72–3
'March of the Makers' 12, 18
marginal utility analysis 79
marginalism 148, 149
market forces/economy
    'Big Bang' (1986) 12
    competition *see* competition
    and economic equilibrium *see*
        economic equilibrium
    emerging economies *see* emerging
        economies
    Hayek and the supremacy of market
        forces 7
    'invisible hand' 3–4, 6, 11, 16, 24,
        181, 189, 193, 202
    and *laissez-faire* 4–5, 11, 25, 77,
        131–2, 214, 220
    and Marx 4
    self-righting markets 24

supply and demand *see* supply and
    demand
Marshall, Alfred 4–5, **76–94**, 125, 149
    on approach to economics 94
    and the backlash against
        globalization 292
    and the Cambridge School 93
    and decentralization 91
    Economics of Industry 77, 79
    and education's role in reducing
        inequality 81, 91
    and inequality 81, 89–92
    and Keynes 126
    and *laissez-faire* 4–5, 77
    legacy 92–4
    life and times of 77–81
    marginal utility analysis 79
    and Marx 80
    and poverty 81, 91
    Principles of Economics 77, 79–80, 81, 93
    and utility theory 81
Marshall, Mary, née Paley 77, 93
Marx, Heinrich 53, 54, 55
Marx, Henriette, née Pressburg 53, 55,
    59
Marx, Jenny, née von Westphalen 51,
    54, 58, 59, 75
Marx, Karl 4, **51–75**
    and agriculture 70, 71
    and the backlash against
        globalization 292
    Capital 51, 60, 62, 70, 72, 144
    and capitalism 57, 61, 74, 148,
        155, 292
    and China 52, 62–3, 70–75
    and class 51, 56–7, 61, 70, 292
    Communist Manifesto (with Engels)
        51, 56–7, 70–71, 72
    communist theories 51, 60–63
    *A Contribution to the Critique of
        Political Economy* 60

Marx, Karl – (*cont.*)
doctoral thesis 54
The Eighteenth Brumaire of Louis Bonaparte 58
and Engels 51, 55, 56–7, 60
journalism 55, 57, 58–9
life and times of 52–60, 75
and Marshall 80
and rate of profit 73
and Ricardo 60, 70
and Russia 51–2, 59, 62
on service sector workers 74
surplus value theory 60–61
and the Young Hegelians 54–5
Marx, Laura 60
Marx, Louise 53
Marxism 51, 60–63, 72, 75, 144, 155, 175
and the Austrian School 175
and unemployment 60–61
see also Marx, Karl
Mason, Edward 153
mathematical economics 99, 100
Mauritius 239
May, Theresa 76
Meade, James 199
median income 7, 86, 87
Menger, Carl 148, 175
mercantilist policies 24, 25, 28, 38, 39, 49
see also Corn Laws
Merkel, Angela 276
Mexico 249
middle class
China 84–6
and economic growth 67
and economic inequality 83
and European revolutionaries 51
income 291
and industrialization 13, 26
and Keynes 124
and Heinrich Marx 53

as proportion of world population 264
and Schumpeter 149
social resentment 86
US 83, 208–9, 291
Mill, James 34, 35, 60
Mill, John Stuart 15, 51, 60, 73, 90
On Liberty 222
Principles of Political Economy 90
Minsky, Hyman 2, 118–19
Mises, Ludwig von 149, 175, 181, 225
Mitchell, Wesley 218, 227
mobile phones/smartphones 160–61, 162, 163–5, 166–9, 203
monetarism 107, 220, 226
see also Friedman, Milton
monetary policy 7, 8, 120–21, 130, 176–7, 179, 214, 225, 227, 228, 236, 237
and Friedman 214, 215
tools 213 *see also* quantitative easing (QE)
see also central banks
monopolies
and Marx 57, 71
natural 91
and Robinson 198, 202–3, 211–12
and Schumpeter 156–7
and Smith 27, 28, 29
and Sraffa 197
monopsony 202, 210
Mont Pelerin Society 184
Morgenthau, Henry 218
mortgage-backed securities (MBS) 233
mortgage lending 114
and the 2008 financial crisis 232–3
sub-prime 118, 190, 232
Myanmar 252, 255–8
Myrdal, Gunnar 187

Napoleon I 57
Napoleon III 58

Napoleonic Wars 39, 40
national/official statistics 14–15, 23
    China 63
    UK 14–15
    US 104, 227
national debt 37, 38, 141
    Austria 176
    and central banks 237
    China 12, 68, 69, 253
    and creditors 251
    and debt forgiveness 258
    and deficits 131
    euro area 120, 134
    and foreign exchange reserves 251
    and investment 138
    Japan 117, 119, 275
    major economies 119, 133
    owed to foreigners 251
    and quantitative easing 135
    and Ricardian equivalent 141
    UK 37, 38, 119, 130–31, 133
    US 119
    Vietnam 254–5
National Health Service (UK) 202
National Infrastructure Commission
    (UK) 137, 276
Navigation Acts 39
neoclassical economics 9, 77, 99, 128,
    148, 202, 269–72
    convergence hypothesis 271–2
    'neoclassical synthesis' 124
    New Neoclassical Synthesis 132
    see also Fisher, Irving; Marshall,
        Alfred; Solow, Robert
Neoclassical Synthesis 124
    see also Samuelson, Paul
New Classicists 131, 132
    see also Lucas, Jr, Robert
New Deal 129, 155, 218, 227, 230
New Institutional Economics 240–41
    see also North, Douglass
New Keynesians 132

    see also Stiglitz, Joseph
New Neoclassical Synthesis 132
New Rhineland News (Cologne) 57
*New Rhineland News: Review of Political
    Economy* (London) 58
new trade theory 47
New York Herald 104
New York Times 182–3, 221, 287
New York Tribune 59
Newcomb, Simon 107
Newsweek 221, 224
Niemeyer, Sir Otto 126
Nissan 43, 44
Nixon, Richard 223, 225
Nokia 160–61, 162, 163
non-tariff barriers (NTBs) 285
Nordhaus, William 295
North, Douglass 8–9, **239–64**
    and the backlash against
        globalization 293
    and development challenges
        240–41, 260–64
    doctoral thesis 242
    *The Economic Growth of the United
        States from 1790 to 1860* 242
    and institutions 8–9, 240–41, 243–5,
        250, 261–3
    *Institutions, Institutional Change and
        Economic Performance* 242–3
    life and times of 241–5
    Nobel Prize 240, 242
    path dependence theory 245, 248,
        253, 260, 263, 293
    and Smith 243
North, Elizabeth, née Case 242
North Korea 46, 196–7, 201
Northern Rock 232

Oak Ridge National Laboratory 43–4
Obama, Barack 12, 284
Occupy movement 7, 172, 173
oil industry 20

Organisation for Economic
  Co-operation and Development
  (OECD) 5–6, 92, 138, 207, 210,
  263–4, 272, 273, 278
Osborne, George 12
Overseas Development Institute (ODI)
  247–8
Oxford University 7, 15, 77–8, 268
  Balliol College 15, 77–8

Paine, Thomas 53
Paley, Mary 77, 93
Paris Peace Conference 126
path dependence theory 245, 248, 253,
  260, 263, 293
  see also North, Douglass
Peel Banking Act 40
Philips, Lion 53
Philips (electronics company) 53, 163
physical capital 266
Physiocrats 16, 25, 70
Pigou, Arthur Cecil 91, 93, 199
Piketty, Thomas 5, 76, 82, 87, 88
pin-making 24
Pinochet, Augusto 220
Ponzi finance 118
populism 284, 287–90, 292, 296
Portugal 46–7, 48, 134, 239
poverty
  aid 248
  and development *see* economic
    development challenges
  eradication/reduction 2, 63, 84–5,
    245–8, 249, 260–61, 264
  frictional 247
  and Marshall 81, 91
  and Marx 61
  and median income 86, 87
  people lifted from 84–5
  in South Africa 258–60
productivity
  and agriculture 247, 257
  'benign neglect' of 276
  Britain's productivity puzzle 22–3,
    273, 278
  and computers 269
  and economic growth 6, 265–6,
    272–4
  and education 245
  and factor reallocation 64–5
  and Germany 206
  and Hayek 186
  incentives 71, 102
  and industry/industrial revolution
    26, 252
  and innovation 6, 21, 145
  and investment 281
  Japan 274–5
  and jobs 211
  labour *see* labour productivity
  and land 38
  low 73, 278
  and Marshall 79
  moving into higher sectors of 13, 211
  and pricing 24–5
  raising 6, 21, 145, 266, 272–4, 275, 281
  and Schumpeter 153
  and secular stagnation 9, 265, 274
  slow economic and productivity
    growth and the future 265–82
  and specialization 24
  and technology 43, 269
  total factor productivity 266, 269
  and trade 38
  and wages 201, 204–5, 209, 273, 274,
    278
Prohibition 97, 101
protectionism 28, 33, 35, 36, 38
  agricultural 35, 38, 222 *see also* Corn
    Laws
  Navigation Acts 39
public-private partnerships 137, 139

public investment 136–8, 155, 277, 281
and Keynes 129, 130, 136–7,
140–42, 293
public spending 132, 141
general government spending *see*
government spending
public investment *see* public
investment
squeeze 20, 123 *see also* austerity
Puerto Rico 239

quantitative easing (QE) 117, 120,
134–5, 190, 213–14, 234, 236–7
Quantity Theory of Money 106–8, 116
see also Friedman, Milton;
monetarism; Equation of Exchange

Rand, Ayn 224
RAND Corporation 268
rate of profit 73
rational expectations theory 132
Reagan, Ronald 131–2, 223, 225, 226
recession/depression 5, 19, 59, 69, 82,
136, 237, 272–3
debt-deflation theory of depression
5, 97–8, 112–16
Great Depression *see* Great
Depression (1930s)
Great Recession (2009) 1, 5, 7, 9,
13–14, 45, 76, 119, 134, 138, 204,
211, 288, 298
Greece 134
'hangover theory' of 179
Hayek on 179
and Keynes 113, 128–31, 177, 179,
227, 297
Long Depression (1880s) 6, 8,
61–2, 78
second recession (1937–38: recession
within the Depression) 5, 8
in UK 1970s 131

redistribution 5, 88–90, 91–2, 140, 258,
291, 292
Regional Comprehensive Economic
Partnership (RCEP) 286
Reich, Robert 88
reindustrialization 12, 14, 19, 43, 44,
45–6, 64, 257
Reisinger, Anna Josefina 151–2
Remington Rand 103, 110
rent-seeking 37–8
research and development (R&D)
investment 22, 43, 45, 271, 281
China 64, 66, 166, 167, 168
Research in Motion (RIM) 161,
162, 163
retail trade 13, 35, 36
Rhineland News 55
Ricardian equivalence 141
Ricardo, David 2, **32–50**, 73, 75, 141
and the backlash against
globalization 292
and class 36, 40
comparative advantage
theory 4, 46–9
and the Corn Laws 34–5, 36,
39–40, 297
*Essay on the Influence of a Low Price
of Corn on the Profits of Stock* 34
The High Price of Bullion 34
international trade theory 37,
38–9, 297
as a landlord 34
life and times of 33–8
as a loan contractor 33–4
and Marx 60, 70
*On the Principles of Political Economy
and Taxation* 33, 34–5, 36, 48
and Schumpeter 37
and Smith 38, 49
wealth 33–4, 36
Ricardo, Priscilla 35

Robbins, Lionel 176–7, 178, 184
Robinson, Austin 197
Robinson, James 240–41, 263
Robinson, Joan 7, 48, 177, **194–212**
   The Accumulation of Capital 196, 201
   and the AEA 199–200
   and the backlash against
     globalization 292
   and communism 196–7
   Economic Philosophy 201
   The Economics of Imperfect Competition
     195, 198, 199–200
   Essays in the Theory of Employment
     195, 200
   and imperfect competition 195, 197,
     198, 201–4, 209
   Introduction to the Theory of
     Employment 195–6, 199
   and Keynes 198, 199
   and Keynesian economics 195–6,
     198, 200–201
   life and times of 201, 212
   and monopolies 198, 202–3, 211–12
   monopsony theory 202
   and Schumpeter 200
   and unemployment 211
   wage determination theory 209–12
robotics 43–4, 46, 208, 269, 281,
   288, 296
Rodrik, Dani 14, 166
Rolls-Royce 20, 22
Roosevelt, Franklin D. 97, 116, 230
   New Deal 129, 155, 218, 227, 230
Russia 18, 250, 251, 254
   1905 Revolution and Lenin 62
   and Marx 51–2, 59, 62

Samsung 163, 164, 165, 169
Samuelson, Paul 2, 10, 47, 99, 124,
   146–7, 153, 196, 268–9,
   294–5, 297

   and the backlash against
     globalization 294–6
   Economics 295
   factor-price equalization
     theorem 296
   Nobel Prize 295
savings 65, 130, 140, 179–80
   for capital investment 179–80
   and inflation 108
   and Keynes 127, 130–31, 140
   and the 'paradox of thrift' 140, 176
Say, Jean-Baptiste 60
Schmoller, Gustav von 148
Schumpeter, Anna, née Reisinger
   151–2
Schumpeter, Gladys, née Seaver 149,
   150, 151
Schumpeter, Joseph 6, **144–71**
   and the backlash against
     globalization 293
   as banker/investor 151
   Business Cycles 150, 154, 155
   and capitalism 144–6, 155–60
   Capitalism, Socialism and Democracy
     144, 150, 154, 155, 171
   'creative destruction', innovation
     and 144–6, 152, 156–71
   'The Crisis of the Tax State' 151
   and the Econometric Society 153
   economics 155–60
   and entrepreneurs 6, 145, 148, 150,
     151, 156–7, 159–60, 165, 170–71
   on Fisher 96
   and Hayek 176
   History of Economic Analysis 154, 171
   and Keynes 154–5
   legacy 170–71
   life and times of 145, 146–55, 171
   The Nature and Content of Theoretical
     Economics 149–50
   and perfect competition 156, 194–5

and Ricardo 37
and Robinson 200
Theory of Economic Development 150
wealth 145, 151
Schumpeter, Romaine Elizabeth, née
    Boody 154
Schumpeter Group of Seven
    Wise Men 153
Schwartz, Anna Jacobson 8, 180,
    226–31, 238
Schwarzenegger, Arnold 215
Scottish Enlightenment 15, 27
Seaver, Gladys Ricarde *see* Schumpeter,
    Gladys
secular stagnation 9, 265, 274
self-interest 25, 28
services sector 3, 12–13, 14, 20–23, 49,
    145–6, 273
    China 13, 67–8
    and deindustrialization 13–14
    financial services *see* financial
        services
    global trade in services 19
    human capital investment 22–3
    invisibility of 41
    liberalization 42, 50
    'manu-services' 22, 41–2
    and Marx 74
    move away from 12
    and national statistics 14–15
    output measurement 23
    productivity and innovation 21
    and Smith 14, 26
    Trade in Services Agreement (TiSA)
        42, 285
    UK 12, 13–14, 17–19, 20–23, 41, 42,
        49, 145–6, 273
    US 13, 145–6, 273
shadow banking 68–9
Shiller, Robert 111
silver 24, 38, 106

Singapore 86, 159, 239, 257, 261
Skidelsky, Robert 124–5
skill-biased technical change 87, 288
skills shortage 276
small and medium-sized enterprises
    (SMEs) 137, 152
smartphones/mobile phones 160–61,
    162, 163–5, 166–9, 203
Smith, Adam 3–4, **11–31**, 64, 75
    and the backlash against
        globalization 292
    as Commissioner of Customs for
        Scotland 29
    economic freedom 29, 224
    on 'invisible hand' of market forces
        3, 11, 24
    and *laissez-faire* economics 11, 25
    legacy 14–15
    life and times of 15–17
    and manufacturing 16
    and Marx 60
    and North 243
    and Physiocracy 16, 26
    on rate of profit 73
    and rebalancing the
        economy 24–30
    and Ricardo 38, 49
    and the services sector 14, 26
    and state intervention 4, 12, 16,
        24–5, 27–8
    The Theory of Moral Sentiments 16
    The Wealth of Nations 3, 11, 16–17,
        26, 28, 31, 38
social capital 67, 262
social networks 67, 262
social services 67, 151
socialism
    communist *see* communism
    vs welfare state capitalism 172, 173
Solow, Barbara ('Bobby'), née
    Lewis 267

Solow, Robert 9, **265–82**
    and the backlash against
        globalization 293–4
    with Council of Economic
        Advisers 268
    doctoral thesis 267
    economic growth model 266,
        269–72, 278–81
    'How Economic Ideas Turn to
        Mush' 282
    John Bates Clark Medal 268
    and Keynesian economics 268
    life and times of 266–9, 282
    Nobel Prize 282
    Presidential Medal of Freedom 268
    and technological progress 266,
        269–71, 280–81
Sony 163
Sorrell, Sir Martin 22–3
South Africa 258–60
South Korea 159, 239, 250, 251,
    257, 261
Soviet Union 4, 51–2, 62, 256
    and China 62, 71–2
    Cold War 51–2, 75
    collapse of 4, 172–3, 189, 261
    see also Russia
Spain 6, 134, 239
specialization 24, 28, 40
spontaneous order 175
Sraffa, Piero 197, 199
stagflation 131, 187
Stanley Black & Decker 43
state
    government regulation 27, 30,
        191, 225
    intervention in the economy 2, 4–5,
        12, 16, 24–5, 27–8, 88–9,
        140–41, 222
    laissez-faire 4–5, 11, 25, 77, 131–2,
        214, 220

STEM (science, technology,
        engineering and mathematics)
        workers 43–4, 45
sterling 18, 19, 229, 249
Stigler, George 219
Stiglitz, Joseph 5, 76, 82–3, 132
stocks
    and Fisher 95, 103–4, 105, 111
    and interest rates 82, 138
    US railroad 59
Strachey, Lytton 126, 127
Strahan, William 29
Strong, Benjamin 227–8
Sturzenegger, Federico 41
Summers, Lawrence 9, 193, 265, 274
supply and demand 4, 11, 24
    see also market forces/economy:
        'invisible hand'
Sustainable Development
        Goals (SDGs) 246

Taiwan 159, 239, 251, 257
Tanzania 248
tariffs 19, 29, 50, 223, 285
taxation
    and austerity 6
    devolved powers of 277
    flat 223
    for government deficit
        spending 141
    before Great Depression 191
    and inequality 88, 291
    and investment 277, 281
    Japan 275
    and Marshall 89, 90, 92
    negative income tax 223
    to pay off national debt 37
    Pigouvian tax 199
    progressive 90
    and Reagan 225, 226
    redistribution through 88–9, 90

Schumpeter on 151
Smith on 11, 25
Taylor, John 190, 191
Taylor, Overton H. 153
technology
  ICT *see* information and
    communications technology
  inequality and technological
    change 291
  institutions and technological
    progress 244
  new technologies and economic
    growth 144–5, 269–71, 280–81
  robotics 43–4, 46, 208, 269, 281,
    288, 296
  and Solow's economic growth
    model 266, 269–71, 280–81
  and unemployment 46, 208, 281
  and wages 208
telecommunications industry 21
  mobile phones/smartphones 160–61,
    162, 163–5, 166–9, 203
temporary workers 207, 208, 210–11
Tennessee 43–4
term auction facility (TAF) 234
Thackeray, William Makepeace 144
Thailand 250, 285
Thatcher, Margaret 132, 188, 192, 226
total factor productivity
  (TFP) 266, 269
Townshend, Charles 16
Toyota 166
trade
  on basis of comparative advantage
    4, 46–9, 297
  Britain as largest world trader 35
  changing face of 284–7
  creation of 'winners' and 'losers' 9,
    10, 49, 288
  deficits *see* trade deficits
  and deindustrialization 18, 32

distributional impact 48, 291
expansion 9–10
exports *see* exports
free trade *see* free trade
German 206–7
and globalization 9–10, 283, 284–7
new trade theory 47
non-tariff barriers 285
patterns changed by advanced
  manufacturing 44–6
and productivity 38
Ricardo's model of international
  trade 37, 38–9, 297
in services *see* services sector
and specialization 40
surplus 18, 38, 49, 66
tariffs/barriers 19, 29, 50, 253, 285
trade-to-GDP ratio 63–4
Transatlantic Trade and Investment
  Partnership 286
Trans-Pacific Partnership 285–6
between UK and US 30
voter backlash 10
and wages 296
WTO *see* World Trade
  Organization
trade deficits
  current account deficit 18, 32,
    41, 249
  and Ricardo 32–50
  significance of 32–3, 49–50
  UK 4, 18, 23, 30, 32–3, 40–42, 50
  US 30, 32, 42–3, 66
Trade in Services Agreement (TiSA)
  42, 285
trade unions 60–61, 206, 209–10
  decreased unionization 88
Trans-Pacific Partnership (TPP) 285–6
Transatlantic Trade and Investment
  Partnership (TTIP) 286
transport facilities 27

Trier, Germany 52–3, 54
Trump, Donald 12, 283–4, 285, 287, 290, 292, 293
Trumpism 287–90, 295, 296
Turkey 250

Ulyanov, Vladimir Ilich (Lenin) 62
unemployment 5–6, 91, 131, 190, 194, 205
    disguised/hidden 6, 211
    and economic growth 279
    and the Great Depression 6, 111, 128, 155, 216, 228
    and hysteresis 279
    long-term unemployment rate 5–6
    and Marxism 60–61
    and Robinson 211
    and robotics 46, 208, 281
    in South Africa 259
    stagflation 131, 187
    U-6 rate 211
    US 111, 128, 155, 205, 211
    youth 6
United Kingdom *see* Britain/UK
United Nations 245, 246, 264
United States
    and the 2008 financial crisis 1, 5
    'America First' policy 283–4, 287, 293
    American Civil War 59
    anti-big business sentiment 156
    Banking Acts (1933 and 1935) 231
    car industry 43, 44
    Cold War 51–2, 75
    company mergers 156
    Council of Economic Advisers 225–6, 268
    deindustrialization 12, 14, 42
    the dollar 108–10
    Fed *see* Federal Reserve
    GDP 111, 208, 228, 230

    and the gold standard 108–9, 116–17, 229, 230
    in Great Depression 112, 208, 218, 227–31
    and Hayek 182–3, 185–7
    housing market 232–3, 235
    industrialization 12
    inequality 82, 87, 92, 290
    institutions and economic success 244
    interest rates 189
    labour force growth 265
    laissez-faire 131–2
    manufacturing 12–13, 18, 42–3, 146, 288
    middle class 83, 208–9, 291
    National Bureau of Economic Research (NBER) 227
    National Industrial Recovery Act 191
    New Deal 129, 155, 218, 227, 230
    productivity and wage growth 205
    rebalancing the economy 13, 30
    reindustrialization 14, 43, 44, 45–6
    reshoring 44, 46
    services sector 13, 145–6, 273
    stagnant/low wages 1, 7, 194, 208–9, 287–8
    trade deficit 30, 32, 42–3, 66
    trade unions 209
    Trans-Pacific Partnership 285–6
    Transatlantic Trade and Investment Partnership 286
    Treasury 233, 234, 235, 256
    Trumpism 287–90
    UK trade with 30
    unemployment 111, 128, 155, 205, 211
    Vietnam War 224
    War of Independence 17

USSR *see* Soviet Union
utility theory 81

Vereinigte Stahlwerke 152
Versailles, Treaty of 178
Vienna 147, 149–50, 175, 184
  Austrian Institute for Business
    Cycle Research 176
  stock market crash 151
  University of 147, 149–50,
    153, 174, 175
Vietnam 73, 224, 252–3
  Communist Party 252
  institutional challenge 252–5
Viner, Jacob 217, 219

wages 36
  and competitiveness 206
  and employment levels 203–4
  and globalization 205–6
  and imperfect competition 195, 198,
    201–4, 209
  and inflation 205
  median 7, 86, 87, 207–8, 287, 296
  minimum 223
  negotiations/bargaining 206,
    210–11
  Nixon's controls 225
  problem with low pay 7, 194, 204–9
  and productivity 201, 204–5, 209,
    273, 274, 278
  Robinson's theory of wage
    determination 209–12
  stagnant 1, 7, 194, 204, 205, 207–9,
    287–8, 296

and technology/automation 208
and trade 296
Walkman 163
Wall Street Journal 221, 237, 282
Wallis, Allen 218, 219, 224
Walras, Leon 148
Wang Jianlin 84–5, 86
Wang Sicong 85–6
Washington Consensus 256
Weber, Max 148
welfare state 6, 87, 92, 130–31,
    140, 175
  socialism vs welfare state capitalism
    172, 173
Westphalen, Ferdinand von 54
Westphalen, Jenny von (Jenny Marx)
    51, 54, 58, 59, 75
Westphalen, Johann Ludwig von 54
Whitbeck, John 289
Wiko 163
Wilson, James 49
Wilson, Woodrow 109
wine 46–7
Wolff, Wilhelm 59
Woolf, Virginia 127
World Bank 63, 142, 239, 247
  and poverty 245, 246, 247
World Trade Organization
    (WTO) 9, 19, 42, 50, 65, 253, 283,
    285–6
WPP 23

Yellen, Janet 119
Young Hegelians 54–5
youth unemployment 6